About the Author

Chris Howell is dedicated to improving the effectiveness, formality, technicality and professionalism of testing within games, as well as improving the perception of game testers and testing in general.

With over 10 years' experience, Chris has worked as a tester, test engineer and test manager. He studied Computer Science at university and then progressed quickly through the ranks of two of the industry's most celebrated companies, Microsoft and Zynga.

He started his career at Microsoft's UK publisher test team, testing Xbox 360 video streaming apps and other first party apps that supported the launch of the Kinect camera and Xbox One. Chris then spent two years working on some of Microsoft's biggest AAA titles as a test engineer, specialising in the test planning for the online services and multiplayer features of Fable Legends and Forza Horizon 3, the latter of which was a launch title for Windows 10.

In 2016, Chris moved to Zynga's UK game studios to work within the development teams on Dawn of Titans and the hugely successful MergeDragons! He's currently lead test manager on MergeDragons!, leading the team of test managers and analysts on the project. He continues to hone his skills by regularly testing, logging bugs and writing test plans.

Chris is an evangelist of adapting software testing techniques into the game domain. He holds one ISTQB certificate at foundation level and two at advanced level. He's given countless workshops, presentations and training to the teams at Zynga, and at the Game Quality Forum Global, one of the first dedicated conferences for game testing. He has been a speaker for the conference every year since 2019 and expects to talk again in 2022.

Modern Game Testing

A Pragmatic Guide to Test Planning and Strategy

Chris Howell

Modern Game Testing: A Pragmatic Guide to Test Planning and Strategy by Chris Howell

Published by Modern Game Testing Company Ltd
60 Culver Lane, Reading, RG6 1DY

moderngametesting.com

Cover by Troubador Publishing Ltd

Typesetting by Troubador Publishing Ltd

Editing and proofreading by Word Service Marketing Communications Ltd

ISBN: 978-1-7397115-0-4

To my partner Zoe and my son Tom, for tolerating all my talk about testing and for filling my days with love and laughter.

Acknowledgements

Everything I've learned about testing video games has come from working alongside some of the smartest and most passionate people I've ever met. Not just other testers, but all the talented designers, developers, artists and producers I've worked with. Writing this book wouldn't be possible without the benefit of their time and knowledge.

I'd like to first thank all the test managers at Microsoft who saw my potential and promoted me into the test engineer role to write my first test plans for Sesame Street Kinect TV – Fraser Murrell and Rich Levy in particular. Fraser was also the one who trusted me to write the test plans for several small projects, like the football World Cup app, Brazil Now. Those small projects were fantastic practice learning about testing holistically for an entire project, and paved the way to planning for larger projects years later. Thanks for the trust and support, Fraser.

Many of the senior staff at Microsoft also contributed considerably to the current test planning and writing style that you'll see in this book. The emphasis on test analysis, the test design framework and many of the small practicalities that make my current testing so effective can be attributed to various members of that team. I'd like to call out Lewis Reid, Tom Brisbane, Luke Harris, Martyn Sibley and Bob Ferry. I learned a lot from you all.

I'd also like to thank the whole of Zynga for the training and support over the last five years, without which I wouldn't have learned so much or reached so many testers. They've funded all my ISTQB training, flown me to India and Poland to meet and train our outsource vendor test teams, as well as various cities in Europe to speak at the Game Quality Forum. Thank you Zynga for being such a fantastic place to work and for the support you've given me.

Lastly, I couldn't not mention Miles Monty, my current manager at Zynga who, I can safely say, has been the biggest advocate of my work and of the creation of this book. Miles excels at removing all obstacles and distractions so that I have more time to improve our test strategies and share my knowledge with the rest of our team. Without such a great manager looking after my interests at work, I wouldn't have the energy or willpower to sit down and write this book in my downtime. Thank you for all the support, Miles.

Contents

0   Introduction   **xi**

  0.1   Why am I writing this book?   xi
  0.2   Who should read this book?   xii
  0.3   The scope of this book   xiii
  0.4   How to use this book   xiv
  0.5   Building a career in games testing   xv

1   Core principles of games testing   **1**

  1.1   What is games testing?   1
  1.2   Quality assurance vs. testing   3
  1.3   The goals of quality assurance   5
  1.4   The goals of testing   7
  1.5   An intro to how we test   14
  1.6   The fundamental test process   18
      1.6.1   *Test planning*   21
      1.6.2   *Test analysis*   24
      1.6.3   *Test design and implementation*   25
      1.6.4   *Test execution, monitoring and control*   28
      1.6.5   *Test reporting*   30
      1.6.6   *Test closure activities*   32
  1.7   Test formality   33
  1.8   The test design framework   36
  1.9   The psychology of testing   44
  1.10   A business case for testing   47
  1.11   Core principles: games vs software   49

2   Project lifecycles   **57**

  2.1   Introduction   57

2.2   The software development lifecycle   59
2.3   Waterfall development   68
2.4   Agile development   72
2.5   Similarities between QA and production roles   76
2.6   Source control and branching   77
2.7   Test levels   91
2.8   Project lifecycles: games vs. software   102

3   Test types and terminology   105

3.1   An introduction to test terminology   105
3.2   Test levels   106
3.3   Test areas   107
3.4   Test activities   113
3.5   Test types   120
3.6   Test terminology conclusion   129
3.7   Test types and terminology: games vs. software   131

4   Test analysis techniques   133

4.1   An intro into test analysis   133
4.2   Test conditions   139
4.3   Key considerations during test analysis   151
4.4   Test input reduction   163
        4.4.1   *Equivalence partitioning*   *163*
        4.4.2   *Boundary value analysis*   *173*
        4.4.3   *Code explanation and caveats*   *179*
4.5   Combinatorial test techniques   181
        4.5.1   *Decision tables*   *186*
        4.5.2   *Non-Boolean combination techniques*   *192*
        4.5.3   *Tool support for combination test cases*   *202*
4.6   Applied test analysis   203
4.7   Test analysis: games vs. software   208

5   Test design techniques   213

5.1   An introduction to test design   213
5.2   The goals of test tasks   216
5.3   Test granularity   222
5.4   Test writing styles   223
        5.4.1   *Test task style guide*   *224*

	5.4.2	*Scripted test style guide*	*234*
	5.4.3	*Unscripted test style guide*	*246*
	5.4.4	*'The detective' writing style*	*254*
	5.4.5	*'The science experiment' writing style*	*256*
5.5		Art and content-heavy test writing	258
5.6		Test case abstraction	262
5.7		Pitfalls of test writing	263
5.8		Non-functional test orientation	268
5.9		Writing for your audience	271
5.10		Test organisation	273
5.11		Influencing factors	278
5.12		Test design: games vs. software	283

6   Major areas of game testing   285

6.1	An introduction to game test domain areas	285
6.2	Platform integration	288
6.3	Third-party SDK integration	290
6.4	Platform certification requirements	292
6.5	Regulations and age rating compliance	293
6.6	UI, menus and navigation	295
6.7	Game environment	297
6.8	Content (Characters, weapons, items, etc.)	300
6.9	User generated content (UGC)	302
6.10	Game modes (campaign, co-op, skirmish, etc.)	305
6.11	Game progress and retention	307
6.12	Online services	309
6.13	Multiplayer	312
6.14	Live events, sales and AB tests	315
6.15	Audio, music and sound effects	317
6.16	Player profiles and file I/O	318
6.17	Identities and cloud save	320
6.18	Hardware and peripherals compatibility	321
6.19	Tutorials	324
6.20	Telemetry and analytics	325
6.21	Anti-cheat and security	328
6.22	Settings and configurations	331
6.23	Performance	332
6.24	Tooling and debug	336

7   **Test management**   **339**

    7.1   An introduction to test management   339
    7.2   Test estimation   340
    7.3   Managing test execution   346
    7.4   Test reporting   350
        7.4.1   *Reporting metrics*   *355*
    7.5   Test team structure   357
        7.5.1   *Testing sub-teams*   *358*
        7.5.2   *Common team structures*   *361*

8   **Afterword**   **369**

Introduction

0.1   Why am I writing this book?

This book aims to document a foundation of knowledge which already exists across the games testing industry but has yet to be organised into a concise, easily-read format.

Games testing as a profession is under-represented academically. General software testing books, whitepapers, courses and certificates are out there, of course, but many people starting out their career in games testing find it difficult to 'translate' these learnings into the gaming space.

I've spoken to many QA managers, QA analysts and testers who have completed software testing courses. They often tell me they either can't see how the techniques apply to their work, or they think that the processes described are too heavyweight and have no place in the 'Wild West' that is the gaming industry. In short, they see them as an unnecessary administrative burden.

There are many areas in games which simply don't exist in software and, for this, we must create our own unique test processes. Each chapter of this book will feature sections highlighting the differences between games and other software to illustrate this point.

For example, have you ever seen a software test technique focused on 3D models or particle effects? Or one that tracks virtual environment test coverage across an open world map? Art and content testing is a huge uncharted territory for game testers.

Some test processes are also completely unique to games: the lack of customer requirements specifications being a good example. Many software teams are building applications where the client is supplying requirements criteria which forms the basis of User Acceptance testing. In the games industry, we are essentially building a product *secretly* in the hope that the eventual customer will like it when it is launched. This creates unique test challenges which we'll cover in this guide.

With little academic grounding, games test professionals are industry-taught and, of course, every company has their own terminology and process. So when they move to another company, they have to change the language they use and adopt new terminology. It also means that when they get together, there is no universal communication protocol or, worse, they use the same words to mean different things. (I say *retest*, you say *regression test*.)

In this book I'll collect and define the most widely and correctly used definitions of games test terminology, so that teams can share them and build a common vocabulary.

Finally, the games testing profession has grown a lot in the last twenty years. No longer can companies pull people off the street to play their games and find bugs, certainly if they're building anything more complex than Mario (or Flappy Bird if you want a modern reference!). Bigger and more complex games are being built each year, and with each new development, dedicated testing professionals are even more essential to the success of those projects.

My hope is that this book will provide a foundation benchmark for the knowledge teams need and can refer to as their work and careers evolve.

0.2   Who should read this book?

The core topics in this book will be of most direct value to those who hold the title QA analyst* or QA tester. Likewise, anyone who is wanting to take their first steps in a game testing career will find all the content here valuable.

Test leads and managers may already be familiar with some of the content, but should still find it helpful to fill any gaps in their experience and to formalise some of the experience they already have. The last part of the book also touches on test management and higher level team strategy, which test leads in particular will find insightful.

In general, anyone holding a role within the manual testing side of the discipline should find the topics discussed and defined here useful. I wrote this content with myself in mind, and focused on the information that I would have found the most helpful in the first years of my career; I didn't even know about the academic side of software testing until at least year three, for example.

---

*   Throughout the book I'll be referring to those who create test strategies and write manual tests as QA analysts and those who execute manual tests as testers. In my career we've actually referred to the analyst role as a test engineer or a QA engineer. The use of that job title is inconsistently adopted, so we'll just use the more common title. Wherever you see QA analyst referenced, just understand that this can be referred to as different job titles depending on the company.

On the topic of outsource vendor test teams and publisher test teams (explained in more detail in chapter seven, **Test management**): these teams are further away from the core of project development and so are often excluded from valuable learnings, difficulties and other intricacies of a project. For this reason, the holistic view provided here should be particularly insightful for these teams, providing the missing pieces of the test process and the wider business. The wider context and reasoning should be very useful on the journey to becoming a better test team.

Automation test engineers may also find this content helpful if they have strong technical knowledge but are looking to learn more about test techniques and the test process. Other disciplines within a game studio that work directly with a test team will find it helps create a more cohesive relationship with the test team as they will understand their work more deeply.

Through the pages we will introduce topics such as risk analysis and quality best practices – techniques that *everyone* on a game team can adopt into their work. I also want the reader to understand more general issues, like setting the perspective of who is responsible for quality of the product, which is also a valuable lesson for everyone on the team.

0.3   The scope of this book

The content here is intended to provide a foundation of knowledge for the core of modern manual games test planning techniques and strategy. So, some areas which *could* have a much deeper discussion and explanation have been summarised for the sake of brevity. Some of these areas are less academic and are a matter of debate amongst the professional community. For these, I've given a viewpoint that should allow the reader to understand the topic and follow up on the discussion elsewhere.

Since the topics have been chosen to focus on manual testing, automated testing will not be discussed in detail, nor will quality practices concerning the writing and structure of the code itself. Important as these topics are, they will be introduced but not discussed in detail.

Similarly, I do not cover any 'white box' test techniques which involve looking at the code directly to assess the quality of it or test coverage through it. These are complex and would require a whole other book to describe in adequate detail. On the topic of looking at the code to plan testing through the 'routes' of logic, I've never seen anyone take this style of approach in games projects, so I haven't included it. These technical topics are, in practice, the work of software engineers and automation engineers and not something that QA analysts would realistically get involved in. Instead, they are an evolution of this book's content for those who want to take the next step and learn more specific and technical areas of testing (which, by the way, I definitely encourage!).

While a technical understanding of code is an advantage for manual test staff, it's not necessary to be successful and I don't assume you have any experience of software code.

The core content focuses on test techniques to add to your toolbox when writing and running tests. This is supplemented by contextual knowledge about projects and the principles of games testing to provide the 'when' and the 'why' of testing. It's important to stress that all of the test techniques and processes described here have been directly applied to real game projects and are explained through the use of game project examples. There are no theoretical, academic examples which haven't already been tried and tested in the real world, on real projects.

0.4 How to use this book

I recommend you read the first three chapters to gain a basis of knowledge, and then either carry on reading the chapters in the order they are written, or jump straight to the content you are interested in.

The techniques outlined here are intentionally flexible and can be adapted to shape the will of the user and the project requirements. Wherever possible, real game project examples are used to provide context and help you apply the lessons learned to your own day-to-day work. Every project is different, so while some off-the-shelf techniques may fit well, others will need work to apply them effectively.

The tester's toolbox

> **The sum of a tester's skills and experience forms a 'toolbox'**
> **which they can draw upon when a new problem arises.**

Each skill, technique or piece of experience is a tool in this box, and the more tools in there, the more likely it is that they'll have a relevant solution to effectively tackle different problems. This doesn't mean that you have to go apply these tools to *every* test problem you have, or that you should change the way that you work all at once. If you can't think of a use for some of the techniques here, don't force it, but don't reject it as irrelevant to your work, either. I would encourage you to understand it and store it for later retrieval. Like physical tools, test processes and techniques require practice to use them effectively. I've found identifying the right technique for a particular job is often tricky as there are so many choices to make throughout the fundamental testing process.

While I try and cover as many practical, real-world examples as possible here, the processes and techniques can only make you a better test professional through experiencing and practising them in the workplace. Driving instructors will tell you that you only really start learning how to drive after you pass your driving test and venture out onto the roads. It's the same thing here. Applying techniques to your own and your team's style of work can be hard. If you think you see something that is useful to you, discuss it with your team, present to them your idea of how you want to bring it into the project, or run a small trial and see how you found it.

If we removed some of the more formal test planning and analysis processes that I work with today, there would be an outcry from the QA analyst team of chaos and disorganisation. But when we first trialled them, they were time consuming and some parts turned out to not be helpful to us. Over time, these planning processes were trimmed down and adapted to the stage they are at now, where the team has practised them so frequently, they hardly take any time at all.

0.5   Building a career in games testing

It's entirely possible to build your life career around testing games. There, I said it. It's not just about *surviving* in the workplace, I'm talking about *thriving* in the workplace and making a massive success of it, in every sense of the word.

Let's talk about money first. In 2019 the BBC reported that the games market in the UK was worth more than video and music industries combined, a total of £3.86bn ($4.85bn)[*]. By choosing a career in games testing, you are choosing to be part of that massive industry. If you choose a stable and reputable company, then there is no reason that you can't enjoy the stability and wages of such a large and profitable industry. With esports and video streaming of games on the rise, plus the growing popularity of mobile gaming, there's no sign of the market shrinking either. More so than ever before, games testing can be a legitimate and lifelong profession. With this book to guide you, you can solidify that choice and make the most of it.

I've talked already about the inconsistencies of games-testing roles across different companies within the industry. It's an unfortunate reality that some companies and people don't value manual test strategy as a worthwhile endeavour, or hold any respect for those that choose to pursue it. Some testers may also find this perspective reflected in the salary offered for testing roles.

Related to this issue, and part of the reason behind it, is that many view games testers as a group whose job it is to try and break the game, or to simply play it and

---

[*]   3rd Jan, 2019. https://www.bbc.co.uk/news/technology-46746593

look for bugs. Many junior testers also think that this is their role and begin to openly critique and criticise the game that has been created by others on the team. As you can imagine, this leads to resentment and negativity, causing test teams to be perceived as problem-orientated and not part of the 'solution' of creating and making the game better. Unfortunately, I've met quite a few junior testers like this, exhibiting a negative attitude and damaging the reputation of the profession for the rest of us.

This book aims to not just instruct on hard skills of game test strategy and technique but, more critically, show that our day-to-day work is conducted with a goal of improving the perception of games testing as a professional discipline. If you act professionally and treat others with respect, others will act professionally towards you and treat you with respect.

It's my ambition, with this book, to separate the image of playtesting and undirected breaking of games, from the conscious and structured pursuit of greater game quality.

Core principles of games testing

This chapter is going to introduce why testing is necessary and what the goals of testing should be. I'll talk specifically about the type of work game testers are expected to do and outline what games testing definitely *isn't* about. There is a difference in scope between quality assurance and testing that is also important to define.

Other topics in this chapter will introduce some of the higher-level testing processes which will provide context to some of the more granular topics later on.

1.1   What is games testing?

When I speak about my work with friends outside of the games industry, some of them think that my job is to check the quality of other companies' games. That I'm some kind of reviewer who works on a team which tells you if your game is good to release or not, and perhaps also to give you my opinion on how fun I think it is.

Have you ever seen the movie 101 Dalmatians? The guy in the film is a game maker. At the end of the film they're all sitting in this boardroom. The boss's kid is sat at the end of the table playing the finished game, with the guy, the girl, the boss and all of the dogs watching in high anticipation. The kid finishes it, tells the guy he liked it and then promptly leaves. Everyone cheers, massive success.

I think that some people assume this is what games testing is about – that it's like testing a toy. It's the little kid in the film giving his final verdict on the product that you've made. So, to burst that bubble, the role of game testers is not to provide a critique on the game or to rate its 'fun-factor'. For lots of die-hard game fans who are super passionate about video games and have opinions they want to share, this reality can be difficult.

While there is a time and a place in every game project to talk about game design and balancing, in the projects I've worked on this has always been firmly driven by the design or art team. They will define the process for how and when they want wider project team input.

If you really want to review and critique games, I would suggest a career as a games journalist or a designer.

As a final note on this topic, Consumer Insights tests let you put early versions of your game in the hands of people selected because they already like the genre of game that you're making. Video cameras are set up to capture the controller or mobile device and the screen. The player is given instructions and they are recorded while they play the game.

The aim is to get early insights into how players interact with the game and what parts they get stuck on. They are usually asked to fill out a questionnaire afterwards. This process is also *not* games testing. The people taking part in these sessions are either volunteers or receive a small cash reward or vouchers.

Next, let's talk about whether being a good gamer also makes you a good tester. In 95% of scenarios, being really good at a specific game or a type of game isn't going to land you a job, and actually it's very unlikely that you'll live within working distance of the company that makes *that* game that you play. Some people investigate games testing because they want to turn their hobby into a career and want to be paid for playing the game they spend all their time on.

This choice is actually feasible now: it's called eSports.

With most of the projects I have worked on, I haven't played them in my spare time. Some of them weren't even built for me as a target audience in mind (children's games for example). You don't need to spend every waking hour playing games to be a good tester. On the contrary, some of the best test professionals that I've met hardly play games at all in their spare time.

You wouldn't expect software testers to be 'fans', for example. The team who tested Microsoft Word or Adobe Photoshop *probably* didn't spend their spare time getting really good at word processing or technical drawing. We can refer to this genre and project-specific information as 'Domain Knowledge' and I've found that it can be fairly easily picked up after moving to a new project team. The only exception to this rule is that some game teams will sometimes try to hire subject matter experts if the game is competitive and they don't have anyone on the team that already fits this profile.

A good example of this is fighting games using arcade sticks. The team will need to be able both to execute the characters' complex moves and balance the difficulty levels of the AI opponents.

Another example is competitive racing simulation games, both using a controller and with a steering wheel. Some of these games have loyal fans who would react badly if new content was released in an unbalanced way or if the game was too easy. This is probably the only instance where being good at a specific game is going to help you as a tester and, even then, I want to stress that this would purely be a supplement to the core of the testing role.

The aim of quality processes – and testing as one of those processes – is to guide a single project throughout its development. The progress from concept through to public release will take months and years for the team, with most test staff remaining on the project for a large part of that project lifecycle.

Unless you are part of a big company with multiple projects on the go, you most likely won't have a choice of projects; so really, you will just be working on the project which needs you and it will be a permanent fixture. This can be slightly different for outsource companies who are facilitating test services for multiple game studio clients. In this environment you would be more likely to move freely between projects.

1.2   Quality assurance vs. testing

It's important to understand the distinction between quality assurance and testing. It's so widely misused and misunderstood that having a well defined understanding of both terms will help guide you through day-to-day conversations in the workplace.

There's a difference in scope between the two terms. Quality assurance talks about all processes across the entire project that are designed to maintain a level of quality in the delivered work, while testing is a subset of that group, being just one of those processes. Testing is a specific activity to gather information about the current state of the product (how healthy it is). Quality processes outside of testing includes things like the review process, checklists and workflow procedures which prompt the team to perform certain actions, eliminating human error and communication error.

A good way to separate the two terms is to ask yourself, who is responsible for quality and who is responsible for testing?

A test team can't be responsible for the quality of work produced by every person on the project team. Even if you had a QA analyst for every member of the team creating content for the game, he or she would have to understand the work as intimately as the author of that work and be able to accurately assess the quality of it and spot any mistakes. Many quality assurance practices are also technical practices and owned by the code teams on the project; processes like coding standards and code reviews. These are the responsibility of the code team and nearly always beyond the influence of the test team.

Listed here are some activities and processes which have been categorised into QA processes and testing processes.

Quality Assurance	Testing
Static analysis code tools	Test organisation + strategy
Unit tests	Test designs
Coding standards	Test review and quality control
Code reviews	Test progress + monitoring
Design spec reviews	Test reporting
Tech spec reviews	Test tools and automation
Risk analysis	
Release process	
Incident management	
Operational monitoring + tools	

Figure 1.1

This is confusing because many people use the acronym QA (Quality Assurance) to talk about test teams.* Many testing roles also have titles like 'QA Analyst' or 'QA Tester' and commonly refer to the whole discipline as 'QA'. Because it *is* so ill-defined, there's quite a lot of controversy whether testers exist primarily to *assure* the quality of a product. 'Assure' means to make something certain to happen which, as we've highlighted already, would be an impossible task for testers. To dispel this view, some game studios have taken to rebranding their test teams as 'Quality Essentials' and 'Quality Assistance', showing that their role is more akin to quality consultants.

The content covered here will mostly focus on testing specifically, with some quality processes introduced in later chapters. This is because more junior members

---

*   One of my personal hates is people substituting the word 'test', 'tester' or 'tested' for just 'QA', to a point where the sentence doesn't make sense anymore. I see posts online from recruiters saying things like "We need QA's!" and I think to myself, "We all need quality assurances all right, but how are you going to do that?". Another personal favourite is, "Can I get this QA'd?". "Can I get this quality assured?" and I think "I don't know, can you? You tell me, you created it!". We can't communicate effectively either because we're unaware or lazy, so let's get it right.

of the games testing profession will start out their career only thinking about testing and not about the bigger quality process picture. Other quality processes outside of testing are also out of reach of vendor teams and remote publishing teams since most of these processes are applied close to the creation of the game itself, onsite in the studio.

It should be the case that as testers mature throughout the course of their career, they start to consider the greater scope of game quality and extend their thinking beyond just the immediate tasks of testing. However, only those who work within a game studio and are in more senior positions will have a reasonable influence on these quality processes, because they require buy in from other project stakeholders and influence how the entire team conducts their work. We'll cover this more in the next section.

1.3   The goals of quality assurance

We've already established the larger scope of quality assurance and also that it's mainly focused at the source of project development, within the game studio. Generally speaking, the goals of all QA processes are primarily preventative measures to decrease the chances of mistakes being made which might later lead to errors. The processes that don't prevent mistakes are designed to catch them as quickly as possible after they've been made. You might recognise these types of processes as just 'best practice' protocols, which teams usually adopt over time anyway.

The aim of quality processes is to maintain the velocity of completed work while producing fewer mistakes along the way. They can be as much about increasing the efficiency and effectiveness of a team as they are about increasing the quality of the work being output.

Since quality processes are discipline-specific, they need to be tailored to each discipline, too. Coding standards and the team's code review process will be different to the art review process and the content pipeline which is followed when working on new art content for the game. These hint at why quality assurance has such a large scope when compared with testing.

It's also why you will find test managers working so closely with the production discipline and others within the business who manage the lifecycle of work (sometimes also known as Product Manager or Scrum Master role). The process is a collaborative effort between the person in the test manager role with the process knowledge, and the discipline lead with the domain knowledge of the area. Good test managers can influence best practices and processes across an entire game project team. When this is done well, the discipline leads start to appreciate the stability of the work and, before long, wouldn't want to proceed without it.

Quality at source

We couldn't talk about quality assurance without mentioning the term 'quality at source' which you may have heard a few times.

This term refers to those quality processes that are as close to the source of creation as possible. You will find talks and discussions on how different teams are striving to achieve better quality at source. 'Upstream quality' has the same meaning and takes its terminology from the waterfall software development model which we'll cover in the next chapter. 'Shift left' also means the same thing and makes more sense if you view the software development model as a flow chart in chronological order.

All it means is that teams are endeavouring to improve quality at the source of creation because they know that it leads to less mistakes, therefore fewer bugs. Put another way, unlike most testing initiatives, these activities focus on bug prevention instead of detection. They are proactive measures. Senior test staff within a game studio will be involved in decisions about how the project team plans and conducts their work to achieve better quality at source. Armed with information about quality at source and a few ideas, the tester can influence the rest of the team to improve this initiative.

The error cost escalation model

The error cost escalation model gives greater business weight to the 'quality at source' strategy and shows that the later in a project lifecycle we fix an error, the more expensive it is to fix that error. There are several examples online of businesses which have collected real data to support this conclusion. A somewhat extreme example is a NASA whitepaper[*] talking about the cost of software failure. It's not hard to imagine how expensive it is to fix a software bug when the shuttle is already *in space*.

It's similar with the design of a new game feature. If we can review the design specification sufficiently well enough to identify a flaw in the proposed design flow, then the flaw can be fixed in the design before a single line of code is written to implement the new game feature. Changing the design could take a few minutes, but fixing the same error after the code was written would probably take a couple of hours. If it was left even longer and other game components were built upon that feature then they'd have to be edited to fix the issue as well, which would take even longer. If the error was only found once the game was live, then it would have to be included in a patch or fixed on the server, or perhaps the game would have to be taken into

---

[*]   https://ntrs.nasa.gov/archive/nasa/casi.ntrs.nasa.gov/20100036670.pdf

maintenance, and maybe online players given compensation. Fixing a bug when the game is live is the most expensive and least desirable route to a fix.

1.4   The goals of testing

Why do we test? The most common and obvious answer to this question is 'to find bugs'. I get it. As a process, test effort goes in and bugs come out, simples. But this is only part of the answer. There are more questions about why we log bugs. Since, as testers, we spend a great deal of time performing test activities in our work, it's definitely worth taking the time to understand all the reasons we do it and what the true goals are.

Let's define some of the generic testing goals which you could apply to all software, then I'll muddy those waters with some game testing specific goals.

Does testing directly improve the quality of the game?

This is the first clarification to make and it's something of a common misconception about the reasons for testers to exist: that testing as an activity alone directly increases the quality of the product. We see it all the time in online forums and in articles on video games – reports of released games being buggy and shots being fired at the test teams for missing those bugs. "The test team must be rubbish" they say. "They should hire me instead and I'll find those bugs".

There's an assumption there that if a bug is found, then it gets fixed and the quality of the game is increased. But this isn't the case. Stakeholders on the project team collectively balance bug fixing with other project priorities, deciding how to best spend the valuable work time. There are many factors which can influence this decision making on the 'if', 'when' and 'how' to fix bugs.

For example, it's common to have multiple sub-teams within a project, working on different parts of that project, each one managing its own time independently, and each containing key stakeholders who have an input to the decision-making process. Those sub teams may have different priorities and a varying velocity of new work they can get through, and so may make different decisions on how many bugs they can fix. Game teams will also have varying quantities of specialists who can fix different bugs on the project, influencing the rate of bug fixes being made in each area. Engine and systems code, gameplay code, UI code, server code, design data, 3D models, animation, sound, environment, visual effects are just *some* of the different specialist skills that require those specific people on the team to fix bugs in those areas. The lesson here is that not all bugs are created equal. This lesson is also *more* true within games than other software because of the much greater range of specialists.

So, does testing directly improve the quality of the game? No it doesn't. Instead, it's more accurate to say that testing collects data about the quality of the game and presents it to the project stakeholders so that they can use it to make decisions.

This also brings us back to the question of the testing goals. Bugs are *just one* form of data that we collect about the quality of the game. Other forms of data include things like test pass/fail results, red/amber/green health ratings, performance and reliability data, to name a few. The point is, we're collecting bugs and other test data as a record of the quality of the game and doing it in sufficient detail that action can be taken to improve the quality.

As a brief aside, I'm using the word *stakeholder* to refer to a person who has a business interest in the feature or project that is the target of decision making. Stakeholder is also a role, not a job title, and in some teams it might be assigned but otherwise it would be decided on the fly. It's common for embedded test leads to be stakeholders themselves in project decision making and so, in this sense, they must wear two hats: their testing hat, where the priority is to collect quality data objectively; and their stakeholder hat, which is to provide a subjective opinion on project decision making.

It's all about risk

We collect data about the health of the game because we're uncertain. We're uncertain whether it's stable, whether it's balanced well, if the latest feature that was integrated into the game didn't break some other previously healthy part of the game. It's exactly the same as any other uncertainty, like wondering if you remembered to lock the door after you left the house. There's a chance that you did lock it, and there's also a chance that you didn't. If the risk is high enough, then you might return home to check it, eliminating that uncertainty.

A risk is an unknown that has a chance of a negative outcome. On the other hand, an opportunity is an unknown that has a chance of a positive outcome.

Test activities are all based around risk analysis and mitigating actions for those risks. We test because we are uncertain (about mistakes) and that uncertainty could have a negative outcome (errors manifesting as bugs). By testing and collecting data we are making what is unknown, known again, eliminating the uncertainty. For example, "We thought there might be bugs in the code and now we've found some of them through testing, we are more certain that this was true."

A large part of effective test planning is driven by good risk management, and knowledge of this is particularly required by QA analysts and QA managers. You will also be able to read up on risk management strategies from outside games and apply them to your work, too, since this is one of the more generic areas.

To develop this idea further, we can say that collecting bug data confirms our uncertainty that there *are* quality issues with the game, and collecting positive test results confirms that specific areas function correctly without errors. Put another way, positive test results give us confidence and help us get clarity, even if we don't find bugs. This brings us back to the myth that the goal of testing is to find bugs. Not finding bugs is great; it means the game is healthier and we have the positive test results to back up the data and give confidence to the stakeholders. (This assumes that sufficient testing has been carried out to collect the data, of course.)

Lastly, it's important to note that we can never fully eliminate uncertainty. Just because *one bug* is found in an area, it doesn't mean that we've uncovered all of the unknowns. There could be more bugs remaining hidden. Similarly, a positive test result doesn't mean that a feature is bug free, since each test still only covers a specific scenario. This becomes useful when we communicate our confidence and certainty based on test results. Understanding and analysing test data into a format that can be communicated is mainly the job of QA analysts and when done well, it takes a surprising amount of time and energy.

Industry tales: The gatekeepers of quality

Through widespread uncertainty about the goals of testing – among testers and other disciplines alike – an unhealthy relationship often develops between the test team and the rest of the project team. This commonly manifests through an incorrect culture where the test team is held responsible for the quality of the product. Other disciplines think that the test team owns all quality processes and that they exist to take 'the burden of the responsibility of quality' off of their plate.

Similarly, some testers enjoy wielding this power by blocking releases ("The quality of this isn't good enough to release!") and fighting the quality corner during project meetings ("We need more time to test, we need to allocate more time to bug fixing, we need to fix this bug because I think it's really bad") This approach creates opposing goals between the test team and the rest of the organisation which leads to a discussion in the absolute best scenario, but in most cases allows continuous conflict, distrust and adversarial relationships to fester between testers and the rest of the team. These are the game teams you might hear about in the news or through colleagues, where the test team is openly reprimanded when bugs are found in a released product.

'Finger pointing' and blaming become the tools for dealing with these failures, deepening the rift between testers and non-testers even further. This culture also contributes to the perception of testers being negative, counterproductive and just out to find problems in the work created by others.

I've worked with people who have been in these teams previously and have skewed expectations and perceptions of the current test team. This was during projects where I was working in the embedded QA analyst role. These individuals haven't ignored me outright, but have been indifferent, uncooperative or disrespectful when we started working together. After a couple of months working in the same feature development pod, through consistent testing competence and a good attitude, I've gained their respect and trust, and (I hope) changed their view on what good game testers look like. To build these relationships, I would be overly communicative about the intentions of my work and how I could add value to the work they were doing. By doing this I would attempt to reset their expectations of me and the test team.

I actually found that when I raised the topic of who was responsible for quality, a majority of my colleagues from other disciplines were in agreement that it was their responsibility too, and had the right attitude towards it; it just required someone to start the discussion. While I've painted a negative picture here, the same majority of non-test colleagues have been great to work with from day one. I hope that as the game testing discipline improves, these negative attitudes will continue to reduce.

I once spoke to past colleagues who were working on another project within the same company; some of them were QA analysts and QA managers, while others were producers, designers and developers. They all gave me their perspective at different times about the same problem that had been continuing for many months and years. There was a breakdown of trust between members of the test team and the development pods that they worked in. The QA analysts had given up trying to cooperate with some of the other team members and had started to withhold information because they felt they were not being listened to. One of them told me that he knew there were severe bugs with the current release but wasn't going to escalate it and that it would "teach them a lesson" when they discovered it. The producers and other team members saw the QA analysts as roadblocks to getting the work done and were working around them by making requests directly to the external team of testers who were executing the tests – so worsening the relationship.

The ongoing reactions from both 'sides' had made the situation gradually worse over time, but what had initially sparked the animosity?

The clue that alerted me was the way the QA analysts would speak to me about conflicts over the quality of the releases and how the project leadership wasn't listening to their concerns. The test team had adopted the role of the guardians of quality and were in frequent conflict over the agreed quality benchmark for each release. This stance had labelled them as blockers to the release of game updates and a problem to be appeased or circumvented wherever possible. The project had some high profile bugs that escaped testing and went out into the live game on several occasions, triggering hotfix releases and retrospective follow-up meetings to diagnose what had gone wrong. Sure enough, I heard that the test team bore the brunt of these failures and had a particularly difficult few weeks each time it happened.

It's part of working life that we may have to work with people that we don't get along with. This can't be helped and might have been true for some members of this team more than most. Regardless of this speculation, the test team had set themselves up for failure by taking the 'guardians of quality' stance and had worsened it through poor attitudes and use of soft skills. This scenario might sound familiar: this isn't the only team I've heard of with this problem. I can't overstate the importance of remembering and evangelising the true goals of our work as testers: capturing data to help inform project decision making. Not capturing data and making decisions privately, only to then present those decisions to the other project leaders.

I read once that the test team wins when the business wins, and I couldn't agree more. This example shows us how important it is to align the goals of testing with the goals of the project team and of the company.

Industry tales: "Everything has to be tested"

In other scenarios, the attitudes of non-testers could be neutral, but they would still have a misunderstanding of my role on the team. Do they need to test their work or was I there to test it for them? Would they be stepping on my toes by carrying out some of the testing themselves? If my schedule was full, could they include a feature if they promised to test it all themselves?

Many non-testers I've spoken to believed that testing was a verification that the game component worked correctly. They saw it as a straightforward and obvious activity. The last question in the examples above is one I've actually been asked quite often. My work time is usually at capacity, with no opportunity to take on planning for more features. So when someone wants to increase the scope of a sprint by including an additional feature, they come to ask if they can include it on the condition that they test it themselves. Their perception of what constitutes 'testing' is usually an over-simplification of the work that I would carry out, so I've needed to approach these requests with diplomacy and select follow-up questions to ask in return.

I'd ask how risky the change was, why they wanted it and how the change stacked up against the priorities of the other features that I was planning for. I would gather information about the request (test planning, essentially) through these questions and then identify what the scope of testing might be (test analysis) before making suggestions as to how we could include that feature and achieve what that person wanted.

Here, again, it was good that the person had raised the request in the first place. They could have just included the feature without telling anyone about it – which does happen by the way. It was important to thank the person for raising the request and take a solutions-orientated approach to it. Testing time will always be in demand: do *not* be tempted to wield this power over people who make requests of you by saying that you are 'doing them a favour', or by taking a large intake of breath and hissing like a car mechanic who's about to quote you an enormous sum of money to fix your car. "I can fix it, but it's going to cost you!". Such reactions to requests are not going to win you any trust or influence, both of which you will need to carry out your testing work effectively.

This type of request stems from the belief that everything must be tested. Test teams commonly communicate that all new work must go through testing, regardless of what it is. So, these feature addition requests came to me because the owners weren't sure how to approach the problem but knew 'the test team will want to test this'.

The assumption that everything needs to be tested is wrong and these scenarios were a great opportunity to explain why. Remember that testing is all about gathering information, and we usually gather information because we are unsure about something. Instead of jumping directly to how long it might take to test the change, I would ask questions to gather information about the unknowns related to the change. How much risk did the change carry? Would our planned testing mitigate the risks anyway? Would we even need to run dedicated tests for it? Would manual testing be an effective way to mitigate the risks? Were there other ways we could mitigate the risks without changing the test schedule?

Never just test for the sake of testing. Remember what testing is trying to achieve and use this to navigate these types of requests. I can guarantee it will save you time, win you respect and inform those non-testers around you.

Testing captures data to clarify doubts (unknowns or potential risks, essentially) that these changes might contain bugs. The point is that we can assess this level of doubt before we even consider testing, remembering that testing is the solution to these quality risks.

When properly analysed, many of the small changes I've been presented with carried very low risk. It would have been easy to insist on testing that didn't present a good return on the time investment. i.e. performing more testing than was warranted, given the risk level of the change. Many of these small changes would be tweaks to the balancing of the game that we had already adjusted several times, or additional telemetry events that used the existing analytics system. If the change was to adjust the game balancing, this told me it didn't require any code edits and was a data adjustment to a value using a system that we had already tested. Because we had high confidence in the code which read that value, we would have also have high confidence that the value could be changed without causing bugs. If we had already adjusted the value at least once before, this gave us even further confidence in the proposed change.

Sometimes, requests like these were to make the change to the live game remotely, as soon as possible, given that we wouldn't need to release a game update for it – meaning that the change would go live as soon as testing was done.

These data changes could be deployed remotely and immediately. If confidence was high and the stakeholders were in agreement, I had no problem saying that I was happy to go ahead without testing at all. On the live ops projects I've worked on, small changes were being deployed into the live game very frequently, at least once a week. So, recommending testing for each and every change where it wasn't required would have both placed a huge burden on the test team and slowed down the team's ability to deploy changes to the game. In some of these scenarios, the live ops test team would run their testing on the live game and would be able to perform a quick check to make sure the change had applied correctly, nothing else. This was done as a quick and easy sanity check.

I've found that recommending testing for a change needs to be based on logical, sound decision making. If anyone thinks that you are just testing for the sake of testing, or testing because that's the way things are done for all changes, they may lose confidence in your decision making and reiterate their alternative viewpoint again. When discussing if and how much testing needs to be carried out, the person I'm speaking to is usually the subject matter expert for that change too, so their opinion carries more weight on the final decision. This also means that they are in a prime position to know if the need for testing the change was incorrectly assessed.

1.5   An intro to how we test

Now that we know *why* we test, we should begin to understand *how* we test and talk about some of the different types of testing.

The information on testing as a data gathering activity was aimed to summarise all test activities under a single banner. Practically, there are more granular reasons for capturing data on the health of the game. Each area we're exploring has its own data format and method of capturing it effectively. So, different test activities are required to achieve this.

We capture performance data on metrics like framerate and memory usage to check that our game runs well on the hardware its planned for; we capture game artifacts like logs, videos and errors to help us diagnose bugs; we capture pass/fail test results to give us granular confidence on the game health. On top of these, we also collect metadata on testing itself, tracking the velocity and completion of testing progress so that we can communicate our work progress and provide accurate estimates to the wider team.

We shouldn't embark on these test activities for every project just because it's what we normally do. Instead, part of the test team's job is to identify information that is productive to capture to help guide the project, and then apply the right activities to effectively collect the data in a timely enough manner to be useful

Checking vs. testing

These are two test activities which are often misunderstood. They are both designed for different reasons, to capture different kinds of data. You'll find ongoing discussions on social media and in various online articles and forums on the topic of 'checking vs. testing'; it's a subject that extends beyond games and is something you can read up on further if you wish. It's a great example of how understanding the end goal of the activity allows you to structure and execute that activity much more effectively.

> **Checking refers to the straightforward, specific confirmation of something that was uncertain, to make it now certain. It verifies something as true (or untrue).**

In a game example, checking is frequently used when implementing new features. Each feature usually has some type of specification, design or acceptance criteria that says "when these things are built, we can consider this feature done". To make certain that everything has been included, we can check what was actually built in the game against what the documentation said we wanted to build.

This activity is specific, limited in scope, highly scripted and positive in its method of verification. Note that if the documentation was detailed enough about the requirements of the feature, it could be used to guide to checking without the need for a separate written format (a manual test). Also note that if the documentation was detailed enough, *anyone* could theoretically follow it to perform the check, including automation tooling or an AI.

Checking is usually specific enough that the result is binary, true or false, pass or fail; and so the data we get back from it is a list of pass/fail results. The only supplementary data we provide is if one of the checks fails, in which case it would include the reason for the check failing, which can help us understand how the actual result differed from our expectations.

Attributes of checking:

Specific – Checking asks closed questions to get a binary answer. Checks ask closed questions like "Does it do this?" (a yes/no answer), but not open questions like "How does it do this?", "Why does it do this?", "When does it do this?" (requires an explanation). Lots of game development teams use a set format for their criteria for this reason, it goes like this: GIVEN ...*something*..., WHEN ...*something else happens*..., THEN ...*the expected outcome shows*[*]

Limited in scope – Checking is intentionally limited to confirm a specific uncertainty, like a feature, and do it quickly. We are focused in our approach and don't get distracted looking for nearby bugs that are not relevant to the check. This is intentional to get the uncertainty confirmed quickly and efficiently.

Highly scripted – Checking defines the exact scenario that we should be verifying and provides all of the prerequisite steps to get us there. It doesn't make assumptions and, because it asks a specific question, it doesn't require any enhancement from the checker. Put another way, the same check, given to a group of people to run individually and separately, should produce the same result from each person.

Positive – Checking is nearly always about verifying that something *does* occur correctly, and rarely about verifying that something *doesn't* occur. The scope of things failing to occur is huge because there are so many ways that failures can manifest. This ties in with checks being limited in scope. If I go back home to check that I locked the door, I *only* check that it is locked. I don't start checking if the lock could jam, if the door hinges could be compromised or if someone could unlock the door through the letterbox. Failure checks are negative and have a hugely increased scope. They also require creative thinking and a great deal more time to create and execute.

---

[*]   More information can be found online on this approach: search "given-when-then"

Driven by documentation – Checking is frequently driven by documentation, whether design specifications, requirements specifications or stories/tasks in the project database. Checklists are either taken directly from this material or derived from it, but the source of the checks come from the author of the document, not a tester. The tester may still have the challenge of figuring out how to perform the checks, but the list of 'what' to check has been created already.

It's important to notice that all these checking attributes give quick and efficient confirmation of the issues that we're checking for. If we expand our previous example of a specific feature to a larger scope of a game update, we want to get confidence that the update hasn't broken existing functionality. In this scenario we're not really interested in finding old bugs or exploring edge case scenarios. Our aim is to feel confident that the update didn't introduce new bugs in the existing game. In this scenario we might use checks to do a positive verification of large sections of the existing game with the goal of building confidence that they have *not* broken. In this scenario, these checks are the quickest way to get through such large sections of the game without it taking an unacceptably long time.

Testing includes everything that you can possibly do beyond checking.

In comparison, testing is almost unlimited in its scope and can vary in its specificity, be positive or negative and as scripted as required. It can be formatted to ask open questions, to find out specific information or to perform a specific task. For this reason, tests can be structured to find and record different formats of data, breaking the binary structure that checks follow. A test can be created to investigate the balance of a game area and provide a subjective conclusion, or to make performance comparisons between two versions of the game where the output is in the format of side-by-side data.

Critically, the greater scope of testing includes not just positive tests, but negative ones too. Negative tests investigate the ways that things could potentially fail so that we can take preventative action. To design good failure tests, testers need to do a kind of 'pre-mortem' on the component under testing to generate ideas on the biggest points of failure, and then figure out a way that they can feasibly test those scenarios.

Later on in this chapter we'll go into more detail about positive (verification) and negative (failure) testing, as well as the split between scripted and unscripted tests.

The last attribute of checking we defined was 'driven by documentation'. The comparison with testing is an important one to make because it feeds into reasons for testing as a dedicated discipline.

Unlike checking, testing is almost entirely designed by the QA analyst creating the strategy, or the tester executing the tests. It's the *added value* that test professionals bring to the business. Over time, testers build a knowledge bank of experience and tools that they take with them and helps them identify what areas to focus testing on. Some of the best testers I've met are simply good at asking the *right questions* that trigger others in the team to take action, without even running a single test!

It's this perspective, this thought process, that drives these types of incisive questions and genuinely effective test direction. These tests require someone to first think of the test as an area that should be looked at, and then have the skills to write a test that will fulfil the idea. I'll go into detail about test analysis – which defines decision-making techniques testers can use to help them decide *what* to test. I'll also cover test design and define some techniques to help testers figure out *how* to test those areas.

Attributes of testing:

Flexible – Unlike checking, testing can be adapted to ask all kinds of questions and achieve different goals. Testing can build confidence in an area by collecting test results; it can be targeted to find as many bugs as quickly as possible; it can be formed as an investigation to collect data and make conclusions, amongst many other goals.

Bigger in scope – The scope of testing is its main defining factor. If they have the time, test teams can test as deeply as they like, exploring whatever scenarios they think productive – whether they're main flow, edge cases, negative or positive tests. Tests are only limited by the minds of the team generating test scenarios and the time the team has to execute them.

Variable granularity – Tests can take on whatever level of detail is required. A test script would define every exact step, while a test session might provide a rough test charter. Varying levels of granularity have different advantages depending on the application. Test granularity is defined and explored more deeply in chapter five, **Test design techniques**.

Variable in intent – Tests can be both positive (verifying that things work correctly) and negative (testing that things don't fail). Written tests for any single component should try and find a healthy balance between the two.

Driven by the test team – Testing, as the activity defined here, is mostly driven by QA analysts and test leads, though it's also common for other disciplines to review test plans and feed into the test scenario ideas. Unlike checking, test design and implementation originate in the mind of the person creating the test plan and don't have an existing piece of documentation to use as guidance.

I said earlier that these two terms are quite misunderstood. This is because many people outside the testing discipline think that testers just exist to perform the checking activity. These same people will also often claim that the test discipline will eventually be replaced entirely by automation.

They are right about one thing: in the most advanced teams, checking is automated and manual test teams get more time to do what they are good at – testing. Many junior QA testers and QA analysts, who don't understand this distinction yet themselves, tend to focus almost entirely on the positive verification surrounding the checking activity. They seem to be unaware that the scope of their work should extend beyond this. Sometimes a project operates at such a fast pace that the test team aren't given the time to perform testing. These scenarios illustrate that it's important for anyone in the test discipline to understand the distinction between checking and testing, so even if their current work doesn't allow them to perform the depth of testing that they would like, they're still able to make a convincing proposal to project leadership to change the project process, instead of accepting the current checking as the correct and only way.

Chapter three (**Test types and terminology**) will go into more detail about specific test activities, and chapter five (**Test design techniques**) will discuss tools that you can add into your toolbox when creating the test plans described here.

1.6   The fundamental test process

The fundamental test process is a template which categorises the key test activities that occur within the lifecycle of testing. The process itself is not specific to game software, but we'll walk through some game project examples when working through the process, to give it more context.

The process is exactly what the name suggests: a series of fundamental steps that define the stages of the core testing process in chronological order. Within each category, we can fit all of the different test activities and techniques that we'll talk about in this book. Since it's chronological, the fundamental test process can remind us of the order in which we should be doing things.

We should think of this as the basic framework we can use to map out the different test skills that we have. These are compartments in the tester's toolbox described in the introduction. As we gain new skills and experience, we can place them in their relevant compartment and, over time, understand how much knowledge we have within each section. This should allow us not just to make more sense of each technique, but, by grouping the techniques into functional areas, we can recall them more easily when we need to make use of them.

The fundamental test process:

- Test planning
- Test analysis
- Test design and implementation
- Test execution, monitoring and control
- Test reporting
- Test closure activities

Being primarily responsible for executing testing directly, QA tester-style roles will use most of the skills that fall into the category of test execution, monitoring and control. These skills are covered in the chapters three (**Test types and terminology**) and six (**Major areas of game testing**).

QA analyst-style roles which plan and write tests will find all chapters useful, but chapters four (**Test analysis techniques**) and five (**Test design techniques**) the most valuable for the core of their work. These chapters cover test planning and analysis, as well as test design and implementation.

Anyone holding a test lead or higher role will find all of the content here useful as a foundation for further reading, but specifically chapter seven, **Test management**. Test management governs the organisation of *all* categories of the fundamental test process, so it sits at a slightly higher level.

Before we go into the details of each step, it's worth noting that the scope of this process can be adapted to fit the scenario at hand. The process can be applied to an entire project and involve a team of testers all working on each step together. This approach is commonly followed in the 'waterfall' software development methodology, where everything is designed in one stage, then built in code and tested at the end. The style of the wider project allows the test team to follow this fundamental test process for the whole project over several months and years. In this scenario, the team will normally have time to approach each test step formally, writing test plan documents and setting up processes from scratch to last the lifetime of the project. We'll talk more about the waterfall methodology in chapter two, **Project lifecycles**.

The process can also be followed on a smaller scale for a specific release or update. This scenario may still involve several of the test team working together, but the timespan will be shorter and the level of formality will be lower. Some of the steps in the process may be followed but not documented, while others may not be necessary at all. An average-size game update might take several weeks to plan and release, but usually no longer than that. The test team know that the lifespan of their work will only be relevant for this time period, and invest in the process accordingly.

The test process also holds true for a single QA analyst working as part of a project pod on a new feature for the game. The analyst will go through the phases of the fundamental test process for that feature, finishing when the feature is integrated or released. Depending on the size of the feature, this might take several days or weeks.

It's normal for small test plans for features to feed into bigger test plans for the release in which they will be included. This in turn, feeds into the test strategy for the project. Each of these fundamental test process layers will be owned by different people on the test team and will also change depending on the organisational makeup on the QA discipline on the project.

While individual QA analysts working within a game studio might be responsible for the test plans for a specific feature, the larger-scale strategy might be owned by a principal QA analyst or a QA lead. Where remote test teams exist, it's also quite common for QA testers to be assigned as the remote owner for a feature and to oversee the execution of testing locally.

So the fundamental test process is useful for the entire discipline and provides a core foundation for the test team to organise themselves around. It also provides consistent terminology that allows test teams to communicate together and outwards to others in the business more effectively.

Top tips - being articulate

Being able to communicate with other non-test disciplines within the studio is incredibly important, because it's very unlikely that they understand the details of your work (when I say non-test disciplines I mean art, code, design, production, etc.). Worse, it is, unfortunately, quite common for non-test disciplines to think they understand game testing, because it's sometimes perceived to be a relatively non-technical and straightforward activity.

> **The fundamental test process, and other terminology defined within this book, gives us a vocabulary we can use to articulate our intentions more clearly and precisely.**

There are discussions that happen daily between different disciplines in a game studio – things like the state of recent feature work, the progress towards the next milestone and how much test time is needed. The team will get together to make decisions on when to start fixing bugs, what features to work on next and when isolated features should be merged into the main body of work. Input is required from all disciplines to make good decisions, with the test discipline being no exception.

During these meetings, the test representative will need to give details of their in-progress work as well as their intentions for the remaining work. It's very common for the decision-making group to challenge each other and ask further incisive questions in order to come to a conclusion. These discussions may also include project management; executive producers, for example, are usually at the core of large tactical decisions within the project.

For this reason, the test representative needs to make sure they are as concise and precise as possible when talking about their test plans and the underlying reasons for their plans. In my experience, people respond positively to sound reasoning and precise answers. They will also come to expect this type of response over time, and are more likely to proactively seek your input in future decisions. Ultimately, communicating in this way helps build trust and confidence in you as a test discipline knowledge holder, and reflects positively on the discipline as a whole.

A good example of this is when other disciplines forget that test analysis and design needs to take place, and expect testing to begin sooner than it can. A client code engineer may deliver a feature late into testing and then become frustrated that testing hasn't begun immediately.

An experienced QA Analyst would be able to explain why it's important to spend time adequately planning testing. An even better response would be to use the topic to suggest that the code engineer involves the QA analyst sooner, and the feature is delivered into testing incrementally.

When you first have these conversations, you might feel unsure because you haven't yet proven the reasoning within your team. You could be thinking, "I'm doing this because the book content suggested it and it sounds like a good point". After you've had some success yourself, you will be able to enter these discussions with more conviction. I strongly encourage you to practise your communication style using the terminology here and develop it further.

I'd also suggest you take time to prepare for meetings where you know your input will be required and decisions will be made. Don't make the mistake of appearing disorganised, because it will undo the trust you've earned. Make sure you know what you're going to say and can explain the reasoning behind it, use the correct terminology and have the data to back it all up (if it exists).

1.6.1 Test planning

This is the first stage of the test process and has the biggest scope, because it asks questions to help establish and understand the problem at hand. Once the problem has been identified, the remaining stages of the process involve designing and running a test solution that solves the problem.

The test planning phase builds on the reasons for the testing and defines the 'why' of the test plan (What are the test goals?).

For this book, we'll focus on test planning for a specific game area or feature, since this flow is the most applicable to QA analysts and QA testers.

Before writing any tests, the QA analyst will gather all the information about the work completed, to help them understand it as much as possible. The success of the later stages will entirely depend on the way the analyst has interpreted the work, so this foundation is very important.

There will be information on both what was intended to be built and what was actually built, and the analyst will need both of these pieces of information to make their test plans. In the best possible scenario, there will be a design specification and a technical specification, but rarely have I seen this actually happen! It's currently popular amongst game design teams to use short-form design documents, sometimes called 'one-pagers', because they're intended to summarise the design of a feature in a single page. The feature will also have an entry on the project database which tracks the bugs and the work. This is usually called a 'story' or 'task', and will contain some form of acceptance criteria saying, "We will consider this feature to be done when it meets this criteria."

In the most well-organised teams, the acceptance criteria is a moderately detailed bullet-point list of things that the feature will do. This acceptance criteria list also starts to define specific details of how the feature will technically function. For this reason, it's sometimes expanded upon during development. Other times, the story or design may be very sparse, out of date, empty or non-existent.

The process will change slightly depending on the feature or change that the test-planning is for. Features built in code will have different documents and formats than game content built by environment artists and level designers. Consider the design for an open world map within a game, for example. It's less likely to have a long written description of the design or wireframes. Instead it may have a map split into sections, complete with a key and annotated points of interest. It's also more likely to have a set of rules to which the whole environment needs to conform, rather than defining criteria for specific areas.

Some features are driven by the code teams as a project necessity, rather than by design choice, so don't have a corresponding design document. A good example of this is integrating Software Development Kit (SDK) updates into the game's code. SDK version updates are common with the graphics engine used by the game (e.g. Unreal engine, Unity engine), and for the platforms on which the game runs, too (e.g. iOS SDK, Android SDK, Xbox (XDK), PlayStation SDK).

Code framework components that need to be built to support future features are also common, along with non-functional features to improve performance and reliability. In the best scenario, these changes have technical specifications which detail the changes and the code team's own risk assessments. Frequently they have no documentation at all, with the exception of a story or task in the project database. Even then, you will find that these features have sparse information in the acceptance criteria, because they are often forced upon the project team as compulsory updates from the SDK owner and don't change the way that the game functions. I frequently see acceptance criteria like this:

- *"The game should be updated to Unity version 2018.4.11"*
- *"The game should not break after taking the update"*

Understanding any changes to the game and the risk that they carry can be very challenging for the QA analyst to plan testing around. Regardless of the variables discussed above, the QA analyst will invariably need to go and speak with the people carrying out the work. If documentation exists, the analyst can use it as a starting point for asking questions about the feature. If it doesn't, the analyst will need to speak with the authors and have them describe the feature while taking down notes.

The goal of the QA analyst with both of these approaches is to understand the change and assess the risk, so that the correct mitigating actions can be taken later in the fundamental test process.

This is also a great opportunity to get the author's opinion and thoughts on the feature. Do they think it's a big change? Are they concerned about specific things? Do they have scenarios that they think require testing? How confident are they in the stability of the work?

Gathering test-planning data like this via asking the *right* questions is a skill in itself, and something that analysts will need to practise to get right. This planning activity also falls into an area of soft skills in communicating effectively with other people; a skill which requires conscious practice over time. Mutual respect and understanding between team members are the multipliers making this activity truly successful.

Through the course of collecting information about a feature, the QA analyst should be looking for the source of truth on which to base their testing. It's likely that if documentation *does* exist, the testers will be using it as a reference during testing, creating bugs where the document varies from the running feature. So it's important that the analyst agrees with the author what feature reference material can be used for this purpose – what is 'the source of truth'?

Later on, when a discrepancy is found between the source of truth and the game, one of the two will need to be updated to fix the inconsistency. The formal term for the source of truth is the Test Oracle – the source we will use to determine the expected results of tests and use as a comparison against actual results. I don't think I've ever heard anyone actually use this term in a game studio, however, where referring to the 'source of truth' is more common workplace language[*].

When no documentation exists, the intended design may be only in the mind of a designer and the technical design will be in the mind of the engineer. It's common enough on games projects, particularly in small teams, for the details of features to be worked out through a conversation in front of a whiteboard or in an instant-messaging channel. This example is simplified, and instead usually involves several specialists who will each contribute their own skillset to the creation of the feature. In these scenarios, when the test team are unclear about the expected result of a test, they will contact the relevant specialist on the feature team to seek clarification. Documenting who the feature stakeholders are and who the point of contact is for various questions is part of the initial test planning process, and will help testers later on know who to speak to for specific areas of testing.

This list of people also forms the audience for test reports in the later stages of the fundamental test process. Links to documentation, the database stories for the feature and the point of contact list are documented in the test plan itself. This test plan can come in any format the team prefers and will be the root work item to which the further stages of the feature test process link.

1.6.2 Test analysis

> *Let's talk about test analysis. This activity defines*
> *what you plan to test but not yet how.*

The test analysis begins almost immediately and in parallel to test planning, when the QA analyst begins to investigate the feature and speak to others on the team about it. Through conversation and investigation into the feature, ideas of what should be covered in testing will surface and need to be documented.

The test analysis phase exists to provide a map of 'things that need to be done' so that tests can be written later, using that map as a guide. For this reason, this step becomes increasingly more important the larger the scope of testing is. Practically, it starts as a list and quickly becomes unwieldy, so evolves into a tree structure with areas and subareas of things that need to be tested.

The process is like preparing to write an essay: making sure you've mapped out the beginning, middle and end; ensuring all the sections are consistent, don't overlap and

---

[*]   Just because the current teams I've personally worked in don't use the 'correct' terminology doesn't mean that this should stop us from aspiring to improve this in the future. This actually supports the point we made earlier about being articulate in our communication style.

don't leave gaps between the content of each. If we go straight into test writing without first analysing what needs to be done, we're much more likely to make mistakes in the writing and end up with a less effective set of tests. The worst case scenario means areas will be missed entirely from the test analysis, letting potential critical bugs remain undetected.

I personally find that without a mind-mapping exercise to take the time and think about test analysis *before* writing the tests, I end up having ideas while I'm writing the tests that force me to go back and edit the approach I've taken to some of the tests, making changes to areas I've already written.

Retrospectively updating tests to include new steps or additional direction is always going to be messier and more error-prone than getting it right the first time. When this happens I also find I have a large set of tests all in progress and none of them complete, instead of just working on them sequentially, one at a time.

Test Conditions

Test conditions are the output of the test analysis phase where each condition refers to a specific scenario that needs to be tested.

Later on when tests are written, they are created to satisfy these test conditions with the aim of capturing all of the conditions by the end of test writing. Practically, I've found when writing tests that it's common for a single test to satisfy multiple conditions, with just a minority of tests targeting a single condition each.

A basic example might be creating a test condition to test a mobile game feature on mobile devices with a notch in the screen. Since this can be done in parallel with other tests, it can be satisfied 'passively' during testing. The technique requires a little practice and requires going through the process of creating tests from a set of test conditions at least once. This is because it can be difficult to figure out the granularity of your test conditions: how specific do you want to be with each condition? Are you expecting each condition to be satisfied by an individual test?

Identifying what needs to be tested is one of the core parts of the QA analyst role and also something which QA testers are likely to contribute to. For this reason, chapter four on **Test analysis techniques** will cover the creation of test conditions extensively, giving practical guidance on what you need to consider when planning your testing.

1.6.3 Test design and implementation

The design phase covers all of the tactical details of how you're actually going to test the areas identified during the analysis phase.

Good test design is about choosing the test activities that will be most effective for each part of the test plan and then creating each test with the appropriate structure and writing style that is most effective for that activity. Should you use scripted testing throughout the plan, or would a focused exploratory session be more effective for parts of it? Will you need tools or automated tests to execute some areas of the plan? If the plan has a large section for regression testing, do you need to write new tests or can you reuse existing tests? These questions and many more are answered during the test design phase. Once again, the QA analyst must search this compartment of their testing toolbox for test activities they can use within their plan. The more test activities they know, the more likely they are to have an effective approach for each part of the plan.

Practically, designing tests and implementing them fall under the same activity, where the output of that activity is tests that are ready to run. It's unusual to have a separate written document which specifies test design because of the increased work involved, and because it duplicates a lot of the content within the tests themselves. The method of implementing the tests will change depending on the test writing tools that the team use but, regardless of the tool specifics, the organisational work that was done in the analysis phase will be brought forward and used to structure the tests themselves.

Test teams will usually create 'work items' for their test tasks in the same database that stores bugs and the development work. Tools that lend themselves to scripted, step-by-step manual tests are also used in a standalone capacity or in parallel and linked to test tasks within the database. Most database tools support linking between items so that test tasks can be linked to their corresponding development task as well as any bugs found while testing, enabling traceability between them. Parent tasks and sub-tasks are also a common feature in database tools, allowing the QA analyst to create sub-test tasks that correspond to the sub-areas detailed within the test analysis. There are many ways to slice test task organisation and it's down to the QA analyst to find the most straightforward and efficient organisation.

Test design and implementation is a blank slate for the QA analyst and there's plenty to consider when writing tests. Chapter five on **Test design techniques** later on will aim to provide practical and detailed guidance when embarking on this task.

Included in the test design are investigations and decisions into the feasibility of the test conditions. How difficult and time consuming will they be to run? Knowing this, are all of the tests worth running? Some areas in game testing are within easy reach and only require a set of steps guiding the tester to a specific area of the game. But other tests target hard-to-reach features or are difficult to set up.

Hard-to-reach areas include features like AI logic, where what is displayed on the screen is only the surface layer of multiple code components interacting together, usually in a somewhat unpredictable way. To surface the correct information, these areas can require debug, logging or tooling requests to the code team before the tests can be run effectively.

Tests that are difficult to set up usually involve populating the game with data and getting it into a specific state. A player profile is a good example of this because it stores so much different information on the state of the player. Tests could require that a player has finished all side challenges and has a score above a certain amount; that the player is in a full multiplayer squad with 24 other players; or even that the tester checks an event that only occurs once within the game and would need a way to reset the state easily to retest the same scenario. Some of these scenarios can be set up through the 'brute force' approach of just playing the game to make the required progress. This can be easy for the QA analyst to write, but such approaches are wasteful and unrepeatable for the QA tester. Good QA analysts will strive for more effective ways to run their tests.

Other considerations are more directed towards the effectiveness and sustainability of the tests themselves. QA analysts have many test approaches at their disposal, with a majority falling into the main categories of scripted tests, unscripted sessions, with a verification or failure focus. There are further decisions of granularity, which is the question of how much detail to go into when writing tests. The QA analyst will adapt their tests according to who is going to run them and where those people are located. Remote testers might require more supporting documentation and context, whereas writing tests that the analyst is going to run themselves (or run locally by other experienced QA analysts) would benefit from being more concise and direct.

The material covered in this book will provide a guide to navigating all of these decisions when test writing, but similarly to the test analysis phase, each new feature brings its own unique test writing challenges. Encountering these during your day-to-day work will provide more context and ideas to the examples given here. While aspiring QA analysts will still find the content helpful, improving your test writing is an incremental process, and I would encourage readers to return to the theory content at intervals between writing tests for different features. This will help promote connections and ideas between the 'toolbox' of techniques here and the actual reality of their workplace.

Career Advice – Test Ownership

On the topic of incrementally improving your test writing skills, I've found that the downside of specialising in a specific area of games means that you're much less likely to be faced with work that challenges you.

The reality of games is that some areas are very repetitive and can become boring after the initial problem-solving phase. I've seen this occur for analysts owning the test plans for content areas like environment, characters or live ops events. A template set of tests is written for a single character model and perhaps improved over the time of testing many different characters in the game, but ultimately it becomes a copy-and-paste job. I've noticed something similar when implementing and running in-game events for live operation projects which are increasingly more popular.

There is value in being able to execute a test plan and do it repeatedly and consistently over time – it's good work experience to have. But the advice I would give here is to recognise how broad your work portfolio is, and speak to your manager about moving your test ownership to unfamiliar areas in the future or taking on smaller areas of ownership in unfamiliar areas, while still maintaining your main specialism. It's extremely valuable to get exposure to different game areas because it gives you a wider appreciation of the project work, expands your tester's toolbox and makes you more flexible as a test professional.

The main attribute we care about is increasing the tester's toolbox. Test planning for different game areas will force you to think about testing differently and with a fresh approach. It's great for challenging the way you currently work and forcing you to adapt.

To use a stereotypical analogy, testing planning the same game area repeatedly is like repeatedly putting a square peg in a square hole in one of those wooden games for children. You already know the square peg fits in the square hole; move on to one of the other shapes already! The other shape slots are different game areas and won't accommodate your 'square peg' test approach.

Recognise when you are no longer learning new things and move on.

1.6.4 Test execution, monitoring and control

This part of the fundamental test process has a much bigger focus on the QA tester or whichever other role is going to be executing the tests.

After assigning the tests to be run, the QA analyst's job isn't done; tests aren't forgotten about to await the bugs to come back. There's frequently ongoing conversation between those writing tests and those executing tests, clarifying questions on the details of testing, complications that arise during testing itself and the escalation of major bugs and test blocking issues. Teething issues when running tests should be expected, particularly if these specific tests are being run for the first time or the game area is new to the testers. I would say, in fact, that tests being run *without* questions and clarifications is the exception to the rule. This only happens when the testers are familiar with the test that they're running and the testing itself goes well.

As well as the internal loop of dialogue during individual tests, this phase includes monitoring the progress and results on the broader scope of testing; where that's a scripted test pass or a set of test sessions. The aim is to identify if the current test velocity and results are favourable. This is why the section includes monitoring and control as well as execution – the key point being that it's an iterative process where early test results feed back into the decision making for future test execution. Test results from a day's testing answer questions like: do we need to run this test again? Do we need to test more deeply into some of the areas covered in testing today? Do we need to retire the test because the results show that it's no longer effective?

'Control actions' is a term that refers to things that you do as a direct consequence of unfavourable data. For example, we monitor the test results to check the health of the game and the velocity of test execution over time, and if these results aren't favourable we can take control actions to move them towards a more favourable result.

Examples of control actions to speed up the rate of test execution could be deprioritising other tests running at the same time, or increasing the number of people running tests. There are many different reasons why you might take control actions depending on the reason for running the test in the first place and the results that came out of it. The point here is that tests are not 'fire and forget' for the QA analyst, they require an evaluation and a conclusion. Some test approaches lend themselves more heavily to a quick and iterative feedback loop like this. Test sessions are a good example of this, where the most formal process sees testers complete a session of no more than a few hours before meeting up with their QA lead or QA analyst to debrief on the session and decide next steps. The intent is to approach the testing in small chunks and use the test results as a primary driving force for further test writing. The opposite of this is long passes of scripted tests on large areas of the game that take a team of testers several days or weeks to complete.

Because of the popularity of remote test teams, the discussion and monitoring of test execution has added challenges. Where the tester and the test author are in the same room, it's a simple thing to gather around the screen showing the game and talk through problems with a live example to aid communication. With remote teams, greater effort is required to organise group instant-messaging channels for different purposes and be more disciplined with the way you communicate. Screen sharing, video capture and screenshot tools can be extremely helpful here, but require everyone in the team to be set up with chat headsets and the correct software that they can join a quick private call with anyone at any time (and also be able to share the video feed from the device that is running the game through their computer).

In the teams of testers that I've worked with, this rarely happens. Instead, we've had to laboriously type out complex problems and suggested solutions to each other. Furthermore, remote test teams mostly exist for cost reasons and are often not even in the same country or speak the same native language as the game studio team.

This can further confuse communication, particularly when talking about technical and complex problems.

Because of these limitations, test monitoring needs thorough planning and dedicated time allotted to be set up in an effective way, *not* as an afterthought. Much frustration can be mitigated by well-written tests and supporting test documentation from the QA analyst, as well as clearly-expressed expectations before tests are run.

This foundation aims to highlight this problem during test execution so that you can take note of it and help mitigate it during your own work. However, solving these problems permanently is a test management task and beyond the scope of this book.

Finally, there's a lot of work that goes into the scheduling of test execution, defining when tests will be executed and in what order. These schedules also contribute to test team size decisions and (avoidance of) overtime planning. On big projects, QA analysts will find themselves competing for test execution time if they don't organise their work together correctly, making combined test planning a requirement of efficient test execution.

Further organisation is required to deliver tests into the team of testers so that they know what they should be working on at any one time. Tests can be assigned to individuals to work through in order or assigned to sub-teams (squads) to work through as a group. They can be added to a prioritised list for testers to pick from, or they can be assigned as daily tasks to the team as a whole. It all depends on what's most effective for the project.

In small projects with just one or two people writing tests, this isn't really an issue and the team can afford to be more casual about their planning and organisation. The same can be said for projects which have a slower velocity of work and don't have tight deadlines.

We'll delve into test execution more deeply in chapter seven, **Test management**. While it *is* labelled as management, this topic is actually very helpful for QA testers, analysts, leads and managers alike, because they're all involved in the process in some capacity. All of these roles need to be on the 'same page' in their understanding for it to work effectively. I've also struggled to find documented techniques or case studies on test execution. There's certainly much less available than test analysis and design. I think it's an area which is assumed to be straightforward after the hard work of test planning is done, so we'll aim to right that wrong within the content here.

1.6.5 Test reporting

Earlier we identified that the goal of testing is to collect data to inform project decisions. These decisions, by proxy, lead to bugs being fixed, milestone dates being changed and other decisions which lead to a higher quality game.

Test reporting takes all the collected test data and presents it in a meaningful way. Don't be put off by the word *reporting*. It doesn't have to mean long form emails full of colourful charts. The test team can decide how formal each of their reports needs to be and whether they should be sent out or kept somewhere people can access it.

A formal format might involve an email to the project leadership on the final state of testing a feature, showing bug data and test coverage data, each filtered in different ways to provide unique perspectives. Such reports are usually designed to give the reader a quick summary and then provide all of the supporting data should they want to read into it, with the aim of not requiring any follow up clarifying questions.

The outcome of testing can also be reported verbally or through an instant messaging channel presented on a wall-mounted screen in the office or updated on a dashboard somewhere. The point is to conclude the testing and provide some closure to the activity. It shouldn't be a case of 'no news is good news'. Sometimes, stakeholders don't care about the data itself but are more interested in the analysis and conclusions that the test team have drawn from the data. They don't want to have to analyse it and draw their own conclusions. With this greater scope of reporting in mind (i.e. not just emails) we, as testers, need to remember to take the time to evaluate the test data and then report back to the wider project team on the results.

The output of testing is also used to feed back into further test planning and trigger other follow-up actions. This is particularly true of agile projects where test writing is more likely to be done iteratively. Even if the QA analyst doesn't intend to report the results to others on the team, the evaluation of that data is still essential to the analyst's future test planning work. For this reason, test reporting is as much for our own benefit as it is for the benefit of others on the team.

On the topic of data types included in reports, recorded bugs are 'error reports' themselves and the most basic form of reporting that all projects will capture. Other types of test data are added depending on the feasibility and requirements within the project. In the chapter seven (**Test management**), we'll go into detail on common test metrics and test reporting within game projects. When we say 'metrics', we're talking about known systems or standards for measuring things within the project. Metrics as a terminology isn't specific to games or even software, for that matter, so you can do your own further reading online if you're so inclined.

We'll also talk later about the different levels of reporting within a game test team, giving a few different examples of team breakdowns that can create the need for different reports.

As a quick example, consider a remote team of testers who have squad leads for each group and a test lead who manages the whole team. These squad leads might collect the output of their squad's work and informally report this into the test lead, who then collates all of the output into a single daily or weekly formal report.

The remote test lead would then send these reports to the embedded test team within the game studio or to the studio project team directly. These reports will sometimes provide information for the internal test team to action directly, and other times will feed into further reports that the internal QA analysts or leads might be creating themselves for features or the project as a whole.

At each of these levels, there are different reasons for each report to exist and different audiences they are addressing. Since this is a foundation, we'll outline the types of reports that testers, team leads and analysts might create. Whether you're creating new reports or altering existing ones, making your reporting successful is a lot about understanding what will be most helpful to your readers and anticipating questions they might have. This is true for all levels.

I assume if you're reading this and already working in one of these roles, you're serious about being good at your job and want to advance to a more senior role. Understanding other roles you are reporting to, what their work is and what is helpful to them, will make your reports better, but also put you in a better position to move into those roles in the future.

By showing that you understand their needs through your communication and reporting, you also show that you understand the role.

1.6.6 Test closure activities

This is the last section of the fundamental test process and captures a selection of small activities that should be carried out before starting the process again for the next release or feature.

> *This section mainly exists to ensure good hygiene for all of the test processes. It is as much about personal organisation as it is about team organisation.*

Tests that are complete need to be closed in the database, and any scripted test passes need to be closed in their own tools. Most scripted testing tools have a button to lock the test run so that it can no longer be edited. Doing this triggers the QA analyst to check the state of bugs found in each test and look for any that haven't been actioned in some way. When testing for a feature or a release is completed, any active bugs lingering around would mean they haven't been considered during the test reporting and so are unknown to the project team.

Bugs will need to be resolved (as fixed or otherwise), intentionally postponed to a future release or placed into the bug backlog. For the live ops projects I've worked on, features were created and then immediately released into the game (within a few weeks). For these projects, it was normal for the QA analyst to create a final report for a feature at the same time as the test closure activities. Using the process to close down the tests and review the bugs is a great way of reminding yourself about the full details of testing. The report also marks the end of testing for a feature and lets everyone know that once issued, all the sub tasks relating to that feature should be closed.

All of the work items in the project database (bugs, stories, tests) will be associated to a sprint, release, milestone or other measurement of work. Teams will also have boards that track all of these work items within the current 'period' of work. By making sure our test work items are always up to date, we're keeping the boards accurate and helpful for the rest of the team, showing them the true state of testing at any single time.

Some tools also require that you close all individual items of work assigned to a milestone before you can mark that milestone as complete and close the entire thing. So if you're near the end of a cycle of work and the whole team is preparing to wrap up and move onto the next milestone, these test closure activities will be a direct prerequisite to the work of someone else to close down the milestone.

Retrospectives and other feedback items are a common feature of test closure too. Test closure is a good opportunity for the QA analysts to provide feedback to the testers who executed the tests, using specific examples from the test notes themselves. This is particularly true when the team of testers is remote and feedback needs to be more clear and concise, and doubly so if the remote team is also a separate vendor company the game studio is paying for their services.

Project teams will also hold retrospective or 'post-mortem' meetings to review how they performed during a release or large piece of work (this also happens after something has gone wrong). Test closure is a great time for all members of the test team to record their own retrospective notes on what went well and what could be improved in the future. This is another area where recording notes while they are fresh in your mind is hugely more effective than trying to recall the details during the meeting several weeks later. Even if these processes aren't set up on your team, any tester who proactively records their own retrospective notes and provides valuable, actionable hindsight to the rest of the team will be showing their ability to improve the team as a unit.

1.7   Test formality

If you've ever done any kind of training course at work, or studied for a minor qualification, you might have sometimes thought, "This seems like a lot of work" or,

"This is far more comprehensive than anything we do at work, we'd never find the time for it".

Often, training courses and academic papers present the most formal and heavyweight version of the topic they're defining. The good ones explain how to pick and choose parts of the material and still have it function properly; they don't enforce adoption of every granular detail all at once. This allows the content to be used without massive up-front investment, and means teams can trial lighter versions of the same content, building up the process over time. In a similar way, the content is modular and allows the reader to pick only the parts of the material that is helpful to them.

Games testing, and all of the content described within this book is exactly like this. Nearly every new test team I've joined has had parts of their work which were extremely casual, undefined and not organised. Sometimes there are good reasons for this, too. Only you know the limitations of the team and the project you are working with, so as you start to think how you would apply the learnings here, you should consider how much return you will get from investing in each new technique or process. This consideration should apply to each item of work that you have, whether it's a feature, a release, a milestone, or the entire project.

Consider some of the following influencing factors to help you decide the level of formality to apply to each piece of work. This will give you the best 'bang for buck' on your time investment.

Risk analysis – Many contributing factors feed into risk analysis, such as features that are large or complex presenting a higher chance of things going wrong. Any risk analysis that identifies a high likelihood or impact risk is worth having a comparatively formal test plan. We'll talk more about risk assessment later on, but for now just know that the outcome of this activity plays a large part in how casual or formal your approach should be.

Available time – The time you have to execute the work is probably the biggest factor influencing your ability to apply more formal testing techniques. The velocity of the project team affects this, as well as how much other work you personally have. Projects that invest in bigger test teams obviously have more time per-person to invest. Having done it myself, I can guarantee that finding the time to research and trial new test techniques is the biggest hurdle you will face. Once you read something in this book that you would like to try, you need to book time out of your week to begin working on it.

Desired level of quality – It's important to understand the goals of the wider project team and what, as a group, you're all trying to achieve with the testing activity.

Understanding this goal more deeply will allow you to invest your time appropriately. It's no secret that many smaller game projects and indie teams don't have the capacity to release a product to the same level of quality as a AAA title. Testers need to understand the level of quality the wider project team are trying to achieve, and adopt a correspondingly formal approach. You could create the most comprehensive test plan in the world and use it to explore every pixel of a feature, but if the project team only have the capacity to fix the top 5% of severe bugs, then you could have used your time more effectively.

The goals of the test activity – Each test plan and section of a test plan may have its own specific goals depending on what you're trying to achieve with the activity. For example, sweeping through a feature to capture easy and obvious bugs might not require a formal approach to be effective, but a test to capture comparison performance data would require good planning to make sure the data captured was representative, accurate and comparable. I've also seen the same effect when creating plans to reproduce rare crashes for which we didn't know the cause. My original plan was too informal and ended up causing a mess of inconsistent and false-positive test results. Complex test investigations require a sufficiently formal test plan.

The last idea we should cover on the topic of test formality is the fact that teams don't adopt effective test techniques and processes overnight. Introducing new techniques from this book to your work and that of your team won't happen quickly. It's important that you understand this and don't lose heart that change isn't happening as fast as you would like. Formal techniques and processes take more work, and when I've proposed these to my teams in the past, there has sometimes been resistance due to the increased effort required (also sometimes seen as unnecessary admin). However, in many cases, we've gone from trialling a new technique to liking it and then, eventually, to depending on it. If I suggested we remove some of the formalities to these teams at the time, there would have been an outcry. It takes time and persistence for positive change to happen, and when this is done correctly, test teams will naturally mature over time.

As an exercise, consider how formal your current work is and where you could make the biggest improvements. A good place to look are the tests that are being written and run, asking yourself these questions:

- How many of your test activities each day are written down or recorded?
- For the tests that are created, how much detail is included in each test?
- How much time is there between a test being created and being run?
- How much free exploratory testing do you do compared to more structured testing?

- How much written preparation do you do before writing tests?
- How much do you lean on the documentation to guide your testing?

As you read through the content here, compare it to your work and perform a self-evaluation to find out where you can make the biggest improvements. Doing such an exercise regularly will help you identify areas where you can make the biggest impact with the smallest effort.

1.8   The test design framework

We developed this framework while I was working in the publisher test team at Microsoft, and the general concept has served me very well since. It's a basic division of test design across four quadrants: scripted and unscripted, verification and failure. It also serves as a good introduction to more specific test design and gets you thinking about the balance of your test approaches without even going into the topic of test design in great detail.

I've included the framework in this section of core principles because it's such an immediately understandable topic and requires no additional work to implement. Nearly every test professional understands scripted and exploratory tests as terminology from the earliest stages of their career, with verification and failure terms following in short order. This principle is continuously helpful for different test roles and within different projects; particularly if you have a tendency to fall into the rut of only working in a certain way. I've fallen victim to this myself on many long projects, approaching each feature in exactly the same way without properly considering my approach.

Scripted Verification	Scripted Failure
Unscripted Verification	Unscripted Failure

Figure 1.2

The primary purpose of the framework is to act as a reminder of the balance of each test type within a test plan that you're creating. You ask yourself if you've considered each quadrant during test writing and then correct any over-indexing of a specific type. There usually isn't an equal balance. Verification tests tend to take up the majority and the remaining distribution is tweaked depending on the feature in testing.

Scripted tests – These test types are highly granular and take the form of test scripts, test cases or directed test sessions. We know that scripted tests have specific attributes that make them good at certain tasks:

- Quick to run – They direct the tester straight to the target of testing.
- Confidence building – Pass/fail results provide granular and methodical confidence in the areas tested as well as the progress of testing so far. You know what has been done, what the results were and also what is left to do.
- Deterministic – Five people following the same test should all produce the same result. The test can only be interpreted in a single way and is repeatable. Similarly, running the same test again will produce exactly the same result.
- Easy to follow – The more granular a test is, the more likely anyone will be able to follow it. These tests rely less on the experience of the tester executing the tests and are less open to interpretation. Good for less experienced teams.
- Low bug yield – Scripted tests find fewer bugs than more open tests because they don't allow the tester to explore as many tangents during testing. Scripted tests don't allow for the testing itself to define which test to run next.
- Game area use – Verifying the logic and behaviour of code features that are created within a game, because the behaviour itself is deterministic and limited. It's good for use as checklists for content-based testing (art, sound, etc.) but needs to be supplemented with unscripted tests. It's not good for testing environment, characters and other vast areas of content.

Unscripted tests – These types of tests range from free exploratory (sometimes called ad-hoc testing) to test sessions which define a test charter.

The common attribute of these tests is that they allow and encourage the tester to self direct at least some of the testing. Free exploratory allows the most freedom, while test sessions will define a mission statement or test charter to direct the testers exploring to a specific area. Regarding the scale of how 'free' the testing is, it's worth calling out that the negative attributes will be more severe the more open-ended and free exploratory testing is.

- Long to run – Exploring takes time – at least twice as long as scripted tests, but often closer to three or four times as long. You don't know where each session will lead when you start it, making it unpredictable. It's also difficult to determine when testing will be complete.

- Poor reporting and coverage – Unscripted tests produce test notes and bugs only. Sometimes this might include a red-amber-green health rating, but it's not common practice. Because of this, knowing what has been tested already and what remains to be covered is extremely difficult, as is using this data to communicate testing to others. Completed exploratory test time doesn't give the same confidence in test coverage as scripted tests.

- Indeterministic – Five people running the same test will produce different outputs because the test is open to interpretation and leans on the experience of the tester. Similarly, unlike scripted tests, there is value in re-running the same test because you won't necessarily get the same result.

- Difficult to run (effectively) – Unscripted tests provide much less detail to the tester, instead relying on their expertise and skills. Experienced testers really like this freedom, but more junior team members will find these tests difficult to run and may not be able to complete them as effectively.

- High bug yield – Unscripted tests statistically find more bugs than scripted tests. This can be because the freedom allows the tester to quickly target buggy areas and capture easy bugs ('low hanging fruit'). It also occurs because the tester has time to investigate strange scenarios for which you would never proactively write specific tests, but are instead discovered 'on the fly'.

- Game area use – Good for verifying vast areas of content (like a game environment) due to scripted tests being unfeasibly detailed when trying to verify each individual item in a scene. Good for testing other areas of content like models, textures, lighting, sound, visual FX, animation and so on, due to the huge combinations of the setup and the variance in each piece of content. Good for testing AI behaviours and AI systems working together, since they're difficult to test deterministically during scripted testing. Poor at testing non-functional areas like performance and complex features due to the often very deliberate test steps that need to be taken to test effectively.

Where scripted and unscripted tests categorise the test approach, verification and failure categorise the test intent and form a separate list. The two lists form the combination quadrant shown above, with four categories in total.

Verification testing – This test type includes all positive testing, which is testing what a feature does, rather than what it doesn't do. Verification testing overlaps heavily with checking, which we described earlier when comparing 'checking vs testing'. We defined checking as limited in scope, driven by documentation, highly scripted and nearly always positive. You should view checking as a subset of the overall verification testing activity, where checking is essentially the scripted-verification category. As the quadrant above shows, verification doesn't have to be scripted or always driven by documentation. There are game areas which call for unscripted verification tests. In these cases, we're still performing positive testing but the feature under test doesn't lend itself well to granular scripts. Let's look at the attributes of verification testing.

- Highest priority – Verification testing is the highest priority for the test team and usually the first test type to be run. It makes sense to check positive scenarios before moving on to more adventurous and complex negative ones. In essence, these core positive tests should pass before moving on. A failed verification test nearly always results in a release blocking bug.
- Driven by documentation – The success of verification tests are driven by the details given in the supporting feature documentation as well as the gap analysis skills of the test author to ask incisive questions against the design. Usually, this is all the information that is needed to create good verification tests. In the best cases, the acceptance criteria and design docs are detailed enough to provide all the information, but when this isn't the case, a conversation with the design or code team will easily supplement this.
- Easiest to create – Verification tests are generally easier to create than failure tests. The tests themselves are more straightforward and there's generally more information about the way that features should work rather than the potential ways that they could fail.
- Easiest to run – Positive tests are also the easiest for the testers to execute too. Unlike negative tests, these tests will define exactly what the expected outcome of each step is, and the tester will have documentation and other resources to refer to. This is particularly true for scripted tests of this type, because they provide the most direction.
- Over used – It's common for test authors to *only* focus on verification tests and to just 'translate' design documents into a set of test steps. Frequently done due to time pressure or because these tests are the easiest to write, verification tests are generally counted on too much.

Failure testing – This test type includes all negative tests that aim to identify ways that a feature could fail. This includes things like edge cases as well as both known and unknown error scenarios. This is also where a majority of the bugs hide. It's normal for the 'main flow' of a feature to work fine and only start failing when some additional component is introduced, or limitation applied. In the context of 'checking vs. testing', failure testing very much embodies the spirit of the testing activity. It's worth calling out here that failure testing is not simply destructive testing, which is usually characterised as a button-mashing, cable-pulling type activity. Destructive tests are instead a (brute force) subset of the greater scope of failure testing. So, when you see the word 'failure', don't immediately think of 'destructive'. Let's look at its attributes:

- Driven by the test team – No documentation or guidance exists to define potential failure scenarios. They're primarily created from the experience in the minds of the QA analysts writing the tests, or generated through discussion and process kicked off by the same QA analyst. In this way, the ideas generated within these tests are the value that the test team brings into the company. Scripted failure tests are more often driven by the experience of the test author whereas exploratory failure tests lean more heavily on the experience of the testers executing the session.

- Difficult to create – Identifying good, valid ideas for failure testing is difficult and requires experience and continuous practice. The tests themselves are less straightforward because you don't know what you will find before the test is actually run, so instead these tests follow more of an investigative style of testing. They're also difficult because they require a much more intimate knowledge of the area under testing, understanding how it works 'under the hood' before potential areas of failure can be identified.

- Difficult to run – Failure testing generally requires more skill and experience from the tester to navigate it effectively. Like any unscripted testing, failure tests usually provide areas of potential failure to investigate, leaving some of the finer details up to the tester. Failure tests also have more difficult set-ups because they attempt to increase the complexity of the test scenario to surface bugs; furthermore, they more commonly involve the use of tooling and debug to introduce limitations on the test scenario. Use of network restriction tools is a good example of this. Like the QA analyst, the tester needs a similar level of 'under the hood' understanding of the feature, requiring familiarisation before the test is run. Junior testers can struggle with these tests, particularly if they are unscripted and provide little guidance.

- Often neglected – These tests are often not included in planned testing at all, instead leaving testers to find the same bugs by chance during free exploratory testing (a much less effective approach). Non-test professionals will not notice that these types of tests are missing either, so it's really up to the QA analyst to make sure they're considered during planning.

- Highly valuable bugs – Bugs found during failure testing are often highly valued by the team because they've identified a 'real player' scenario which failed because it wasn't considered earlier in development. These are the kinds of bugs that are met with responses like, "Great catch!" and, "Great idea, we didn't consider that".

When planning tests, it doesn't require much effort to consider which test types are right for your test plan and which you think need more attention: it's just a thought process. I frequently see a strong focus on scripted verification tests, with unscripted verification added as an afterthought to the end of each test (e.g. an extra step onto the end of every test case that says something like, "Spend an additional 30 minutes performing exploratory testing in this area", which is an easy to write but not very effective strategy).

Failure testing is usually neglected because we find it easy to write tests for known and obvious failure scenarios, but don't try hard enough to write tests aimed at finding unknown and deeper failures. This is primarily because obvious failures are usually documented and have their own error messages within the game. Going offline during an online-only feature is a good example of this. It's easy to consider during testing because we know that there should be a 'network disconnection'-type error dialogue. In some ways, you *could* argue that you can verify the UI and messaging within these error dialogues and this would then be categorised as a verification test. It's really up to the QA analyst planning the testing how they want to organise it. I'd recommend categorising any known (planned/designed for) failure scenarios within the verification section and leave the failure testing to identify new, unknown failures.

Lots of further attributes play into the decision-making when writing tests. Some of the descriptions here might have given you some ideas already. If the test team is quite junior, then exploratory and failure testing will be less effective and test writing will need to provide much more guidance. If test execution time is short, then you may need to have a heavier bias towards scripted tests for both verification and failure, because these test types will be the quickest to run. Similarly, if the 'bottleneck' is a limited time to prepare tests, but there is a surplus of (experienced) test execution work power, then the most effective strategy might be to focus on unscripted tests which require less time to create.

I mentioned game area usage within some of the attributes: sometimes a feature area doesn't lend itself well to a particular type of test and there's little we can do about this. For example, capturing performance or stability data nearly always requires a scripted approach for it to be effective because there are so many variables that can affect the recorded performance data. Careful consideration needs to be taken to decide the inputs of the testing: hardware, graphical settings, player profile and the actions of the tester can all influence the test results. Without such a detailed approach, the resulting test data would be meaningless and not comparable to the agreed benchmarks.

Content areas that are unique to games testing also present similar limitations to the approach we take to test writing. Consider the 3D model of a character and writing a granular scripted test to look for visual issues on the character. If you were to write it in a scripted way, such a test would have to be laboriously detailed, take a long time to write and would be difficult to maintain. A snippet of the scripted test might look something like this:

- *Verify the buttons on the jacket have undistorted texturing*
- *Verify the buttons on the jacket have the correct material for lighting*
- *Verify the buttons on the jacket are not geometrically distorted during animation A*
- *Verify the buttons on the jacket are not geometrically distorted during animation B*
- *etc..*

You might think I've chosen an exaggerated small detail of a single part of the overall character model, but I've seen many bugs logged against small details of character models like this. This might be the only character that wears a jacket so it's not even the case that you can write a single test for all characters. The test still needs to cover the entire model and any item that they're compatible with (e.g. weapons, clothing).

These types of tests are much more effective if a less granular approach is taken – somewhere between a directed exploratory test and a scripted test case. Consider the following comparison test snippet:

For each of the following tests on this character, use the debug free camera to explore the character from all angles. Be on the lookout for any visual issues you see during this test, using the linked concept images as a reference. Spend at least 30 minutes exploring each component before moving on.

- *Check each section of the core model is textured correctly and that there are no irregularities with the geometry*
- *Inspect all visual FX and sources of light on the model*
- *Inspect all idle animations, looking for stretching geometry and other temporary visual issues which occur during the animation*
- *…*

A more generic approach not only allows the test author to re-use the test for a wider range of characters, but it makes the entire exercise more concise and easy to follow. The instructions to the tester are a lot simpler.

Promotion of test scenarios

Before we move on to another topic, we should briefly touch on how this design framework can be developed over the lifetime of a feature area.

At Microsoft, we had an ideal methodology: bugs and other outputs of the unscripted testing would form a basis to update the scripted tests with new test scenarios that uncovered known bugs and risky areas. In essence, once unscripted testing had uncovered a buggy scenario, we'd add that scenario to the scripted tests and so they would mature over the course of the project. Similarly, as we identified new failures within the game through failure testing and those were handled through fixes, any new error handling would be migrated from the failure tests into a new verification test for the error dialogues and so on. The promotion of test scenarios followed this order.

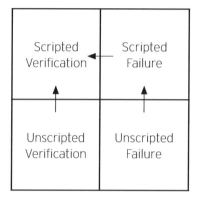

Figure 1.3

This promotion flow is another good reminder of the intent of each type of testing and the strengths they have. The promotion is particularly useful if the project runs a lot of regression testing against existing areas or if test re-use is high on the project in general.

If you have a franchise game that shares its code base with the next game release in the franchise, it's well worth doing this test scenario promotion so you'll be well-equipped to tackle the next project. This makes sure that discovered 'unknowns' are recorded in your scripted tests forever, and running unscripted tests on the next project doesn't re-discover the same bugs you found before. If this is done correctly, further unscripted tests can be directed towards new, uncharted waters and to find further bugs.

For further detail on scripted and unscripted testing, we'll be talking about all test types in chapter three, **Test types and terminology**. We'll also be covering the difference between test scripts and test cases within the 'scripted testing' category.

1.9   The psychology of testing

The discussion has always been ongoing about why a dedicated test discipline needs to exist and why software engineers and artists can't simply test their own work. This discussion is even more pronounced within games testing because game quality can be so subjective. The answer to this discussion is an important principle to take with you into your work, and the aim of this section is to outline the specifics so that you can make better decisions and have more effective conversations on this topic.

> *The topic centres around test independence, which is a measure of how intimately the tester (or anyone) knows the work and the creator of that work.*

The closer you are to a piece of work, the less independent you are from it, and vice versa. Low test independence means that you are more highly influenced by your closeness to the author and the work, and you're less able to review it in a fair, objective and unbiased way. Conversely, those who have high test independence will be able to view a piece of work with 'fresh eyes', having never seen it before and not having had background information from the author. These people are much more likely to be able to provide a fair and complete evaluation of the work. You may have actually heard of the term 'fresh eyes testing' being used when new testers are put on a project or a feature that they haven't seen before.

To aid in our explanation of why this is the case, we can look at a trivial non-software example of writing an essay.

Most of us have been asked to write a long-form essay during our time at college or university and remember spending so many hours writing it that the words blur together into some kind of crossword puzzle. We usually ask a friend to read it through and check whether it makes sense. Why do we do this and not just read it through ourselves? The answer is because as the creator of the work, we have a unique perspective on it and we're less likely to notice mistakes that we've made.

Creators know the most about the work and are prone to making assumptions about how much others know too. Creators also know what they are trying to achieve or communicate and will view the work from that perspective – their view is via their personal filter. By having someone else review the work, the creator gets an outside opinion.

Let's take this example a step further and consider that a close friend of the essay-writer might still not give unbiased feedback, because they're influenced by maintaining their relationship with the friend and not upsetting them with a potentially harsh evaluation. The friend might also have the author explain the essay beforehand and give them some background information on what the key topics are, or they may have been speaking about the topics casually over time. This contextual information prepares the reviewer to understand the essay better and influences their evaluation of it, usually providing a more favourable review than someone who is reading the essay 'cold'. Authors and creators go through this process for any work they know is going to be published into the public view and will undergo the scrutiny of other people who have never met or spoken to them.

The ideas discussed here, the creation of work to be published in the public view and the interpersonal nuances of the evaluation of that work all directly apply to the creation of video games. Unlike other software, games are also hugely subjective. They're arty, fun, challenging, engaging and thought provoking, and how they are received is highly influenced by each player's own opinions and tastes.

Many other pieces of software (that is, non-entertainment software) exist to perform a specific function, so it's clearer how well they are performing that function. During testing, feedback can more easily be given due to the objective nature of the project, "It was intended to perform this function and it doesn't do it". The intended function is logical and clear. The engineer who created the feature isn't going to react negatively. Sure, there will still be non-functional tests like usability which introduces an element of subjectivity, but it's limited when we compare this to games.

In games, there are many areas of content creation which are highly affected by test independence. I've worked side by side with artists and I know how long it takes to create things like 3D models. If I see a minor inconsistency between the concept artwork for a character and the final 3D model of that character, I'm probably less likely to raise it as a bug than someone who doesn't have such a close working relationship with the artist. Perhaps the face of the model isn't the same likeness as the concept; maybe the walking animation of a character doesn't quite look right… how close does it need to be before you raise it as a bug?

There are many areas of game content where the intended design isn't binary or even logical, but a perspective of what looks good or not. I've seen a lot of bugs like this where the creator has said "I intended for it to look that way because I think it's better," and the tester or other person has disagreed. Test independence is even more important for games for the reasons discussed here. Games are very subjective creations of artwork. They're published into the public view and they receive critical reviews from the media as soon as they are live.

In modern game projects, there can be several layers of test independence depending on the structure of your organisation. Test teams embedded within game studios will have the lowest level of test independence as they are closest to development and receive the most business pressure. Remote publisher test teams have more independence because they're physically in a different location and have a weaker relationship with engineers and artists. They can conduct testing in a calmer environment, partially shielded from influences within the studio itself. These teams are still owned by the same business, though, and will be influenced by business pressure to deliver work and conform to the business needs.

Remote vendor test teams and crowdsource test companies have greater test independence than both in-house and remote publisher teams. They have the perspective of having tested projects for multiple different companies, giving them a more objective view. They have no personal relationships with the individuals creating the game content and regularly don't speak to them directly at all. These are the teams most likely to provide objectivity. You have to remember that they're still paid by the game studio and have a business interest in keeping their customers happy, so will still respond to requests and certain pressures from the studio.

Lastly, consider an independent review group not paid by the game studio or with any affiliation to it, such as an age-rating review group or a legal group. If they are reviewing the game for something specific, they'll have the greatest level of test independence and will not be influenced by any factors at all. Legal groups reviewing games compliance to recent European GDPR law is a good example of this.

By now you may be thinking that game test teams should always strive to have as much test independence as possible to achieve maximum objectivity, because that sounds like the best way to get true feedback on the game features. That assumption would then lead to the conclusion that game studios should always use external companies to perform their testing, right?

Unfortunately, it's not as clear cut as this. The greater the test independence, the lower the business and technical understanding of the project. Being more independent means that you are frequently 'out of the loop' and so your project contributions are more likely to be out of date, incorrect or not aligned with the current focus of the project. I've personally experienced this with live ops and agile projects which progress very quickly. A successful test discipline will need a mixture of people with different levels of test independence to effectively test a game project, which is why it's common to see embedded game studio test staff as well as a larger external team either at a publisher or vendor office. Embedded test staff are best-equipped to understand the needs of the project and the business. They also form the bond between the test discipline and other disciplines required to build the game.

In conclusion, I'd stress the importance of evaluating and recognising your own level of test independence. If you have low independence, you can identify areas of your bias and attempt to balance them when making decisions. Knowing your biases is the first step to better decision making.

A common example of low-independence decision-making will be, "We still have active bugs in the release. Do we release on time and take the risk on the bugs or do we delay the release and choose to fix the bugs?".

Conversely, those who have high independence can recognise that they may have a low understanding of how the project and the business is performing or might not be up to date with the current priorities of the project. Is the project focusing on building new content? Is it working towards a major new feature? Is it trying to stabilise existing features? How financially successful was the current or last project? Asking questions will build a better understanding of the project needs, allow you to make better day-to-day decisions in your work and counteract the disadvantages of being so independent.

1.10 A business case for testing

Why do dedicated test staff exist?

We talked about one reason for this in the previous section of test independence, but that alone wouldn't be enough to justify spending thousands of dollars on testing. Another relevant question might be, how do businesses decide how much money they're going to spend on testing and testers?

It's normal for game studios to scrutinise new hires and expenditures, because they know that everything they spend needs to be recouped by the profits from the game. While this is true for all businesses, video games have proven to be a *particularly* volatile business and the string of news articles telling of game studio closures attests to this fact. Companies invest in dedicated test staff partly because they know about the Error Cost Escalation Model that was introduced earlier in this book. They know that finding bugs after release will be more expensive to fix, so this alone presents a financial saving through investing time upfront to find those bugs. I think most people wouldn't necessarily know the name of this model or the specific stages, but they'd understand enough to recognise that preventative measures are financially better than reactive ones.

Games that are not operating as a service and are instead released in whole on a specific date can fail financially in a massive way if the initial release isn't received well. A buggy initial experience can make or break a game release. Even if those bugs are fixed a few weeks later in a patch, the damage can be too late to reverse. Bigger titles have a very large marketing investment in the pre-launch period which can't be refunded or cancelled as the money is already spent. This multiplies the pressure to release the game on time and to ensure the quality is high enough to create a 'buzz' in the industry.

Unfortunately, the amount of money that should be invested in testing is difficult to determine accurately. The 'Cost of Quality' theory helps us break down the costs to understand them better. It defines four cost groups: the cost to prevent bugs, the cost to detect bugs, the cost of internal failures and the cost of external failures.

This is a quantitative approach you *could* take to help you understand the total costs of testing and quality in general. I'll be honest, though, and say that I've never seen any game studio management apply this technique to help them plan how much money they are willing to spend on each quality measure. Without significant time investment, this exercise doesn't produce accurate information which the team can action.

So, we've discovered that it's difficult for companies to understand exactly how much money they need to invest in testing and we've also discovered that many managers know that they have a financial incentive to invest in it, but, if pressed, would be unsure of the details. On top of this (somewhat fuzzy) foundation, the value that testing brings is sometimes difficult to pinpoint for non-QA managers within a game studio.

I've seen teams flounce good quality and testing practices when releasing a product and just 'get lucky' with the release. This can create the illusion that they did everything right, and that repeating it will also produce a good result. Testing can be a little bit like buying car insurance in this way. If a motorist buys the cheapest possible insurance, the insurer's roadside recovery could be entirely ineffective without the motorist realising it. They would never find out about the poor roadside recovery until they need to make a claim. If they 'get lucky' and never claim, they would continue with the insurer under the false confidence that they are providing a good service, even when they aren't.

The value that testing brings is an advanced topic that we won't cover in detail here but is something that test managers will be interested in for future reading. For the scope of this book, it's sufficient for us to understand that there needs to be a business case for the test team and that the studio test manager will be advising the studio leadership on the investment required (or be directly responsible for it).

As an aside, I'll briefly explain the working process that I *have* observed in the teams that I've worked in.

Senior test managers or test directors would use their experience of previous projects to make an expert estimation of team sizes and testing investment. Many embedded teams (mainly of QA analysts) also have a ratio of engineering to QA team numbers that they try to stick to. For example, for every five engineers creating game features, there needs to be one embedded QA analyst responsible for test planning for those features. Test managers will use this ratio, amongst other project factors, to influence their decision making. The number of testers (executing tests) can vary wildly, however, and don't have the same type of ruling. Instead, the tester team size will be either be decided directly from the combined test estimations of the QA analysts, or the test manager will use the estimations to help their own team size planning.

It's important to know that these types of decisions are being made and who is making them. It will also help you make better decisions yourself during your day-to-day work and give you an appreciation of the wider business. As testers, we need to remember that testing as comprehensively as we would like doesn't always equal good business value. Similarly, testing too little doesn't make good use of preventative measures and exposes too much financial risk when a poor quality game is released.

Understanding these holistic business goals is crucial to building a respected and effective test discipline. Without considering business goals, some testers can become adversarial to other disciplines and stubbornly argue for more testing time and greater quality without solid reasoning. When this happens, testers become frustrated and unhappy with their work, which can have a downwards spiralling effect. In the worst cases, the QA team ends up being seen as a barrier to success and something to be worked around and undermined where possible.

The clearest response to this is "The test team only 'wins' when the business wins." This means releasing a game that satisfies your company's criteria of a successful release. Finding release-blocking bugs and delaying a release is *not* winning. Blocking a release or cancelling a feature due to insufficient quality is not winning either. Working on earlier detection and prevention so that the team don't have to delay releases in the first place is, however, a winning scenario. Understand why the business hired you and your work will be more impactful for it, and people will notice this.

1.11   Core principles: games vs. software

Here we'll recap on the main differences between games and other types of software on the topics that we've discussed in this chapter. As we introduced early on, many game testers attending software testing courses and reading up on software testing theory find it difficult to translate the learning into their workplace. I've spoken to colleagues and other test managers at industry conferences that don't find software testing techniques helpful at all and, instead, ignore them when searching for training for their teams. Others admit that it can be useful but see it as a *'nice to have'*, something to supplement actual project work experience which they see as more valuable. Some vendor companies providing game testing services will use software testing certifications to bolster their company profile, usually having all their managers undergo certain training. While this is good to see, practically speaking I haven't seen these learnings filter down to the level of the testers executing the tests on game projects.

My view here (and one of the main motivating factors for creating this book) is that games testing can learn a lot from the more defined and mature testing that goes on in the software world. Many software applications can be life-critical and/

or are forced to adhere to certain international software quality standards. Programs to manage vehicles, aviation, machinery, medical devices, chemicals, sensitive data, for example; all of these could have life-threatening impact if they failed. For these reasons, software testing standards, training and certifications have evolved out of the workplace through sheer necessity. Why would we not try to learn from that evolution? All it takes is to understand what others have done in the software world and adopt it to our own work in games. This might require minor alterations to make the learnings work for us, or at other times we might have to recreate the same idea in a brand new way. This can be difficult because it requires time, effort and innovation on our part, but I can guarantee that it's worth it.

And so, in these chapter endings, we'll outline the differences between software and games, identifying the unique challenges that game testers face. Through better understanding of the differences, you will get more out of the content of this book and you will be better equipped to translate software techniques acquired elsewhere into your own work in game testing.

Business need

We talked about the business need for testing and the importance of understanding the bigger picture in the projects that we're working on. Outside of games, it's common for software teams to be independent specialists who create applications for other companies, i.e. their clients. They do this because it's expensive to create software and to hire new staff, yet nearly every business will need a website and certain internal and external tools to operate. This makes it more cost effective to contract an external team of experts to do the work, with the flexibility of adjusting the resource going into the project without having to build and disband teams themselves. There are, of course, some larger companies employing permanent teams to develop and maintain their own programs (the software giants like Apple, Google and Microsoft are good examples of this). And so lots of software testing case studies and theory material, because it is born out of industry experience, will gravitate around the narrative of creating and testing a product for a business customer. From this narrative, specific testing challenges and processes are introduced into testing theory – scenarios that would appear unfamiliar to any game tester.

Contract work *does* exist within games (teams creating games or other game middleware for external clients), but this time it's the minority. Most game companies are creating and selling their own product directly to customers (the players). This means that there are fewer external influences and no business client to be satisfied during development. Potential customers who might buy the game don't see it until it's nearly complete, and any news that *is* shared about the product is entirely on the decision of the project team only sharing *when* and *what* they like. This creates a different relationship between the creator and the customer, changing the dynamic of the business and the way it operates. Let's look at some specific examples of how this practically impacts testing.

No external product specification

In the normal contracting arrangement, the client company produces requirements documentation and the development team uses it as a basis to create designs and build the software. The team directly builds to the requirements provided to them with varying degrees of creative freedom. This creates certain stages within the fundamental test process and the project lifecycle that include the use of requirements documentation and quality reviews from the client. For example, user acceptance testing is an activity that is performed from the viewpoint of the user. In this activity, testing is intended to ask, "Did we build what the customer wanted in the first place?" Or put another way, "Does the software solve the problem it was commissioned to solve?".

This type of testing disregards internal designs and tech specs as the source of truth and takes a more holistic view of the product. Games are created without such requirements for new players that are yet to experience it. They are created *secretly* in the hope that players will enjoy the product once it is released. Since the game is owned by the company making it, requirements documentation is less of a strict requirement and more like loose charter that is followed throughout development to create a product that will be popular and successful in the current game market. Unlike nearly all other software, games are also not built to solve a particular problem, which makes it very difficult to test them holistically and objectively against the reason for their existence. It becomes very difficult for us to answer the question, "Does it fulfil the brief?" because the brief is essentially to make a fun and engaging product (and even then I'm generalising).

Games require a different approach to user acceptance testing and other parts of the testing process that involve interaction with the end-user, as well as anything that challenges the reason for creating the software in the first place. This topic can go down quite a deep rabbit hole, so we'll stop here. For this foundation, identifying and understanding this difference is enough to save us much frustration and confusion when talking about requirements documentation and user acceptance testing.

Incomplete and changing requirements

Continuing the topic of requirements specifications, it's a common case study in software testing to have vague, non-existent or incomplete requirements from the client. A lot of the time, they don't know the details of what exactly they want, or their requirements change over time, adding more requests onto what the software does or changing its purpose entirely. Changing requirements is a challenge for the entire development team, the test team included. During testing we need to refer to a point of truth frequently and if any of this information is provided by the client, then getting it in a complete and up to date written format can be a real challenge.

Games development can have these same problems, but not for the same reasons. Requirements specifications generally don't exist at all, because there isn't anything that the game is *required* to do. Instead, teams start directly with design concepts which are later replaced by more detailed design specs and technical specs. Game development teams still have to deal with the changing of the project focus, but these changes are more due to different influences within the company steering the project in certain directions. Studio heads, project discipline leads and other senior management all input into steering the large technical and creative project decisions.

Just as with an external client, late reviews with senior company members *do* happen, when design feedback is given at a stage which is too late for the development team to make any meaningful changes. Whether the team tries to accommodate the late feedback is down to the strength of the individuals on the team. Games that begin development with more of a blank page also have more decisions to make, making it unfortunately quite common for the team to spend time on a feature idea/concept before scrapping it and trying something else. This is particularly true for companies that are creating a new IP (Intellectual Property) rather than building on existing ideas. In this way, the process of creation is more fluid, creative and subjective within games.

This is probably truer for the more senior test roles because they're more involved, but it's important for testers to understand the process of creation at the company they are working at. Who are the main decision makers? How are steering decisions made? What is the creative process? How stable/likely to change are the current project decisions? Knowing this helps testers apply the correct level of test scrutiny during their work and know when the direction of the work is likely to change. The end result is that the right questions are asked to enable the testers to align themselves with the vision and creative process of the project in an effort to better understand and predict changes in work direction.

The product is more subjective (and art-heavy)

The broadness of game design makes it difficult for the test team to understand the goals of the game and whether the finer details of the design are intended or not. Even when feature components or whole projects have a clear objective that everyone is aligned with, there are always subjective elements of the work that will be interpreted differently by different people.

This is particularly true for games because they contain such a large component of content amongst the code logic. When I say *content*, this covers all brands of creative work outside of code that goes into a game. Unlike other software, artists and creative members are part of a group that is at least as big as the code engineering teams within a game project. What one person finds difficult and frustrating about the game, another might find easy. The strategic layout of levels, the visual look of characters and items, any interaction or functional game logic choice; there are endless small decisions made during game development that are too granular to define within design documentation.

> *Is that bush supposed to be in this corridor? It's kind of in the way and it's not in keeping with other environment props in this area. I don't know if that's intended design or not. The balanced axe weapons are classified as throwing weapons so I can't equip them with my barbarian character class, I don't know if that's intended or a design bug. What's more, the historical period in which the game is set, does in fact show barbarian types using this weapon.*

The vastness of game artwork and virtual environments almost certainly compounds this subjectivity far beyond what we see in other software. Small design decisions are much more numerous when creating and testing content compared with testing code based logical features.

Industry tales: Subjectivity and context in bugs

Forza Horizon had in-game radio stations you could tune into to play different styles of music as you raced around the map. I remember one of our team logged a bug whereby the music was cutting out when they drove through a specific area of the map. To that person it was odd and a little jarring. The bug came back as 'by design'. It turned out that the tester was driving through a beach-side cave and, of course, you would lose radio signal in a cave, causing the music to cut out. The audio and design teams had made a specific choice to cut the music and add realistic cave echo to the car engine sound FX, making the cave route quite epic if you were in the right car. Even though the bug was closed as 'by design', it was still a very helpful clarification of the design. Having the bug now permanently stored in the database meant that the information was visible to others discovering the same curiosity. It's quite common to see the bug database become a point of truth like this, particularly later in the project lifecycle.

The last area on subjectivity takes us to the topic of the content and artwork quality bar. What *looks good* or *is acceptable to release with* can be very subjective when it comes to testing content. Generally, there are far more content bugs created too (compared with code-based bugs), which increases the number of quality decisions needing to be made on each project. Understanding how to navigate this quality bar is an area of uncharted waters for testing and something we'll cover in writing for the first time. See chapter six on **Major areas of game testing,** which will go into more detail about how testers approach testing of specific game content areas and help navigate decision making on the types of content anomalies that should be bugged.

Usability testing

Continuing the topic of intended design, no other software is designed to make things as intentionally challenging for the user as games software. This turns the area of usability testing into a vague grey fog of unknown design intentions. This creates further uncertainties. *Is it intended to be difficult or is it badly designed?* This can be true for many different components of the game, not just the core gameplay itself: navigating paths in a menu system, using a specific item or character, interacting with objects, using the heads-up display.

A good example of this is the Pip-Boy 3000 menu in Fallout 3. There's a quick animation of the character bringing their wrist into view *every time* you call the menu, which some players found very annoying after the game was released. The animation is clearly put there intentionally, but since it is such a commonly-called menu, it's difficult to determine how long the wait needs to be before it's worth escalating as usability bug. I've also seen many hacking style mini-games which are intentionally clunky in design to keep to the theme and perhaps to add a little pressure to the task. We know that design documents won't include every granular detail of a design, so it can take a while speaking to people on the project team before you find the person who knows the true intentions for the game area. Even then, some details are unintended and are positive, so they are made part of the design. Other times, intended designs are bugged and improved. This leads to the cliché, "That's not a bug, it's a feature!". With limited time to iterate on designs, it can be quite common to label negative usability as a part of the intended game experience, turning a bug into part of the game. If you're lucky and the team is honest, the less-than-optimal experience will be kept as a bug and postponed to a future release.

Conclusions

Let's wrap up this first section on games vs. software. We've identified the reasons for the difficulty that game testers experience when applying more formal and heavyweight learning into their work, particularly from the software testing space. It was a fairly big comparison because we introduced a lot of core differences that will be explored more deeply in specific sections of this book. But core differences they are, large topics that I'd encourage you to consider from the point of view of your own work experience and to remember when you continue your work on future projects and teams. Understanding the unique challenges of game testing is the key to improving and maturing the discipline globally. These are just the first steps.

From this chapter, many of the areas have a grounding in software and you will be able to read up further outside of games and have it make sense to your project. The psychology of testing, the goals of QA, the fundamental test process, test formality are all similar across games and software. The difficulty comes with the *application* of the theory. The 'translation' into games is difficult for individual testers to apply alone and takes time, experience and patience. Without dedicated game testing content, only experienced test managers or people moving from previous roles in software testing have had success employing these more formal techniques into their game testing teams. Test managers I've met, report creating their own 'translated' versions of software testing courses and distributing it amongst their teams or setting it up as internal training courses. Others present processes and techniques derived from some original source of more heavyweight test theory which have been customised beyond recognition or reusability. In nearly all scenarios, these adapted processes are kept in silos as internal company processes, yet to be documented in writing or formally shared with the world.

At the end of each chapter, we'll look deeper into the specifics of how the topics in the chapter are unique to games, and call out the differences you'll see in software testing theory. In essence, this book will present its own practical translation of software test theory into the gaming space based on years of real-world game studio testing experience. It will also supplement this translation with brand new theory, processes and learning born out of necessity within game testing and unique to the discipline. For some of these areas that are unique to games, this will be the first time that they are formally recorded and publicly shared.

2

Project lifecycles

2.1   Introduction

This chapter aims to provide a year-to-year and month-to-month holistic view of how game software projects are generally run. Those of you who already have experience within a game studio will recognise some of the material and be able to fill in any gaps in your knowledge. Depending on the type of game, project teams will stick to certain methodologies – so if you haven't moved companies much, you may only have experienced some of this chapter's content. Those of you who work external to a studio or are yet to embark on your testing career will likely have a less intimate knowledge of any of it, so I expect this to be a valuable and complete description for you of the *what, when* and *why* of a project lifecycle. For those with less or no experience, then this chapter will also cement the understanding of what game testing really involves. During the introduction I said that it wasn't about reviewing games other people had made or playtesting games to give your personal critique. Those thoughts might conjure an image of testing a new game every week and having some kind of management process to dictate which game you'll be reviewing next – resulting in a quick project work cadence which sounds quite exciting.

This chapter should set your expectations straight regarding how complete the project will be as you work on it, the length of time that you'll be working on the same area and the choice you have about what games you work on. Testing the same product repeatedly for many months can be a sticking point for new testers wanting to join the industry; as well as the realisation that you won't really have a choice about what projects you work on. Development teams in a single office space will have no more than five active projects and most of the time one primary project will dominate most of the team's resources. You need to genuinely enjoy the work and the project for this to be a sustainable career choice.*

Having knowledge of all the most common ways a game project can be organised will make you more flexible as an employee and allow you to orientate yourself to new companies and projects quicker. I once made the mistake of taking all my experience from a previous company and trying to apply it exactly to the new team. I soon realised that it wasn't going to work and I would have to adapt and develop my experience in new ways. Even though different teams may have the same problems, the solutions will not always be the same. Furthermore, a misunderstanding of project phases and priorities can lead to confusion and frustration for the tester. The stage of the project will heavily dictate your work priorities and what type of bugs the wider team care about. If you go logging polish bugs during a prototyping phase, people will get annoyed and probably tell you to go away! Prototyping is intended to be 'quick and dirty' and the team will mainly care about stability and core loop bugs.

If you're applying for a new role or moving to a new project, having knowledge of the end-to-end lifecycle will allow you to understand where the project is currently at and set your expectations for the type of work you'll be doing when you join it. You may also be looking to fill gaps in your experience and be actively looking for projects which are at a certain phase of their life. There are pros and cons to each stage. Mature live ops projects offer stability of work but with the pressure of operating a live game 24/7. Projects earlier in development are likely to be more randomised and lack good direction, but will be at the more exciting part of the project journey. Be aware that early projects can evolve into different games entirely, or be cancelled. On the other hand, there is pride to be taken in working on a project from the early stages and seeing it through to being released to players many months later. For disc-based games, it's normal for everyone on the team to get their own copy of the game once it's released, which can be incredibly rewarding and a nice memento of several months of hard work. I have a few Xbox One and Xbox 360 games still in their film wrapping at my home. I notice them occasionally and get reminded of fond memories working on them back at Microsoft.

The point at which testing staff get involved in a project varies depending on the location you're working in and how senior you are. Embedded test staff will be the earliest to be involved because they are a permanent fixture in the studio and their

---

*   Note that these facts are true to embedded game studio testers, but slightly less true for publishing test teams and external remote test teams, and even less so for crowdsourced testing. External teams are more likely to switch testers between multiple projects by the same publisher or multiple projects from different game studio clients. This fluidity can be both a blessing and a burden. Crowdsourced testing is the opposite of what I describe here and is a process of signing up to a service where you can choose what projects you pick up and when you test. I'll discuss this separately in further detail, but for the purposes of this chapter we're going to ignore crowdsourced testing.

involvement will only be limited by their commitment to older ongoing projects. Remote publisher test teams and external vendor test teams get involved later on in the project lifecycle because they're usually organised to bring the majority of test execution work power. They get involved in the project and then scale up, bringing testers onto the project in high numbers. There are some practical reasons why it's difficult to have remote testers working on earlier stages on the project, but it's enough that you understand that your proximity to the core of the project will influence the project phases that you will work on.

We noted that seniority influences your involvement, too. Test managers and directors within a studio will be the first to be involved because they will have an input into how the project is setup and will need to plan embedded test team resources for the project. Embedded QA analysts, responsible for test planning, will be involved next, followed by embedded testers who will only get involved when test execution is due to begin. The same is true later on for publishing test teams and external teams. The test managers of those teams will get involved to start planning team resources. It's normal for the most senior test leads and testers on those external teams to be involved first when the new test team is built for the project. When new teams are created to support a project, they are small, and so smart test leads will move the most senior testers into it first.

The conclusion is that, early in your career, you will have the least amount of influence on the work you do and you will likely also be one of the last to be on boarded onto new projects. As you become more senior and/or move closer to the source or project creation, you will see more phases of the project lifecycle.*

2.2 The software development lifecycle

The software development lifecycle (sometimes shortened to SDLC) is consistent terminology that you'll hear across all software, not just in games. It is exactly what it sounds like, it encompasses the life of a software project. Since nearly all software projects are delivered iteratively (think of continuous updates and patches), it becomes a cycle. Within the large lifecycle that spans months and years, there are smaller cycles which span weeks and days.

---

* This is an unfortunate scenario because it's easy for junior testers not to be given the opportunity to experience different phases of a project, which then makes them unprepared when applying for embedded studio jobs or moving teams. If you aren't careful, you can spend multiple years testing without realising that the work you have been doing is only a part of the complete body of testing work that is being completed against the project. This chapter should remedy this and give you the holistic view, allowing you to see parts of the project which you haven't been involved in, but might like to be in the future. This can then help you make decisions about whether to move teams or apply for roles at a different company.

Here we'll start to identify some of the main landmarks in the landscape of a game project – things you will see on every project and which should be directly applicable to your work. Then we'll define the two main methodologies that projects can follow.

Project gates and phases

All game companies will have a way of controlling when and how much of the company resources go into a specific project – such as finance, people and office space. This is usually controlled through a series of greenlight gates a project needs to clear to unlock the next level of company resources. To clear a gate, the project leadership will collect data, amongst other technical and creative materials, to present to the company leadership to get their buy-in for taking the project to the next phase of its lifecycle. The nature of these gates will vary from company to company and will get more rigorous the further a project progresses through its life and the more the company invests in it. Some company cultures mean that the leadership is more interested in a project's creative direction while others will be more interested in hard market data to reduce the financial risk of investing in the project (i.e. they'll want to know if the game style is already proven in the market).

These gates will also align to large phases of the project's development. The name of each gate refers to the phase that is being unlocked. Let's have a brief look at some popular development phases.

- **Concept** – This is the earliest incubation phase of new game ideas. Most teams start with concept artwork and design. It's common to have 'vertical slice' art which illustrates what a very small part of the end game might look like, to get people excited. It could also include key concepts or ideas the game will centre around. Some teams also start with a technical concept (a 'tech demo') which then grows, but this is less conventional. Each company has their own process for greenlighting time spent on new game concepts. Some companies welcome new ideas at any time and encourage their employees to work on ideas continually, whereas others are more restrictive and already have a roadmap of games that they are planning to make.
- **Prototyping** – Concepts that pass the concept review gate are then greenlit for prototyping. This phase approves a very small team to begin building a few core game mechanics in a quick-and-dirty style, so that the team can get an idea about how their idea actually looks on screen when you interact with it. It's very true that some ideas just don't translate well when you play them. Prototyping involves a mixed team of engineers and technical artists – essentially, the minimum required to build something from scratch. Importantly, prototyping code is not supposed to be included in the final

product. So, it's intended that work is done fast and not necessarily well. Testers will sometimes get involved in testing early prototypes to get them ready for demoing, but it's not that common.

- **Pre-production** – This is the first big one. Clearing the pre-production gate means that the prototype is greenlit to start building out the game design and technical design in detail. The investment ramps up in this phase, because it's longer and many more people are involved. The actual work that gets carried out is essentially to create everything that is needed as a prerequisite to building the game in the next phase. This covers a few key areas: team resource planning (which experts are required, does the company have that expertise already, etc.), game design (a more detailed and complete game design) and technical design (how is it going to be built, what are the technical requirements). Test managers are involved in the team planning element of the pre-production phase and embedded testers are sometimes involved in testing prototypes that are converted into production-ready code during this phase.

- **Production** – The biggest, and key, phase of development. Passing into the production phase means that the project has full investment from the company and that all the supporting tech has been built or bought. By this time, the project team should know how long it's going to take to build and have a drafted release date for the game. The team should have a roadmap and all of the team members required should be in place. This is the first phase where the full strength of test teams become involved, and growing as the game grows in size.

- **Soft launch, alphas and betas** – This is a 'soft' gate and kicks in when the team view the game as complete and stable enough to release to a restricted audience. There are several reasons why a soft launch is a good idea, the main ones being scalability and stability. A soft launch is a discreet, no-marketing launch, usually to specific smaller countries or other restricted audiences. It is mainly used for games that will be running as a continuous service. The team will use the time during the soft launch phase to 'polish' the game by fixing bugs and getting it ready for release to their primary audience. It's also a key time for free-to-play games when it's used to understand the purchasing patterns of players – so it's particularly popular in mobile gaming. The approval for this gate is usually quite light and dependent on whether the team needs it at all. Alpha and beta tests serve the same purpose of stability and scalability, but are mainly used for traditional projects with a single paid release. Alpha tests run earlier than betas, but they are also common because the game would be in a much less-finished state. Open/public tests refer to when a test is open to the public to join. Restricted/closed is when the test is invite-only and to a limited audience.

- **Hard launch** – The final gate. Passing this gate means that the game is greenlit for launch and the project either turns into a live service, or the team begin working on content updates. This gate is less formal because it's likely that near-final builds of the game will be shared internally to play, giving everyone in the company visibility on the progress of the game. The company leadership will be playing the game and having more frequent and informal meetings with the project team, too, planning marketing for the launch and contacting partner companies to arrange 'featured' slots in the online stores. By this point, any concerns over hitting the launch date will already be under discussion.

The process I describe here is the most complete version of this model and the most idealistic. You're most likely to see this followed if you're working on a new game IP (intellectual property) or an idea which is new to the company. This happens a lot in mobile, as teams search for new ways to engage their target market and in companies that are open to taking risks by trying out new game ideas. Conversely, you will see a cut-down version of this lifecycle if you work on a franchise game where the team has already released at least one game in a franchise and proven it works in the market. Franchise games will have a much quicker start, not requiring technical prototyping, since they already have all the existing technology they built into the previous game. Concepting will also be quicker and much more limited to the design of the franchise.

Industry tales

Working on Forza Horizon 3 was a great example of a franchise title lifecycle. Because we were acting as the publisher test team at Microsoft, we didn't get involved in the project in the very early stages, but our test managers weren't far behind the embedded studio test team. Regardless of that slightly late involvement, the project came together incredibly quickly and smoothly because they had two games worth of technology and learnings to build upon – as well as all of the imported car simulation technology from the partner team building the Forza Motorsport series. All in all, I worked on that project for less than a year and it was launched during that time. I haven't worked on another project to this day which had such a well-defined and structured path through the development lifecycle. Working on a franchise title had its benefits and taught me a lot about what 'good' looks like. The project went through pre-production, production and straight to hard launch because we didn't need the additional project phases. At the time, the previous Forza Horizon games were still popular and players were active in the online multiplayer. There was no need to scale test the multiplayer through an open beta release because the company had enough data to make them confident about what they could expect. Instead, it was popular at Microsoft to make builds available to other employees across the company and encourage them to play multiplayer on the internal server environment. Email updates would be sent out to organise larger scale playtesting on specific days, as well as getting as much of the test team as we could to postpone other ongoing tests and join in the playtest during those times.

On the other hand, my more recent work at Zynga on mobile games-as-a-service projects has been a great example of requiring and using the entire project lifecycle and gates. The size and style of the mobile game market means there is a big focus on concepting new ideas and getting prototypes into the hands of players to prove before additional investment is committed. This has been easier thanks to the popularity of the casual games genre on mobile, and it's been more visible to me because I've been working directly in the game studios with these projects. Being involved in ideas from their early inception and seeing them evolve through their lifecycle has been both a challenge and a delight. With the games themselves being smaller, we have more game projects in development at the same time too, allowing us to switch between projects which are at different stages of their lifecycle. The company is very open to anyone presenting new game ideas and investing in anything that shows genuine merit. Involvement in early project lifecycles is very common, with many prototypes being built. Additionally, greenlight gates are used diligently and projects without strong supporting data are slowed, changed or cancelled; an ethos which is refreshingly brave and confident for the industry!

Deliverables

Projects are also orientated around certain key deliverables which add major landmarks to the project lifecycle: prototypes, playable demos, soft launch releases, hard launch releases, content releases and game updates. These are all major deliverables in a project's life where the agreed date is difficult to move and something needs to be submitted, usually a version of the game. It's possible for teams to have multiple deliverables in progress at the same time too. A sub-team might be working on polishing a small playable demo while the majority of the team continue working on the final release. Testers, like everyone else on the project, should make sure they know the date of the next major deliverable because it's likely to be a very hard deadline.

Milestones

Milestones define more granular, soft goals the project team will be working towards, and are different for the two major project types we're looking into next, waterfall and agile. Milestones also define smaller phases of development and provide the main source of information which tells the test team what parts of the project are available for testing. Nearly all of these milestones structure development in the later stages of the project, telling us when certain components of the project are complete. Let's go through some of the most common ones in chronological order.

- **Code complete** – Defines the point where all of the code is implemented and only bug fixing remains. This ultimately means that no additional changes or additions will be made to the code beyond fixing what is there already. It can be applied to features, releases or entire projects. This milestone is very important for testers because testing before this means that we are essentially testing a work-in-progress and so we can't just go bugging everything that we see. For this reason, it's normal for only embedded staff to be testing pre-code complete features.

- **Content complete** – Defines the point at which all of the final artwork has been added to the game. Creating artwork and game content takes a *really* long time, period. The art team will be continuing to create all sorts of content to populate the game well after the code complete milestone. In many scenarios, the underlying code constructs also need to be in place before the content creators can see their work in the game. Before this milestone, placeholder artwork may fill parts of the game or areas will be unfinished without their final polishing. The content complete milestone means that all content existing in the game is intended to be seen by players and no placeholder artwork exists. While the test team will have tested earlier versions of the content, this milestone allows the team to test the entire games content in its finished state without doubting that any sections may not be finished.

- **Feature complete** – This is sometimes the same as content complete. It defines the point where *everything* has been implemented and only bug fixing is left. Code and artwork should already be done, but this milestone also includes game data and any other miscellaneous components of the game project. Game data is the stuff that will define all of the thousands of values that make up the game balancing. Up until this milestone, the values might be placeholder or test values used during development, but afterwards they should all be set to their final values, which players will see. Sometimes, projects will also be waiting for external dependencies or integrations to finish development products before final versions are integrated into the game. This milestone takes another step towards project completeness, where the game is now pretty close to what players will see in real life. This milestone is really *the* milestone. After this, anything is fair game for bugging.

- **Code freeze** – This is a less common milestone. It defines a point where the code is locked down and no further changes, including bug fixing, are allowed without a group review. The milestone can apply to entire projects, releases or features. It's more common with large single-release projects which are approaching their global launch date. It's intended to reduce the chances of code changes destabilising the game at such a late stage. Committing changes to the game can be locked down through tooling, forcing review conversations to happen and requiring a password to bypass the lock. This is a good quality milestone to have and the test team management should work with the production team and code leadership to make sure it is upheld and the process is correct. Some teams I've worked with refer to locking the code down as being 'under embargo'; e.g. "Hey everyone, the release branch is now under embargo, if you want to commit something please come and see a producer."

- **ZBB (Zero bug bounce)** – Defines the date where there are no active bugs and any new bugs need to be actioned (either fixed or postponed) within 24 hours. This usually involves existing bugs being reactivated rather than brand new bugs being found. The intent of this milestone is to prepare for the actual bug zero date, because experienced project managers know to allow time for a little back-and-forth between code and the testers confirming the bug fixes. This is especially true for the last few bugs in a big project where the total number of active bugs has been reduced quickly to meet the deadline. It's called a bug bounce because the active bugs chart trends towards zero and then bounces, returning each day to zero. Theoretically, we also expect the bounce to be high at first, with multiple active bugs each day, then settle down over several days towards the actual zero bugs milestone. This milestone is generally only used for large projects which have been in development for several months.

  When this milestone is hit, the team may decide to create their first Release Candidate build (sometimes called a master* build or RC). This is essentially a potential candidate for the build that will be released to the world. At this point, the team is expecting more bugs, but hoping that they won't come. With each new bug that the team decides to fix, another release candidate is made.

---

*   'Master' refers to the code branch that the release candidate build is created from. I'll explain branching later in this chapter.

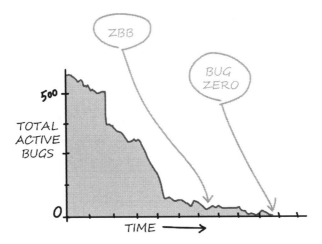

Figure 2.1 In theory, the active bugs graph should hit zero at the ZBB date and then 'bounce'
as bugs are found and resolved each day. However, most bug databases don't record the data
frequently enough to see it reach zero before more bugs are found.

- **Bug zero** – An obvious one. This defines the date when the project should have no active bugs. The project management (including the test manager) will have been planning and working towards this milestone over many weeks, calculating the rate at which the test team are finding new bugs as well as the rate bugs are being fixed by the code and content teams. Glide slopes of active bugs down towards bug zero show how the team are tracking towards the milestone. The ZBB milestone also provides a check of realism several days before this zero bug milestone is due.

    When the project is truly at bug zero, the final **Release Candidate** becomes the build that will be uploaded to digital stores and sent away for manufacturing onto disks. Some teams refer to this final candidate build as **Gold Master**. There are several other smaller jobs that still need to be done, but this is the last major milestone for testers. After this, glory awaits!

Sprints

Sprints are the next-most granular level of development. We're now looking at the day-to-day and week-to-week progress of the project. You'll hear this term a lot and it's not specific to games development. While sprints are primarily associated with agile lifecycles, they are also used in other project types. The entire body of work for the project is broken down into smaller chunks to be completed within each sprint, adding much needed organisation and progress tracking to the project. This is because software (games included) is so vast and complex to create, it would be extremely difficult for it all hang together in a cohesive and complete way without breaking down the work into manageable parts.

A sprint can be anything from 1 to 8 weeks, but 2 to 4 weeks is the most common. It allows the team to commit to bigger sections of work in one go, but isn't too long that the work becomes unwieldy and unfocused over time. Both of the main software development lifecycle techniques have sprint work at their core, making it a very universally useful concept to understand. Sprints will have planning meetings to define their content and a surrounding process which tracks the items being worked on and by whom, and their current progress. Embedded QA analysts will be integrated into this sprint process, attending the meetings and contributing to work estimations and other decision making. There are entire training courses and certifications dedicated to the different ways a team can organise their work through sprints, so we're not going to delve into the detail here. For this book, you should just walk into the next sections with the understanding that newly completed game components will be delivered into testing each sprint and that embedded QA analysts will be involved in this process.

Development teams are also broken down into small sub-teams, each running their own sprints and planning independently. This is done for the same reason as sprints: because it breaks down the project into smaller pieces of work that different parts of the team can create independently. Team size is ideally seven (±3) to be effective but, practically, they become whatever size the game component requires to be built. As a general rule, there should be one embedded QA analyst per sprint team. These test roles will be the closest to the source of development and in the family of game testing job roles, will be the closest to working with other disciplines.

In the section on **Test Levels** later in this chapter, we'll go into more detail about the types of testing that take place in a sprint team, and then how those game components come together into the main game and need to be tested again in another test level. This chapter should start to paint a picture, illustrating why it's necessary that teams have 'layers' of test staff in the studio, in the publisher office and in remote testing locations. By understanding how businesses organise their game development, testers in different teams will gain an appreciation of how their work fits into the greater project testing and quality strategy.

Industry tales

I started my career in a publishing test team at Microsoft. I was there for about 5 years in total. In the first few years I never saw or spoke to the development team making the app I was testing. Our test managers would have contact with the development team and organise what work arrived and when. I just remember getting daily builds, running the test plans against them and not much else. My exposure to the bigger project workings was very limited. It wasn't really until a few years later that I moved to a QA analyst role (the role title was actually Software Test Engineer at MS) and was asked to travel to the development studio during key times of our project. We were lucky enough that the Microsoft-owned studios we worked with were all based in the south of the UK, so we could travel there and back easily for just a day's work. I went from working side-by-side with a floor full of people in the test discipline to spending some of my time in the studios where there were no testers at all and everyone belonged to different areas of expertise. Apart from the enjoyment of meeting people I had been remotely communicating with, I found the variety of perspectives and opinions to be extremely refreshing.

The first big project I worked on as a QA analyst was Kinect Sesame Street TV for Xbox 360, which was being developed in London by the Soho Productions team. I have fond memories of travelling into London to work with the team there and getting to know some of the team more personally. Later on, I moved to the Fable Legends project and began travelling to the Lionhead office in Guildford one day a week, every week. The exposure to the internal workings of the development team was both incredibly helpful for my own work and made remote communication easier, because the team knew who I was. Being located physically close to individuals on the development team meant that I was exposed to many desk-side conversations and decision making, ideas and discussions that wouldn't be written down or recorded anywhere.

It also became pretty clear that the game studio buildings themselves were kitted out with way more cool stuff than we ever had at our central publisher office at MS Headquarters – it was difficult not to get excited about the project when you were there. Their walls were plastered with concept artwork and quirky office accessories, including highly branded reception areas which showed off their previous projects. They had better hardware, bigger screens and trendy kitchen spaces for you to each lunch and chill out. In short, they were exciting places to work, full of creative buzz and great people. I learned and gained so much from just spending some of my time there that I knew if a job opportunity to work in a studio came up, I would take it.

2.3 Waterfall development

This is the first and most traditionally popular style of the software development lifecycle. It's called the waterfall model because the flow chart showing the stages of the lifecycle follows a sequential style that looks like a waterfall. It's widely used across the software world, so further reading online is an option if you want to find out more.

Waterfall SDLC diagram

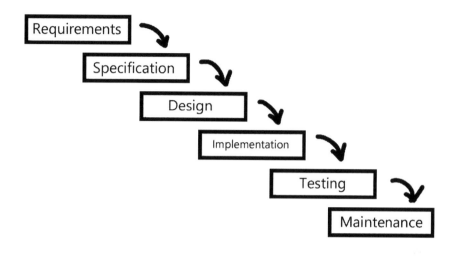

Figure 2.2

The main characteristic of this development model is that each stage of the lifecycle follows sequentially from the previous one, and no stage is worked on after it is completed. This also means that the scope of the project is entirely defined up front, providing a clear roadmap for the remainder of the project.

Each stage has strict entry criteria that must be fulfilled before it can start. For example, before the design phase can begin, the specification phase before it needs to reach a minimum percentage of completion. The exact entry criteria for each phase is defined by the team and varies in formality. The theory is to completely finish one stage before moving on to the next but, realistically, the stages overlap quite heavily because there is a business advantage in starting each stage as early as possible. So, teams will identify parts of each stage that don't require prerequisites before work can begin. For example, some of the coding implementation might begin on the engine of the game before the designs are complete, because the team has already made a decision about which graphics middleware to use and this work can begin without knowing the exact details of the game design.

In this way, each project team is likely to vary how strictly it follows this process, performing some of the work in parallel wherever possible. In a typical game project, each of the waterfall phases will take several months to complete, and so each stage requires supporting documentation and work velocity tracking to make sure it's on track and everyone on the team is aware of the holistic plan.

In this model, the testing phase is near the end of the waterfall and starts when most of the other activities have already been running for several months.

Testing won't necessarily wait for implementation to completely finish. It's more likely to be the case that testing begins as soon as some parts of the project, at least, are finished. Regardless, testers working on projects that follow this model will generally get involved later on when much of the project has already been defined.

This leads to a deeper discussion within the testing discipline about the right stage of a project at which to get testers involved, along with an argument that testers need to be onboarded onto the project much earlier than the main testing phase schedule suggests. The 'vanilla' waterfall model is quite simplistic in this way and shows testing as something that is done retrospectively, after everything else. But the more a tester learns about effective test strategy and risk mitigation, the more they realise the importance of preventative testing work that needs to be done side-by-side with the creation of the game.

There *are* improvements on the waterfall model, which expand it to include more granular details and give a bigger focus to testing. The V-model is a good example of this. It is covered in software testing books and attaches a test activity to each phase of development, putting greater emphasis on early testing and defining different test levels across the project lifecycle. The details of test levels themselves are defined later in this chapter.

Because this model defines a test activity for each phase of development, it provides a formality and gives weight to the argument that testers should be involved in the project earlier on.

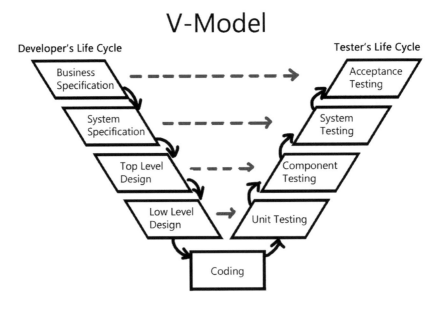

Figure 2.3

Game project use

Firstly, game projects nearly always skip the requirements phase, since this is usually dedicated to collecting information to understand what the goals of the software will be before the team begin designing it. This phase is about defining the problem to which the software will be the solution. Since games aren't solving a specific problem, they proceed directly to the design phase.

This type of development is primarily used for franchise games and those projects that have already developed a 'winning formula'. Many teams use this development model to take what they already know works and improve upon it for their next game.

Games from the biggest companies that have new releases every one or two years are the type that would follow this model. In these situations, the project team has a good idea about how long each phase will take and so is able to provide accurate work estimations over several months. These teams also mitigate the burden of heavy documentation and upfront design effort by re-using work from their previous projects and then building upon it. These are the only game projects that you will work on where the team has a clear and well-documented idea about the scope of the game from the early stages. For the same reasons, these projects are also the least likely to be randomised by late design changes and scope increase during development. In the waterfall projects that I've worked on, the process was followed quite strictly. The phases were defined, the work tracked and the entry criteria for each phase listed.

Pros and cons of the waterfall model

Benefits of the model:

- **Detailed documentation:** Testers love documentation because it makes their lives easier. Waterfall projects will have more detailed documentation across a greater range of projects areas.
- **More time for test planning:** Provided they are involved early enough, QA analysts will have more time to adopt more formal test planning techniques, making their test plans more effective. Increased time for test planning also allows QA analysts more freedom to perform test planning to the best of their ability instead of having to compromise and do what is quick.
- **Clearer project roadmap:** Less randomisation means testers can invest more heavily in test plans without fear that those plans will become out of date.
- **High automation potential:** These projects provide the stability on which the team can invest in longer-term test automation. This is particularly true for franchise titles where the team know that the automation investment will be applicable to the *next* project too.

Drawbacks of the model:

- **Difficult long-term estimations:** Unless you have some good data to reference, estimating for this type of development can be tricky. An example would be trying to judge how long it would take to test the entirety of a game mode, like a single-player campaign. Estimating test time for such large pieces of work can be very difficult and a lot can depend on the outcome.
- **More likely to cause crunch:** Because this type of project is inflexible to changes and often difficult to estimate, they are the most likely to be affected by crunch on the lead-up to a release date. By crunch I'm referring to optional or compulsory overtime work over an extended period to ensure the project meets a deadline.

2.4 Agile development

Agile is the newer software development methodology and has been hugely popular since its inception in 2000. It follows four values and twelve core principles which centre around streamlining the development process and eliminating the painful points of the historical waterfall model.

The four values of the agile manifesto[*]

1. Individuals and interactions over processes and tools
2. Working software over comprehensive documentation
3. Customer collaboration over contract negotiation
4. Responding to change over following a plan

The last point here is particularly crucial. With the old model, many companies found that by the time a project was completed, their competition had moved on and the software was already out of date. Many others would repeatedly update the requirements of the project while it was being developed, asking more and more of it, pushing the completion date further behind the original plan. In this way, the waterfall process doesn't support the changing of project direction very well and many development teams become extremely frustrated with its inflexibility and forced adherence to the original plan. You'll see the same themes from the other values. Note the priority on working software and individual interactions; teams following

---

[*]   https://agilemanifesto.org/

the waterfall model would see meticulously created documentation go out of date, and the time spent creating it lost. To avoid wasting time creating and revising documentation, this model favours progress by delivering the working software itself.

Game project use

This directly applies to game projects too, but for slightly different reasons. As we've discussed, game projects can be a process of exploring what 'works' for the game (things that feel good and play well when trialled) and binning anything that doesn't work. In short, many projects don't start with a fixed plan and, instead, evolve a plan through trial and error.

This creative process does not work well with the waterfall software development lifecycle, which calls for strong up front documentation, causing game makers to turn to the agile methodology. The end result of following an agile methodology means you won't have a fixed roadmap of what the game will contain, but instead build the game incrementally in small parts and choose in each sprint which part to build next.

Put another way, teams will intentionally not commit to large pieces of work that will lock them on a strict path for multiple months. Instead, they will commit to a smaller piece and when it is completed, decide whether to continue on that path or whether to work on a separate part of the game. Agile game projects will have a backlog which contains a priority-ordered list of game components which the team has defined, creating a rough charter for the project. Each sprint, the team will decide what components to work on next and commit to completing them during the next sprint. The backlog list is very lightweight and each component will become more defined just before work begins on it. The key point of this process is that the backlog of potential work is fluid and can be reorganised at the will of the team.

There are many methodologies that teams use to organise working within the agile principles. Scrum is a popular example, and provides a specific framework which conforms to the general agile principles. It provides detail on how to divide and organise the work, how to prioritise backlog items, how to conduct meetings, create work estimates and many other practical details of agile project management. Scrum has a huge amount of free reading online, but for those who really want to explore it in detail there are scrum master certifications which you can take. Some companies (mainly outside of games) have a job title called 'Scrum Master' for this work, which is the equivalent to a Producer or a Product Manager within games. Because all project disciplines work together under the agreed methodology, all disciplines should make it their business to know it in good detail.

Kanban is also worth mentioning here due to its popularity. Kanban is a more specific process, focusing on workflow management and visualisation. A Kanban board essentially shows the work as small pieces, where each piece is moved across columns on the board as progress is made on it. Each column represents a different state of that piece of work: Backlog, To Do, In Progress, In Testing, Done. This is just an example: these columns can be customised to suit your needs. While I've seen some teams use digital Kanban boards to track their work, digital versions can create barriers to customising and updating the board, as well as creating physical challenges when a team of people needs to gather around a screen to review the work. Because of this, low-tech Kanban boards created with dry-wipe marker pens and Post-it notes are popular. It's common to see game studio walls and windows converted into makeshift boards, tracking the work of the various sub-teams within the project. Teams also like to use coloured Post-its to show different types of work, like code, design or art. This has the added bonus of giving an even easier visualisation of the work completed by certain disciplines within the team. While you *can* search Kanban online for further reading, the core process is pretty simple and just understanding it from this introduction is enough for most.

Pros and Cons of agile

Benefits of the model:

- **Increased product stability:** Agile supports a 'test as you build' style of work, making the product more stable during the early and mid-points of the project. Some live ops agile projects have a rule where the game should technically be shippable at the end of each sprint, meaning that all new bugs generated by the work have been fixed in the sprint or closed. No bug fixing is postponed to a later date.
- **Earlier test involvement:** Because of the same 'test as you build' project style, early project components will be finished and ready for testing much sooner than waterfall projects. This calls for much earlier involvement of test teams in the lifecycle of the project. Earlier involvement helps testers generate regression test plans and gives them a head start to mature testing over the course of the project. More test involvement over the course of the project gives the test team a better opportunity to mature and adapt their processes.
- **Predictable use of regression testing:** Building the game in small increments guarantees that the test team will be frequently running regression testing against the existing game after each new component is delivered. The high amount of regression testing is predictable and so can be planned for. However, this is somewhat of a small 'silver lining' to a much bigger drawback that we'll talk about next.

Drawbacks of the model:

- **Less time to write tests:** With each sprint only lasting a few weeks and the tester not knowing what features will be implemented beforehand, there isn't very much time in this model to perform good test planning and writing. There is an unfortunate reality that quick paced agile projects don't give QA analysts a good opportunity to do their best work, limiting them to only lightweight test techniques. At best this results in an upskilling of risk assessment and difficult decision-making; at worst this turns testing into a quick and dirty scramble to test as much as possible in the short time given. Because of the time it takes to write effective scripted tests, I've seen this restraint cause teams to overuse and abuse exploratory testing under the pretence that they don't have time to write anything more structured.

- **More difficult test maintenance:** Agile projects are more likely to cause existing features to be removed or changed, meaning their tests will be out of date much sooner than a waterfall project. Each sprint, the test team will also only have time to write tests for the new features being added that sprint. Both of these factors make it very difficult to maintain the existing set of tests for features that are already built. This impact is multiplied because of the heavy use of regression testing in agile projects, too, making the regression tests less and less effective each sprint.

- **Harder to invest in automation:** Due to the quickly changing direction and priority of the project, it's more difficult to make good investments in test automation that will pay off. Big test automation projects are the most successful when the game lifecycle is predictable and stable. While it is possible to implement automation on agile, it needs to be trialled and implemented in small pieces and requires a quicker return on the investment.

- **Light/no documentation:** This is a big one. Because agile methodologies promote working software as the main deliverable, supporting design and technical documentation is often very light or missing completely. Instead, the use of test oracles are common, meaning the use of specific people as the source of truth, instead of written documents. Less reference material makes test planning and testing more difficult, and means that testers need to rely more heavily on asking clarifying questions of the test oracles. Testers will need to make more assumptions during testing about what is and isn't a bug, relying on their experience more heavily. Test writers will also need to investigate more deeply any sources of information they can gather about a feature, including looking through the committed code and making an assessment themselves. The small benefit of this drawback is that diligent QA analysts can use this environment to increase their technical understanding and their skills in discussing the specifics of new features in person. Great things can come from talking through feature details in this way, so I would recommend testers view this arrangement in a positive light.

- **Unplanned bug debt:** A perfect agile project should create and test a feature component within a sprint, fixing or closing all of the bugs created and not postponing them to a later date. Practically, I've never seen this happen within a games project (and I would bet the same is true for agile software projects too!) Instead, only critical and major bugs are generally fixed during a sprint, as well as any bugs in other areas of the game which have been broken by the new component. Agile game projects grow a backlog of bug debt with each new component that is added and, unlike waterfall projects, they don't have a dedicated phase for holistic project bug-fixing. This can be demoralising for the test team, and creates additional work requiring the team to look through the backlog of active bugs when creating new issues. Lastly, experienced test managers will anticipate this phenomenon and suggest dedicated 'product hardening' sprints which swap new feature development for stability improvements and bug fixes only. They will also create special testing tasks to retest older bugs in the backlog and verify that they are still present in the latest version of the game, ensuring that the backlog remains accurate and prevents it from turning into a dumping ground of out-of-date bugs.

(Final note: we call this bug 'debt' because the project team is postponing the work to a later date, but knows that it *will* still have to be done at some point. Because the work doesn't disappear, we call it a debt)

2.5 Similarities between QA and production roles

Now that we've introduced both of the main project lifecycle methodologies that game projects use, this is a good time to take a slight detour and talk about the production discipline. You might have noticed that embedded testing roles have a close working relationship with the entire project lifecycle, and test managers in particular will have an influence in project planning decision making. Because testing is one of the last stages of the creation pipeline, testers need to be acquainted with project milestones and will frequently use test data to estimate whether those dates are achievable or need to be moved. These factors cause testers to spend a lot of time coordinating with producers (sometimes called product managers or scrum masters). The disciplines spend a lot of time working alongside each other within the studio environment, so if you don't know much about the production discipline when you start, you soon will.

I've known quite a few colleagues who started out in QA and then side-stepped into production job roles. Providing that open roles are available and that you are working in a game studio, this move should be very achievable. Developing this further, the production career path leads to executive producer roles, which in turn can promote into general manager / project head roles. This is partly why you might hear the occasional story about how a veteran games industry figure started out their career within testing. It's obviously a long career path that has its own trials and tribulations but it is helpful to know that there is a precedent for it.

2.6 Source control and branching

In this section we're going to talk about the basics of how work-in-progress versions of the game are created, tracked and distributed internally. Regardless of how close you are to the development team, you should understand how the game is updated and how these updates make their way into a format which you can install and run on your test device. Good understanding of this process helps testers communicate more effectively with other disciplines and ask more precise questions (and asking the *right* question is half the battle of effective communication).

The most common use case for testers is understanding which new build contains the fixes for bugs, so that retesting can be performed. The basics of this process are simple. For example, getting a new build of the game each day that has an updated internal version number (where higher numbers show a more recent version of the game). In modern games, however, the reality is rarely this simple. For a start, versions of the game are duplicated out into separate 'branches' and worked on independently by different sub-teams before being merged back together, meaning that there can be several different copies of the project existing in parallel at any time. In addition to the game code, the server code is treated separately. Art content and game data can also be deployed remotely and downloaded when the game is launched. All of these components will have their own independent version numbers.

So, as well as making sure testers are testing on the correct branch of the game, they have to make sure they are testing the correct versions of the game (client) code, server code and game content too. The complexity and scale of projects creates many different moving parts that testers need to be aware of when performing their testing. If you are still a little confused about this, don't worry: we'll cover 'branches' and 'builds' in the following sections. We'll also dig into the terminology of clients, servers and services.

Consider this an introduction to a large and technical topic. My intention is to describe it in as non-technical a way as possible and not use terminology which is only relevant to specific tools. Test staff that haven't worked inside a dev studio may have never had this experience first-hand, instead hearing just some of the terminology being used, so I'm very keen to provide a complete explanation for these readers.

If you already know the basics of source control and branching, you may find it helpful to skip this section.

Source control

Source control is a software development-specific type of version control and is summarised as a system for tracking and managing changes to code. Source control management software stores a history of revisions (edits) to the code and provides a set of tools which allow team members to perform more advanced operations like reverting any individual change or going back to a specific revision of the code and loading it on their machine.

The software shows all of the revisions that have been made along with details about who made the change, what files were changed (or added/removed) and what lines of code within those files were changed. Each revision also contains supplementary data from the author, usually requiring them to leave a comment about the revision. The source control management software links to a central repository which is a remote server location where all of the code is actually stored.

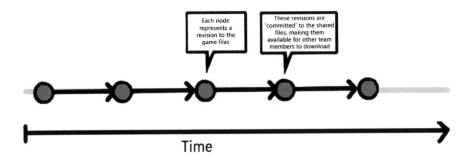

Figure 2.4

Each team member downloads the latest changes to their local machine using the software, and can then make changes to it in isolation, without affecting other people also working on the project files. When they are ready to submit their changes back to the remote repository, they will commit their new code and push it to the remote repository, causing the software to create a new revision which is then available for the rest of the team to download. Downloading the latest changes from the remote repository can be called 'syncing' or 'pulling' depending on the software that the team is using. People might also just say 'get latest' ("Did you get latest?") to refer to the latest changes that have been made to the remote code. Part of the power of these tools is their ability to manage changes from many people, allowing them all to work on parts of the project in parallel without overriding each other's changes.

You might have noticed that while I've only referred to code so far: game teams use these repositories to store all sorts of non-code files too. Game data files, documentation, textures, 3D models, animations, sound, plus a myriad of other asset types are stored in the repository. This is primarily done through necessity, so that it is as simple as possible to download the entire project from one location and run it on your machine. Downloading parts of the project from different locations would be incredibly painful. However, other file types don't work quite so well with the source control software because they aren't text files and so can't show you which parts of the file have been edited and provide counts of the number of changed lines etc. Instead, when an edit is made, the whole file is replaced. For these changes you also need to have the specific software to open that file type, rather than being able to view the changes within the source control software, decreasing the visibility on the changes: 3D modelling software to open models, image editing software to open 2D images, etc. Each commit to the remote repository will have an ID (sometimes called a hash) which can either be numeric or alphanumeric. These commit IDs may later surface in bugs and feature tasks, creating traceability between the change and the feature or bug that it relates to.

Embedded testers (or 'dev QA') will have the most visibility of source control software because they will likely have direct access to it on their computer and can sync the latest project changes in real time alongside the rest of the project team. This allows them to run the game on their own computer, even if the target release platform for the game is not PC or Mac. Nearly all games are built using existing software called graphics engines, which provide a set of tools and technology that the game can be built upon. Most graphics engines come with their own editing software where the game project can be loaded, configured and directly run from the editing software, instead of the target platform. You'll hear people refer to this as the 'editor', ("I ran it in the editor and saw the bug there too"). I can't understate the value of testers having direct visibility and hands-on experience of the project files. This is firmly an area which *can* be described to you, but it's very difficult to understand it until you see it and use it yourself. This is why you can very quickly learn more technical skills just by being in an embedded testing role within a game studio. Depending on how technically minded testers are, they are free to use this exposure of the game project code to upskill themselves through observation first and even experimenting with local changes later on.

This section on source control and repositories has been tool-agnostic. But popular source control tools which you may have heard of include Git, Perforce and Subversion (SVN). When people reference these tools, they're talking about source control.

Branching

We mentioned branching briefly during the introduction to this chapter; it's a topic nearly all testers will have exposure to, but can be extremely confusing without a diagram and an explanation. I find that some testers think they understand it, but then trip up on the finer details during their work.

Let's start from the beginning. Source control tools allow teams to create multiple copies of the same project files, so that each copy can be edited independently from the other. The act of splitting a project into two separate working copies is called branching (or sometimes forking). The name comes from the idea that the main working copy is like the trunk of a tree and copies of it are 'branched off', like tree branches! Unlike trees however, these branches are usually merged back together, combining all of the work into a single place once again. This is called merging.

The simplest and most common case that I will give is the use of branching when releasing an update to a game, a separate working copy of the game is created to allow the final fixes to be made without being impacted by more recent feature development. If a team is releasing version 1, they might develop the features for that version in the main 'trunk' branch and then split it out into a separate branch which will be labelled 'release v1', creating two copies of the project files (trunk and version 1). Once this is done, anyone working on features for the next update (version 2) can add them safely into the trunk branch without accidently going into version 1.

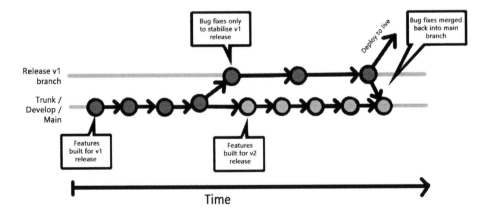

Figure 2.5 – A basic branching example showing how features for two releases can be worked on in parallel

In parallel to this, the version 1 release branch will have fixes and final polishing applied to it to make it ready for releasing; as well as a set of release tests to ensure the health of the release. In this scenario, the version of the project that goes live is the version from the 'release 1' branch. This separate version of the project is isolated from the more recent work that is being added towards release 2. Once the release is published, all of the changes that were made to it are merged back into the trunk so that they are not lost in the next release.

So, we can see that having separate working copies allows the team to both stabilise release v1 in isolation and work on release v2 in parallel. Part of the reason for having separate working copies is stability. New work will generally be the most unstable. Like anything that is 'under construction', creating new game components is disruptive and parts of the game will likely break before it is finished and stability returns. Whereas features that are being prepared to be released will undergo more scrutiny from development and testing to make sure that they are healthy. In most projects, I actually see four levels of working copies (branches) being used, each one with its own level of stability.

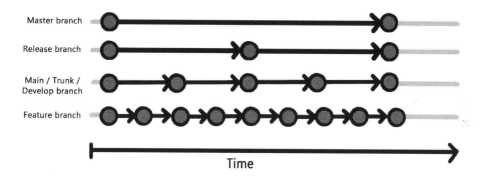

Figure 2.6 – This diagram shows the rate of change in each branch.
Branches with more changes are more likely to be unstable

- **Develop/trunk/main branch** – This goes by different names and is the main working copy of the project files that most of the team will be working on. Smaller fixes and changes will sometimes be committed directly to this branch (yes, we still call it a 'branch') as well as acting as the melting pot for integrating larger features together from different feature branches. Copies of the game will be branched from this main branch, but will nearly always be merged back to it at a later time. Due to this, the branch is also a permanent fixture for the life of the entire project. Because so many people on the project team work directly with these files, the main branch needs to remain stable. If a single person commits broken changes and others on the team sync those changes, work on the project could grind to a halt because people are blocked from further work. You should consider this branch to be constantly moving and continually updated with new changes. Generally, testing on this branch provides testers with a free rein where anything is in scope, since it should always be working and stable. Any changes which are likely to make this branch unstable should be created in the safety of their own branch. This is the place where features are combined, so there is a lot of potential for their integration to cause seemingly random breakages. Because of this, broad, holistic testing is executed on this branch and generally, all bugs are fair game in the main branch.

- **Feature branches** – These are sandboxes for the development of new features or other large changes, where each feature is created in its own branch. Feature branches are created by forking off the main branch and then adding the new feature, so they are essentially main branch code plus the new feature code. Only those working directly on this feature will be working in this branch, so if it's unstable then no one else's work will be impacted by the breakage. The work remains in isolation until it is proven to be stable enough to be merged into the main working copy of the project. Often features also need to be considered complete before they are merged, so that only bug-fixing work remains. Feature branches are numerous and temporary. When testers are working on feature branches they will be testing a specific feature only, and whether that feature has destabilised other parts of the game. Since these branches are early in a feature lifecycle, stability and core functionality of the feature are of the most importance. Smaller bug fixes can be worked out later on. For these reasons, it's very important that testers concentrate their focus on the feature and don't wander too far into areas that are of no importance to this feature branch. Developers of this feature frankly won't care if you've found a bug in another part of the game. Testing in these branches should always be relevant and directly helpful to the feature authors. Testers need to be particularly vigilant if they are testing a work-in-progress, only focusing on those areas that are ready for test and not logging unhelpful bugs that the "feature is not working." That's a really quick way to annoy the feature authors.

- **Release branches** – Release branches are created to stabilise a feature set out the way of the constantly changing main branch. They're created by forking off from the main branch at a predetermined time in the project, before any work has been committed for the *next* release. If teams tried to release directly from the main branch, then there would likely always be new work coming in and creating new bugs, which would be very difficult to keep up with.

Instead, release branches only allow bug fixes and aim to prepare the project for release. These types of branches are temporary and exist for as long as it takes to stabilise the release. For smaller releases, this could just be a few weeks, but for large releases of an entire game, this could be months. These types of branches also exist for other deliverables like playable demos where the team needs to take the full game, lock it to a single section and then polish it, though in these scenarios they might not merge the demo back into the main branch. Testing on release branches focuses on the changes and features being included in the release as well as any trouble areas which are unstable. Testers need to make sure they know exactly what is being included in the release and can spot unintended changes sneaking in. Testers in this branch also need to be more aware that any major bugs, like crashes, exploits or serious performance issues, have increased importance so close to the planned release. Any hint of such issues during testing needs to be escalated and investigated, even if they are one-off or difficult to reproduce.

- **Master branch** – The master branch is used universally across all software projects and represents the currently live version of the product. This means that it is only updated when a new release is published and the files are never edited directly. Instead, this branch is only edited when the final version of the release branch is merged into master, essentially overriding the older version with the code with the files from the new release. This also means that it represents the most stable and releasable version of the project. This is also where the terminology of 'gold master' comes from, referring to the final release candidate build that will be published to the public. The master branch is a permanent fixture of the project and will exist from its first release. As a final comment, some teams choose to back up (fork off) the master branch before overriding it with the code from a new release, so that they have copies of both the current release and the new release. This is so that the team can easily roll back to an older release without actually reverting the merge which can be painful in some projects. I've seen this practise used when projects are releasing frequently (every few weeks) and also when projects frequently update and deploy game data from the master branch. Testing on master branch is a little unique. Testing here will either be live ops testing on the live game or it will be testing a final release candidate build which will be published. Testers should be aware of what the final release candidate build number is (gold master) because it's normal for some tests to be re-run on the actual final files that will be uploaded to a store. On mobile, teams will also upload the build to a testing track of the mobile stores so that they can download and test a build in a way which is closest to the public release.

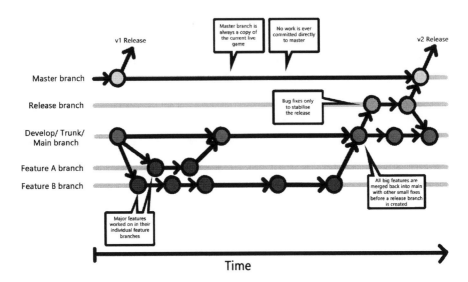

*Figure 2.7 – A complete branching example. This is very
close to the model that many teams use in their real work.*

The testing activities in each branch strongly correlate to various levels of testing which we'll cover in more detail in the **Test Levels** section later in this chapter. The branch types listed here are the ones that I've seen used in nearly all of the projects that I've worked on, but it's worth calling out that teams will use them in different ways and have their own rules for how they like to organise when branches are branched out and merged back together. This process is under the ownership of the code engineering team and is called a 'branching strategy'.

Most teams will *not* have a diagram of their strategy, but instead will have a verbally agreed approach that is led by the engineering leadership. If you are able, I would strongly advise test teams to ask their development teams about the branching strategy and gather around a whiteboard to draw it out and discuss the details. If this isn't possible, find someone on the team who is willing to explain it to you one on one. Those executing tests can get by with a loose understanding of the branches that exist on the project, but any QA analysts, leads or managers need to have a comprehensive understanding of it to perform effective test planning and longer term project planning.

Like source control, this is another area where having a good technical understanding of the topic moves testers into a semi-technical area where they can have project quality and risk discussions with the engineering team about the branching strategy, eventually making their own suggestions and recommendations. As well as building the respect of other project disciplines, this knowledge also helps provide a foundation for good test planning and moves your knowledge from testing into the larger scope of quality practices.

This brings us neatly to the last point I'd like to make about branches and branching strategies. A branching strategy is a quality driven preventative technique for ensuring the health (quality) of the build. Testers should recognise it as a quality tool and have an inherent interest in it, making sure it is being used effectively.

Builds

If a branch is a collection of living, raw files that are updated continuously, a build of the game is essentially a packaged snapshot of those files at a specific date and time.

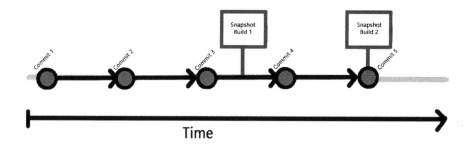

Figure 2.8 – Builds capture a packaged snapshot of the branch files. In this diagram, build 1 contains changes from commits 1, 2 and 3, but not 4 or 5.

All teams that I've worked in will either build overnight versions of the game daily, if it's big or, if the project is small enough, will build a new version every time a change is made.

'Build' is common terminology across all software, but I've also seen 'snapshots' used in a few teams. Builds are created because those raw files need to be packaged into a format that can be executed by the target platform and device, whether that's a game console, a mobile device, a PC or other device entirely. The player's device runs this executable version – they don't have the raw source code on their device. In games, the code is compiled into an executable file, but game assets also go through a process of being compressed and bundled into packages for optimisation purposes. Game assets are what cause games to have such a large file size compared with other software. Because of this, the build process takes longer and is more complicated.

These builds are built daily (the actual frequency is defined by the team) from various different branches and for each platform that the game supports, so it's normal to have multiple copies of each build. Different 'flavours' of each build are sometimes created too, with various levels of logging and debug enabled: full debug, partial debug, performance profiling and release flavours.

On mobile, for example, a nightly build of one branch might contain one build for the iOS platform and one for Android. One project I worked on created 8 different versions on each build at one point, which I'll admit was probably overkill! These are the files that testers pick up and run on their test devices, so it's important that they know which build variations they should be using for each task.

Since each project is set up differently, I can't give specific advice here. Instead, here is some general guidance and things to be aware of during testing.

- Do I need a debug or a release build?
  - o Most testing should be carried out on a debug build so that logs can be captured and testers can take advantage of debug tools
  - o Some tests, like performance testing, are impacted by the addition of debug and so need to be carried out on release builds

- Has my build been created from the correct branch?
  - o Especially important for retesting. If a fix was made yesterday and a tester has today's build, this won't apply if the tester is on a different branch than the fix was made
  - o Testers should be alert around branch and merge dates, in case they need to move their testing to a new branch build

- Use the terminology of 'flavours' to talk about build types
  - o Speaking about a 'release build' can either mean a release flavour or the release branch, so be specific
  - o 'Debug' is also overly generic and can be confusing, so try to get into the habit of saying 'debug flavour build'

- Watch out for special, platform-specific build types and configurations
  - o iOS has enterprise and non-enterprise builds which use different types of licences. Get the wrong build and you may not be able to install it
  - o Some platforms require special builds to perform purchases and other features where the game interacts with the platform on which it runs
  - o Some platforms require the build to be uploaded to a test (alpha) version of the platform store before these same features are enabled. Purchases are a good example of this
  - o Other third-party integrations might also require special builds for the features to function during testing. Twitter, Twitch or Facebook integration is a good example of this.

- Be alert for fixes and changes that have been made on the same day you are testing. Understanding the build system means that the change may have been committed to the branch, but a new build containing the change hasn't been created yet. I occasionally see testers fall into this trap and incorrectly mark bugs as 'fix fail' only to then retest them the day afterwards.

- Large games have large build files and can take over an hour to deploy to your device. Small projects are much more forgiving. Make sure to account for this when changing builds. Some teams use automated deployment tools before testers arrive in the office or simply deploy a new build before they leave the office each day. When I was working on consoles, we could get away with deploying a new build during our hour lunch break.

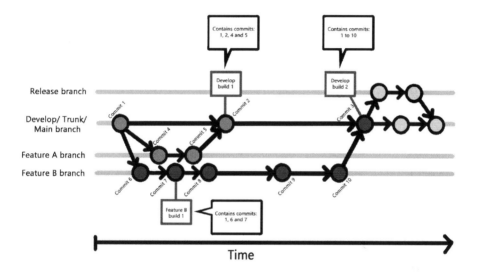

Figure 2.9 – This diagram shows the complexities of creating builds from different branches at different points in time. In this example, any newer build cannot guarantee to contain all older fixes, since they may have been committed on different branches.

I'm going to end this brief introduction to builds by touching on *how* builds are created.

Building a game from the raw, loose files into packages takes time – anything from 10 minutes to several hours depending on the size of the project. Game developers rarely (never) build from their local copies of the project. This is because the build process would use up the processing power of their machine and stop them from working during the process.

Instead, game teams will have dedicated build machines (computers/servers) whose only job is to create builds from the source files. These build machines are mostly computers running Windows or MacOS, but will vary depending on the requirements of the project. It's normal for certain build machines to be setup for each target platform that the game supports. For example, if you were releasing on the Nintendo Switch, you might need a different software setup on the build machine than if you were building for Xbox and Windows.

iOS apps are a good example of this. To build Apple store apps, you need to build the game project on a Mac computer. The mobile teams that I've worked on generally have a 50/50 split between Windows and Mac project build machines. Teams also need additional software to manage the process of taking versions of the project code and communicating with the build machines to create all the build variations. These are called Continuous Integration (CI) tools, and popular names include Jenkins and TeamCity.

To summarise, these CI tools automatically trigger builds on a basis defined by the team (usually daily) and show users which builds are queued and which are in progress, a historical set of previous builds and what branches all of these builds are from. They also allow users to manually trigger new builds of any branch and can be configured by the development team to add parameters to the build to customise it.

They do have further functionality – and there is a reason they're called continuous integration tools – but that topic is beyond the scope of this book. However, testers embedded in game studios will have access to these tools so that they can monitor build delivery to the wider test team and kick off new builds without engineering support when it is required. The understanding of this process is need-to-know for QA analysts and QA managers, because it helps us understand and diagnose when builds fail and don't get delivered into testing. It also helps provide accurate estimations for when new builds will be ready, and tracks 'last known good' builds.

Server code and remote game data

The simplicity of the creation and delivery of builds into testing is disrupted by the introduction of server code, which is built separately and deployed directly by server engineers.

The same applies to many modern games which choose to deploy data packages for the game to remote server storage, where the game downloads this data when launched. Such systems allow teams to configure and update games without publishing a full update for it. The server code runs remotely in a one-to-many relationship with the game 'client' builds, meaning that while multiple users need to install the client build on their device, the server build only needs to be installed once.

Because of this arrangement, the server code is handled separately to the game builds. Some server teams choose to automatically build and deploy the server code each night; others will only deploy when they trigger it manually.

Like the client code, server code also has branches that are used to organise the work. To run each version (branch) of the server code in parallel, multiple server environments are created to which the client builds can connect. At the very least, this will usually be a production environment which runs the live game server code and a development environment which runs the newly developed server code. In practice, teams will have several development environments for different branches of code.

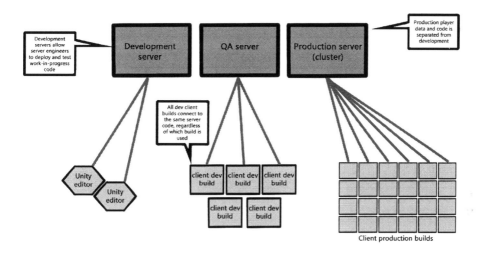

Figure 2.10 – A basic diagram showing the relationship between client builds and server deployments

This topic is technical and deep, so for this book it is enough for testers to understand these core differences between the client build, that runs on your device, and the server build, that runs remotely. Testers should be very aware of server code bugs and the challenges they face!

Industry tales: The mystery of server side bug fixes

When I was working at Microsoft we were acting as a Publisher test team on Fable Legends which was entirely online multiplayer, and had lots of interaction with microservices and the game server for each session. I was a software test engineer and owned the online services and multiplayer test plans, so I was quite heavily involved in knowing the version of the online services we were using as well as the current version of the game server.

We had a small team of testers locally executing tests, but a majority of the testers were in Warsaw, Poland. Most of the test team were very accustomed to getting bug fixes to retest through the daily builds of the client game that we would install on the Xbox kits. But fixes were also made to the online services and were deployed remotely in real time, which was met with confusion and a little frustration by the testers when it first happened.

A bug would be present one minute and then appear fixed the next, without ever installing a new build onto the kit. In the best scenarios, bugs were updated with comments about the fix being a server fix and gave a date and time of when the fix was deployed, as well as where it was deployed. In the worst cases, server deployments would be made that were unhealthy and caused testers to unnecessarily investigate temporary bugs that would suddenly be fixed sometime later. We also had the opposite problem where a resolved bug would be correctly marked with a server commit ID and, while that code had been committed, it hadn't been built and deployed to one of the active server environments and so wasn't actually testable yet. In this scenario, testers would retest the bug and reactivate it back to the server developer, resulting in much back-and-forth bug comments between the tester and the developer, with frustration on both sides.

A large part of the problem was because the testers didn't know when server deployments were made and what version was currently active, so it was very difficult for them to figure out what was happening if they saw anomalies during their testing. Additionally, different versions of the server code were deployed to different environments which were used for different reasons. So, it was important that testers understood which environment their build was using during their test sessions. Because you can't really 'see' the server code as tester, it can appear very techy, under-the-hood and a little daunting. The general architecture of server setups and deployments is unknown and mysterious to most testers, which can cause further misunderstanding during communication and questioning. The same can be said for building game content bundles and uploading them to a storage location that the game client can access. The details of the process are not always visible to the test team.

Given all of these server-side components, I totally understand why some testers didn't like testing it and were hesitant when logging bugs. Double checking sudden bugs with other testers became commonplace. If lots of the team suddenly started seeing multiplayer or network errors, this suggested that something had happened server side and it was best to wait for a fix than try to spend time chasing ghosts and investigating bugs that likely wouldn't be there 30 minutes later.

While I was acting as publisher QA in a remote office, I still called into the daily stand up meetings and visited the studio once or twice a week to work beside the dev teams. Thanks to this direct contact with both the multiplayer team and the online services team, I was able to use the information from our meetings and stand-ups to create basic training content for the team of testers so that they could better understand what was going on in the background. It wasn't easy or quick, but with the increased level of understanding, these frustrations were eased over time.

I should also note that some of the testers appreciated the heightened level of understanding and became enthused by the technical nature of the topic. Once they had a basic understanding of how the server code and environments were set up, it became an interesting and technical testing challenge, rather than a mysterious void of frustration!

This is a great example of how testers require a good level of technical knowledge to do their work effectively, short of being able to write code. It also shows an evolution from the older style of testing stand-alone game clients as a 'black box' into a newer style, where testing is at the very least 'grey box' and requires some knowledge of the inner workings.*

I should provide a last note here that not all of the test team were enthusiastic about this game area because it was difficult and had a steep learning curve, so we continued to work on upskilling the team throughout the project.

I've learned quite a bit since then and I'm now an advocate of setting up preventive measures to keep the test team involved without my interaction. On more recent projects, we have automated alerts in Slack (an instant messaging tool) which fire when server deployments are made or new game data is deployed. If it doesn't exist already, we also put in requests to add elements to the debug HUD showing the tester what current versions of the server and data they are using. This creates much-needed visibility into the remote components of the game that exist on the server.

Furthermore, we build support into our bug database tools to include fields in our bug forms for server and data versions. This applies to the information testers enter when they log a bug showing what the full configuration of the bug is, as well as the bug resolution flow where the resolver can define if the fix was client, server or data and state the specific commit ID or deployment time. Armed with this experience, test managers can input these process measures proactively and prevent later frustration.

2.7 Test levels

Test levels categorise the testing activities that apply to each stage of the development lifecycle we've been defining so far, and strongly correlate to the branches that are used

---

*   See chapter three on **Test types and terminology** for definitions of black box, grey box and white box testing.

for each level, too. Test levels are also one of the core reasons game project test teams have multiple sub teams: embedded test, publisher test and external test. Whether they know it explicitly or not, they are usually each responsible for a test level.

Having this model formalised helps testers articulate what their team is responsible for and understand how their ownership fits in with that of the other test teams.

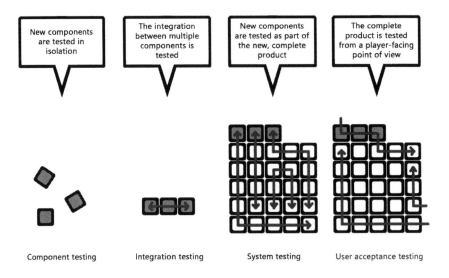

Figure 2.11 – A visual guide to the main four test levels described in this section.

Component Testing

Who: Embedded teams
Where: Feature branches
Scope: A single component (part of a large feature or a small feature)
Duration: Short, 1 sprint

The defining attribute of component testing is that it is carried out against a single game component in isolation. This is the earliest testing run by humans* that is carried out against a component, and is done in the feature branch for that component before it is integrated into the rest of the game code. Some authors go a step further by building and deploying their new components directly to a device which is given to

---

*   There is a test level before component testing, called unit testing. This test level is the earliest level
     and is run by test automation against each of the code functions directly. However, I've seen this
     used so rarely in games that it isn't included within the scope of this book. Furthermore, the unit
     testing level is a specialist technical level that is either written by the developer of the feature or by
     a dedicated automation engineer. This test level is an advanced topic and has been intentionally
     omitted from this book.

a tester sitting nearby. In this workflow, the new component can be tested before it is even committed to the branch.

For this reason, this type of testing is nearly always carried out by test staff embedded in the game studio. Furthermore, the component authors and the tester will be part of the same sub-team (i.e. pod, scrum team) and will be creating and testing the new component as part of a sprint.

Component level testing goals are primarily to confirm that the feature is complete and stable by the end of the sprint. This may sound simple, but each team or individual can have their own definition of what 'done'* actually means. The QA analyst will work with the authors of the feature and the team producer to make sure that what has been created matches the understanding of what the wider team intended. Feature components should have acceptance criteria in the sprint task which need to be fulfilled, at the very least.

The definition I use for 'done' during component level-testing is that the feature fulfils the acceptance criteria and doesn't have any active bugs of severity 1 or 2, meaning that it must be stable, but cosmetic and minor bugs can be tackled later. The way that sprints work means that the team will claim a feature as complete and then swiftly move to the next sprint to start new work, so it's important that all work is *actually* complete before the team moves on. This is achieved by providing direct and rapid feedback on the new component to the authors.

Component testers have a very short space of time in which to understand the new component technically and then set about testing it. In most cases, testing is actually carried out by QA analysts who sometimes have testers to help them out. The component testing level is primarily for verification and involves few or no failure tests at this early stage. Another key focus is evaluating the risk of the new component and asking incisive questions of the authors about the workings of the component and the potential risks involved. In some cases, through the course of this questioning, the tester actually helps define what the acceptance criteria should be, and it is updated during the sprint. The process for these activities is very personal and organic, and differs from sub-team to sub-team.

You can see why this level of testing is only carried out within the game studio: it's something that external teams will have very little exposure to. This process also gives testers the greatest exposure to the production sprint process and other disciplines, making it both engaging and challenging.

Finally, depending on the size of the project, the QA analyst may also own the test plan for other levels of testing too. When this is the case, the component test level provides a good environment for the QA analyst to use the information to perform

---

* Search online for 'definition of done' for further reading. This applies to all software.

test planning for later levels, leveraging all of the technical risk details gained from the authors of the component to feed into the test plans. In other cases, the embedded QA analyst will be responsible for an effective handover of information to a test owner in another test team, who in turn will be responsible for other levels of testing. In both scenarios, the best component test owners will document their efforts so that others can benefit from the conversations that happen during the sprint work. Testers who don't work directly in the game studio will greatly appreciate this information exchange.

Integration Testing

Who: Embedded teams, publisher teams, external teams
Where: Feature branch, main branch
Scope: Multiple components or features
Duration: Short (1-2 weeks)

This test level immediately follows component testing. It aims to verify that several components continue to function correctly once they have been integrated together. This type of testing is increasingly necessary when the components are intended to work together or when they use shared code or other resources. Of all the test levels, this one is the least used and those teams that *do* run it, don't usually define it as an explicit activity, instead including it in another test level less formally.

I would advise using it when components are large, complex or risky. As an example, large features are built by completing a set of feature components over several sprints. So, as well as testing each component during each sprint, you need to test that the components work together to form a complete and coherent feature once all of the components are built. This test level is also used on a selective basis when it is required.

Good examples of this occur when large components are built by separate teams and integrated together. A new game feature might require a new server code component as well as game client components and possibly even third-party middleware updates from other teams. At some point, these different deliverables must come together to form the complete new feature. It's up to the team to choose how big or complex a feature needs to be for them to run dedicated integration testing against it. Similarly, what we define as a component vs. a feature is quite arbitrary and a question of size and complexity for the team. On the topic of third-party software, technically any updates from SDKs (software development kits) on which the game depends would be subject to integration testing; it just so happens that most teams don't label it formally.

Because integration testing is completed outside the sprint structure, it is usually executed by a publisher or external test team. This leaves the embedded test team to continue focusing on the next set of component tests.

Integration tests are also afforded the time of being able to test more deeply than component tests and investigate more end-to-end test scenarios. These tests might have a separate test owner but would likely be planned and owned by the same embedded QA analyst who planned for each of the individual components.

Depending on the target, size and risk of the integration testing, the testing activity would be carried out on a feature branch or directly in the main branch. When planning what to test in this level, test teams will want to both re-run their component tests and supplement these existing tests with new tests which exercise end-to-end feature flows and focus on the individual interactions between components. For testers with a non-technical background, this is a great area to delve deeply into understanding the technical style and format of how game components are interacting, serving both as an educational tool and as a driver for better test planning.

As an example of this, our test team will look through the commit change lists, fixes and known bugs for third-party updates like the Unity or Unreal engine when we integrate those updates into the game. The change lists are presented in a very specific and technical way, making it difficult, at first, to identify relevant information. But given practice and a little guidance from a friendly software engineer, testers can identify changes within the third-party software that the game uses and understand how the game uses it. This information then translates into a list of game areas most likely to be negatively impacted by taking the SDK update, thus narrowing down the focus of integration testing to specific areas which will have the most impact.

For testing features that have been developed in-house, testers should speak to the authors of each component to understand how much integration testing is required and take into account any concerns raised by the authors.

Sometimes a developer might highlight assumptions and limitations about the inputs that a component expects from another component. They might say something like, "When this code is triggered, it assumes it already has the player's server ID and the social media ID from the server and then attempts to sync. I can't think of game scenarios where we wouldn't have that data on the player yet, but you should investigate if that's possible and check that it fails gracefully."

This is a paraphrased example of a conversation I had about a cloud save feature which was responsible for uploading and downloading a player's save game to different devices. We were adding a new social media account into the mix and new code had to be written for both server and client components. In this case, the component of the code the player used to sign into a social media account to link their devices together, like Facebook, was separate from the component that actually handled the player's save data on the server. These components were also written by different people. It was important to see them as two separate components interacting together and test accordingly.

Industry tales: System level changes

Talking about integration testing of SDKs and other third-party updates reminds me about the difficulties of identifying what to test when faced with updates to these components. I've worked in a couple of teams where we had dedicated systems engineers. These are developers that spend most of their time on core project technologies which include both the code that the project team has written themselves and also third-party technology that the game depends on. Almost everything they worked on wouldn't directly influence a player-facing part of the game but would instead modify part of the foundation code, which then had the potential to break or influence some unknown parts of the player-facing behaviour.

Generally, these types of code components are functions that are utilised by many other features throughout the game or are continuously running in the background. They are frequently described as 'low level' because they are the bottom layer of a stack of dependent technologies, where other technologies that are layered on top of them are dependent on them.

Systems that deal with allocating and releasing memory are a good example; as are systems that interact with the device hardware directly, optimising for a specific console or peripherals (these are just a few examples of course, there are many more areas where this occurs). When updates or fixes to this code appeared on our feature list, we would follow the usual route of speaking to our systems engineers about the changes. A normal response from them would be, "You can't really test this change", "There isn't anything to test" or, "It touches everything!". What they meant was there were no changes to directly verify and the scope of the impact from the changes was usually very difficult to determine. Some of our junior QA analysts had trouble test planning for these changes at times because their choice was effectively to test nothing or test everything, neither of which are very effective or efficient options!

It's important that QA analysts tackle this test problem with care and give systems-level changes the attention they deserve, taking the time to really understand the scope of the changes. SDK updates from graphics engines and other third-party tools have always been a source of bugs for the projects that I've worked on, frequently creating very serious bugs too. We've caught some during testing, while others were found in the live game and required hotfixes. Reading SDK change lists and notes is a must.

I would also encourage testers to ask systems engineers to explain the changes to them. Use a whiteboard if necessary, then follow up with incisive questions that might start to give you an idea of the scope of the changes. Fair warning – this can get very technical, very quickly. Systems engineers have a specialist role for a reason. But it's worth it and by being patient and persevering you can dramatically increase the effectiveness of your test plan for these areas (and learn a thing or two while you're there). I've also seen testers neglect testing these changes outright in favour of testing more enjoyable content and gameplay changes. Testers can't afford to be picky in this way. Test managers should remain vigilant if they see that the test team is shying away from these types of difficult-to-test changes.

System Testing

Who: Publisher teams, external teams
Where: Main branch, release branch
Scope: The entire product
Duration: Long (multiple weeks/months)

System-level testing is the most common activity carried out by test teams and is usually the primary reason for larger remote test teams to exist. It looks not just at new components and features, but includes all existing features too. It views the entire new product holistically, considering it as a complete package instead of a collection of individual components.

System-level testing isn't referred to by this name in game testing. More commonly, it's referred to as 'release testing' because it is used to test a release. Other teams don't label it at all, or describe it loosely as 'user testing', 'player testing', 'end to end testing' or some similar variation.

For small projects or releases, system testing will begin once all the features are complete and have been merged into the same branch. For larger projects, it will begin for sections of the project that are feature-complete, even if some other areas are still undergoing feature development. This test level runs over several weeks or months and includes a greater depth of testing compared with previous levels, including the lower priority tests that were not tested during component testing. For us, this means running all the failure and exploratory tests that take a long time to run but are so effective at finding bugs. The breadth of testing is also increased in this test level – tests are carried out more legitimately using fewer debug and stub (fake) components, making each test flow as complete as possible. In this way, tests from earlier levels might be re-run, but this time chained together to form longer and more complex end-to-end flows.

While the levels here are described as discrete activities, in reality component testing will start in a feature branch and then the integration or system testing will act as a continuation of that same test plan. Some tests are re-run; others are run for the first time because they were not included in earlier levels. In this way system testing can contain a lot of different test plans: some continuing plans from the component test level which look at individual features more deeply, others new test plans which cover all features. As an example, non-functional areas like performance are introduced into testing here for the first time, covering new and old features alike.

Some areas of testing lend themselves to being run solely at a system level like this (performance testing is the most effective when all of the component pieces are present), so testers will wait until this level to kick off certain tests. Furthermore, this test level will use a test environment that has more platform and third-party integrations enabled, like sandbox store purchases and social media integrations. As an example, in earlier test levels, testers use debug to test in-game items and access certain areas of the game, but here the test environment* is set up so that they can make test purchases from the platform store directly and have those items appear within the game like they would for real players. Other platform integrations like achievements, notifications and special install features might also only be available in this environment.

As another example, our current mobile project uses a test environment for in-game advertisements which is configured to connect only to test ads, so that testing can be completed without triggering ads intended for real players. These tests are only run at the system level and are effectively the middle stage between the completely clean and stable production game setup, and the dirty, unstable development setup used within feature branches. As a side note, this 'clean'/'dirty' description can be a useful metaphor for the evolution of the game through the different test levels, with each progressive resembling more the production game and less a development work in progress.

The increased scope of this test level is why larger test teams are required. Commonly, this test level has a separate set of QA analysts, QA managers and test ownership because the embedded test team will be focusing on the latest features being built within the sprints. This is particularly true for game studios which have a publishing test team. The publisher team will have their own QA analysts to write larger system-level test plans for each feature area, leaving the embedded QA analysts to work on testing at a component and integration level. I will go into more detail about common team

---

*   A test environment refers to the setup and configuration of the different layers of technology that the game needs to run. The most obvious comparison environments are between the production environment (the live game) and the development environment. These two 'setups' will have separate servers, different game data, different clients with debug toggled on/off and many other similar configurations that are set depending on what the environment is designed for. In reality, there can be several development environments set up for different purposes. This combination of configurations makes up the test environment

structures and their ownerships later in the **Test Management** chapter. I reference the team ownership here because you should understand that this test level commonly runs in parallel to the component test level. When system testing is being run for the current release, component testing for the next release will be running in parallel.

For very large releases, system testing may cover both the main branch and the release branch. Where the scope of testing is very large, system testing will begin in the main branch as early as possible once some of the main game areas are feature-complete. When all of the features are complete, a subset of system tests will be run again in the release branch. In this way, the entry criteria for the start of system testing varies from team to team, depending on the project limitations and the size of the release.

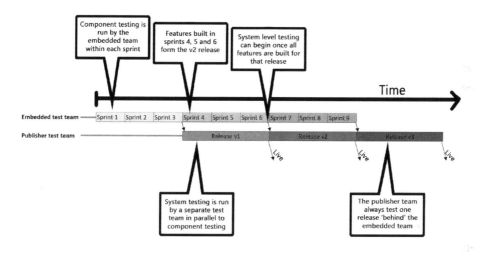

Figure 2.12 – A diagram showing how multiple test teams execute different test levels in parallel

User Acceptance Testing

Who: All test teams
Where: Release branch
Scope: The entire product
Duration: Short (1-7 days)

User acceptance testing is the least-common test level for test teams within the games industry. This is another big difference between games and other software. It looks at how the user is going to use the software as the point-of-truth, and disregards the documentation which is used as the basis for testing in other test levels.

In short, all other test levels ask the question, "Did we build what we set out to build in our designs?" The user acceptance test level, on the other hand, asks the broader question, "Does our final product meet the requirements of the user?".

This means that user acceptance testing can identify bugs which are correct according to the intended design (the behaviour is 'by design'), but where the bug is stating that the intended design is poor and doesn't meet the user expectations in some way. These bugs can't be closed as 'by design' for this reason, since they are logged from the external viewpoint of the user.

This test level makes a lot of sense for most software, because the product is created for a specific purpose and it is important to make sure it actually fulfils that need and doesn't go off on a design tangent during the development process. But games are not created to solve a specific problem and they have no user requirements, which is why user acceptance testing in this format is never carried out on game projects.

This test level is still very important, but game teams must take a customised approach for it to provide good value. Once a game is released and people start playing it, player requirements will manifest organically over time and feed back to the development team through various channels. Players will frequently interact with the game in ways the team did not expect, which can push the focus of further development and testing in new directions. This can be less crucial for one-off game releases but is incredibly important for games that run as a continuous live service.

For live ops projects, user acceptance testing focuses on testing new releases to the service from the perspective of existing players. It considers how the update will impact those players and what game features are important to those players. To run this effectively, testers will use tools to import real player game profiles into the development environment and use these 'mature' profiles to run this test level. The bugs that I see during this process cluster around the existing data that players have in their profiles. If a new update breaks or changes the stats for an item that is important to the player, then that player is going to be very unhappy. Similarly, if game data negatively rebalances a favourite character or the players' in-game setup, making them less effective in the game, then that player will be equally unhappy.

This is particularly hard to catch when long-term players have items and other profile data acquired in a much older version of the game and is no longer available. This can be a common reality for long running live ops games. Testing only the latest update with a fresh profile would not catch such a bug, but loading mature live player profiles, understanding what they care about and performing user acceptance testing is a good start to approaching this test level within game projects.

One-off game releases as part of an existing franchise are a slight anomaly because they can also benefit from this test level. Collecting the most reported bugs and design feedback from the previous game gives a basis for user acceptance testing for the next project. These projects benefit from knowing their audience, using past data to predict the player requirements before the new game is released. It requires good organisation between the QA team, the customer service team and production to trigger this activity and make time in the project schedule for it. Unfortunately, for one-off release projects I've worked on, the team has collected the data from the previous game release with the full intention of using it to drive user acceptance testing, only for the activity to be deprioritised later in the schedule.

Because this type of testing is unconventional and doesn't have a defined guiding document, testers find it challenging to execute. In my experience, testers find it difficult to understand what the goal of the test activity is, and try to refer back to project documentation as their guide or see it as an opportunity to log feature suggestions, defeating the point of the activity. It is difficult to be invested in a game profile that you have imported, even after playing with it for a few hours. Testers will never know a game profile as intimately as the real owner of that profile, who has likely invested many hours of gameplay building it.

Many projects choose to release updates to a limited audience of real players, either through a beta program or with a soft launch of a live ops game to smaller regions before they release worldwide. Even though this isn't carried out by the test team, within games this is the most widely used method of collecting user acceptance feedback and bugs. Test teams should recognise this and get involved in it if they aren't already key stakeholders. For beta tests, they should get feedback from the customer service team and identify specific issues that warrant deeper investigation by the test team.

Test levels conclusion

If you are in the testing discipline, take a minute to consider what test levels you are responsible for and then identify the responsibilities of other test teams that you work with. Labelling these levels more formally and knowing the goals of each level will allow you to coordinate testing more effectively across the project, avoiding duplication of test effort and improving communication between test teams. This understanding is a key requirement for test managers and other embedded test staff, because they're frequently the ones who will be driving the larger project test strategy. Additionally, knowing these test levels also allows junior testers to understand the project test strategy beyond their immediate ownership, giving helpful insight into testing outside of their visibility.

I mention junior testers here because they may not be in direct communication with QA members in the wider organisation or even know that they exist. If you are a tester in a publishing or external test team, I encourage you to use this information to ask your test leads about the wider test organisation and what they are responsible for. If your test lead doesn't have a clear definition, you can suggest that it would be productive to find out the next time they are in contact with other test teams on the project. The difference in scope forms a large part of what makes the test levels different, and understanding it provides a great guide to many of the small decisions all testers need to take during testing. Testers with a good knowledge of this area will have a much better idea about what is in scope and out of scope for their current testing, what bugs are important and what the ultimate goal of their current test activity is.

2.8 Project lifecycles: games vs. software

While this chapter has presented a game project-oriented view of project lifecycles, many of the topics that were covered are relevant to all software. Agile and waterfall software development methodologies apply directly to software projects, as do the accompanying source control and branching strategies.

The section on project gates is fairly unique to games, though you may also see them in software where the company is developing their own new products from early inception. Game projects have such a strong orientation around these gates that you are unlikely to find documentation of them in software testing academia. Further detail on how testing is set up to help navigate the project through these gates is beyond the scope of this book, but there is enough direction here that testers should be able to at least identify these gates in their own projects and understand what they are for. As we've discussed, a lot of software projects are created with specific goals in mind and so don't need such rigid gates in place to release company resources to back the project.

Continuing the topic of project gates and phases, game projects also have a much heavier focus on prototyping and ideation around the art style and core loop of the game during the early phases of the life cycle. This early project phase of throwaway work presents unique test challenges to game testers. During these early phases, documentation doesn't exist and any test plans are likely to become obsolete quickly. Because each company approaches this phase differently, there are very few publications showing what a well-defined test process looks like for game projects during this early phase. Because these test activities are so specific to embedded test teams during a small part of the overall lifecycle, I won't be going into further detail about it in this book.

Finally, while game teams *are* made up by a collection of smaller sprint teams, unlike most software, they are much more cross-discipline. For example, a typical software sub-team might be made up primarily of software engineers of different specialities, perhaps with the addition of a UI engineer. In these sub-teams the ratio of code engineers to artists is very high, and therefore many documented software testing processes are based on this assumption.

An example of a testing process that follows this assumption might be one that tracks test metrics which show the velocity of bugs being fixed over time and is the most accurate when the bugs are as similar as possible (bugs that are fixed in code). With teams largely made up of software engineers creating code bugs, tracking the rate of bug fixes back to the test team can be done fairly accurately. However, because game project sub-teams are cross-discipline, involving a more equal mix of software engineers and artists of various sub-disciplines, the bugs they create can have wildly different characteristics, making many software testing processes like this one ineffective. This is a key difference in the make-up of game development teams, and it filters down to many other areas of project life and test work which we'll cover elsewhere in this book.

Going back to our example, content bugs from artists or designers are typically more numerous and generally quicker to fix. As a result, testers and producers must recognise the differences between these bug types and change their processes to fit – for example, by creating new bug fields to track whether bugs are code or content and then using this to provide a more detailed view of the types of bugs being generated. If teams choose to track metrics like bug fix velocity, they must create separate velocities for content and code bugs. This is just one example of how the unique team composition introduces small challenges into the practicalities of daily test work. The same example applies to many other test metrics which we will cover in chapter seven, **Test Management**.

Expanding on this further, some large game teams will have sub-teams comprised entirely of content creators working towards the same game component. The game environment is a great example of this. For large games with a 3D environment, there will be an environment art and design team that spends most of its project time crafting and polishing sections of the environment. These teams really do break the traditional sprint team mould, disregarding a lot of the software lifecycle processes that we've discussed in this chapter because they were created with software engineers in mind. The same applies to teams of character creators and other large-scale content creations. These are the areas where game development diverges the most heavily away from published software development methodology. In chapter six, **Major areas of game testing**, we'll go into more detail about how testers approach different areas of game testing, and these content areas will be included there.

3

Test types and terminology

3.1　An introduction to test terminology

"Can you define what regression testing is and what re-testing is?" This is a favourite interview question for our team. I was asked it when I joined the company several years ago and we still ask it to this day when interviewing new candidates.

We ask it because many game test teams have their definitions reversed. We did at Microsoft. During my interview, I gave my definitions for each term, told them how we used those terms in our team and then added that I knew it was wrong! I have no clue why this is, but many teams use the term 'regression' to refer to the activity of re-testing a bug to verify a fix. That activity is actually 're-testing', whereas regression testing refers to testing existing areas of the game which worked previously to make sure they haven't regressed in quality. The word 'regress' as a general term, means to go back to a less-developed state. During testing we use regression testing to check that adding a new component doesn't accidently break existing healthy components. The two activities are very different, so it's important that testers using these terms have a shared understanding of what they refer to.

In other areas of testing, terms like 'smoke testing' are overused as a catch-all for any brief test activity or when the person is too lazy to properly define the type of testing that they want to run: "It just requires a quick smoke test.."

This may sound a little harsh, but I've seen it done many times. Furthermore, many testers and game teams use terms that have evolved into company slang or have been abbreviated over time. UAT – meaning user acceptance testing – is a good example, as is halo testing, a lesser-used term.

You will notice that many of these terms follow the format of "<something>

testing", which is confusing when we consider that some of them describe phases or types of testing, while others describe specific test tasks. This adds to the ambiguity when using test terminology.

This chapter defines a list of game test terminology which provides all of the information in a single place, and is both correct and consistent. The list names are newly defined in this book. I wanted to provide additional structure to this list to properly categorise each item, to highlight their differences and describe how they fit together. Many of these terms are not mutually exclusive, and a single test can have multiple attributes from these lists at the same time.

The lists defined below are in descending scope order. Test levels have the largest project scope, with multiple test areas within each level. For each test area, there are many test activities and each test activity has at least one test type associated with it. Definitions are provided for each category inline.

3.2   Test levels

Test levels define the project phase in which the testing is being carried out. They are the largest in scope and can encompass multiple test areas, test activities and test types. Since test levels are defined in detail in chapter two, I won't elaborate here. Instead, each level is defined through its relationship with other test terminology.

Component Testing

A phase of testing that focuses on a single game component or feature. This level can have multiple test areas but they are isolated from one another and may run at different times. Teams can run component testing simultaneously against different features and will refer to them separately. Because this test level is early in the life cycle and focuses on the core functions of the new component, the scale of test activities and test types carried out here are limited. The test types focus primarily on verification and scripted tests. Certain test activities that are specific to in-sprint testing are also carried out here, user story acceptance testing is a good example.

> What we say: *"We've run three out of five planned test sessions as part of component testing, once those are complete we can discuss merging this feature branch into main."*

Integration Testing

A phase of testing that focuses on the integration of multiple game components. This test level usually comprises the integration of test areas for all the components and runs only a small number of specific test activities. Test types focus primarily on verification and scripted tests.

> What we say: *"Once all of the features for the release are in the main branch, we'll run the core feature tests again as integration tests before we move on to wider game system testing."*

System Testing

The main phase of testing and the phase with the largest scope. This phase includes nearly all test areas, test activities and test types.

> What we say: *"The failure and edge case tests will only be executed during system testing once the higher priority tests have completed."*

User Acceptance Testing

A unique test phase which contains specific test activities aimed at testing from the perspective of a player. This phase contains a small number of test activities and is primarily driven by more exploratory test types like persona testing. It can also not contain test activities at all and instead be set up as an alpha or beta program.

> What we say: *"We can try to run user acceptance testing through tasks with the test team or we can focus our efforts on developing feedback channels for our early adopters to achieve the same result."*

3.3   Test areas

Test areas define a test focus for a specific part of the product. They divide the game into sections and further subsections. Test areas are also the main work product for QA analysts, who break down large areas of testing during their planning process. I'll group these into functional game areas and non-functional game areas. Put another way, the goal of test areas is to categorise what the game does (functional testing) and how well it does it (non-functional testing).

Test areas are consistent throughout all test levels, and apply for the lifetime of the project. Generally, each successive test level introduces more test areas into the testing process, with the system level including tests against all planned areas. For example, component testing might only include core test areas, whereas system testing would expand the testing out to lower priority test areas.

Test areas don't refer to specific tasks either; as breakdowns, they define groupings of test activities.

Functional test areas

Functional test areas are unique to each game and labelled by the QA analyst creating the test area breakdowns. Functional testing refers to testing what the game does – its 'functionality'. This definition of functionality is not specific to logical functionality either, it includes areas like graphical functionality too. Later in chapter six, I will list the most common functional testing areas and go into detail about the test planning approach for each. Across the different types of games in the industry, there are many common test areas and many more specialist areas not mentioned here. However, here are a few quick examples:

- **First time user experience (FTUE) testing:** This area focuses on testing the initial game launch flow and experience. Some teams refer to this as OOBE, out-of-box-experience.
- **Platform integration testing:** A focus on testing the interactions that the game has with the operating system that it runs on.
- **Multiplayer testing:** Testing of multiplayer modes, matchmaking and other feature areas which support inputs from multiple players.

The following spoken examples refer to the focus of testing, area for tests to target or a set of tests, but never a specific individual test. Test areas also allow us to talk about test coverage for a game area even if tests don't exist yet, since we're talking about the area, not about specific tests.

> What we say:
> *"Are we going to look at platform integration as part of that test plan?"*
> *"When are we going to be running those FTUE tests?"*
> *"John is the multiplayer test owner."*

Non-functional test areas

Non-functional test areas are mostly generic across all game and software projects, though some feature much more prominently within games. They test how well the game is performing in each functional area and include areas like performance, stability and usability testing. Like functional areas, the scale of non-functional testing included in any test plan is defined by the QA analyst.

Ownership and organisational test planning around non-functional test areas can become confusing if they are categorised incorrectly. Where different QA analysts own functional test areas like multiplayer and FTUE testing, they need to recognise that non-functional areas apply across all of the functional areas that they own.

By definition, functional and non-functional areas overlap entirely. Every functional area needs to consider non-functional tests within it. This means that it wouldn't make sense to have a dedicated performance testing owner who needs to know *all* the functional areas. Instead each feature owner should be responsible for all non-functional testing in their areas.

The same rule of organisation in these areas applies to planning and writing tests. While it is fine to have dedicated performance tests, they need to be thought of as being orientated 'across' functional areas.

FTUE - Tutorial dialogue tests
FTUE - UI tests
FTUE - Navigation flow tests
FTUE - Performance tests
FTUE - Stability tests

Figure 3.1 – This is a feature area breakdown sample and shows an incorrect thought process for non-functional test areas. See that the non-functional tests of stability and performance are an addition to the functional areas and displayed as a flat list. Functional areas and non-functional ones are wrongly shown as mutually exclusive.

	FTUE - Performance tests	FTUE - Stability tests
FTUE - Tutorial dialogue tests		
FTUE - UI tests		
FTUE - Navigation flow tests		

Figure 3.2 – This is an area breakdown sample and shows the correct thought process for non-functional test areas. See that the non-functional tests of stability and performance slice across the functional areas, showing that you should consider non-functional tests for each functional sub area. These are represented as each box in the figure. Every functional area should consider every non-functional area within it.

Here is a list of the most important non-functional test areas within games:

- **Performance testing:** This describes a large area and focuses on testing the game's speed and responsiveness. This area is large enough to be broken down into several sub areas, each looking at a different aspect of performance. Graphical performance, load times, network performance and server performance are just some of the areas where performance testing is applied. All of them, not testing what the component does, but how well it does it. Graphical performance is particularly important in games, due to the heavy focus on artwork. Because performance is so crucial to games, I've covered it in more depth in chapter six.

  What we say: *"As part of the performance testing pass, we're going to look at loading times, memory usage, CPU utilisation and GPU utilisation."*

- **Load testing:** This is a sub-area of performance testing that is worth calling out separately. Testers will likely have heard of load testing, but most will not be involved in it due to its specialist nature. Load testing analyses a system's performance under high traffic. For games, this nearly always refers to remote services used by the game (like a login service which holds the player database) or the multiplayer game server. While large groups of testers can work on this together to apply load to the service, it is still nowhere near the load that players worldwide will put on those servers once the game is live. Specialist load testing tools are used by the project's server code team to simulate real player load while the test team checks how the game client handles that high server load. Teams also use beta programs to slowly introduce players into their game to help them load test.

  What we say: *"We'll start applying load to the login and cloud save services at 2pm. The team should focus on testing those areas of the client under load and include these details in any bugs that they log."*

- **Stress testing:** This is another popular sub-area of performance testing that's worth calling out separately. Stress testing is like load testing but has a wider scope beyond adding network traffic to a service. For example, graphical performance can be stress-tested by playing the busiest scene in the game on the maximum graphics settings. While it doesn't have to be, stress testing in games frequently refers to worst-case scenario performance testing. It looks to apply the worst-case combination of conditions until the component fails or until the maximum realistic stress is applied. The theory is that knowing the worst possible performance scenario allows testers to ignore other more ideal performance combinations during their testing, cutting down on test time. Knowing the worst case sets a benchmark which the team can work around. Stress testing is also used in other areas of performance testing: as an example, testers will frequently stress the network connection to the device under test to check how it handles the poorer connection. Note that unlike load testing, this test is just local to that tester and their connection, whereas load testing impacts all devices using the target server.

What we say:

"I'm going to try that bug reproduction again but this time stress the network during the test."

"Have you included a stress test in the levels test plan? If so, do you know yet which level has the worst performance?"

- **Stability testing:** This looks at measuring the rate of crashes and other fatal failures which stop gameplay. Stability testing features prominently in games due to the broad range of hardware that games are expected to run on. Additionally, games will intentionally push the limits of hardware to make the game look as good as it can do. This applies as much to mobile games as it does to console and PC games, simply because games will frequently grow to the limits of each platform. When testing feature components, stability testing is hardly ever referred to by its name or run as a dedicated task. This is because other functional and non-functional areas will cover stability passively, often finding crashes and fatal failures 'accidentally' through the course of testing. Those that are responsible for test planning just need to remember that it doesn't come completely for free and should be written into test cases for other areas. However, the exceptions to this are a few specific test activities – BVTs and smoke tests – which we'll cover in the next section and look at basic stability of the build. These two test activities are dedicated stability tests.

What we say:

Developer: *"Do you run any stability testing against the daily builds?"*

QA analyst: *"Yes, we run an automated BVT."*

- **Localisation testing:** This describes all test activities involved in translating the game into different spoken languages, and covers checking that translations are correct (text and audio dialogue) as well as testing for functional bugs like text bleeding out of UI elements or being cut off (because the length of words and phrases can differ greatly between languages). Confusingly, one of these activities requires the tester to speak the translated language, while the other doesn't. The latter is called functional localisation testing, the former is just localisation testing. Because translation is such a specialist area, there is a separate localisation team* that would normally deal with both the translations and most of the testing of those translations after they've been integrated into the game. Localisation testing can also include themes, images, jokes and slang that would not translate well into other languages. Localisation specialists refer to this process as transcreation, because it requires scrapping the direct translation and recreating it in the target language. This is a unique and interesting area for games; the communication style within the game is very casual and often complex for character dialogue.

What we say:
Tester: "This test case for the new feature includes a check for localisation in each language, can I run that?"
QA analyst: "Yes, we should just check each of the new strings has a localised version, logging bugs for any that are missing. We should also log bugs for cut off text and overlaps. I don't expect you to check the translations though."

- **Security testing:** Testing to determine how vulnerable the game code is to cyber-attacks, cheat hackers and cheat tools. It's a specialist area which I'll introduce in chapter five. Even then, there are several technical areas of security testing which are beyond the scope of this book. 'Pen testing', short for penetration testing, is one example. Because this area contains a selection of very different test activities, it's rarely referred to as just 'security testing'. Instead the individual test activities are referred to directly.

What we say:
QA Analyst: "Do we have to run security testing against our game server?"
Server Engineer: "No, we use a third-party provider to host our game server and they manage that risk for us. If we hosted it ourselves then we'd have to worry about that."

- **Usability testing:** This describes testing how intuitive and easy the game is to navigate. It's an area which is rarely run in game testing because the in-

---

*   It's fairly common for testers to get into localisation testing because they are multilingual, then later move to functional testing and up through the functional testing career path. This is a good route if there are no entry-level functional testing roles in your area.

game experience is heavily dictated by the design team and is very subjective. This test type can still be run against menus to look for friction within flows. Friction in this sense refers to how many clicks or taps it takes the player to perform a certain action. Too many clicks means the flow has high friction and could be made more efficient; important for upselling flows and in-game stores. Instead of this test area, game teams run balancing testing to assess the relative difficulty and game economy. This is actually a functional area within games, which we'll cover in chapter five. If I had to choose the closest test activity that fits into this test area, it would be playtesting: it usually involves the entire multidisciplinary development team and aims to capture early design feedback. During this activity, the test team enables capturing the type of feedback the design team is looking for. While we don't label this activity as usability testing, the bugs that come from it are usability bugs.

What we say:
"We should log a usability bug for the special offers shop flow, there is way too much friction in it. It takes four taps to reach the shop and then you have to scroll to the end of the list to discover the special offer. Instead, we should have a 'special offer' badge that links players directly there from the main menu."

There are other non-functional test areas, like portability tests, maintainability tests, interoperability tests and scalability tests that I've not included in this book because I haven't seen them used in game projects. Furthermore, many non-functional areas, like security testing, are also outside the scope of responsibility of game testers below manager level and will be included in more advanced reading.

3.4   Test activities

Test activities are the testing tasks themselves, which are created, run and closed once they are done. These activities can take on any format – a scripted test pass, an investigation, an exploratory session, a playtest, to name a few. A test activity is constructed from single or multiple test types, which are defined in the next list. Unlike test levels and test areas, which are active throughout the project, test activities have a much shorter life and are only relevant while they are being executed.

For each of the functional and non-functional test areas I defined earlier, there are as many test activities as required to sufficiently cover testing for the area. Additionally, new instances of test activity might be created if tests need to be re-run. Specific test activities also exist for other reasons. Retesting is an example – a global activity that exists as part of the bug life cycle. Build verification tests (BVTs) are another good example, being run against each new build independently of any active test areas or test levels.

Here is a list of the main test activities:

Smoke testing

This test activity is run to check the stability of a build or a game area to make sure it is stable enough for more comprehensive testing to be carried out. It's intended to provide broad coverage quickly and only looks for major stability issues and test blockers. The purpose is to scout the area and give the go ahead for larger testing activities to begin.

Earlier I hinted at how overused and misused this term is; testers should not use this term to refer to other small, brief or light test activities. A colleague told me his way of remembering the goal of this test type was to refer to the origins of the term in mechanical testing. Plumbers use smoke to test new sewers and pipework for leaks before running a test with water in the pipes. The engineers only go ahead with the full water test if the smoke test passes. Like in software, the impact is much lower if the smoke test fails than if a major issue is discovered during the larger test effort.

Smoke tests can be run for multiple reasons: against each new build or against large components of the game before big test passes are run against the component. This is particularly useful when components are new and the test team is not sure whether the feature is stable enough to test against yet. It's normal for a team to write a game-wide smoke test that anyone can reuse, so it doesn't need to be recreated by each test owner. The test owner needs to just choose the parts of the smoke test that are relevant to the game area that they need to smoke-test. Smoke tests should not take longer than an hour or so for a manual test, because the intention is for it to be very brief and very broad. If it takes longer than this it is likely too detailed.

> What we say:
> *"The scripted test pass is estimated to take four work weeks, so let's schedule a smoke test first thing on Monday before we commit to the full scripted pass."*

Build Verification Tests (BVTs)

This test activity, sometimes called 'daily smoke tests', are smoke tests that are specific to new builds. The intention is to check the stability of the build before any other testing is carried out against it. A lot of time can be wasted testing against unstable or broken builds, and the impact of this is multiplied by the size of the test team. Teams will tag the last known stable build as 'last known good' (LKG) to direct everyone to the most up to date build.

When I worked on console games, the builds were huge (60GB to 100GB and beyond) and would take about 45 minutes to deploy to our dev kit consoles over the network. For these projects, deploying a broken build even for a modest team of 20 testers creates an immediate impact of 20 work hours lost to redeploy a new build.

So how does running a BVT solve this problem?

BVTs are run manually or through automated tools. Because they are repeatable and frequently used tests (usually daily), they are commonly the first goal of any automated testing effort, making automated BVTs quite common. An automated test can check the stability of a nightly build and then automatically deploy it to all dev kits on the test team if it is healthy, making the new build available to the team when they come into work for the day. Other teams have test leads or chosen BVT testers who start work early and run manual BVT tests against new builds, lowering the impact before the rest of the team picks up these builds later in the day. In some cases the BVT testers kick off build deployments to the test team early if the BVT test passes, performing the same job as the automated tools.

What we say:
"I'm running the BVT now, I'll send a message out on the health as soon as I'm done and you can pick up the build. Please wait for my signal."

Acceptance testing

This test activity is easily confused with the user acceptance test level, so readers should be careful and note their differences. This test activity is run by embedded testers during development sprint work as part of the component testing level. It should be called 'acceptance criteria testing', because its goal is to run testing against the acceptance criteria defined in development tasks or user stories within each sprint.

This test activity is only used in projects following agile methodologies where testing is carried out during, not after development. Acceptance testing activities are always a verification test type and are mostly scripted, but can also include exploratory testing. Because it is only carried out by embedded testers, some acceptance testing might not be written down in test tasks. Instead, it's performed by testing and recording the results directly into the relevant user story or task.

What we say: *"Have you completed the acceptance testing for that user story yet? The end of the sprint is tomorrow."*

Play testing

This activity is unique in its creation and goals. Play tests are usually directed towards a specific test area for a new feature and are run in the component testing level, where the design and code team are still able to make changes easily. It is always a focused exploratory test activity, directing the play testers towards specific functionality, asking them for certain types of feedback and letting them explore within those limits.

Unlike nearly all other testing activities, play testing is an opportunity to play the game, not to test it. Testers are being asked to play and provide their subjective feedback on the game. It's the closest to what many people imagine game testers do every day. Play tests are usually requested by the design team or a prototyping team once they are ready to receive such feedback: it's not an activity generally scheduled by the test team.

While functional bugs are found during playtests, the goal is to capture early subjective feedback. It's primarily run within the game studio with the other disciplines, but some teams do send builds out to external vendor test teams for play testing too. This usually happens when the team is small, doesn't have the time themselves, or want a fresh perspective from people who haven't played the game before. Some teams also combine play tests with closed alpha multiplayer tests, getting as many internal employees as possible to play multiplayer features together remotely. This is a popular approach for any games which focus heavily on multiplayer gameplay.

> What we say: *"Let's run a playtest on the prototype build this Friday lunchtime. We'll look at the new battle flow and get pizza and beers in for the team."*

Regression testing

This activity focuses on testing existing healthy areas of the game to check they haven't reduced in quality due to the addition of new components or some other change. Regression testing of the existing game needs to be carried out whenever something new gets added, which becomes a bigger task each time the scope of the existing game grows.

Regression testing should feature in nearly all test areas: adding new components will always affect parts of the existing game. For single-release games, the team will test each component as it gets delivered and then regression-test it again later on once larger parts of the game are finished. Regression testing can be fairly limited for those projects. However, live ops games operating as a continuous service will feature regression testing heavily because they're updating the existing game frequently with new content.[*] For this reason, it's important that test teams for these projects have a solid regression testing plan. Regression activities themselves are primarily scripted

---

[*]   Many mobile games release as frequently as every week, increasing the importance of efficient regression testing.

verification, because their goal is to check broad areas of functionality as efficiently as possible. Rather than writing separate tests for regression testing activities, test teams will instead create a test plan reusing core tests written for each feature component.

The challenge with regression testing is in identifying which areas of the current game are most at risk of regression when a change is made. Testers can't simply test the entire existing game every time a new feature is added and trying to do so would be a waste of resources. Identifying what to test is the job of the test analysis phase, and planning for regression testing is something that we'll cover in chapter four, **Test analysis techniques**.

> What we say:
>
> *QA manager: "What regression testing are you planning to run with the new feature release?"*
>
> *QA analyst: "Last time this feature was changed there were a lot of UI regressions, so that will be a big focus of our regression testing this time."*

Retesting

Also called confirmation testing, this test activity describes the action of following the reproduction steps of a bug after a fix has been committed for it, with the aim of confirming whether the fix was effective. Bugs that are confirmed as fixed during this activity are closed; otherwise bugs are reactivated with updated details. This is the activity that, confusingly, many teams refer to as 'regression'. If this applies to your team, you should speak to your colleagues about updating your terminology. Since this term is consistent across all software, you can also cross-check the definition given in this book with other online publications, if you still aren't convinced.

Because the retesting activity is orientated around bugs, it has no association to any test levels, areas or types described in this chapter. It's really a miscellaneous activity in this way. There are two popular ways that test teams conduct retesting.

One is to assign all fixed bugs back to the tester who logged the bug, then each tester is responsible for clearing their own retest queue each day. Where possible, this is the best method to use because the tester who created the bug is essentially the subject matter expert of that bug and is best situated to retest it effectively. We've used this method during most projects I've worked on, with the first two hours of each day being allotted to retesting, before planned testing begins.

The second method is to have a dedicated retesting sub team retesting all of the resolved bugs each day, regardless of who they were created by. This method is less likely to delay retesting because the tester is on holiday or ill. It is also more effective if the test team members change frequently. On the other hand, testers take longer to understand each bug and the result of testing is more likely to be a false positive (the tester closes the bug as fixed when it isn't fixed), especially if the bug does not reproduce one hundred percent of the time.

There is an exception to this test activity on game projects with a very high number of art bugs. Where large numbers of low-severity art bugs exist for a game area like the in-game environment, the artists might fix the bugs through their own polishing tasks on an area-by-area basis, rather than working through the bug list order. Testers will do the same by re-running guided exploratory tests against a specific environment area and then bulk-closing all the bugs for that area. They do this because it's more efficient than working through each of the bugs one by one, navigating to each area of the in-game world as they do so. I have also seen very low-severity content bugs closed without retesting for the same reason that the impact of the bug is not worth the time commitment of retesting.

What we say: *"This performance bug has been improved but may not be completely fixed. Please retest and add new results for us to review."*

Halo testing

Halo testing is a lesser-used term, but you will hear it from time to time so I wanted to include it in this list. Halo testing is when a tester performs additional testing around a fixed bug after they have retested it. Whereas retesting calls for the tester to follow the reproduction steps exactly, halo testing is an exploratory test. The goal is to look for similar and knock-on bugs that may have been caused by the fix. Anyone with experience with software bug fixes knows they are rarely straightforward. Anecdotally, fixing one bug causes two more to appear, and trying to fix those might cause the original issue to appear again.

The goal of halo testing is to anticipate this and provide additional testing around specific bug fixes. To help, those fixing bugs should provide good context about the nature of the bug fix so that the tester can risk-assess whether to perform halo testing. High profile bug fixes can also be identified by the QA analyst owning the testing for the feature area where the bug exists.

What we say:
Developer: "The fix for this crash is to re-write the code for this component. It's risky because it touches lots of other areas of the game. Please make sure to test it thoroughly."
QA Analyst: "Thanks for the information, I'll write a halo test task to supplement the bug retest."

Sanity testing

Sanity testing is another lesser-used term; it's spoken about but rarely written down as sanity testing. Sanity testing is carried out when the target of testing has very low risk, as few changes (or none at all) have been made to the build. In these scenarios, the change to the build is so minor that testing is not expected to find any bugs, but the team has agreed that a brief test should be carried out regardless. This is done because the risk is *near* zero, so there is a small chance that issues could be found. This test activity is a slight anomaly because the actual test activity will be something else (a smoke or regression test most likely) and sanity is the reason that it is being run. You could say that the word 'sanity' is used because finding an issue is so unlikely that it would be insane, so the check is made to maintain sanity and make absolutely sure.

A good example of a sanity test being run during real projects is when a production release candidate build contains the exact same code and content as a previous production release candidate build that the test team have been testing on. While the new build should be exactly the same as the previous one, there is always a small chance that some issue occurred generating the build files. If the new build is the one to be uploaded to the online stores (ready to publish to the public), it needs a sanity test run against it. However unlikely, the two builds may be different.

A further example is when this production build is uploaded to each of the online stores the game is released on. Testing the build by installing it locally is not the same as downloading it from the store page, even though the files should be the same. The test team will perform a sanity test against the build downloaded from the store page in case the files were corrupted during the upload or some other hidden problem occurred. In these scenarios, the chance of failure is very low, but the impact of failure is very high. So, sanity tests are carried out.

> What we say: *"We're going to run the RC test pass on the master gold build and then we'll run them again for sanity once the build has been uploaded to the store page."*

Static testing

Also called static analysis, this test activity is a unique activity because it's the only one that doesn't test the product while it is running. Static testing involves testing the project files and the supporting documentation directly. Depending on the target files, static techniques look for errors, inconsistencies, omissions, ambiguities or any other bugs in the data. This test activity is carried out before any other test activities and therefore usually only run by QA analysts within development sprints as part of the component testing level.

Static testing is mostly run against designs and other supporting documentation and rarely run against the code itself by the manual test team. However, when software engineers review each other's code before committing it to the project, this is a form of static testing too. The goal of static testing is to find issues as early as possible, before they cause failures when the product is running. If static testing can find an error in a design document before that faulty design is written into faulty code, it can be fixed before it even becomes a bug in the game.

This mentality relates back to the error cost escalation model we defined earlier in this book. Static testing activities are not labelled as static tests and are not normally tracked formally as tests, either. Instead, they take the form of documentation reviews where questions or issues are raised as comments on the documentation pages.

Finally, QA analysts peer reviewing each other's test plans is also a form of static testing, but this time the testing is against the test plan itself. Experienced QA analysts can make a big impact on testing just by asking good incisive questions about documentation, using their experience of past testing to predict where potential issues might occur.

What we say: *"Once the design documentation is complete, can you send it out to the team for review?"*

3.5   Test types

Test types are the last category in our terminology list and define techniques that can be applied to any test activity. A test activity can use a single test type or a mixture to achieve good test effectiveness. So, unlike the other categories above, test types are not mutually exclusive, and a single test activity can be a combination of types.

Two of the most effective – and common – combinations are scripted verification tests and exploratory failure tests. The types listed here require different approaches to test writing and are each effective at achieving certain test goals. Test authors need to choose which techniques from this list to apply to each test activity to best achieve the goal of that activity. In chapter one, **Core principles of game testing**, we introduced the test design framework where we said that the test area influences what type of testing is applied. Some test areas lend themselves more to certain test types and it's down to the experience of the test author to know what combinations work the best. The test design framework also showed the matrix of test type combinations made up from scripted, exploratory, failure and verification tests. I defined that design framework as a core principle because it shows us the core test types that should be considered for *all* test plans. The list of types here includes lesser-used types that have more specialised usage or are less common, but still useful nonetheless.

Verification testing

Also called checking or positive testing, verification testing is a test type to check that game components function correctly according to their design specifications. Verification tests are the most common test type because they're the easiest to write, the easiest to run and are the most obvious starting point for any test plan. Verification testing is most effective when combined with scripted testing but can also be used with exploratory tests types for specific game areas.

The direct opposite of verification testing is failure testing. While these two test types can be combined in a single test activity, I have found that it isn't very effective and makes the focus of testing too large. I would encourage failure and verification tests to be split up wherever possible. I defined this test type in detail in chapter one, so I won't cover the same ground here.

Failure testing

Commonly forgotten by QA analysts, but critically important; failure testing defines a group of testing types that focus on identifying ways that the game might fail. Failure testing is also sometimes referred to as negative testing, which helps with its definition as being the direct opposite of positive (verification) testing. Failure testing has a large scope because there are so many ways a game component could fail. Specific techniques for failure testing depend on the game area; failure testing guidance is given for certain areas in chapter six, **Major areas of game testing**. Most of these techniques are referred to as general failure test types but, because this is a large area, there are some specific subtypes which you will hear in use. Here they are:

- **Destructive testing:** This test type defines a subtype that takes a brute force approach to finding failures. Destructive testing is essentially the sledgehammer in your test toolbox. It describes a style of testing that includes actions such as button mashing, repeated screen tapping, simultaneous input, power cable pulling, network cable pulling, device power button usage, Wi-Fi toggling, airplane mode toggling, as well as the abuse of in-game controls including rapid and repeated navigation, constant backgrounding of the game application, spamming of specific actions and extreme actions that real players would never perform. This is one of the first types of failure testing that testers learn and it can be effective when applied with a little precision, rather than blindly across all game areas.

  The important takeaway is that destructive testing is just one small part of failure testing. As a test area owner, I don't want testers to be executing all my failure tests by just pulling cables each and every time. While destructive testing has its place, most effective failure testing needs to be more structured and precise. I consider this to be the software testing version of the popular quote, "If your only tool is a hammer then every problem looks like a nail." Many junior testers can go a long time without evolving their failure testing beyond basic destructive testing, something I've observed through many interviews with test candidates.

What we say: *"The aim of this test is to perform destructive testing techniques during the game loading sequence to identify potential failures."*

- **Interruption testing:** This type of failure testing focuses specifically on interrupting the natural game flow with actions that take immediate effect. This type of testing can be very effective to force failures to occur consistently that real players might only see by chance, one in 100 times. This technique is applied most effectively to target areas like game install flows, FTUE flows and other heavily scripted areas, cinematics, loading screens and other transitions, game save operations with local storage, cloud save operations and any communications with the game servers. The interruptive action could be player input or performing some system level change that the game has to respond to. Minimising the game to navigate back to the operating system for example, will stop whatever processes are running in the game and send it into a suspended state. Some of the best interruptive tests are also triggered remotely and force their way into the active gameplay window: notifications, calls, messages and game session invites are some great examples. Sometimes the presence of the interruption itself causes the game to handle it at a vulnerable time and lead to a failure; otherwise the tester may have to action the interruption which will then cause the failure. A good example of this would be receiving a multiplayer session invite during a loading screen and accepting it so that the game deeplinks straight into the game lobby of the multiplayer session. This is exactly the kind of edge case that interruption testing aims to test.

What we say: *"Part of this test is to investigate interruptive scenarios during the game launch sequence."*

Scripted testing

This is a test type characterised by highly directed and detailed test steps which make up each test. Scripted tests tell the tester what steps to perform and what the expected result for each step is, with the outcome of the test being a pass or fail result. While I defined the attributes that all scripted tests have in the section on the test design framework in chapter one, here I will list sub-types of scripted tests and define the differences between them. I should also note here that scripted testing should never refer to automated test scripts. If you are referring to automation scripting then say 'automated tests' or 'automation scripts', otherwise this becomes very confusing.

- **Test suites:** A 'test suite' is terminology used in some popular scripted testing tools which allow test teams to manage groups of scripted tests. In these tools, tests are written as master copies that are never executed directly. When these tests are executed, a separate copy of the tests is created from the master copy. These master copies are grouped into sets – called test suites – for organisational purposes. As an example, a team would have a test suite for each major feature in the game and would create an instance of that test suite if they wanted to run those tests. Test suites are organised in this way so that the master copy can easily be updated and found without searching through previously executed instances of those tests. Otherwise, if you were to create a new test by copying one of the previous test executions, then updates to the tests could easily be lost depending on which execution you used. This organisation also creates traceability between multiple runs of the same test suite, allowing you to see historical results of that suite.

  What we say: *"The test for player login is outdated, so I'm going to update the login flow test suite so that it reflects the latest design."*

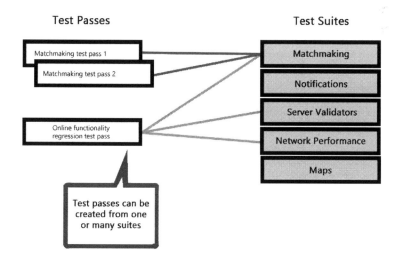

Figure 3.3

- **Test runs / test passes / test cycles:** These refer to instances of test suites which have been created for execution. In more general terms, these are a collection of scripted tests, copied from one or multiple test suites and grouped to be executed as a compiled set. Each test run can be customised by selecting only desired tests from each suite too, allowing QA analysts to choose only priority one and two tests, for example. Test runs are also given their own name and description to help identify them. The length of a test run can vary. While scripted test runs would traditionally run for several weeks, many teams prefer the flexibility and quicker results of shorter runs; there is no defined limitation. Finally, while I've categorised this as scripted testing terminology, many teams use these terms to refer to all groups of tests that are being run together, regardless of what type of tests they are (including exploratory tests).

  What we say: *"The test pass is scheduled to start on Monday and estimated to take four work-weeks. We'll have a team of four working on it, so I expect it to be complete by Friday."*

- **Test cases and test scripts:** These terms refer to individual scripted tests. Each test will have steps, with each step having a pass/fail result and the test having a final pass/fail result. While most testers use these terms interchangeably, there are subtle differences in their granularity.

  Test scripts provide the most granular test direction, give zero freedoms to the tester and have zero ambiguity. Test scripts are detailed enough that you could theoretically use them as a guide to write an automation script. As an example, if you had an isometric view battle game and had a test for a certain battle, the test steps would define exactly where to move each unit and what actions to take throughout the battle. In reality, test scripts are rarely used to this extreme unless it is absolutely necessary, because they take so long to write and because they are very fragile, becoming outdated easily. The benefits of test scripts are that you can give them to the least experienced testers (or non-testers) and still get good, consistent results. QA analysts might use this technique for very high priority tests which have to be executed in a very specific way, or when outsourcing, for example, where they don't know how experienced the testers are. I'll talk further about choosing the right test types for your testers in chapter five, **Test design techniques**.

  Test cases still provide the tester with specific test steps, but omit lots of information that would be redundant to an experienced tester who is familiar with the game and the project. Test cases are more readable and easier to maintain for this reason, providing only the necessary information and using the experience of the tester to fill in the blanks. Tests still have specific steps that pass or fail, but provide more holistic direction. In the same example – testing a certain battle of an isometric battle game – a test case might only direct the tester to complete the level and use all of the units available in the battle, allowing the testers to work out the exact moves. Test cases are more focused on the end goal of what the test is trying to check, rather than hand-holding the tester through the steps to get there. I've seen lots of tests written where the writer has fallen into the trap of writing the test in an unnecessarily granular way. I've frequently found tests several months after they were written to check if I can reuse them, only to see that many of the details given in the tests have changed or been updated. This is a painful learning curve for new test writers and something I will be also covering in detail in chapter five, **Test design techniques**.

Exploratory testing

Also called unscripted testing, this test type is characterised as the opposite of scripted testing. It gives the tester greater freedom to explore tangentially from the focus of the test activity. The benefits and drawbacks of exploratory testing were covered in the section of the test design framework in chapter one, **Core principles of games testing.** Here, we will list all the different terms that are used to refer to this test type, calling out specific differences where they exist. Exploratory testing and scripted testing are not binary and actually exist on a sliding scale of granularity and test direction (where exploratory techniques have lower amounts of both). The term exploratory testing is used to refer to any test type that sits on the less granular side of that scale. Given this, readers should use the terms exploratory and unscripted to refer to the group as a whole. In reference to different test areas, exploratory testing is primarily used for functional tests and is generally too informal to capture good data against non-functional areas. Furthermore, because exploratory testing takes longer than scripted testing, it's primarily used as a supplement to scripted testing during the system testing test level and user acceptance testing level. Exploratory testing doesn't normally make up the majority of the team's test efforts, nor should it. Let's define the specific types you will hear:

- **Focused exploratory testing:** This term refers to exploratory test types that provide structure to the exploration. They limit the testing to a specific area by providing details about what is in and out of scope for testing during the session. Other focused exploratory tests use test goals, mission statements or test charters to provide some focus to the exploratory test. Well-organised focused exploratory tests also timebox each test activity so that the results can be reviewed before too much time is invested in the test. Timeboxing also provides pacing for the exploratory tester, allowing them to go off-piste from the test focus, but reminding them that they have to return to the focus of the activity before the time is up. Focused exploratory tests are sometimes recorded and comprehensive notes provided about the testing; other times they are less formally executed.

What we say: *"We're running several exploratory tests tomorrow, but they will be focused exploratory, so testers should read the test charter carefully before starting the test."*

- **Ad-hoc / free testing:** These terms refer to exploratory testing which has no given focus or limitation on scope. It frequently doesn't have a time limit given either. This type of testing is entirely self-directed, essentially allowing the tester to define their own test plan within the session and then execute it iteratively. In the hands of experienced testers with good ideas, free exploratory testing is a powerful tool. However, it's frequently abused by lazy test planners or by teams claiming they don't have time to conduct more formal test planning. Furthermore, unlike focused exploratory testing, which is usually written down and tracked as a test activity, free testing is usually executed without tracking any test data apart from the bugs that are produced. This creates problems when trying to reproduce tests that found good bugs, and means testers could unintentionally overlap their test coverage with other testers, creating inefficiencies.

What we say: *"After you have finished the test pass, spend the remainder of the day running ad-hoc testing."*

- **Session based testing:** This type of exploratory testing is heavily organised around short exploratory sessions of no more than a few hours each. The tester and their test lead have a debrief after each session to review the results and define the focus for further sessions. Test sessions iteratively define the overall test direction in this way, rather than defining it upfront like scripted tests. The tester will use the session test results to make recommendations for further test areas to run sessions against, and discuss whether they feel the area of test focus has had adequate coverage or requires further sessions. Each session is intended to be short so that the course of testing can be adjusted quickly, and to cut down on the expensive time investment of longer, more open exploratory testing.

What we say: *"We are going to be running a series of test sessions against the new feature. Everyone should take note of the session time estimations and then report back once the first sessions are complete."*

- **Persona testing:** This type of exploratory testing is used during the system test level and sometimes for the user acceptance testing level. It's a type of exploratory test where the tester adopts the play style of a certain demographic of players to uncover bugs that might otherwise be missed. This usually involves interacting with the game in ways which the tester might not normally use and gives the tester a usability perspective on how certain players might perceive parts of the game. A classic example would be a 'completionist' persona that rushes through the game so they can complete all of the achievements or trophies within the game. Any problems with unlocking achievements will annoy this type of player. Free-to-play games will also use personas to adopt the play style of both paying and non-paying players. This test type adds structure and a focus to exploratory testing. It's also one of the only test types that causes the tester to play the game, rather than test it.

What we say: *"Once all functional system testing is complete, we'll run exploratory test passes, starting with the personas that we identified in the meeting last week."*

Black box and white box testing

These are two test types which define whether the tester has visibility, and understands the inner workings of the game component that they are testing. Both terms are used colloquially, but rarely written down because it is obvious whether the testing is black box or white box, making any labelling superfluous.

Black box testing does not take into account the inner workings of the game. This is what most manual game testing is, because the tester doesn't have visibility into the code or internal structure of the component. In a metaphor where the game is the box, the tester cannot see inside it and testing focuses only on the inputs and outputs of the box. Black box testing is frequently carried out on the basis that testing doesn't *need* to know the inner workings and that the output of what the player sees is the most important test focus anyway. For this reason, black box testing is also sometimes referred to as a behavioural test technique, though I've never heard this actually used within game teams. Negatives of black box testing include troubleshooting problems and analysis of test outputs, because these activities can be very difficult when you don't understand how a component functions. Without technical support, black box testers can be left to make assumptions about test outputs and are in danger of misinterpreting results.

Also referred to as structural testing, white box testing is when testing has full visibility into the internal workings of the game and can test internal components directly. In our metaphor, the box is transparent and the tester can look beyond the inputs and outputs of the system as a whole. This test type includes unit tests, automation and static analysis of code. White box testing can investigate much more deeply into bugs to not only identify the failure, but perform a root cause analysis to find the fault. White box testing can also set up more complex testing scenarios through directly interacting with game code, testing areas where black box testing cannot reach. This type of testing is carried out by technical roles, usually either software engineers or test automation engineers. The main negative of white box testing is that it can become disconnected from the holistic goals of the output the player will see, and focus (sometimes unnecessarily) on the quality of specific components.

You may hear 'grey box testing' as a term, too. This usually refers to black box testing being carried out by manual testers who have a partial understanding of the internal workings of the component. Many manual testers strive to increase their knowledge of code and work closely with the technical project disciplines to better understand the inner workings of the product they are working on. An example of this is testing with network tools that view or manipulate network data. Knowing which game components send and receive network data will allow testers to read network logs more easily, increasing their chances of identifying bugs.

Another common example is understanding the difference between warnings, errors, exceptions and crashes and correctly identifying them during testing. When manual test teams say they want to be 'more grey box' in their testing, this is what they mean. In terms of test activities defined earlier, while they won't be labelled as 'black box' tests, QA analysts writing tests will need to consider how technical their tests need to be and provide adequate explanations for the tester to execute the test. Successful technical testing requires some training or knowledge handover before test execution begins.

What we say: *"The test team should attend the engineering talk about the new feature because it may allow our testing to be more grey box."*

White box test techniques in games

Before we finish defining terminology, it's worth taking a quick detour to talk further about white box testing techniques in real game projects. Some software testing books and qualifications define various ways testers can use white box techniques to plan testing and track test coverage. These focus on techniques that measure test coverage via tracking which lines of code have been exercised by the testing. These look at logical functions like IF statements and aim to test each of the outcomes of the statement.

Test coverage is measured as a percentage of the code paths tested. Other techniques describe measuring test coverage by tracking the number of code statements (lines of code that contain a logical statement) covered by testing.

I've never seen these techniques used in game the projects I've worked on.

My advice is that non-technical testing roles can safely ignore these testing techniques. The closest comparison to these would be software engineers writing unit tests for the feature components they have implemented. Even in this scenario, the engineers wouldn't try to capture that coverage through lines of code tested. For QA analysts to use code paths to plan and measure manual test coverage would be both incredibly time consuming and not worth the time investment. Similarly, as we've discussed, most game testers perform black box testing and don't have access to the game code to guide such testing.

3.6   Test terminology conclusion

These categories show us how each of the terms fit together, providing a scope and a reason for terminology in each category. When you hear new terms being used, you can determine whether it's a different name for one of the terms already listed. If not, you can use these categories to work out whether you are talking about a test level, area, activity or type.

   Testers should store these lists as compartments in their testing toolbox and draw upon them when executing tests or planning for testing. It's very easy to repeatedly use the same, most common test terms, and become lazy during planning. Instead, these lists are a good starting point to remind us of the full range of tools available during testing work. Correct and consistent use of test terminology when test writing will make the intent clearer to testers executing them and increase the overall effectiveness of the testing effort. The correct use of terminology also helps communicate with other disciplines. If testers can describe their work more clearly, discussions and decision-making with other team disciplines will be more valuable.

Test planning scenario

To conclude this chapter, I'll use some of these terms in a theoretical example of a feature where the test plan is owned by a QA analyst and executed by some QA testers.

Mo is a QA analyst working within a game studio. He's part of the feature development pod within the studio team. They're working on a new in-game event type for their game which is running as a live service. The feature team is developing the new event type in a feature branch called 'raid-boss' because the new event features a cooperative raid boss.

Mo started work by reviewing all the design documentation and listing questions against it. He knows that static testing will help his test planning and may also find early bugs in the designs. He does this during the sprint before the engineers begin coding the feature. The feature will take several sprints to be completed and only parts will be delivered each sprint.

During the first sprints, Mo carries out testing himself. Mo needs to work quickly and complete his testing before the sprint ends, so he will use exploratory verification tests to quickly scout the feature without having to prepare scripted tests. During this time he's only testing against the new event components in isolation, and not taking account of other features being developed by other development pods in parallel. He's testing at a component level against the raid boss event as a test area.

During the development sprints, some of Mo's testing activities will aim to verify the acceptance criteria in each of the stories in the sprint. This will make up his acceptance testing, which he can use to confirm that the new work defined in the stories is complete and stable enough to close the story, marking the new work as complete. Before the sprint ends, he will need to test and close all stories that the pod is working on during the sprint.

Mo is unlikely to be performing any testing beyond basic verification; partly due to time constraints and partly because he plans to perform the majority of testing once the development of the new event type is complete and has been merged in the main branch.

During the sprints leading up to the completion of the feature, he makes plans for the system level testing and ensures a good balance of test types are included in his test plan. He also defines a test area breakdown for the new event type, defining the major areas and sub-areas of testing the feature.

At this point, he will create supporting test planning documentation and write the test activities that the test team will execute later.

Once all the sprints that contribute towards the development of the feature are complete, Mo and the feature pod will decide together if the feature is stable enough to merge the feature branch back into the main branch of the game with other new features that will be included in the next game update. Mo will consider various factors to decide whether he needs to run integration testing or whether his planned system testing will satisfy the same purpose.

When the feature is merged in the main branch, the team of QA testers may run a smoke test of the feature to verify its stability before committing to the larger system test plan Mo has written. He will now start working on the next feature development work as a new sprint starts, leaving the test team to run the system testing against the epic raid event feature. At this time, Mo and the rest of the development pod will be working in a freshly created feature branch while the test team perform system testing against the separate main branch. The two testing workstreams are now running in parallel.

This system testing will include a mixture of test activities and test types within those activities. Mo will have decided what balance of scripted and unscripted testing to use in the test plan, based on factors like time constraints and the experience of the test team. Mo determines the order of test execution, deciding that scripted verification is the first to be executed, and arranges for the team to run longer exploratory sessions into different test areas afterwards. Some of those exploratory sessions have a failure testing focus; others are investigations to answer specific test questions that arose during test planning.

Once all of the system-level functional and non-functional testing is complete and bugs have been actioned, the test team may join the studio project team to run some internal playtests of the new event type before it goes out to real players. This will act as a final review for the team to see what the event is like and also provide test coverage of a 'rehearsal' of the event, as it would be run in with real players.

3.7   Test types and terminology: games vs. software

Play testing is a good example of a term that is unique to games. The organisation and goals of a play test aren't defined outside of the gaming space. Because this activity is usually only run within the game studio, remote test teams might also only have a rough idea about the setup for these tests. This uniqueness and difficulty is compounded when setting up mass multiplayer playtests. Outside of games, software will use internal betas or 'dogfooding' instead, which is where teams use the product they are creating on a day-to-day basis, becoming a user of the product. QA analysts in a studio should remember the effectiveness of play tests and become an advocate of running them.

Aside from play testing, all of the terms listed here are consistent between games and other software, which is great because it means that game testers can use software testing resources online as reference material, carrying out quick searches to recall and define terms easily. Game testers will find, however, that most of the terms are interpreted differently for games and, as I discussed in the introduction, the difficult part is translating each test level, area, activity or type into the gaming space.

This chapter omits many software testing terms that are not common or relevant to game projects. This is the main difference in terminology; with gaming, a specialised subset of all software, there is a greater set of terms within software that do not apply to games. This can confuse junior game testers reading books or taking part in training when they see terms and associated processes defined which they don't see in their game projects. Game testers and QA analysts should use the lists defined in this chapter as core techniques, mastering them before investigating further options. The terms listed in this chapter should be a suitable set of tools to tackle 95% of test planning scenarios that QA analysts and testers will face within game projects, with only advanced test activities requiring more specialisation.

Test analysis techniques

4.1   An intro into test analysis

Test analysis techniques define what needs to be tested without yet explaining how exactly it will be tested. Test analysis is really the core work of the QA analyst*, making this chapter an important part of this book.

Deciding what needs to be tested may sound initially obvious. Surely you just test whatever feature is being created by the development team? While this is true, test analysis takes that feature and dissects it into small pieces, allowing testing to be considered for each individual piece, and nothing to be forgotten. We introduced this as part of the fundamental test framework in chapter one and referred to it as creating a map of what needs to be tested. It's a good way to think about this part of the test creation process.

Test analysis is part of the first stage of the fundamental test process and is realistically carried out in parallel with test planning activities. Planning is finding and organising information to be used for the test analysis. This chapter assumes that you've completed all of your test planning activities, so you have your source of information to analyse. That information will likely be incomplete, slightly out of date and exist in multiple locations. Some of that information might only exist in the minds of other team members, which you will have extracted by speaking with them and asking incisive questions.

---

*   The clue is in the name! This chapter also helps us solidify the difference between the role of a tester (someone who executes tests) and a QA analyst/test engineer (someone who plans and writes tests), a differentiation which is still a grey area for many.

The techniques in this chapter will help you make sense of that information, translating it into a list of things that need to be tested. It will help you identify important areas and irrelevant technical details. The larger a feature, the more daunting this can be, leaving you wondering where to begin.

Earlier I described this process as similar to planning the structure of an essay before you begin writing it. Like an essay, writing is going to be ineffective unless a good foundation is put in place to structure that writing. If QA analysts choose to focus on the wrong areas during their analysis, it won't matter how well-written their tests are, because they're focusing on the wrong areas.

This is why I consider test analysis (planning the tests) to be more critical than test design (writing the tests). Test design is more forgiving when tests are badly written, because this usually results in more questions from the testers, and these problems can be ironed out throughout test execution. However, getting the test analysis wrong and focusing testing on the wrong areas can waste huge amounts of test effort, which is compounded the larger the test plan is and the more testers you have executing it.

As a quick side-step into an advanced topic, by allocating teams of testers to execute a test plan, QA analysts are effectively spending the company testing budget by allocating those testers. As we know, budgets are limited and wasting test effort through poor test analysis is also wasting the company budget. This is doubly so if the team is using an external test vendor whom they are paying for by the hour. The spend is very apparent on the monthly invoice. For this reason, QA analysts would do well to remind themselves, as they carry out their test analysis, of the business case for testing.

Tools for your toolbox

Each of the following techniques are helpful for different types of features as the focus of testing, helping the QA analyst breakdown and understand large and complex game components. It's important to note that not every technique will help with every feature, and choosing the most useful techniques for each situation is part of the work.

Many find it difficult to apply these techniques to their games testing. This is largely because they can't link a technique to a particular test analysis problem, or try to use the wrong technique for the wrong feature, or for all features in testing. This is where our 'toolbox' analogy comes in. You don't use every tool for every job; you need to pick the most appropriate tools. Similarly, you might not be able to use a new tool immediately, but will need to store it until the appropriate test problem presents itself.

In addition to matching the techniques to the appropriate problems, QA analysts should also decide whether to use these techniques at all for each test plan. The techniques listed here are the most heavyweight versions, requiring the most amount of work when they are used. This greater investment in test planning only provides a good return on that effort when the feature under test is suitably large, complex or risky. Smaller features don't require such rigorous planning and can be approached with cut-down versions of these techniques or without using them at all. It's perfectly fine for QA analysts to change the formality of their test analysis from feature to feature, as long as this is a conscious decision and they are choosing how much time to invest based on the complexity and risk of the feature, and not just because test planning with lower formality requires less effort.

Pitfalls of test analysis

There's an unfortunate reality that test analysis is overlooked by many test teams, who instead proceed straight into writing tests and forming the structure organically during that process. Many testers and junior QA analysts don't yet appreciate that the structure of the test plan needs to be created by the test team and not just be a straight copy of the development task breakdown. Development tasks organising the creation of features are rarely in a helpful breakdown for test planning. The organisation of development tasks is usually done from a technical and discipline perspective, with sub tasks for a gameplay code engineer, more for the UI code engineer – for example, separating the tasks by discipline. I've also observed a lot of junior QA analysts who view test writing as a direct translation of the design documentation into verification test cases. When you follow this misguided flow there doesn't appear to be a need for test analysis at all.

> *Design: "The feature should do X"*
> *Test: "Test that the feature does X"*

Basing testing solely on verifying what is included in the design documentation and simply translating that information into written test cases will make test analysis very limited in scope and miss critical areas of testing. Test analysis should be the opposite of this lazy approach: an open mind-mapping exercise that attempts to identify the widest possible scope for a test plan. It's incredibly important that test teams don't fall into these traps and instead perform test analysis as a fresh and independent activity.

Goals of test analysis

The goal of the test analysis phase is to create a plan for the tests to follow when they are being written. As well as defining what needs to be tested, test analysis helps organise testing into sections and subsections so that test writing can progress easily and effectively.

If you have seen any test suite before, you will know that a single suite can span hundreds of individual tests and configurations. Embarking on test writing without a good plan leads to inconsistency, gaps and duplication across the tests. There is nothing more painful than having to go back through large sets of tests and make edits.

Test analysis is also important for efficiency in the test planning process. So you need to invest some time to get it right the first time when test writing, which in turn helps avoid late reorganisation or editing of already-written tests. In the next sections, I'll explain how I approach this task and give some examples of what a game feature breakdown looks like in different formats. Once it has been used to plan the tests, the analysis is redundant: the tests become the main point of reference for the test plan for the lifetime of the project.

This means it's difficult to decide how much time to invest in test analysis and how to formally record the outcome. Some of the examples I'll give will also show how the test analysis stage can be used as a living document, effectively recycling the breakdown for other purposes later in the fundamental test process.

Industry tales: The QA analyst role

Early in my career, near the end of my time in a QA tester role, I was executing tests written by others and started to have ideas and opinions about what areas our testing should focus on. I used the exploratory test time given to me to focus my testing on those areas and I wanted the opportunity to write my own tests and choose the test direction. I think this is a natural progression for testers as they gain enough experience to move into the QA analyst role. However, like many other testers, I didn't appreciate the amount of support work that goes into test writing. We had test leads who would organise the test execution and manage the test team, but we also had separate software test engineers (QA analysts) who would own the test planning and writing. So, most of my communication was with my test lead and I didn't know a lot about the test creation process, however much I thought I did.

For the same reason, testers moving into junior QA analyst roles can struggle or, worse, spend a long time writing ineffective test plans through poor test analysis and design. While good testing experience is a prerequisite for effective test analysis and design, it *is* still a different skill set. This means that being a good tester does not immediately make that person a good QA analyst.

The QA analyst role in games can be difficult to move into. You can't build your skillset or experience until you actually work in the role, and there's very little training content to help you. This test analysis chapter intends to bridge that gap and describe the core work of game project QA analysts, providing clear guidance and techniques on how to tackle this component of the test planning process. I'm writing it from the perspective of information that I needed when I was a tester in this position. This is applicable to QA managers wanting to upskill their analyst teams, analysts wanting to improve, and testers moving into the analyst role.

When I eventually got to be a QA analyst, it was a new role created because there was a big project coming up. The application process involved writing a top-level test plan for this new project, on a given template. This was a written document rather than a spreadsheet, so it was quite text-heavy. I did a bit of research and put quite a lot of thought into the plan. The new project was heavily focused around streaming video, and I had already done quite a lot of testing against video streaming apps on Xbox that had heavy elements of services and network testing. I applied my learnings from the past projects to the new test plan. I was a senior tester, what we called 'TA2', short for test associate level 2, but not yet test lead. The decision to use a test plan as the application for the job was great because it tested the applicants on their planning and organisation skills, rather than just their ability to execute tests. I want to call this out because it's an entirely different skill set and the hiring managers knew that. What I was doing in that test plan was test analysis.

Industry tales: The real state of the QA analyst role

Because there's so little guidance and standardisation around the QA analyst role, those whom I've met have varied wildly in competency. There's definitely a lack of consistency around how QA analysts conduct their work and the type of work that they are expected to do, as I've seen many times when interviewing external candidates for these roles.

The confusion partly comes from an uncertainty around the difference between the role of testing (QA tester) and test planning (QA analyst). Testers are directly assigned work to complete as part of a larger test team, while QA analysts work independently and are left to organise themselves and their work in whatever way they see fit. Yes, they'll have a test manager to rely on for guidance, but this is very hands-off compared with the relationship between a tester and their test lead.

There are quite a few QA analysts who have been promoted into the role but still have the mindset of a tester, approaching features by testing them directly themselves, or by writing tests and then immediately running those tests themselves. Because no one else sees these tests, they are usually lower in quality and formality. This approach lacks the power of delegation, allowing multiple testers to execute test plans more quickly, as well as depriving the QA analyst of the experience of organising test execution.

QA analysts in this position can struggle to organise their work and identify new sources of work in the game studio. Unlike a test team, no-one in the studio game team will assign the QA analyst work. Instead, developers, designers and artists will expect the QA analyst to pick up the feature work as they go along, in addition to proactively involving themselves in specific discussions that they care about. Many junior QA analysts are not so proactive because they aren't experienced enough to approach work in this way. If left unchecked, this can lead to the QA analyst thinking that they're doing well when they are actually underperforming. This is much more likely with embedded test roles because other disciplines mostly don't know or care what the QA analyst role does. Remote teams made up entirely of test staff are more likely to have well-defined roles and QA processes. This is fine until the person wants to move to another company with a more mature test team.

Test writing is also commonly self-taught, leading to varying test quality from person to person. With many teams not peer reviewing test plans, this can also go unchecked for a long time. As a non-technical activity, test writing can be seen as easy and something that anyone can do, creating a false sense of confidence. This is definitely not true of any but the simplest of test plans. More developed test teams will have test writing style guides and test planning processes that everyone on the team adheres to, in addition to peer reviewing guidelines. Test consistency between different test writers is also important. However, the reality is that many teams don't have these guides and processes in place, and test writing is left to each individual.

To make things worse, many managers outside of the testing discipline don't understand the difference between test roles that execute testing from provided instructions, and those that are self directed and need to plan for testing. When interviewing for embedded QA roles, it's normal to include the hiring manager from the testing discipline, plus a producer and technical manager from the code discipline. Many young or small teams also don't have test managers in the studio at all and instead have QA analysts reporting directly into studio leadership.

In a previous team I worked on, one of our QA analysts moved to another project internally and we needed to make a new hire. I was surprised when other managers proposed we ask our remote testers to own the test planning and write the tests remotely while we searched for a new candidate. I suggested that it might be possible to mentor a tester into the QA analyst role only if they were in the local office, had the right attitude and we had the time to do it. We did exactly that a few months later as the team grew. The point is that uncertainty around the QA analyst role is much higher outside of the testing discipline, with many viewing the roles of QA tester and QA analyst as the same thing. Studio game teams hiring their first QA team members are at risk of falling into the trap of bad hiring decisions, as are game teams which don't have strong QA leadership.

Because of this reality, I'm highly self-evaluating of my work and always look for ways to improve it. Likewise, I'm a huge advocate of sharing knowledge and helping QA analysts on my teams improve. It's a large part of what inspired me to write this book. There's so much potential for improvement and enjoying the fruits of that improvement.

4.2   Test conditions

Test conditions are a list or table of what needs to be tested, and the primary output of the test analysis phase.

The techniques listed in this chapter will help you correctly identify and prioritise your test conditions for different types of features. The techniques are a supplement to the creation of test conditions, allowing you to plan for bigger and more complex features. If you want to introduce test conditions into your test planning, you can start by just introducing test conditions themselves, generating the list using your current skill set and project experience. Then you can introduce some of the other test analysis techniques later to help you build *better* test conditions. I'd recommend this approach as it will provide the easiest learning curve.

Before we dig deeper into those techniques, I'm setting the scene with test conditions to give you a clear picture of the end goal of the process. They're called conditions because tests are written to satisfy those conditions. Any single test can satisfy one or many conditions, so it doesn't necessarily need to be a one-to-one relationship. I write test conditions in a brief format, being careful not to delve too much into how I might test those conditions. Let's take a theoretical example so we can see what test conditions actually look like.

A new feature has been added to include a single upsell popup within the game which gives the player the opportunity to double their rewards in exchange for some in-game resources like gold or crystals. The popup appears at various entry points throughout the game. Some test conditions for the feature could be:

- Test the UI layout of the new payment popup
- Test actioning of all the buttons on the new popup

- Test for the standard UI sounds when actioning the new popup
- Test the new UI on different screen ratios, at least 4:3 and 16:9

Note that these are written in short form lists: they don't need to be full sentences. I usually write my test conditions as if I were writing a reminder to myself. While being 'quick and dirty', it should still be clear to other people what each condition is referring to. As my list grows I will start to prefix conditions that are similar, grouping them together. If a single test condition is too broad in scope, I'll create a sub-list under it and go into more detail.

Here's an evolved version of our test condition list snippet.

- UI – Test the UI layout of the new payment popup
- UI – Test the new UI on different screen ratios, at least 4:3 and 16:9
- Audio – Test for the standard UI sounds when actioning the new popup
- Upsell – Test actioning all of the buttons on the new popup
- Test that accepting the offer removes and gives the correct resources
- Test that the offer cancel button dismisses the popup
- Test that the close ('x') button dismisses the popup

Note that I've started to group all test conditions that focus on the visual components of the feature, prefixing them with 'UI'. It's useful to group similar test conditions together because it helps keep the list organised as it grows. Additionally, there is a good chance that some similar conditions can be satisfied by the same test. Having them next to each other in the list will be helpful when tests are written.

I've also broken down the test condition about actioning the buttons into more specific conditions that should be covered during testing. Knowing how much detail to go into requires a little practice, but I would advise that too much detail is better than too little. For example, you shouldn't have any 'catch all' test conditions like, "test all of the new feature UI", "test the newly introduced characters" or "test on multiple different devices". Such broad and vague test conditions will not serve as a very good map during test writing and should be refined first.

Test condition formats

I like to use three different formats when creating test conditions. Each has its own level of formality. For smaller features, I use quick and lightweight 'throwaway' formats. For larger and longer running feature development, I use more complex and heavyweight formats which allow the organisation of larger test sets without becoming a mess.

Lists: A list of bullet points is the most lightweight format and it's the one used in the example above. The list can include sub-lists to provide a basic breakdown where needed, but using this method for large breakdowns makes the list hard to read. I most commonly use this format for small, quick or low-risk features.

The time you spend creating the test conditions needs to be relative to the time taken to write and run the tests. If it only takes two days of work to write the tests, then there is little value in spending more than a couple of hours on the test conditions as the prerequisite step. In my more recent work where we are developing small features and releasing them every few weeks, I use this format to quickly plan for multiple features within a two week sprint, with each list taking up to an hour, maximum, to create.

When using this format, the test condition list can be included directly into the parent task for the test plan within the database (the same database that the bugs and dev tasks are stored). Bullet points and rich text formatting are nearly always supported, allowing you to create the list in the most appropriate place for your team, wherever that is.

Here's a multiplayer matchmaking example of the list format (note – this is just a snippet, the complete list of test conditions for a matchmaking system would be much larger).

- UI – Test the matchmaking menu is visually correct
  o Test each of the dropdown UI matchmaking options
  o Test the tooltips when hovering over each control
  o Test the loading spinner animates

- Matchmaking inputs
  o Test that players of similar level are matched
  o Test players are matched by region first

- Networking – Test different network setups
  o Test matchmaking with an open DNS
  o Test matchmaking on different network connections
    - Wired
    - 3G, 4G
    - Wireless

Tables: A table format allows you to add additional data onto each test condition by including further columns after the list of conditions.

A common addition is to assign priorities. These help decide the order in which the tests are designed and executed later on. Tables also allow for traceability to be added to each condition, which can be done by adding columns linking to the relevant dev task and test for each test condition. I usually add hyperlinks to the test tasks and tasks within the database, which makes it quicker to access the relevant information in the database and also serves as a test design progress tracker. This setup allows you to track which tests satisfy which test conditions and shows conditions which are yet to have tests written for them, providing progress tracking through the test design process.

By creating traceability, you won't have missed anything in your test plan, because all of the dev tasks should be accounted for in the table (i.e. You have test conditions for all documented feature components and you know which components map to which test conditions). I usually use this format for test writing that takes longer than three days or if the feature presents some bespoke consideration that needs to be captured within a table.

Tables don't require much extra effort to create, but are useful if the feature documentation is disorganised and you need to gather it in a central location. The same is true for slightly bigger features which are made up of multiple development sub tasks: this format is useful to organise the dispersed task details into a single place, combining it with the documentation information.

For these bigger features, it's recommended that you use a shared documentation tool for your test condition table, like Confluence, OneNote or Google Docs. Large tables placed directly within your database start to look ugly and become difficult to navigate. Instead, I create a test analysis section within the QA area of our company-shared documentation and then provide a link from the database test plan to the corresponding page. These tools also provide more advanced formatting options like basic colouring of cells, increasing the readability of table sections.

Lastly, you can use the table format to store other types of supplementary information – it doesn't have to be limited to the examples given here. You could add a column to categorise the test conditions by test type (verification/failure) to provide an easy way to view the balance of the plan. You could also add a column for additional notes, something I almost invariably do.

For example, when we integrated 64-bit Android support into our last mobile project, we knew that both our development build process and our release candidate (master) build process would need to be updated to produce 64-bit versions of our app. Because of this, we chose to perform a subset of the tests again on the master build, so added a column to the test condition table to tag tests that should be rerun on the master build.

Here's the matchmaking example again, but in table format with some supplementary information.

Test Condition	Priority	Dev Task	Test	Notes
UI – Test each of the dropdown UI matchmaking options	1	PROJ-201	PROJ-240	Private/public options, character selection, password selection, game modifiers, game length
UI – Test the tooltips when hovering over each control	2	PROJ-201	PROJ-240	Dropdowns, map selection, game list filters
UI – Test the loading spinner animates	3	PROJ-201	PROJ-240	Consider testing on different aspect ratios?
MM Inputs – Test that players of similar level are matched	1	PROJ-205		Rookie levels (1-5), Intermediate levels (6-12), Pro levels (13+)
MM Inputs – Test players are matched by region first	2	PROJ-206		Can we use a VPN for this? To investigate.
Networking – Test matchmaking with an open DNS	2	PROJ-211		
Networking – Test matchmaking on different network connections (wired, 3G, 4G, wireless)	1	PROJ-211		Investigate whether this is our game code, may be lower risk.

Figure 4.1 – Test condition table format

You'll notice that some of the comments consider *how* these components will be tested. While test analysis only focuses on what is tested, it's natural to start thinking about test design and how you will write tests to satisfy the test conditions.

The notes section of this table is a natural place to start the test design process. You should still aim to finish all test analysis before starting to write the tests, but the test design notes and follow-up actions can help prepare you for test writing.

I find this particularly useful to identify and prepare anything that will be needed as a prerequisite to running the tests. For example, this could include tests that require tools and tool configurations, player profile data setups, new debug controls, new debug HUD elements or supporting game data like balancing numbers. Notice the inclusion of debug in that list: test analysis is the perfect time to identify new debug tools that you might need to test the feature. If you identify this need early enough while the rest of the team are still creating the feature, then it's much more likely that they'll be able to code in the new debug while the feature is being created.

Test breakdowns: Some of the teams I've worked with use spreadsheet breakdowns as a tool to document their feature area test conditions in the test analysis step. This is the most heavyweight format for creating test conditions and I highly recommend spreadsheets for maximum flexibility and formatting when creating the breakdown.

The main difference between the breakdown format and the standard test condition table is that the former puts a large focus on splitting the test conditions across several columns. These let you quickly define a tree-like structure, where each successive column is an increasingly granular sub-area.

This approach works really well when organising large areas of testing into smaller sections – useful for large features where it can be difficult to decide where to begin. I start by defining my major areas of testing and then place test conditions within those major areas, allocating each to the most logical sub-area. The spreadsheet can include the same supplementary information supported by the table format, but allows a much greater amount of information to be displayed on screen at once, allowing for easier visual navigation of the test plan. I also use spreadsheet features to freeze, hide or collapse rows in the test condition table for easier viewing.

Let's take the same example of the matchmaking test conditions that we used earlier and show them in the breakdown format.

This breakdown allows us to organise more of the specific details of each test condition from the table format. If we take the matchmaking UI as an example, writing out a test condition for each individual element will get tedious very quickly. Conversely, writing 'test all UI elements' is too vague and may cause some to be missed during test writing. The test breakdown format allows test planning to create test conditions in a quicker notation format. When creating breakdowns, you can create as many columns as you need to breakdown the testing into suitably small pieces. In this way, the breakdown format allows the test analysis to be much more explicit about individual scenarios and configurations that should be tested.

Main area	Sub area	Sub sub area	Sub sub sub area	Notes	Dev Task	Test	Priority
UI	MM screen	Quickmatch filter dropdowns		Private/public options, character selection, password selection, game modifiers, game length	PROJ-201	PROJ-240	1
UI	MM screen	Map selection	Selection control		PROJ-201		1
UI	MM screen	Map selection	Map preview	Mini preview auto-gen, spawn points, size	PROJ-201		1
UI	MM screen	Tooltips		Dropdowns, map selection, game list filters	PROJ-201	PROJ-240	2
UI	MM screen	Error dialogs		Can't find match, game ended, no network,	PROJ-201		2
UI	MM screen	HUD	Button legend		PROJ-201		1
UI	MM screen	HUD	Play again' button	Only appears after playing a match	PROJ-201		1
UI	MM screen	HUD	Console window		PROJ-201		2
UI	MM screen	HUD	Screen ratios + resolutions	On mobile, tablet, widescreen, super widescreen. 1080p, 4k.	PROJ-201		2
UI	Misc areas	loading screen	loading spinner		PROJ-201	PROJ-240	3
UI	Misc areas	loading screen	loading tips	Covered elsewhere?	PROJ-201		3
MM inputs	By level	Rookie (1-5)		Test that players of similar level are matched. Test matchmaking preference, create two games and check which is joined?	PROJ-206		1
MM inputs	By level	Intermediate (6-12)			PROJ-206		1
MM inputs	By level	Pro levels (13+)			PROJ-206		1
MM inputs	By level	Extended search		Test relaxation of searching restrictions over time. i.e. If players of similar levels can't be found, then search more broadly	PROJ-206		1

Figure 4.2 – Test condition breakdown format

The breakdown format has several benefits. Because they're created from spreadsheets, these test analysis breakdown documents can be easily modified to generate test progress reports. The analyst just needs to turn the test breakdown into a pivot table and then create a separate tab which can be formatted into a dashboard of metrics and graphs. As mentioned before, this is mainly useful for capturing a very high-level view of test progress across the project area. We would look to other test tools to get more specific test data. QA managers can create a separate file that references the data within the QA analyst's feature breakdowns, easily combining the data to show project-wide test metrics.

I generally only use this format when it's absolutely necessary, due to the time it takes to create a new sheet for each feature. For this investment to be worth it, the test writing should be estimated to take at least a week and the test execution several weeks or months. You're most likely to see it on franchise game projects where the project team is working over a couple of years on the next release in the franchise and has a fairly solid plan for the game's development. In terms of the project development style, waterfall projects which favour upfront planning provide good conditions for this style of test analysis. The investment can be made with relative certainty that the plan will not need to be changed.

Additionally, for waterfall projects the *entire* game needs to be broken down during test analysis, making each feature area massively more complex than a team running an agile project and delivering smaller feature components every few weeks. The 'everything at once' style of waterfall actually necessitates this heavyweight analysis approach for test analysis to be effective.

Agile projects however, present a much trickier challenge for this format of test analysis. QA analysts within agile projects will be test planning for smaller feature components on a much shorter timescale, preventing them from carrying out longer term test analysis investment. The challenge of the agile project QA analyst is to identify when a sufficiently large feature arrives on the schedule that requires this format. For agile QA analysts accustomed to a 'quick and dirty' work style, larger features can present a shock during test planning if they aren't sufficiently equipped.

Industry tales: Multiplayer test planning for Forza Horizon

When I was a software test engineer at Microsoft, I worked on Fable Legends as the multiplayer and online services test owner and later as the multiplayer test owner for Forza Horizon 3.

These projects had features that were developed over several months and required the test breakdown format of test analysis. Forza was a particularly good example of this because it was also a franchise title with a strongly defined development roadmap. We used the breakdown format for our test analysis of each game area we owned throughout the lifetime of the project. It was important that we planned well and took care when test planning, because it would be serving as our guide for the following 18 or so months of testing.

The areas of ownership were sizeable: the whole of the single player campaign to one person; multiplayer and online sections to another; all of the environments and character models to another. The entire game was divided up between four or five of us in this way and we each owned a few of these areas over the course of the project.

When you are planning for test areas this large and complex, some of the sub-areas can almost require a test plan of their own. It's up to the QA analyst to decide whether they think a sub area is worth its own test plan. These breakdowns have good flexibility and can be adapted and personalised by each QA analyst according to their needs, adding in additional columns for notes, tracking and traceability.

This table below shows part of my multiplayer breakdown on Forza. The overall test analysis was broken down into each multiplayer game mode and then a separate section (shown here) for features that were global to all the modes. Note that breaking down the areas in this way meant that when writing the tests, I would be much less likely to accidently duplicate these tests in different areas of the plan. The test plan notes in this example are mainly self-serving, acting as a reminder to myself during test writing. These 37 lines were just a small section of my test breakdown. In addition to this global section, I had sections for online freeroam, playground games, online adventure, car meets, matchmaking and network. The full tests analysis totalled 172 lines! This is a great example of the scale that test analysis can reach and the requirement for good organisation.

Area	Sub Area	Sub Sub	Sub Sub Sub	Test Plan Notes
Global	VOIP	Basic Verification		Basic verification. Should be tested in each game mode. ALL VOIP TESTS ARE CROSS-PLATFORM
Global	VOIP	Full Session Verification		A verification of VOIP consistency + quality across a full 12 player game session. Xbox + PC
Global	VOIP	Device Types (cross-platform)		Stereo headset, chat heatset, kinect. PC Peripherals
Global	VOIP	Enabling + Mute Controls		VOIP enabled, disabled, Mute myself, mute other players.GUI is updated
Global	VOIP	Platform Chat prioritisation		A test to verify platform party chat vs. in-game chat
Global	VOIP	Platform Privacy + Settings		Does the title comply with platform/profile settings for communication over voice and text
Global	VOIP	Failure + destructive		Controller pulling, headset pulling, ethernet pulling, bandwidth throttling
Global	Anti-Grief	Idle Kicking	PC	
Global	Anti-Grief	Idle Kicking	Xbox	Players being kicked from online sessions due to being idle. Should be tested in a range of game states + across both Xbox and PC
Global	Car Horns	Basic MP Verification		Custom car horns heard by other players, a variety of horns play different sounds and can be heard by other players, Switching horns functions correctly
Global	Car Horns	Logic + Anti-grief		Geoposition logic for hearing car horns + anti-grief logic for repeatedly sounding horns
Global	Car Horns	Failure + Griefing		
Global	Platform	Privacy + Settings		Real-name sharing, Joining Multiplayer games
Global	Game Parties	Creation + Invites		Functional verification of game parties across both platforms. Each platform can setup, invite and accept invites
Global	Game Parties	Failure + Errors		Full parties, error messages, cross-platform play, destructive tests, complex leaving and joining scenarios (creating + joining while being in different states)
Global	Game Parties	Party Leader Options		Verification of the party leader options. Leaving the party, submitting to matchmaking etc.
Global	Game Parties	GUI + Data		Would need to test each of the available status' for players. GUI needs some testing, but is mostly ported from Anthem
Global	Multiplayer UI	Player List		Functional verification, GUI, gamercard links, Gamertag display, display on PC
Global	Multiplayer UI	Misc.		Exploratory verification on miscellaneous menus, GUI, Prompts, notifications + pop ups that is specific to Multiplayer
Global	Private	Basic Verification		Basic functional verification of differences
Global	Private	Leadership		Leader transfer scenarios + Specific Options (leader leaving, leader Kick player, Mak option to "Make Session Leader" for other player, make party leader,
Global	Private	Leadership		Flow for leader starting events and other players being notified of Event starting + the event and being able to accept
Global	Private	Game Modes		Online Freeroam, Online Aventure, Co-op
Global	Private	Failure + Destructive		Leader ethernet disconnect, leader crash,
Global	Transitions	Currency Gain + SP Progress		Failure tests here
Global	Transitions	SP -> MP (limbo)		
Global	Friends Icon	Max Icons Failure		
Global	Friends Icon	Online functional verification	PC	
Global	Friends Icon	Online functional verification	Xbox	
Global	Friends Icon	Synchronisation Failure		
Global	Friends Icon	UI, Position + Synchronisation		
Global	Synchronisation	World Sync	TOD, Traffic, Weather	
Global	Synchronisation	Cars Sync	Liveries, Cars, Tu	Local and remote paints are consistent
Global	Synchronisation	Smashables + Collision		Stuff that is already smashed on my screen is also smashed on yours, New stuff we smash appears smashed on both clients
Global	Synchronisation	Transitions + Waits (post-race/pre-race, car select)		
Global	Synchronisation	Frame-rate tests	cross-platform	Might be a fair bit of overlap with PC framerate and Sync testing
Global	Synchronisation	Frame-rate tests	high/low	Might be a fair bit of overlap with PC framerate and Sync testing

Figure 4.3 – Breakdown snippet from a Multiplayer test plan on Forza

After mapping out my test conditions, I started to track which of those test conditions I had written a test for, including the work item number in the sheet once the test was written. At the time we used Team Foundation Server to store the tests, a Microsoft database tool that you can use through Visual Studio. By creating this in a spreadsheet we were each able to create a formula which detected the number of tests written and tracked our test writing progress automatically over days and weeks.

With test design being such a long task for the QA analyst group, this tracking was a great way for the project test manager to make sure test design progress was on track across the whole project. This is also a good example of how the spreadsheet format really adds value to test analysis; the integration of formulas and graphing provides a very low effort solution to other test problems during the fundamental test process.

My test breakdown included a set of supplementary information, shown separately. Figure 4.4 shows the supplementary data that I added to my sheet. These additions are essentially repurposing the test analysis document into a tracking tool which can be used and updated throughout the project. The reason for doing it this way is primarily for the sake of efficiency – why create a separate tracking document when you can just use a document you have already?

Delivered / Available	Code or Content?	Template Test Case	Area Health
Yes	Code	94368	Average
Yes	Code	N/A	Average
Yes	Code	94376	Good
Yes	Code	94377	Good
Yes	Code	94379	Good
Yes	Code	94376	Average
Yes	Code	94380	Poor
Yes	Code	96615	Average
Yes	Code	94385	Poor
Yes	Code	107581	Average
Yes	Code	107439	Poor
Yes	Code	107438	Average
Yes	Code	107557	Average
Yes	Code	107482	Average
Yes	Content	94390	Average
Yes	Content	94393	Good
Yes	Code	94408	Good
Yes	Code	96603	Average
Yes	Code	94431	Average
Yes	Code	94418	Average

Figure 4.4 – Breakdown format supplementary information

The next most important thing was to understand in what order the feature components were going to be ready for testing. What could we start testing and what was still in development? The column 'delivered/available' tracked what test conditions were ready for testing. I would frequently get questions from the testers on whether a bug they had found was in scope and could be bugged. My test condition table was an easy source of information to answer these questions. One of the aims of the test execution schedule was to make sure that test execution was completed at roughly the same rate as new features being delivered into testing. If test execution was too slow, this would cause a backlog of things that needed to be tested but hadn't yet been tested. This column allowed us to track the percentage of the feature area that was available for testing against the percentage of the feature area that we had tested already, making sure the two were aligned.

Let's review the general use of each of these columns and provide some wider usage examples.

Delivered/available – The first column tracks the delivery of the features into testing which can be very helpful for long and complex lists. I've seen this type of tracking used by QA analysts in different ways, particularly for features which have multiple stages of delivery. Consider a game environment or levels which can go through various stages of creation: white box assets only, final assets, polish and dressing, lighting, etc. The QA analyst can use their test breakdown to track the delivery of each level or part of the environment. This type of planning will help the QA analyst coordinate when to run each of their tests during the test execution phase of the life cycle.

Code or content – This refers to the origin of the feature component. Is it created by the code team or created by one of the creative disciplines? It was used in this example as a way of assessing risk and as a reminder of who on the team to speak to about that component.

Test case ID – We said earlier that test analysis tracks what testing is planned and the details of how it's tested are written into the tests themselves. This column tracks which areas have had tests written for them, showing test implementation progress. You could write 'yes/no' here, but inserting the test ID means that this column also doubles up as useful traceability, allowing the QA analyst to find the associated test much more easily. In the case where the test analysis is updated with new information, the analyst can more easily find and update the associated test.

Area health – This is an example of test results tracking at a very high (non granular) level. Many of the individual tests and their results will be distributed across your test tools so it can be difficult to collate them into a single place and get a complete picture of the entire game area. Instead, the test breakdown document can present a useful place to track health or other similar test metrics in this way. It doesn't have to be a health indicator; the QA analyst could choose to input bug numbers or test case pass percentages into here instead.

To finish this case study, the screenshot below shows the summary tab of how this test analysis sheet can be collated into automatic tracking and reporting.

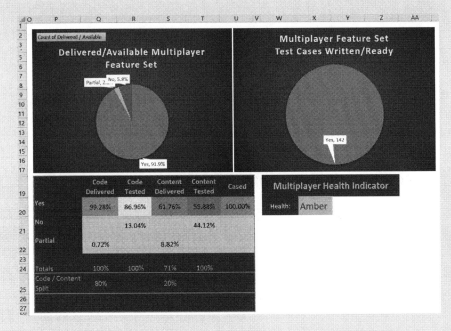

Figure 4.5 – The reporting tab for the multiplayer test breakdown on Forza

During the project, we took the test analysis document a lot further than just using it to create test conditions. They were built from the start to serve multiple purposes throughout the project and were intentionally similar between each of the QA analysts, so that the data could be collated together by our project test manager.

This setup made test progress reporting very easy when a top level summary was required. Built-in reporting from test tools are designed to create test reports from specific test passes and aren't very good at collecting information from a variety of different test activities together. This is particularly true if you have a mix of scripted tests and exploratory sessions. To solve this problem, I really liked the 'area health' solution we used, which provided a rough measure of feature health based on the quantity and severity of bugs in that area. In exploratory sessions, testers could provide a health rating themselves within the session template, while scripted pass/fail results would need to be assessed while I was updating the test condition sheet. Even though this sheet would need to be updated manually for the area health ratings, it would only take thirty minutes each week and more than made up for it in test reporting and tracking.

4.3 Key considerations during test analysis

Regardless of which test condition format you choose, much of the creative process of identifying those test conditions remains the same.

In this section I'll describe the steps I go through when creating test conditions and the mindset that should be adopted when trying to identify test scenarios. I'll also list the main benefits of creating test conditions instead of moving directly to test design. I'm very aware that many QA analysts might still view this step as a 'nice to have' and unnecessary added work to the test creation process. Because of this, I will also describe the direct benefits of this process that I've seen during my own work and illustrate just how impactful it can be.

Verification as a foundation

Positive verification testing is the easiest and most logical place to begin when creating test conditions. Most of the information about what the feature should do has already been collected from various sources during the test planning phase.

I begin by breaking down the feature verification into manageable sub-areas so that every function of the feature can be categorised into one of those sub-areas. I then continue by writing test conditions for each individual piece of functionality for the feature and assigning that test condition to the most logical category. You should try to organise individual test conditions and their groupings so that anyone looking at the list in the future will be able to search and find the information in the most appropriate category.

During testing, there are nearly always questions like, "Are we testing for XXX?" or, "Have we included scenario YYY in our test plan?" Logically-categorised test condition groups will help answer these questions quickly for anyone looking at the list (or if you need to reference the list to check the answer).

Once this is complete, the test conditions should capture everything that needs to be tested to verify all new functional changes introduced by the feature. Before moving on, take a moment to re-review all of the feature information and make sure you have everything covered. I find the process of creating test conditions forces you to consider deeper details about the feature, prompting clarification from the designer or developer. This is a great time, early in the test planning process, to iron out any ambiguities in the designs. Being skilled in the test analysis process means learning to 'read between the lines' of the documentation and then including those hidden details in your test plan. Similarly, you should try to identify what details are *not* included in the designs that you thought would be, and then follow up with questions to fill any gaps.

If the feature has started being developed already, there may be an early version which you can run. Exploring work-in-progress features is a great way to see how the designs are being interpreted. The act of navigating through flows – even if they aren't finished – nearly always prompts additional questions and ideas about how components of the feature will function.

Taking the time to perform these additional steps will make your positive test conditions more thorough: they shouldn't be thought of as optional. It's not possible for the design team to document every small detail of a feature, so taking any documentation at face value without investigating more deeply will result in a basic and insufficient set of positive test conditions.

Many inexperienced QA analysts might stop here, having exhausted all of the information that was presented for the feature. But there is more work to do.

The remaining test conditions are created by the QA analyst on the basis of their past test experience or from techniques which they use to extract yet even more information about the feature. Once the verification test conditions are complete and the feature categories set, the next stage is to move on to identifying negative test conditions – those identifying ways in which the feature might fail.

We discussed failure testing earlier in this book, so by now you should have a good idea about the types of tests that I'm talking about. I aim to have some failure tests in each feature category, with at least 10% of the total test conditions being failure tests. For many feature components, this will be much higher, with more like a 50:50 split between positive and negative tests. Some areas naturally present themselves as having a high potential for failure, making this process easier, while potential failures in others are more specific and require extra work.

A basic example of easily identifiable negative test conditions is a multiplayer login flow. The verification test conditions will have covered all of the core login scenarios, but most testers will know that a feature like this is susceptible to network failures. There are a lot of network-related reasons why a login flow might fail, so the test conditions should identify these and include them in the test analysis. The important point here is that failure testing is entirely identified and driven by the QA analyst.

No-one will instruct the test team to test these failure scenarios, they will not be included in the documentation and (frequently) no-one will be checking that these tests have been considered. But there could still be big quality consequences if they are not tested. This loops back to the core of the QA analyst role: being responsible for identifying what needs to be tested, given any feature as input.

If the idea of having to think up failure tests feels a little daunting, don't worry. Asking the right questions about risk and potential failure lets you gather helpful information for this task. I'll give some more guidance on this, and the techniques throughout this chapter will also guide you.

Fresh labelling and breakdown

Each feature has a user story describing it and a set of sub-tasks defining the individual pieces of code and content work needed to create that feature. It's really easy to copy the title and description of a feature user story from the database and paste it as the title for your test condition table and your test plan. But don't be tempted to do this. Design documentation, technical specifications and user stories are usually written from the perspective of their relevant disciplines. This means that tasks may have technical names that are perfectly accurate for the author, but are too detailed or technical for a tester. I find this is particularly true for 'under the hood' code components which support player-facing features; the test plan should focus on the player-facing result of the underlying change. Copying the titles of other documents is likely to cause confusion for the testers who will be running the tests, triggering more questions than usual. It's much better to read all of the supporting material and then paraphrase technical terminology into a more easily understandable format.

In addition to the terminology itself, copying the breakdown of subtasks for the feature is also a mistake which can lead to ineffective test analysis. Development tasks are usually divided by discipline and in a format which is not helpful for testing planning. Feature creation is also broken down according to the time it will take to create each component, *not* according to the test effort that will be required to test it. For this reason, simply copying the development task breakdown and using it for test analysis will lead to testing being focused on the wrong areas or missing areas entirely.

An experienced QA analyst will know which important details to extract directly from the development tasks, but will create the rest of the test analysis fresh. As well as being a lazy approach, I've found that too much copy/paste work doesn't trigger the same creative thought process, decreasing the number of test conditions that are identified and the number of incisive questions generated.

Test plan scope

For those test planning as part of a team of QA analysts working on a project, test analysis should take into account what is included in the test plans of other QA analysts. Test plans should complement each other, not duplicate effort by testing the same areas or creating gaps between test plans.

This is slightly easier when working on agile because it's common that each QA analyst will be assigned to a feature pod (a sub-team), making the division of test work clear. But it's a much more important consideration for projects where the division of work is more fluid. Missing areas of project testing, because each QA analyst assumes another has covered it, would obviously be a catastrophic planning failure. Because of this, caution is essential, even if it means a small amount of overlap between test plans.

A good example of this is performance testing. QA analysts must agree on whether they will each test the performance of their respective features or whether one of the QA analysts will take test ownership of performance testing across the entire game. In this example, I've found that it's productive to have a dedicated performance testing owner for the entire game, but to allow individual test plans to include specific performance investigations purely as a supplement to the overall performance testing plan. This clarification on test scope will ensure that all QA analysts on the project are aligned in their approach and know what to include in their own test analysis.

Non-functional and compatibility tests

The example of performance testing is a nice segue into this section. You will remember from chapter three that I defined non-functional testing as how well the software performs each piece of functionality, including testing of areas like stability, performance and usability. In nearly every case, non-functional requirements will not be included within the designs or other documentation for a feature. Because of this, it's the responsibility of the QA analyst to consider whether the feature will have implications for non-functional areas like performance and then include test conditions for this.

Performance is a huge area for games, and QA analysts will need to identify specific sub-areas that the feature might impact, like loading times, framerate, memory use, storage use and network utilisation.

I start this process by identifying non-functional areas and then speaking to the creators of the feature to get a more technical assessment on non-functional implications. Artists and content creators will know the file size and quantity of new assets that are being added to the game, providing guidance on memory and storage use. Code discipline team members are also a great source of knowledge for a variety of game-wide performance information, QA analysts would do well to seek them out when confirming performance suspicions.

Non-functional test areas also include hardware, platform and other external considerations. This is another instance where the feature documentation will not contain any details on how it is expected to function on different hardware setups, leaving this up to the test team to consider. QA analysts must be adept at identifying features which will integrate with hardware and platform setups differently and then include these within the test analysis.

A common example is UI testing on different screen sizes and ratios. Any feature that implements a new UI may see bugs when the feature is tested on a mobile device that has a notch in the screen or when run on an ultra widescreen display (21:9 aspect ratio). It's also quite common for games to implement variable quality settings for different hardware setups, downgrading visual elements and turning off certain visual effects in an effort to make the game run smoothly on less powerful hardware. This is most common on mobile and PC platforms.

Test analysis should take this into account and test visual changes on different hardware setups to check each quality level of the added feature. The key question to ask here is, "Will this feature behave differently on different operating systems and hardware?" Some features have heavy integration with the platform the game is running on (e.g. achievements and trophies) while others will have very little (e.g. enemy AI). It's up to the QA analyst to identify and assess the need for compatibility testing.

These types of unspoken and undocumented complications arise frequently when developing new features in real game projects. The new feature may interact with or impact the platform in ways that weren't considered during design or development. It's not uncommon for test planning to identify a new complication that then triggers a new design for the feature, which is then included in the feature implementation.

Industry tales: 'Out of memory' crashes

The implications of new features on game performance are overlooked alarmingly often on the mobile game projects that I've worked on. The problem with mobile devices is the vast range of hardware performance available, with low-end devices and old phones still being popular.

Across multiple projects, I've seen recurring problems specific to the temporary memory that is available on the phone (the RAM or random access memory). Devices with 2GB or more RAM account for most of the market and would run our apps fine, but there are still a lot of mid-range devices that have 1GB or less. The iPhone 6 and iPhone 6 Plus are prime candidates for this, being mid-range and still very popular. The 6 Plus variant, in particular, has a bigger screen and a higher screen resolution, but yet both have 1GB of memory.

Quite often our mobile projects would be using near the memory limit of these devices, meaning that any small memory increase could tip the memory over the device limit and crash the app. A small memory increase could be caused by any unsuspecting feature addition that, on the surface, did not appear to have any performance implications. We usually found about these crashes after the feature had been released to the production game, through our automated crash reporting tools. It would usually start with a small subsection of the player base who both had these devices and also had been playing the game a long enough time to have lots of content on their profiles.

Late game players running on low end devices is the worst-case scenario for many mobile projects, and became something that we tested frequently (and still do to this day). The lesson is to be very cautious of new content and visual effects being added by small features and to always remember to include performance testing into the test analysis for such features.

Lastly, if you are curious about the performance of other iPhone models, you'll be happy to know that the next model, the iPhone 6S, did double the memory to 2GB. Since then, the memory in devices has been a consistent upwards trend which has outpaced that which most apps need to run. Top end models now support 8, 12 and even 16GB of memory, far beyond what any current app would need. Additionally, there are still Android devices on the market with 1GB of RAM and less, but many of these are in the low-end performance bracket and not very popular, reducing the impact on our projects. We found that, typically, mid-range and above Android devices would support more RAM than their comparative iOS devices.

Regression tests

While the majority of every test plan will focus on the new thing that is being added or changed, regression testing of existing areas also needs to be considered. I defined this earlier as the testing of existing, healthy game areas to make sure that they haven't gone backwards in quality. (Put another way: running tests to make sure the new feature hasn't broken some existing healthy feature.)

I initiate this process by adding a regression testing section to my table of test conditions and then start to investigate what existing features are at most risk of breaking. Past experience is a good guide here, particularly if you know of game areas that break frequently. Begin by including these in your test plan if they have a connection with the feature.

Some associated game areas at risk of regression may also be obvious from a player-facing point of view, while others may require a conversation with the feature creator. Player facing regression areas can easily be added to the test plan, but there are often 'under the hood' links between features that exist in the code but aren't visible to the player. This is common when two features depend on some common framework code within the game.

The end result of this process should be a list of existing areas to test and some notes about their relative risk factor. Regression testing is usually a lower priority than new feature verification, but the risk of breakage can vary wildly. Some new features in real game projects are very isolated and have minimal interaction with existing game components. In this case, QA analysts don't need to force fit regression tests. Other features, however, have no new player facing changes and present a test challenge which is *entirely* regression testing.

This is an area where many teams have generic regression testing test passes which cover large areas of the game after new features are added, so that individual feature owners don't need to worry about it during their test planning. While this is effective, testing a majority of the existing game is an inefficient use of testing time and becomes a larger task with every release, as more new features are added to the existing pile. Instead, QA analysts should try to be smarter about the regression testing that is required, identifying specific areas of focus during this test analysis phase.

At the very least, targeted regression testing carried out at a feature plan level can be used as an effective supplement to wider game regression testing. In the perfect scenario, test teams should be able to drop generic 'catch-all' regression testing entirely in favour of more targeted regression testing which focuses only on the risky areas. However, realistically, identifying all areas that are at risk of regression is an almost impossible task; games can break in weird and wonderful ways, making this a challenging area of test planning.

Prioritise

Prioritising your test conditions helps decide both the order of test design and test execution, by writing and running the highest priority tests first.

Since it's such a quick activity, it's always worth adding priorities, regardless of the format that you use for your test conditions. I will introduce test execution strategy later on in chapter seven, **Test Management**, where I'll talk more about the reasons for ordering testing by priority and the benefits that it brings.

Prioritise your test conditions into three groups: priority one, two and three. Priority one should be all conditions that are 'must test', priority two should be all conditions that are 'should test' and priority three are test conditions that are 'could test' (if you have time). Three priority levels is a good number to apply the technique.

Any more is further work and doesn't add much value to the process. I find that a majority of my test conditions are priority one with a small subset of deeper failure and exploratory tests being lower priorities.

The inclusion of priorities in your test analysis might prompt the question, "How do I decide what is high priority for testing?" This is a very good question. The answer is that each feature will have a different set of priorities for what is the most important focus of testing. However, there are some general rules that I follow. The core 'golden flow' verification of the feature is always priority one. These are the tests that check the feature does what it was designed to do. Other types of verification further away from the core flow, including exploratory verification tests, are also usually priority one.

Deeper exploratory tests that take longer to execute, regression testing and failure testing are usually priority two. They should be tested, but if you had to choose, the verification tests would come first. Priority three tests are usually those that take a long time to run and don't present a good return on testing investment. These tests are good as a backup if the test team finishes other lower priority testing early. On agile projects where time is scarce, I expect that priority three tests will not be run at all, and plan accordingly.

Sources of information

Identifying what needs to be tested doesn't mean the QA analyst sitting alone in a room, thinking up ideas. There are many sources of information that can be used to provide direct information on areas that need to be included in testing.

Past experience: Ideas from past project experience don't always come naturally and easily during your work. QA analysts should consciously identify previous features they have tested in the current project or previous projects, looking for similarities that they can use to fuel their test analysis. Snippets of information come to me in the form of, "I know that when XXXX is changed, then YYYY usually breaks." I have seen trends like this across multiple different game projects: trouble areas that persist across projects and bugs that you see again and again. If you find it hard to recall this information, try searching through previous test plans in your project database or look through archived documentation pages for past features or projects.

Bug hotspots: Every game has bad neighbourhoods – areas of the game which generate the most bugs and seem to generate the same bugs repeatedly, even after they've been fixed. Search the bug database or ask the rest of the test team for information on unstable areas that are close to the feature you are test planning for. If there are unstable areas or recurring bugs linked to the feature in some way, the test analysis should include a regression testing section to target those areas, and retesting of specific bugs.

Existing feature bugs: Many features are improvements to existing features, replacements for existing features or built on top of existing game framework components. Test analysis for a new feature should search the database for existing bugs with the current old version of the feature and aim to retest those bugs as part of the regression testing area of the test plan. Bugs with framework components can also be retested to make sure that they, at least, have not been made worse by the feature addition. If you are unsure about these details, you should be able to speak to the code engineer who implemented the feature to get this information.

Nearby features: Many features interact with other game components and features, sometimes in unlikely and complex ways. This can also happen when two new features are being implemented at the same time by two sub-teams, where bugs found for one feature will impact the other. Test analysis should identify nearby features and make sure those features are considered in the test plan. This might mean adding tests to check the integration between the features, or it might mean retesting the bugs for the nearby feature. This is a question of scope: "How far-reaching are the changes for this new feature?" Changes that have a heavy impact on nearby game areas are a challenge to plan for, but this consideration at least allows you to know about them.

Reviews: All QA analysts should endeavour to have their test conditions peer reviewed by other QA analysts on the project. This is actually the single, most helpful method of gathering information and new ideas during test analysis. Other members of the test team who are experienced with test planning are best placed to identify gaps in the test plan and provide ideas from their own experience. When the team is busy, this can sometimes be difficult to organise. But the reality is that giving up some of your time to review someone else's test plan will increase the chances of them returning the favour when you need your tests reviewed. The time investment is mutually beneficial.

In addition to a peer review from other members of the test team, you should get a review from the creator(s) of the feature. There are multiple benefits to this (which we'll talk about next) but, primarily, the feature creators will be able to provide the best feedback on whether they think testing is focusing on the right areas. Even today, I include scenarios in my test analysis because I think those areas are going to be unstable and good sources of bugs, only to be told by the code engineer that the code for that component was straightforward and is unlikely to cause any problems. Getting review feedback and buy-in from the creators of a feature can be difficult because you're asking them to give up their time, but it's invaluable for any test plan.

Benefits of test analysis

It's no secret that many game test teams don't conduct test analysis at all, or rather they include it with test design on the fly as the tests are being written, giving it little thought. When I've spoken to past colleagues about more heavyweight test planning like this, some test managers see it as not applicable to their projects or an ineffective use of time. This is particularly true when the techniques are being introduced as part of a training program which the company would have to pay for. For these reasons, among others, some game test teams don't trial these techniques to see the benefits that they can bring. It *is* extra effort, but the benefits far outweigh the time investment. In this section, I'll list the benefits that I've seen and demonstrate the great impact they can have when implemented well.

Test planning for large or complex features: Performing test analysis as a distinct step in the planning process provides more value the larger the feature is. I would recommend that it's actually a strict necessity for the largest project features, because they present such a difficult organisational challenge. However, QA analysts need to have some experience creating test conditions before they tackle the next big feature that is coming up on the project. Without practising the technique beforehand, you will not be well equipped when a feature arrives that absolutely requires it. So, while many test teams can get by without test analysis as a distinct step, the benefit of having experience with it essentially 'unlocks' test planning for more substantial features for the test team. In addition to larger features on current projects, bigger and more complex games may be created by the studio in the future. This technique allows the test team to scale to these new project sizes.

My final note for this particular benefit is to consider that there is a scale of project sizes too, beginning with small, casual, mobile games and ending with AAA console and PC game projects. In the casual, mobile game projects that I've worked on, these sizeable pieces of work only arrive a couple of times each year, limiting the opportunity to apply more heavyweight test analysis. Yet all of the console projects that I worked on required test analysis for all features throughout the course of the entire project. The opportunities for this benefit will scale relative to the size and complexity of the overall project.

Project area breakdowns: While most embedded test teams will be working within the predefined feature pod teams of the game studio, publisher and external vendor test teams may need to create test plans for entire projects, dividing up the test responsibility amongst the team. When I worked on Microsoft game projects, we were acting as a publisher test team for each game studio. In this example, the system-level testing for the entire project would be divided amongst the QA analyst publisher test team.

Breaking down an entire game project into testable areas is the epitome of test analysis; it's large, complex and needs to be watertight. Having experience with this technique for features allows test managers to apply the same process for a project and evenly assign ownerships to the QA analyst team with confidence that no test areas have been missed.

As a QA analyst, I've also been solely responsible for small projects in the past: companion apps, websites and event apps. These small projects were also a prime target for test analysis. Having experience in the technique allows QA analysts to approach these unique test challenges with confidence, even when they are the sole test owner for the project.

Peer reviews and dev reviews: Getting feedback on a test plan is incredibly important; no test plan should be created in a silo. The most difficult part of reviews is getting others to spend their time conducting the review and to give it their full attention. This can be easier for peer reviews from other QA analysts, but much more difficult when approaching feature creators because they aren't responsible for the test plan and have no ownership of it. This means that most people will see the review as less important than their current work and are more likely to say they don't have time to do it, or rush it without providing any good feedback. These effects are multiplied when the review is on the tests themselves, because they are usually both high in number and in detail.

I have reviewed scripted tests myself in the past; it takes a long time and it's difficult to remain focused after you've looked at thirty tests and have another forty to go. Reviewers are more likely to get bored, scan the long list of tests and give an answer like, "It's very comprehensive, it looks good to me". Which, actually, isn't very helpful.

When reviewing tests, most reviewers are also not sure what type of feedback they are expected to give. So when tests are reviewed directly, the feedback is mainly on the test design: commenting on how understandable the tests are, highlighting typos and broken links to documentation and so on. This means that feedback on the test analysis is nearly always missed. I said earlier that test analysis is much more important than test design, causing this review style to miss the most valuable feedback – highlighting gaps in the test plan.

Acting on feedback from reviews of tests is much harder if you've already written them. You may have to re-edit a selection of the tests or reorganise tests to include new areas. I *really* dislike going back over work that I've already completed, so I find this approach both ineffective for getting valuable feedback and also painful when feedback is given.

Performing the test analysis as a distinct step provides a much better basis to give and receive feedback. Not only is it much easier to persuade others to review a short list of what you plan to test, but the feedback itself will be against the test analysis and not on the test design.

I find this particularly true when approaching feature developers to review my test analysis. With test conditions, I can wrap the review with the context of, "This is what I plan to test. Do you think I'm focusing on the right areas and are there any areas I should add in?". By doing this, I'm directing the reviewer to give me a specific type of feedback which is most valuable and letting them know what I'm requesting from them. It's also much easier for others to view and easily understand a test plan in this format, creating fewer obstacles to an effective review. In our teams, most team members outside of the test discipline don't have direct access to test case tools either, making a direct review of the test cases even harder because they have to find the company's guest account details before they can even conduct the review.

I regularly use this process with different feature creators on the teams I work in. As well as benefiting the immediate test plan, I'm indirectly getting them involved, invested and interested in test planning in general. When this is done repeatedly over the course of a project, the wider game team builds an understanding and respect for the work that I'm doing. So, this activity can make a tangible impact on long term collaboration between the test team and other game studio disciplines.

Recycled as living documents: Earlier I defined the test breakdown format of test conditions and provided some examples of the types of additional information you can store within that format. For particularly large or long-running test plans, the test analysis can double up as a living document to track the progress and results of testing throughout all stages of the fundamental test process, far beyond the test analysis phase.

Normally, test teams will use test case data to report directly on test progress and test results health, but I find multiple problems with this approach. A mixture of exploratory tests and scripted sessions makes collating types of results together difficult; test suite reruns make collating results from multiple runs messy; test cases capture data at far too granular a level to provide a concise summary; and this data set doesn't include other types of information that we might also want to track.

In my work, the last point on that list is the main additional requirement I have. Using one of the examples I gave earlier, the test analysis document is an ideal location to track the delivery of features into testing. Knowing what is ready for testing and what is still being implemented is incredibly helpful during test execution, particularly if you aim to start testing as early as possible (which is usually the case). This document provides an ideal foundation for any type of customisation that you might be interested in tracking.

Whether you use the document purely for your own tracking or whether you intend to use it to report the state to the wider team, the added value increases the return you get on the original time investment. This is an important benefit, since 'not having enough time' is the primary reason given by QA analysts for not conducting test analysis as a discrete step in the first place. When done well, this process reduces the effort spent on tracking and reporting later in the fundamental test process. In my experience, QA analysts will be busier the further into the test process they are.

When using spreadsheet tools, the potential for reducing repeated manual effort is increased even further. Formulas can be created to collect data automatically across all of the test conditions, but code can also be added to the spreadsheets to create more advanced automation and reporting. Data connections are added, linking multiple sheets together and automated reports created and emailed (or instant-messaged) to team members.

As a brief aside, many embedded QA analysts report that they don't have time to work on tracking test progress and reporting on testing to the extent that they would like. Frequently (and wrongly) bugs are seen as the only output that is required from testing, with other types of test reporting dropped entirely. Recycling the test analysis document allows QA analysts to avoid this bad habit by reducing the amount of work needed to provide important tracking and reporting.

4.4   Test input reduction

One of the first tasks during test analysis is to decide which inputs you want to include in your testing. Including every possible input would provide comprehensive testing but would likely take too long (and bore the testers to death executing each test). However, too few inputs wouldn't provide adequate test coverage. The topics and techniques in this section will let you understand how to plan tests efficiently by only testing the most important inputs. It includes several different techniques that mainly cover numerical test inputs; but when thinking about how the topics apply to your own project, you should consider the wider goal of reducing the test inputs down to an efficient set.

4.4.1 Equivalence partitioning

Equivalence partitioning is one of the most broadly applicable techniques, in the sense that it can be applied easily to every feature that comes through testing. It's also one of the first techniques listed in software testing academia, making it a good place for us to start.

The purpose of this technique is to reduce the number of tests that need to be run by grouping any inputs that are identified as being equivalent.

Essentially, it's a technique to improve efficiency by removing redundant tests. Many game QA analysts might be doing this for some of their testing already without realising it – but doing it unconsciously creates an inconsistent application of the technique, limiting its effectiveness to just the obvious cases. In this section, I'll give a classic software example using numerical inputs, then I'll go into some game project applications that use numerical inputs, as well as some that don't. The real power of this technique lies in the ability to apply it to the wider set of game features that are not numerical and to take a more holistic view of test input reduction.

Software testing example

Imagine you need to test a flow where the user enters their date of birth so that the application can calculate the user's age. Do you input every single possible date of birth into the application to test the logic? No, that would take you a huge amount of time and wouldn't be effective. So, how many date of birth values should you try?

Let's imagine the application needs to know the user's age to figure out if they are over eighteen. In this case you might test a date of birth that is under eighteen and one that is over eighteen – so two tests. But how have we reduced the huge number of possible ages down to two test inputs? In this scenario, we consider all ages below eighteen to be *equivalent* and so we don't test them all – they will all follow the same code flow and produce the same output, and we've calculated that all ages over eighteen are also equivalent. This is the basic principle of equivalence partitioning, identifying partitions of equivalent test inputs where testing one input in that partition will provide test confidence for the entire partition.

For numerical test inputs, it's normal to see equivalent partitions represented in a visual format. Here's an example using our simplified date of birth test input for determining if the user is over eighteen. Note that this is purely a visual guide as I introduce this technique, I've never drawn this out during my actual work. Furthermore, this only really applies if we're looking at numerical inputs in a sequence.

Figure 4.6

You'll notice that I've included limits of 1 and 150 to the scale. I've made some assumptions here about the oldest valid age that someone can be, as well as the valid date of births that the software actually accepts. Let's assume we've spoken to the feature developer or looked at the code directly to confirm this.

The two equivalent partitions identified so far are both valid test input partitions, but what about invalid test inputs? Failure tests, essentially. Let's assume that in this theoretical scenario, if a date of birth entry calculates the user's age as zero or below, an error is displayed. The software also produces an error for ages over 150. Using this information, we can include additional partitions onto the scale which identify invalid test inputs.

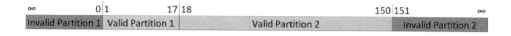

Figure 4.7

In the same way that valid ages between 1 and 17 would all produce the same positive output, any invalid ages of zero and below would produce the same error output. There *is* value in testing these invalid inputs, but we can apply the same rules of equivalence to reduce the number of inputs that we test. For example, inputting a date of birth which gives an age of negative 10 is the same as inputting a date of birth which gives an age of negative 1000, since they both belong to the same partition.

Before moving on to some game project examples, I want to emphasise that the partition boundaries are identified through inspecting how the software actually handles the test input. This requires at least a grey-box understanding of the underlying logic of the feature and, in most cases, will require the QA analyst to speak with the feature developer. Equivalent partitions shouldn't be guessed or assumed. They need to be driven by logic.

Game examples using numerical inputs

There is a broad set of obvious numerical examples which can be seen within game projects and applied directly to test analysis. Nearly every game that exists uses numerical data structures to control the game balance, progression and player profile.

Consider a basic levelling system that uses two numerical counters – experience and level – to track player progress. Players gain experience and, when they have enough, they go up to the next level and the experience counter is reset to zero. If you were to test a new feature that unlocked immediately for high level players only (e.g. levels 30 and over), would you test *all* existing player levels? Would you test *all* experience values between levels? Probably not. You would have to understand how the logic of the feature unlocking worked, but it's likely that two valid partitions of player levels would exist (>=30 and <30).

We had this exact example on our last mobile project. Characters within the game had levels that went up to 60 and they would unlock item and skill slots at certain level milestones. There were up to six slots you could unlock for skills and six slots for items. This was actually the maximum unlock potential and only available for the highest rarity characters (five star rarity). Characters of lower rarity (one star to four star) were capped at lower levels with fewer slots for both skills and items.

Here's a visual guide for these level partitions. We didn't use this for testing, but it helps illustrate the large number of possible inputs.

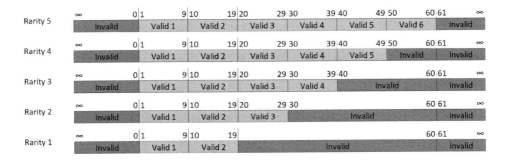

Figure 4.8 – The possible levels for characters of each rarity. Rarity 5 characters could level up to 60, whereas rarity 1 characters were capped to 19.

Throughout the project, we had a lot of regression tests for features using these characters, and their level nearly always had some influence on the logic on the feature. The level would be used to calculate army strength, which would then be used to find quick matches against equal strength opponents. You could also fuse the characters together which would level up one of them, consuming the others. This fusion provided a greater output the higher the level of the fused characters. In addition to this, many areas of the game UI would display stats, unlock states and character progress based on this same data. The frequent choice was, "Do we need to test all character levels for this feature or can we just choose a sample of levels?". Additionally, we would need to ask, "Are all rarities equivalent or do they each need to be tested?". With up to 60 levels, duplicated out across five rarities, the potential test input was substantial, making equivalence partitioning and test input reduction a common theme in this test area.

I will add here that testing a character at a specific level involved a great deal of manual work to spawn the character and then level it up, even with the use of assisted debug controls. Frequently, setting up test inputs during game testing isn't as simple as just inputting the values, so reducing the test inputs is even more essential to efficient testing. Many software examples of this technique focus on inputting values directly into fields, like inputting a font size into your word processor. Such trivial examples are rarely seen within game testing and make the translation of those techniques into the gaming space difficult.

You may also notice that for rarities one to four, I haven't merged the invalid partitions together. This is because the game would perform an initial check on all characters to make sure they weren't over level sixty (if they were, this usually indicated a player was cheating and had hacked their account!) and then further into the feature specific code it would perform other checks on the level. Because the game was handling these invalid inputs at different times, they would produce different outputs and so were not considered to be equivalent.

As I said earlier, equivalent test inputs are entirely contextual based on the feature under test. So, for some features, a rarity one character at level eight would be equivalent to a rarity five character at level eight, because the feature wasn't considering the rarity value in the logic. In this scenario, all of the rarities belonged to the same equivalence partition, meaning that we could run the test with just one rarity and be confident that if one worked, they would all work.

Rarity 1	Rarity 2	Rarity 3	Rarity 4	Rarity 5
Valid				

Figure 4.9 – All rarities were considered equivalent for some game features

Conversely, some features would only be available for rarity five characters. They could equip special items that were locked for lower rarities. For these features, rarities one to four were part of the same invalid partition, and rarity five was in its own valid partition. This meant that we didn't need to test each lower rarity value as an invalid input; we could just test that one could not equip the locked 'rarity five' items and be confident this would apply to all invalid rarities.

Rarity 1	Rarity 2	Rarity 3	Rarity 4	Rarity 5
Invalid				Valid

Figure 4.10 – Weapons locked to rarity 5 had different equivalence due to the rarity-specific logic

Let's move on to some other common game project examples of equivalence partitioning using numerical inputs.

Game design data is frequently separated from the compiled and packaged game code so that it can be temporarily or permanently modified without releasing an update to the game. This data is responsible for defining a huge number of values which are read across different areas of the game code, a majority of which are numerical values. It will define attributes for things like objects in the game (vehicles, enemies, units, levels, weapons, etc.); balancing and difficulty modifiers (damage modifiers, weighted values, quantity of opponents, scarcity of ammo, etc.); and player-facing settings (screen resolution, brightness, language), amongst a range of more bespoke data values. When new features are implemented in code, the developer will write the logic for the feature in code and connect the variable in the logic to the relevant key in the data file, usually putting in a placeholder value which will be later replaced by a designer entering the actual production game value.

These systems present a challenge for testers: they need to approach testing with an understanding that the value might be changed by the design team at a later date. So instead of testing the single value that has been entered, the tester needs to identify the larger scope of valid values that *could* be entered and test the whole range.

As a theoretical example, a weapon damage buff is added to the game. The value is added as a 'double' data type and defaults to 0.0 which is equivalent to 0% additional damage. If the value is changed to 1.0, this is equivalent to 100% additional damage, if it is changed to -1.0 this is equivalent to 100% less damage. In this example, you would want to clarify with the developer what the boundaries of the value are and whether it supports negative values at all. It's possible that a separate parameter has been added to act as a debuff and the system has been designed to allow multiple buffs and debuffs to be applied simultaneously.

I've seen examples of this scenario in projects where the default value has been tested, but the parameter was modified at a later time to an unexpected value and caused bugs.

But what about equivalence partitioning? In the best scenarios, testers are given (or request) direct access to the data so that they can identify and test the full range of possible inputs for each data parameter.

This can be done through debug controls, through modifying the data files directly or through game tools. Once the range has been identified, the QA analyst can go about identifying equivalent inputs for the parameter. In the damage buff example I gave, testing every possible input would be not just time consuming, but impossible, because of the infinite number of decimal values (0.1, 0.11, 0.111, etc.) Instead, the QA analyst would identify what the valid values are and test each partition.

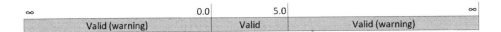

Figure 4.11 – Partitions for a damage buff multiplier, 0 to 500%

In this scenario, it's likely that limits will be hard coded in for the value, capping the buff at a maximum and minimum value. Another common option would be to just allow the value to be anything, but to trigger a log or warning message if an unexpected value has been used, for example if the buff was originally designed to operate between 0 and 500%, then trigger a warning if a negative value is used or if a value over 500% is used.

There are many, many values in games which follow this pattern. They can be presented as static numerical values, but are implemented as sliding values between two limits. Many junior QA analysts don't dig deep enough into a feature to know that the value is configurable, and so are happy testing just the initial game value.

This is great from a test reduction point of view because only one value is tested, but provides inadequate test coverage of the feature logic. More experienced QA analysts will want to understand the limitations of the value and if it's likely to change in the future. Only after some investigation to uncover the full scope of the parameter will the QA analyst be presented with the problem of testing the range of inputs, and be able to apply equivalence partitioning to reduce the test inputs back down to a manageable number.

Industry tales: Configurable values

On the subject of configurable values within games, I think the most common bugs that actually occur from these values changing are within the UI. More often than not, I've seen that the code handles the full range of values well. The sizes of UI components however, don't always accommodate the full range of values that can be displayed within them. I've seen quite a few single-digit values which display fine in their default value but bleed out of their UI container once they reach a double digit value.

On a previous project, we had multiplier values which would display in the format, 'x1.5'. The base game at the time this UI was introduced didn't have any combination of items that could trigger a high enough multiplier to push it over 'x10.0', but later we found that certain high level items would provide enough of a bonus to push the multiplier value into double digits and cause it to extend beyond the UI container it was in. We discovered this was only possible when equipping a specific combination of items to certain characters and causing the multiplier to stack up.

I've had a lot of success finding bugs when considering UI during equivalence partitioning. Two values might be treated as equivalent by the code logic, but will display differently in the UI and so I split them out into different partitions. A good question to consider is, 'Are the maximum and minimum values supported by the code also equally supported by the UI where they will be displayed?' The same is true for extremely large values. Data types defined in the game code will handle values far larger than the game will ever need, while the UI is designed to accommodate a much lower maximum value.

My advice here is to include the visual test of values together with the logical tests and consider both during your equivalence partitioning. You will find that you will want to test values that are logically equivalent, but not visually equivalent.

Further game examples and non-numerical inputs

Lots of 'under the hood' non-player facing numerical inputs exist in games, they just require us to understand more about how the game is built before we can identify them correctly. Game world coordinates is an easy to understand example: moving a character around a world is translating the player input into a numerical format of the character position coordinates. E.g. x:25, y:25, z:50 to x:50, y: 50, z:50. Depending on the context of the game world, these two coordinates could be equivalent and so they don't both need to be tested.

This is why we wouldn't run a test that moves the character to every coordinate on the map. It would be a waste of time and many of those inputs would be equivalent, producing the same output. However, some coordinates could have unique attributes that cause the test output to change. On a car racing game for example, the ground might be assigned different surface types which change the game behaviour (tarmac, grass, sand, loose gravel, etc.). If you were to run a test against each surface type, you'd essentially be taking all of the available position coordinates within the game world and grouping them into equivalent partitions where you expect each partition to behave differently.

This example sounds strange because we've broken the mould slightly by not applying the technique to a sequential range of inputs (the inputs are not in order). The partitions are now seen in three dimensional space and wouldn't make much sense in the visual format that I showed earlier. They are still numerical inputs, we just don't bother to label them as such because there are easier ways to display partitions like this.

Thinking about this scenario in terms of which coordinates are equivalent allows us to understand why you wouldn't test every coordinate on the map and forces us to begin considering how you might break up a huge game world into equivalent parts. We want to find a scenario where we can say, "If one of these things is true, then we can conclude that they are all true." This allows us to perform one test and have confidence in the entire set. If I perform a test to check increased braking distance on a patch of grass within the game, can I deduce that *all* patches of grass will produce the same output or do I need to test each individually?

Let's continue with the theoretical example of the game environment for a moment. Many game worlds are built up by reusing assets from a more limited palette that the team have created. A forest is made by placing copies of the same few tree and bush assets. A town is created by placing copies of the same few building assets. A smart test approach to testing tree collision would be to recognise that the forest is built by reusing the same assets and deduce that by testing a source asset once, you could have confidence that the same test applied to *all* copies where that tree was used. Put another way, you wouldn't need to test the collision of every tree in the forest, you could just test each type of tree once and calculate the rest as equivalent.

This is the first example I've covered where we are moving away from equivalence partitioning of numerical inputs and have started to identify equivalent groups in other types of tests where they might be less obvious. I said earlier that part of the difficulty of this technique is identifying equivalence outside of the trivial numerical examples. The following game project examples are intended to give you more ideas about test input reduction outside of numerical inputs, giving you the best possible chance of applying it within your own projects.

I recently carried out test planning for a large localisation change that was made to our game. Hundreds of the strings for a particular language had been swapped out for slightly reworded versions. They weren't new strings, they were straight replacements. Nearly all game projects I've worked on have set up a localisation spreadsheet which contains all of the game translations and where the game code has no hardcoded text, instead picking the text from the localisation file when it is launched. This means that if no new strings are being added, the localisations in the sheet can be updated without changing a single line of code.

The question was, did I need to verify every single localisation change or could I test a subset of them? There were hundreds. Finding them all within the game to check them would have taken days of the test time. Instead, I grouped the changed strings by game area: strings for items, strings for characters, strings for UI elements and popups, etc. We were able to verify a few of the new translations for each game area and get confidence in the entire set, hugely reducing the test effort. I had confirmed that this approach would be sufficient with the rest of the feature team to confirm the game was handling these in the way that I expected.

Another common use case, which applies to many different game projects, is the use of test input reduction when choosing hardware configurations to test on. The mobile projects I've worked on support a vast array of mobile devices across the different popular operating systems. Android OS, in particular, is available on a huge number of devices. As with the other scenarios above, testing every supported device wouldn't present a good return on the investment of test time. Instead, most test teams use industry benchmarks to rank devices by their relative performance and group them into low, medium and high performance groups. This is simple to do using public information about each device's performance. By grouping them like this, you can test one device belonging to the high performance group and assume that all devices of that group would perform in a similar way. We use this technique on our current project.

On a past project, the game had system-level code which detected the hardware that it was running on and automatically tuned the game's graphical settings to optimise the game for that device. We were able to use the same classifications the code was using to choose our own equivalent testing groups of devices. This was actually a mobile project again, which isn't too common. But this kind of hardware categorisation logic is very common with games running on Windows and Mac.

Other equivalent partitions we identified for hardware devices included grouping devices by the type of texture compression that they used. We had a project that supported four different types of texture compression for Android devices (ETC, ATC, PVRTC, DXTC). In this scenario, in addition to grouping the devices by relative performance, we also grouped them by the texture compression they used. Each type had a separate expansion file (Android .OBB file type) that was created alongside the main build file (Android .apk file type), so they were using a completely separate set of assets. In this scenario, when running graphical regression tests, we knew to group the devices by the texture compression that we used and just test one device from each group.

Industry tales: When separate platforms become equivalent

In nearly all cases, testing on one platform is not considered equivalent to running the same test on another platform. This is because there are parts of the game that react uniquely to the platform, causing bugs on one that are not seen on the other. In addition to this, there are platform-specific features which only function correctly on the platform for which they are intended (e.g. achievements, notifications, payments, etc.). This is enough to cause testing to either be entirely duplicated out across supported platforms, or to at least ensure all testing is split evenly across them.

One of the projects I've worked on had chosen the former and were duplicating out all of their testing between iOS and Android, doubling the test effort required for each test task. It was a high profile project, so I understood the need to be thorough with the testing. We couldn't afford to have high severity bugs escaping into the live game. This approach was being taken both for new features and live events that were being created in data and deployed to the live game every two weeks or so. However, when we reviewed the historical bugs for the project, very few were platform-specific, and none of those were event bugs. So, we had over a year's worth of live event bug data suggesting that we were spending a lot of time duplicating tests for each event that wasn't required.

This showed the importance of not applying equivalence partitioning on a broad basis, as in our case, across the entire project. We had many features where it was still important to consider the platforms separately, but that wasn't the case for the live event testing. We couldn't have reached the same conclusion at the start of the project without that supporting data, but with it we were able to redefine our equivalence partitions for event testing, making testing more efficient.

I wrote earlier in this book about testing for the sake of testing. In this scenario, it was easy to include tests for both platforms even though they weren't required. The effort to duplicate the tasks was minimal, and testers were still able to execute the event testing on schedule with their team of four.

So, you might think, if you had the time, why not just test both? Such decisions are a frequent occurrence for QA analysts and managers. The consequences of the decision aren't immediately apparent, but testing time spent unnecessarily is time that can't be spent on some other test activity. In our case, we had the option to divert or reduce the number of testers involved in testing live events, which would have a positive influence on our test budget. Just testing both platforms would have been an easy approach, but this was useful to highlight the importance of using our testing time efficiently.

4.4.2 Boundary value analysis

This technique is commonly listed in software testing books alongside equivalence partitioning because they share similar attributes. It's also applicable to many features that appear during game development, if testers know where to look!

Its purpose is to identify 'interesting' test inputs around boundaries: inputs that are the most likely to find bugs. By focusing on testing the interesting inputs out of the total scope, we could also say that it contributes to test input reduction.

During this section I'll help define what we mean by boundaries and why values around these boundaries are of interest to us. As before, I will go through a basic software example before moving onto some game project examples that I've come across in past projects. Like the previous technique, the difficult part of applying this in your work will be identifying the boundaries for each feature, so I'll be providing a selection of examples to give you more ideas.

Software testing example

Let's take the same example of entering your date of birth so that an application can calculate your age and deduce whether you are over 18.

The input boundaries can be found at the edges of the equivalent partitions we identified. There are three logical boundaries in this example. These are almost always where we expect the behaviour of the application to change.

There is a boundary between the age of 17 and 18, where 17 is the last possible value that categorises the user as 'under age'. The next value, 18 – causes the application to follow different logic. These two inputs are interesting to us for this reason: they identify where we expect the application to behave differently. The boundary values we would use as test inputs are the date of births that would give ages 17 and 18 (depending on what the current date is). The other boundaries in this example are situated around 0 and 150, and represent the boundaries of valid ages that can be input into the application. We can apply the same logic to these, where the boundary values would be 0, 1, 150 and 151 respectively.*

To increase the precision of these boundary values we can look at the actual day the user was born instead of just the year. The two boundary values for the 'under 18' boundary would be a date of birth where the user turned 18 today and one where the user is 17, but will turn 18 tomorrow (they are only one day short of the boundary). How close you are able to get to the boundary will depend on the data types being used within the application. Date of birth will use a 'date' data type, where the precision is to the nearest day. If the application were to ask the user to input their age directly and store it as an integer (a whole number), then the boundary values could only be as precise as the nearest whole number. Likewise, a data value which supports decimal places would support boundary values more precisely.

0|1   17|18   150|151

Figure 4.12

---

*   I've made a mistake in this example, did you spot what it was? It is valid to have an age of zero. This would just represent a date of birth where a person has not had their first birthday yet. If this was a real application, an age of -1 would be invalid, but 0 and 1 would be valid. Since this is a fictional example, it doesn't matter too much for us. Remember that the identified boundaries are contextual based on the data types and logic of the application under test and so vary from application to application.

In some scenarios, three boundary values are chosen; the value before the boundary, the boundary itself and the value after the boundary. In the example of the 'under 18' boundary, these would be 17, 18 and 19. I'd recommend this is chosen depending on the context of the feature you are testing. Data structures and logical operators used within code often create 'off by one' type bugs where the maximum limit of a list or logical boundary could be incorrect by one value. So it makes sense to test one value on either side of the boundary. In many test scenarios, adding this into your test doesn't require much additional effort, so you might decide that it's worth it anyway.

In this example, the numerical value is being directly input by the user, but this isn't always the case. Frequently, boundaries will need to be tested by setting up the test input data indirectly to reach the boundary. Boundaries also come in many formats; the maximum allowed length of a text string, the minimum allowed limit of a list, the minimum supported software version. Dynamic data structures like lists are a common target for boundary value analysis because they're populated during the runtime of the application and so there's a greater chance the user could do something the application wasn't expecting, like emptying the list or filling it over it's maximum intended capacity. The dynamic data structure (whether it's a list or something else) could be storing anything: integers, strings, complex data types or even further data structures.

Frequently, the boundaries are also configurable and not hardcoded into the application, making identifying and testing them even harder. For all these reasons, QA analysts will need to speak to the feature code engineers on their project to understand how the logic of the application works and where the boundaries are being populated from. This is another area where a grey- or white-box understanding of the application greatly benefits test effectiveness. The more QA analysts and testers understand how the game components work 'under the hood', the more likely they are to be able to identify boundary values for testing.

Game project examples

The most common target for boundary values I've used within my projects is the use of lists. There are many areas where lists are used within all types of game projects and they're nearly always populated through player actions, meaning the player is able to manipulate each list at runtime.

Consider all the information that makes up the player profile for a game: lists of weapons and items, customisations, user generated content like game replays and skins, skill lists, modifier lists, progression counting lists, characters, vehicles, collections of unlockables like stickers. Players can have multiple save files and customised character templates within those save files. Game UI is also littered with lists of options, items, content and packs. All of these lists and similar data structures have minimum and maximum designed values, they might have default values, they might have values at which they trigger different game logic and they're all controllable by the player at runtime. Because of the dynamic nature of how the game data is populated, many bugs are found at the boundaries of lists.

However, unlike the software example I gave where the input values were on a sequential scale (input date of birth values were in date order), the data within these lists isn't always in a specific order. Instead, many of the boundary bugs that I see are less to do with the data and more related to the population of the list or other data structure.

Testers don't need to test every single increment when populating a list, but would do well instead to identify interesting increments that trigger unique logic. There are a lot of these interesting values that might not be specified in design documentation either, requiring an exploratory approach to identify them.

Below I'll give some examples of bugs within game UI and navigation which is dynamically updated based on the data that populates it. This is particularly prevalent when games create their own unique UI elements, instead of using standard off-the-shelf controls which provide a more stable experience in other software.

Other areas with boundary value bugs are in scenarios closer to the software example I gave. When a single value meets some criteria, then logic is triggered within the game. This is quite common for any value used to track the player's progression through the game. Many modern games are complex enough that they track a number of different values to track player progress. I'll give some examples below of both types of boundary bugs that I've seen.

User-generated content

Many games allow the player to create their own content within the game and even share it or sell it to other players. I worked on a few projects for the Xbox where players could record and edit snippets of gameplay, as well as take screenshots to share with other players. These recordings had separate size and length limits, as well as having a limit for the total amount of game cloud storage they were able to use. In addition to this, there was a "low storage" warning when the player was within 10% of their storage limit.

For this project, having an empty clip list was an 'interesting' boundary value because the UI would display a different message about how to capture game clips instead of displaying the clip list for the player. Similarly, there were other areas of the game, like sharing video clips, which would behave differently if you had no clips to share.

We also tested boundary values around the 10% storage warning and the maximum storage limit. The interesting range came when you were near, but hadn't yet exceeded, the storage limit. The game would actually allow you to upload the final clip even if it pushed you over the limit, since the game didn't know how large the final video clip would be and if it would fit within the remaining storage quota that the player had.

As well as testing the actual logic around these boundaries, we were also interested in how the game UI and messaging communicated and represented this information to the player. It would have been a very poor user experience to reach the end of the clip editing process only to be told that it couldn't be saved because there was no storage quota left. The point is, we found a bunch of bugs around these interesting values for clip file size and clip storage. It wouldn't have been useful to test the cloud storage being filled at 10% and then again at 20%, and then again at 30%, or 35%. These values were simply not *interesting* to us because they all behaved in the same way and were very unlikely to yield unique bugs.

User Interface boundary values

A later racing project I worked on had car customisations and liveries that the player could create and sell for in-game currency to other players, as well as an in-game auction house. These pieces of user-generated content were subject to the same types of boundaries: empty lists, full lists and other interesting values in between.

We saw some of these when each list became long enough to require a scrollbar because it didn't fit within the UI panel. In most cases, the content list should have become automatically scrollable, but we still found a few UI bugs around this boundary. I've seen bugs in this same scenario when the UI panel uses pagination instead of scrolling. This style of UI panel usually has navigation buttons (next page/previous page) that only appear once there is more content than can be displayed on a single page.

So, populating the list with two or three items isn't interesting, but reaching the limit for a page which causes a new page to be created and navigation buttons to be visible definitely is. Bugs I've seen around these types of lists include a new page appearing one item too early so that the first page is full and the second page is empty; populating a list with enough content to create multiple pages and then deleting the content again, causing the additional pages to remain visible and empty; and scrolling and pagination bugs on different screen ratios because the screen supports a different number of items per page which causes the boundary to move.

Progression and unlocks

Many numerical boundaries are tested within games without formally identifying them as boundaries. The game logic needs a way to track the player's progress through the game and this is frequently done through numerical parameters. Once the player's profile satisfies some criteria, it triggers a game event to unlock something or progress them further into the game. This might be as direct as reaching a threshold of experience points or it might be satisfying multiple different thresholds, like getting a number of kills within a time limit in a first-person shooter. Many testers might focus their testing around verifying the unlock functionality and not spend too long looking at the actual values that trigger the change in logic (i.e. the designs say that the unlock occurs, so testing focuses on following what the designs specify). It's tempting to be content that the event triggers once the conditions are satisfied, however, good bugs can be found by testing the boundary values around the progression unlocks.

I've found bugs for features where the player needs to claim or purchase an unlock after they've met the criteria. So, they make progress and unlock an option, but then need to perform an additional step to claim the unlock.

Consider a buggy scenario where the player has more resources than are required for the unlock and the excess resource is lost after the purchase. Some games have players 'spend' their experience to level up or purchase nodes on a skill tree to level up. In these scenarios, having the exact amount of resources might work fine, but having resources beyond the required limit may cause the excess to be wrongly lost. Conversely, having too few resources and attempting the action should display some messaging or UI to show the player why they aren't able to claim the unlock.

Game environment boundaries

As equivalence partitions can be found within the game environment, the same can be said for boundary values.

All game environments will have boundaries, regardless of whether it's a 2D or 3D environment. The most obvious boundaries can be found at the edges of collision meshes, which represent solid surfaces that the player can collide with. Teams testing game environments will perform tests along collision mesh boundaries looking for areas where they might fit through gaps, falling through the floor or inside objects.

Gameplay logic is frequently orientated around map locations and areas too. Consider a 3D multiplayer game where you have to capture and hold an area of the map. That area might be a custom map shape or a set radius around a map coordinate, forming a circle. Either way, it will have game logic that triggers when the player is inside that zone, activating the 'capturing' state; and different logic which triggers when the player is outside that zone.

The software example I gave earlier was a single value on a one dimensional scale; this is the same application but applied to a three dimensional shape and the input values are player coordinates. A mediocre test might verify that the 'capturing' logic is active when you are inside the zone and deactivated when you exit the zone. A better test would probe areas of the map along the boundary. Maybe it intersects a piece of badly placed scenery, or another nearby capture zone which was designed to be separate; perhaps it extends into a building and allows players to activate the logic from a position that would circumvent the level design. Because the test is operating in a 3D space, there is a range of boundaries instead of just one value, so we would be extending the boundary theory of 'before, on and after' to apply across the full range of the 3D boundary.

This last example is stretching the original intent of this technique quite a bit. However, I would actually encourage this in your own work. These techniques need to evolve and be customised to solve the unique test challenges that testers face within games. If QA analysts and testers approach these scenarios by thinking of them as logical boundaries that have values before, on and after the boundary, then they are going to be better equipped to remember to test these values during their work.

This applies to testers performing exploratory testing as well as QA analysts writing tests. The 'boundary value' mindset is more important than trying to apply the base technique too rigidly to your test planning. If you find yourself remembering the technique and applying your own version of it, then that's a win, as is remembering to consider interesting values at boundaries and incorporating that into your test planning in other ways.

Finally, boundary logic is commonly presented to the test team through documentation, so we get that basic information 'for free' and can include it in our test plans without much thought (e.g. races unlock at level 13). However, these test analysis techniques are helping us identify *what* should be tested, which helps us remember that we should be defining that ourselves and not just copying whatever information was given to us.

Only confirming the logic given is a lazy and insufficient test approach. Boundary value analysis provides a tool to help us generate ideas for additional tests and should be used to test beyond the basic information provided. Don't get caught out by taking designs at face value and neglecting the generation of ideas for additional tests!

4.4.3 Code explanation and caveats

Before moving on from this section on test input reduction, I want to briefly provide some insight into the underlying logic of boundaries, the equivalence partitions between them and the reason that testing is able to reduce test inputs without compromising on test confidence.

I'm going to give some examples of common code operators, so if you're already familiar with basic code logic, then you can skip this section. I'll finish with an example where some code logic doesn't lend itself to these input reduction techniques. In the real world, QA analysts will be able to speak to feature developers to understand the rules of equivalence for a feature rather than looking through the code directly.

However, as I've described previously, it's very helpful to build an understanding of this stuff.

Let's consider a trivial example of a feature which follows different logic if a whole number input is 5 or over. All code uses a selection of 'operators', with a very common one being the 'if' statement. You use it if you want to run some code only when the statement is true and you can use mathematical expressions to define that statement. The following pseudo code runs some other code if the value of the variable 'input' is 5 or more (note: This is also equivalent to just being larger than four. >=5 is the same as >4)

```
IF input >= 5
     Run some code when this is true
```

Note the use of the 'is equal to or greater than' expression. Just like in mathematics, this operator doesn't differentiate between input values six and seven; they're both greater than four and are treated the same. Now consider the following pseudo code.

```
SWITCH input
     input = 1,2,3 or 4
              Run some code
     input = 5
              Run some other code
     input = 6,8,9 or 10
              Run some different code
     input is anything else
              Do nothing
```

This pseudo code takes the 'input' variable and then runs different code depending on what its value is, but it uses a different logical operator: the switch statement. This code could be trying to achieve the same final result as the previous code. It's performing some logic for all values below 5 and different logic for all values above 5, but it's structured in a different way and has defined more special cases. 5 is a special case because it's handled separately. This logic defines an upper bound of 10 for the input; anything over 10 and the code does nothing.

More importantly, with this method, each possible value of 'input' has to be explicitly added to the code, meaning that each individual value should be included in testing and you could *not* say that testing inputs 6 and 7 are equivalent. Indeed, in this example I've intentionally forgotten to include 7 in the pseudo code to show that testing 6 would show the correct result, but testing 7 would produce a bug, because it was missed during implementation.

This shows how the logical flow of the game code can lend itself to test input reduction, and when it doesn't. In some scenarios, you will still need to test each and every input. The lesson is not to blindly apply these techniques to all test plans, but to correctly assess the needs of testing through finding concrete information about how the game actually handles the inputs.

If this was a bit technical for you, don't worry. QA analysts will never be looking through code themselves to make these conclusions. Instead they would speak to the creators of each feature, share their test plans and discuss what test inputs are relevant. I get good responses from asking questions like, "Does the feature differentiate between these inputs?", "Is this feature platform agnostic?", "Are there any specific inputs which you think we should test?", "I've chosen to just test a sample of these inputs, what are your thoughts on that?". As ever, effective test input reduction relies on a good relationship with the feature creators that you're working with and an ability to have technical conversations with them.

4.5 Combinatorial test techniques

Combinatorial test techniques focus on tracking and organising tests when there are multiple different test inputs that combine together to form a larger matrix of test combinations. For example, testing against Mac and Windows would be two configurations which would be multiplied out to four combinations if you wanted to include tests for both Firefox and Chrome across both Mac and Windows.

Browsers		Operating Systems	
		Windows	Mac
	Chrome		
	Firefox		

Figure 4.13 – A simple test matrix of two operating systems and two browsers

Because test inputs multiply when they are combined, the resulting test matrix grows very quickly. Adding one more browser to this setup (Safari), adds two combinations to the resulting matrix. Adding a further additional operating system (Linux), adds three more combinations the resulting matrix, bringing the total to nine. This growth trend continues exponentially with each additional input configuration that is added.

		Operating Systems		
		Windows	Mac	Linux
	Chrome			
Browsers	Firefox			
	Safari			

Figure 4.14 – A simple test matrix of three operating systems and three browsers

In this basic example, we only have two lists of input configuration: operating systems and browsers. Adding additional lists, like versions, into the mix very quickly creates huge combinatorial explosions of tests. If the test coverage includes an additional list with just two values, the number of potential configurations doubles.

Game client v1.0						Game client v2.0				
		Operating Systems						Operating Systems		
		Windows	Mac	Linux				Windows	Mac	Linux
	Chrome						Chrome			
Browsers	Firefox					Browsers	Firefox			
	Safari						Safari			

Figure 4.15 – A simple test matrix of operating systems, browsers and game client versions

The techniques in this section help us identify, organise and prioritise these test combinations so that testing stays effective and efficient without getting bogged down. Testing large combinations of inputs is a common occurrence within nearly all game projects, making this section one of the more widely applicable topics in this book.

Games share the normal environment combinations that are seen in software testing: different operating systems, versions of those operating systems and hardware that they run on. I've worked on projects across console, PC and mobile, and they all need to consider these basic configurations, but all in slightly different ways. (This isn't what I'll focus on in this section, but it's a good way to introduce combination testing.)

Different test environment combinations are easily identified, and the resulting test matrices are relatively small, making any formal techniques superfluous. It's the *gameplay* test combinations that we're most interested in here. Games, by their nature, present a huge number of permanent choices and small options to the player which testing needs to consider. I'll start with the immediate environment combinations before moving onto the more interesting gameplay combinations and the combination test techniques that we can use with them.

Environment combinations

These feature in every project. When planning testing for these combinations, a majority of the test confidence can be gained passively during other testing. The combination test matrix is created at the start of the project (or may exist from previous projects) and the screens, hardware and OS versions are split up across the test team so that each combination is being exercised at any one time.

The idea is that the tester is likely to notice bugs unique to that combination while performing other tests. Where the number of combinations is larger than the test team, devices with different setups will be rotated in and out throughout testing. For these environment combinations, a good test setup will make sure each configuration is being tested individually, while a great test setup will make sure combinations of configurations are being tested and have a way of tracking that test coverage.

- **Screen types (resolutions / aspect ratios):** Every project I've worked on needed to consider the type of display that the game will be shown on. When I started out on Xbox 360 projects we were interested in testing across the more common widescreen screens and the older 4:3 ratio 'square' screens. On modern projects, it's more likely that console and PC games will be tested on standard widescreen ratios (16:9) as well as ultra-widescreen ratios (21:9). This is actually common for mobile games too, with many phones having odd screen ratios. A recent obsession with adding notches and hole-punches into the screen to accommodate the device sensors has increased the need to test against a broader range of individual devices. PC and console games will also be interested in testing different screen resolutions, with 1080p and 4k screen resolutions being the main modern configurations. Scaling bugs are sometimes seen for higher resolutions, while any screens that are not the standard widescreen ratio may see bugs with the game HUD wrapping around the edge of the screen incorrectly. New monitors also offer G-Sync and Freesync proprietary technologies that help eliminate screen tearing specifically when running PC games. These screen types will have to be combined together with different hardware types to make sure not just that each display type works, but also that all combinations of displays and hardware are included during testing. Freesync and G-Sync require the PC to have a supported graphics card from the owning manufacturer to be enabled in the game but, of course, testing would want to include the reverse scenario too (testing the incorrect hardware and screen combinations). With extensive use of visual technologies and custom UI within games, graphical artefacts on different setups are a common occurrence, making this area a high priority for any game project.
- **Hardware setups:** The hardware running the game is the other side of the

combinatorial matrix from the screen type. Mobile games are fortunate here because the screen and the hardware are tied together on the same device, so players have less opportunity to mix and match the two. In this case, you can test each hardware configuration individually without creating a combination matrix with the screen types (it's still required, but to a much lesser extent). On console and PC however, there is a much broader selection of hardware that the game needs to run on, and many games have adaptive graphics settings which are adjusted according to the performance of the hardware, meaning that the game will be visually different across different configurations. Unlike a lot of other software, the relationship between the application (the game) and the hardware is complex and heavily integrated, increasing the priority of testing different hardware setups. This was less of a problem for consoles of previous generations (Xbox 360 and PlayStation 3 era), because their hardware didn't change. But current generations of game consoles have a selection of slim, standard and pro versions which have different insides, increasing the number of supported configurations for console titles. Many game projects release on PlayStation 4 variants, Xbox One variants and PC. Some even release a downgraded version of the game on the previous gen consoles, adding further hardware setups. You can start to imagine how the list of supported hardware grows quickly for these cross-platform projects and explodes out into a large matrix when you multiply it against the different screen types – at the very least doubling that list to cover it on 4k and 1080p resolutions since the latest consoles support both.

Mobile games are more like PCs: the hardware is so varied that test teams need to take a more precise approach. Apple and Android are the major platforms, with Amazon and Microsoft devices occupying smaller platforms. The variation of iOS devices is limited, making testing across all of their devices possible. Android however, runs on devices made by a huge number of manufacturers, creating a list too large to test (and not worth the company money to purchase all the devices). Instead, Android devices are grouped by attributes such as memory limit, processor type, texture compression type and benchmarked performance. My experience is that some of these attributes can be tested individually, but a few of them need to be multiplied out. A common case is multiplying out a certain memory limit (e.g. 1GB devices) with phones and tablets, since tablets sometimes have the same amount of memory, but their other components are higher performance and the screen is different.

- **Operating system versions:** The test consideration for operating system versions is pretty standard and the same as you might expect in any other software. On consoles, we never considered the OS version because it hardly ever changed. When it did change, it was a one-time test effort rather than a consistent consideration throughout the project. Mobile is slightly different because there are a greater number of iOS and Android operating system versions in use at the same time, and also because there are greater differences between each OS version. For platform integration features like push notifications, it's normal to create a combination test matrix of operating system versions against each supported platform.

- **Game client versions:** Testing different versions of the game client is mostly applicable to games which operate as a continuous service and do not require players to update to the latest game version before they can play. In this scenario, players on different versions of the game can play together if the game is multiplayer. Live game events can also be published to different versions of the game. When we run live game events on my current mobile project, the testing covers two game versions and is then multiplied out further if the event requires it. For games that allow multiplayer on different game versions, the client version is another variable you add to the already huge matrix of multiplayer test combinations.

Talking about potential game environment combinations should have helped you understand the full scope of the problem that combinatorial testing presents. Each list of variables needs to be identified and the appropriate variables multiplied together to form the test matrix. Then it needs to be included in the test plan in a way that can be organised and tracked, which gets more difficult the larger the matrix is. As with the other techniques, creating it also relies on correct analysis of the game components and their relationship to the environment – it isn't something that should be guessed.

In my experience, many people don't organise their configurations in a test matrix and instead proceed directly to forming a list from memory that can be input into a tracking sheet or into test cases. While this works fine for small lists, it's likely to mean configurations for anything larger or more complex may be missed. The techniques in this section will look into larger test matrices and how they can be generated using a process, cutting out the need to think-up or remember specific combinations for the list.

Gameplay combinations

Earlier I described each of the techniques in this book as tools in your toolbox, each to be deployed when you face the corresponding problem. When planning feature testing, these combinatorial tools are some that I use the most frequently. Gameplay and configuration choices, which are at the core of so many games, seem to create a breeding ground for complex combination matrices. Consider customer service reports from players who are experiencing issues. The CS agent will have to ask a number of questions to understand more about the player's profile before they can begin to troubleshoot it: what they were doing, how they were doing it, what methods they used and what game settings they enabled. These questions are narrowing down all of the choices the player has made into a single, unique setup where this bug exists.

Trying to unpick and organise a complex system into tests covering each area, that don't overlap and also don't miss areas can be difficult, frustrating and time consuming. In many ways, these techniques help the QA analyst organise chaos. They show you where to begin and how to find a path through, when finding a logical place to begin can be the most difficult part.

I've found these techniques don't just pave the way for test design to take place; they provide a perspective that allows me to understand complex gameplay systems in the first place – an obvious but important prerequisite to effective test planning.

Working through complex systems logically generates ideas and questions I note down and take back to the feature author. I go as far as to say that, even if you don't formally use the combination matrix as the basis for your test design, the thought process it provides generates enough ideas, questions, curiosities and starting points for further investigation to make it worth the investment.

Thinking about testing as a combination of different configurations and options can be really difficult, however. Different gameplay choices can appear as mutually exclusive and it's not always obvious that they might have an impact on each other. This is even more true when features and configurations are presented as separate components to the test team. Unlike the feature authors, testers don't have the insight into the code to see the logical connections that tie them together.

Many game projects (like other software) are also made up of sections of legacy, complex or messy code which can create a web of unseen dependencies between feature components. When this is the case, even the feature authors may not be aware of the impact that one area can have on another. And so, with gameplay combinations, it's up to the QA analyst to discover the connections and fit the target of testing into a combination matrix.

4.5.1 Decision tables

I'm going to kick off these techniques by talking about the use of decision tables for organising battle outcomes in the last mobile project I worked on.

Decision tables allow us to calculate the total number of possible input combinations for a system that we are trying to test, where each unique combination is a test case that we can run.

It's a great example of organising something in a way that generates ideas and questions, and doesn't appear to be a combination test problem when you first approach it. First, I'll give a quick overview of the technique.

Software example

Decision tables are a great way to organise combinations of inputs where each input only has two possible values, most commonly a Boolean type, true or false.

		1	2	3	4	5	6	7	8
1	ID Valid?	N	Y	N	Y	N	Y	N	Y
2	Passport Valid?	N	N	Y	Y	N	N	Y	Y
3	Admin access?	N	N	N	N	Y	Y	Y	Y
	System Access Outcome	N	N	N	N	N	N	N	Y

Figure 4.16 – A basic decision table with three Boolean inputs. The user needs all inputs to be true to get access to the system, which is represented in the final row

A decision table is organised with the inputs down the side and the final row representing the expected logical output for each input combination. With each input only having two possible input values, it allows us to mathematically calculate the total number of possible test combinations. The total number of combinations is calculated as follows.

$$\text{Total outputs} = 2^{\text{Number of test inputs}}$$
$$8 = 2^3$$

Because we have three inputs in this scenario, the number of columns in the table is 8, illustrating each possible combination of inputs. After finding the number of columns for the table, the true/false values for the inputs can be entered, starting with the bottom row and working upwards. These are entered in the same pattern each time. The bottom row is divided down the middle and into two parts; the next row divided into four parts; and so on until you reach the top row. The 'outcome' row or rows is/ are unique to each feature and can be completed according to the expected outcome of each combination. The expected outcome doesn't actually have to be a Boolean type either, you could add any output you like there. In the example above, the user is only allowed access to the system if all of the inputs are true. The remaining seven outputs all deny the user access. If the system design were to change and not require a valid passport, the outcome row would change.

This technique shows all possible *and* impossible outputs of a system, meaning that some of the combinations shown in the table couldn't be tested if the software doesn't allow it. Perhaps the UI takes the user's input individually and shows an error if one value is false, stopping the user before they can input the remaining values. Many times, inputs are 'unlocked' only when other inputs meet a certain criteria. Once the table is filled out, we can identify which combinations are possible and which are impossible. Rather than striking through impossible inputs and forgetting about them, I have a better idea. I just label all of the impossible inputs as negative tests! After all, testing that a feature *doesn't* do something is just as important as testing that it *does* do something. In other words, it provides a reminder that testing should include tests to make sure that the software correctly handles that specific impossible input combination.

Industry tales: Decision table for battle outcomes

My last mobile project was an online real-time strategy battle game for mobile, where players formed alliances of up to 50 players and were presented together in the same world of up to 50 alliances, making a potential total of 2500 players together.

The game allowed them to browse the full world freely and target each other for attacks, at which point they would play a short-form real-time battle game. Since this was part of the core gameplay loop, many new features and changes that we worked on each release would influence and change the battle game, making regression testing of battles a frequent occurrence. We released updates frequently, too: every six to eight weeks, depending on the project phase. Shortly after the hard launch of the game, updates were slower, but a year on, the updates were rolling out regularly and consistently.

Players were represented as castles on floating islands. Around their castles was a series of further resource islands which the player could harvest for game resources. The resource islands were smaller and split into different types – for food, gold and 'victory points'. Each player had just one permanent castle, but could have multiple different and temporary resource islands.

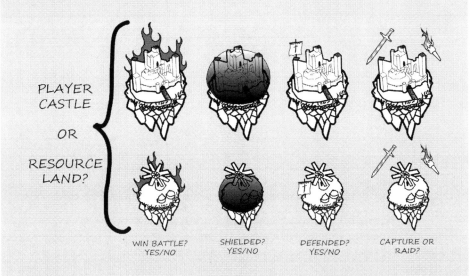

PLAYER
CASTLE

OR

RESOURCE
LAND?

WIN BATTLE?   SHIELDED?   DEFENDED?   CAPTURE OR
YES/NO   YES/NO   YES/NO   RAID?

Figure 4.17 – A visualisation of possible battle outcomes

Players were free to target any opposing player's castle or lands across the entire game world for an attack, with the only limitation being that the attacking player would need an attacking army strong enough to win the battle.

Things began to get interesting when we looked at all of the potential battle outcomes, making sure we tested each one during our regression testing. It started with two options for the attacking player: to capture the land for themselves or to raid it and take the resources it contained, leaving the land itself. The two options had different pre-battle UI to show what you would get from each outcome, as well as the post-battle logic to resolve the resource changes to both player's profiles.

This choice also had a special rule: only the resource islands could be captured, not the enemy player castle. The land could contain an enemy army garrison too – represented by a flag on the land which the attacker would have to defeat to win the battle, making the attack a lot harder.

As well as spawning the enemy army during the battle, these two options would present different pre-battle stats to show the defending unit types and their metadata. Players could also purchase shields for their lands which would block all attacks entirely, and were shown as a blue bubble shield over the land. The shields were a relatively simple flow of just blocking the UI controls which allowed the attack.

Amongst these battle input variables, the result of any battle itself could, of course, be a success or failure. No resources would be taken for failed raids and the land wouldn't have changed ownership for failed captures. On a successful attack, lands were automatically shielded for 24 hours to prevent a player from getting too damaged while they were away from the game.

So, there were many different logical paths for the battle flow and many different actions that had to be taken by the game for each outcome to resolve the battle. It wasn't just a case of winning and losing points. Resources were exchanged between players, additional resources awarded, lands moved, shields activated, the world state updated for other players, UI was updated, defending armies returned to the defender while all attacking armies lost regardless of the outcome.

There were a lot of edge cases, too, like trying to capture a land when your own pool of lands was already at capacity. The capture option was disabled until you increased your limit or made room.

Our regression testing needed to be ready to catch bugs that occurred in any one of these scenarios. Having tests to just check the win and lose flow was not enough. We did originally have tests that looked at win and lose scenarios, and some tests that referenced the capture and raid flows, but they were all separate tests, mainly concerned with checking the flow itself, and didn't reference the battle outcome much.

I noticed that we could organise all of the options into a Boolean format, with the exception that we'd have to split the types of land into just the garrison and the surrounding resource lands. We couldn't expand it out further into the sub-types of resource lands because there were three sub-options there that didn't fit.

	1	2	3	4	5	6	7	8	9	10	11	12	13	14	15	16	17	18	19	20	21	22	23	24	25	26	27	28	29	30	31	32
1 Capture or Raid?	R	C	R	C	R	C	R	C	R	C	R	C	R	C	R	C	R	C	R	C	R	C	R	C	R	C	R	C	R	C	R	C
2 Shielded?	N	N	Y	Y	N	N	Y	Y	N	N	Y	Y	N	N	Y	Y	N	N	Y	Y	N	N	Y	Y	N	N	Y	Y	N	N	Y	Y
3 Defended?	N	N	N	N	Y	Y	Y	Y	N	N	N	N	Y	Y	Y	Y	N	N	N	N	Y	Y	Y	Y	N	N	N	N	Y	Y	Y	Y
4 Garrison or resource land?	R	R	R	R	R	R	R	R	G	G	G	G	G	G	G	G	R	R	R	R	R	R	R	R	G	G	G	G	G	G	G	G
5 Win Battle?	N	N	N	N	N	N	N	N	N	N	N	N	N	N	N	N	Y	Y	Y	Y	Y	Y	Y	Y	Y	Y	Y	Y	Y	Y	Y	Y

Figure 4.18 – A decision table of all possible battle outcomes

With that small concession, we'd be able to create a map using decision tables to see how many possible battle outcomes there were and use it to guide our regression testing. I'd identified five input variables that we could fit into a Boolean format and I put these into a decision table that resulted in 32 unique battle outcomes. I didn't actually bother to add an output row to the table because, as I described, there was quite a lot of different and complex logic which was applied after a battle. It wasn't productive to try and capture that information in a table and I had already achieved what I wanted: a map of all the possible battle outcomes to guide testing.

I called a meeting with all of the QA analysts on our project and also invited the QA analysts on the other studio project if they were interested, creating a group of about seven of us. I knew it wasn't enough for just me to be thinking about our battle regression testing in this way, I'd need to share it with others writing tests for the project and the testers to help guide their exploratory testing. In reality, my ownership was to write test plans for server pod (sub-team) and other more technical test areas, leaving the gameplay and event test plans to the other QA analysts on the project.

A quick side note: like me, you may find yourself with the tools to solve other people's test problems. I can't advocate the use of peer reviews and knowledge sharing meetings strongly enough for exactly this reason. More senior members of the team will also want to evangelise the techniques they want the rest of the team to follow. Getting everyone on board with improvements is essential since no one person can perform all of the test team's work.

The meeting generated some great discussion about the battle game and which of the outcomes in the table we hadn't really been thinking about during our testing so far. After drawing the table up on a whiteboard and proudly illustrating just how many different battle outcomes there could be, there was a brief silence before one of the QA analysts pointed out that many of the outcomes were actually impossible and couldn't be tested at all. After pausing for dramatic effect, I replied and stated that these outcomes weren't impossible at all, they were just negative tests. It was equally as important to test that you couldn't perform an action, like raid a shielded castle, as it was to test that you could perform an action, like raid an unshielded resource land.

On a team where many of the more junior test writers struggled to think up negative tests for their features, this was a great exercise to mathematically and logically discover negative test cases. It gave them solid examples of the types of scenarios they should be including in their test plans.

The table reminded us that many battle outcomes were not equivalent and required separate tests. 'Test that you can't attack a shielded land' wasn't the same as, 'test that you can't attack a shielded castle'. They follow different code paths, so testing one doesn't make the other also true.

Using the shield logic as one example, inspecting some of the columns in the table above shows numerous variations of different tests against shielded targets. There were plenty of opportunities in the complex battle logic to find bugs which were unique to only one of these combinations. Perhaps having a defending army interfered with the logic in some way and only caused bugs when trying to attack any shielded lands which had an army present. Worse yet, maybe this was only true when trying to capture shielded castles when there was an army present. We would never have found such bugs simply by creating a test that 'checked shielded and unshielded lands', or even creating an exploratory test session that 'investigated different battle combinations'. Even the most effective testers on our team wouldn't have been able to organise their exploratory testing in such a logical way as to investigate all of the different combinations.

As with many projects which operate as a continuous service, we were always building on top of this already complex logic. It was only a matter of time before we would need to expand the decision table. Sure enough, a few months later, we added the ability to chain your lands down so that they couldn't be captured by other players. Unlike the shields, the chains were permanent for the resource lands. They only prevented capture, they didn't prevent the land being raided, and because they were used to prevent capture, they weren't available for the castle land. So, here was another Boolean-type input variable to be added into the battle combination matrix (chained and unchained lands) which came with its own unique logic and game visuals.

Another input into the decision table increased our decision table outputs from a reasonable 'we can test all of these with a bit of extra test effort' 32, to a 'this is becoming unfeasible' total of 64. Even if we weren't able to cover all combinations in our testing, the use of the decision table at least allowed us to see the potential scope of what the testing could be, so that we could then make some smart decisions about what was actually feasible and valuable to include in our regression testing each release.

4.5.2 Non-Boolean combination techniques

What happens when you can't organise your inputs into Boolean values? Like the game environment combinations, where each input could have many values and the 'resource islands' in my last example, which had three values. This section will describe some techniques to help you create combination matrices for these more complex input parameters.

For all of the following techniques, I'll be referring to each unique list of values as the 'inputs' and the number of potential values within those lists as 'values'. In the previous section, we had many inputs, but the values were strictly limited to two. For the techniques in this section, the number of values can be anything. When calculating out the resulting matrix, we use the input which has the highest number of values.

INPUTS

Cars	Visual upgrades	Liveries	
2017 Acura NSX	Front bumber	Xbox classic	
1979 Chevrolet Camaro Z28	Spoiler	Retro arcade	VALUES
2005 Ford GT	Bonnet		
	Sideskirts		
	Wheel rims		
	Wheel arches		
	Full body kits		

Figure 4.19 – A sample table showing a list of visual upgrades
and liveries that can be applied to a list of cars

When you increase the number of values in each input beyond two, the matrices also get really large, making exhaustive testing impossible in many cases. Part of the power of these techniques is that they reduce the total combinations down to smaller sets, helping make testing more feasible without lowering test confidence. Once you get comfortable with organising your test inputs and creating combination matrices, the decision of how to actually test such a large test set becomes the next immediate problem. You're effectively having to apply test input reduction to the combination matrix. It's the same thought process we applied in the last section: figuring out how to reduce the total possible tests down to a more feasible and interesting set, without eroding confidence in the testing. These techniques allow you to choose from a minimal test set, an optimised test set and a full test set, which provide convenient choices of incrementing test investment.

Pairwise/all pairs testing

For combination testing up until this point, we've been creating a matrix to capture *every* combination of input: a full set. The all pairs technique, however, picks a minimal test set, greatly reducing the total number of output combinations. You can use tools to generate this minimal test set for you too, which is super helpful and something you would use in practice over trying to manually create a matrix. To use these tools however, you should understand what a 'pair' is in this context and how it relates to larger test sets.

Given the same example above for customisations in a racing game, a full test set multiplies out all values in each of the test inputs.

42 outputs = 3 cars x 7 visual upgrades x 2 liveries

All Triples

	Cars	Visual Upgrades	Liveries
1	1979 Chevrolet Camaro Z28	Bonnet	Retro arcade
2	1979 Chevrolet Camaro Z28	Bonnet	Xbox classic
3	1979 Chevrolet Camaro Z28	Front bumber	Retro arcade
4	1979 Chevrolet Camaro Z28	Front bumber	Xbox classic
5	1979 Chevrolet Camaro Z28	Full body kits	Retro arcade
6	1979 Chevrolet Camaro Z28	Full body kits	Xbox classic
7	1979 Chevrolet Camaro Z28	Sideskirts	Retro arcade
8	1979 Chevrolet Camaro Z28	Sideskirts	Xbox classic
9	1979 Chevrolet Camaro Z28	Spoiler	Retro arcade
10	1979 Chevrolet Camaro Z28	Spoiler	Xbox classic
11	1979 Chevrolet Camaro Z28	Wheel arches	Retro arcade
12	1979 Chevrolet Camaro Z28	Wheel arches	Xbox classic
13	1979 Chevrolet Camaro Z28	Wheel rims	Retro arcade
14	1979 Chevrolet Camaro Z28	Wheel rims	Xbox classic
15	2005 Ford GT	Bonnet	Retro arcade
16	2005 Ford GT	Bonnet	Xbox classic
17	2005 Ford GT	Front bumber	Retro arcade
18	2005 Ford GT	Front bumber	Xbox classic
19	2005 Ford GT	Full body kits	Retro arcade

Figure 4.20 – I've cut this table short for conciseness. The full table follows the same pattern for the other two cars and runs to 42 rows

A quick aside on the topic of calculating all outputs; for the decision tables I used the following formula to calculate the total number of combinations.

$$\text{Total outputs} = 2^{\text{Number of test inputs}}$$

For three inputs, we can expand this out to write it like this.

$$\text{Total outputs} = 2^3$$
$$\text{Total outputs} = 2 \times 2 \times 2$$

This is essentially saying that we can get the total combinations by multiplying together the number of values for each input, and since decision tables limited us to two (true/false) values each, the multiplication is always in twos. However, when we increase the number of values in each input beyond two, this same multiplication rule still applies.

$$\textbf{Total outputs} = \textbf{\# values for input 1} \times \textbf{\# values for input 2} \times \textbf{\# values for input 3}$$
$$\textbf{42 outputs} = \textbf{3 cars} \times \textbf{7 visual upgrades} \times \textbf{2 liveries}$$

This is how we can say that the total complete test set for this racing game example is 42, we've simply multiplied together the number of values for each input.

Notice that a full test set, where three inputs exist, creates a resulting matrix where each output (row) is a unique combination of three values – we call this a triple. In this instance, we've created an all-triples test matrix. You can look through the table and see that it includes all possible triples for the Chevrolet Camaro. At this point you might consider what would happen if there were four, or even five, inputs. Does this still work? Yes. A full test set of four inputs would be an all-quadruples test matrix – unique combinations of four.

All-pairs testing reduces this test matrix down from unique combinations of three, to only unique combinations of two. This means each value (e.g. Chevrolet Camaro) will still be tested in combination with every value from other input columns (e.g. Bonnet), but only in pairs, covering two inputs at a time: cars and visual upgrades, or liveries and visual upgrades, or cars and liveries, but never cars, visual upgrades and liveries together.

This test matrix is an all-pairs matrix generated by a tool. See that each value within the cars column is paired with every value from the visual upgrades column and also separately paired with every value from the liveries column.

All Pairs

	Cars	Visual Upgrades	Liveries
1	1979 Chevrolet Camaro Z28	Bonnet	Xbox classic
2	1979 Chevrolet Camaro Z28	Front bumber	Retro arcade
3	1979 Chevrolet Camaro Z28	Full body kits	Xbox classic
4	1979 Chevrolet Camaro Z28	Sideskirts	Retro arcade
5	1979 Chevrolet Camaro Z28	Spoiler	Retro arcade
6	1979 Chevrolet Camaro Z28	Wheel arches	Retro arcade
7	1979 Chevrolet Camaro Z28	Wheel rims	Xbox classic
8	2005 Ford GT	Bonnet	Retro arcade
9	2005 Ford GT	Front bumber	Xbox classic
10	2005 Ford GT	Full body kits	Retro arcade
11	2005 Ford GT	Sideskirts	Retro arcade
12	2005 Ford GT	Spoiler	Xbox classic
13	2005 Ford GT	Wheel arches	Xbox classic
14	2005 Ford GT	Wheel rims	Xbox classic
15	2017 Acura NSX	Bonnet	Xbox classic
16	2017 Acura NSX	Front bumber	Retro arcade
17	2017 Acura NSX	Full body kits	Xbox classic
18	2017 Acura NSX	Sideskirts	Xbox classic
19	2017 Acura NSX	Spoiler	Xbox classic
20	2017 Acura NSX	Wheel arches	Xbox classic
21	2017 Acura NSX	Wheel rims	Retro arcade

Figure 4.21 – A test matrix for all-pairs coverage. The number of combinations has been reduced from 42 down to 21

To avoid potential confusion, some values in the table are superfluous and are filled in randomly to complete the table. We could mark these values as 'don't care' if we were creating this table manually. If you inspect pairs of values in the table, you'll see this is true for the liveries input column (e.g. the unique pair of 'Bonnet' and 'Xbox classic' is repeated unnecessarily within the table). This is just a consequence of having a different number of values for each input.

Halving the total number of combinations is a pretty big deal when you consider that this is just a trivial example; no racing game I've ever played had as few as three cars! If you load up any (simulation) racing game and navigate through the customisation and tuning menus, you'll see that there are lot more customisation inputs than I've given here; some games allow you to add parts, then apply custom paint to those parts, then apply vinyls and liveries on top of that, in addition to customising a character who appears inside the car. In a full example, an all-pairs matrix would cut down a full test set of hundreds or thousands of unique combinations.

While you could generate the table manually, I'm not going to describe the process because combinatorial testing, by definition, is most helpful for large data sets and doesn't lend itself to being manually created. I use an open-source Microsoft command line tool called PICT, which runs on Windows and takes a text file as input and is able to produce the output test matrix in MS Excel file format – providing a convenient output. However, you can find a big list of available tools at http://pairwise.org/tools.asp or by searching online for 'pairwise' or 'all-pairs' test tools.

The main piece of manual work that you'll need to do is prepare the input lists in the format that the tool requires. While you could write this down, copied from the game at runtime, this is a time consuming and error-prone method. Instead, speak to the design or code teams to get a copy of source data or design documents which provide the data in a more convenient format. I usually see game data created in spreadsheets and then parsed into .JSON or .XML file formats which the game code can read directly from (a good opportunity to try your hand at coding by writing a small script to do it). The spreadsheets that the design team use are the best place to copy this data from, if you can get a copy of the latest files.

Test input reduction example for a car racing game

The theory of using the all-pairs technique to reduce combinations down to a minimal test set is that it's less likely you'll find a bug that only occurs for a unique combination of three or more values; only testing pairs of combinations should, in theory, still catch a majority of bugs that you care about. However, as we know, test input reduction needs to consider the context of how the feature has been created, so we'd need to ask the question, "Does this assumption about bugs apply to the scenario of car customisations for this project?"

You should choose your combinatorial testing techniques according to the depth of test coverage that you require from a technical feature point of view, though I'll concede that I've also had to just base it on the amount of test resources we had available.

I'll describe a typical scenario for these car parts in a racing game so that you can begin to picture what questions to ask and what to look for in your own projects when setting up these tests yourself.

In any racing game where you have real cars in the game, you're going to have a large team of 3D modelling artists – sometimes in the studio, sometimes outsourced to a specialist vendor – creating the models for each car, usually a large quantity for the entire game. These models need to be exact copies of the real thing and, if they have a licence to use the real manufacturer name and badge, the models and badges will be reviewed by the manufacturer too.

Just like real cars, the models can differ hugely, coming in a variety of shapes and sizes that will pose different challenges for customisation. Wheel arches for some cars will be too small to support wheel rims larger than a certain size; the contact points for spoilers differ from car to car; the shape of the bodywork panels will require specific bumpers and side skirts for them to attach properly and so on.

It's possible that sets of generic customised car parts (3D models) are created for the game where each part is compatible with certain car models within the game, just like in the real world. Equally, the team may have to create a full set of car parts for each individual car so that the custom parts are specific to that car. By understanding how the models are created and combined, the QA analyst can work out whether test combinations can be reduced or whether they need to test the full combination matrix. If separate car parts are created individually for each car, combinatorial testing would need to be more thorough, – not just testing a single spoiler type once, but instead testing it across every car.

The same applies to paint and vinyl for the cars, which can be applied in layers on top of the base car and the custom parts. A simple implementation may only allow players to paint the base car and have all custom parts in a grey or a carbon fibre pattern, whereas a more complete implementation would allow players to apply paint and vinyl across all parts. The models for the car parts might be created in a 'paintable' material defined by the game, where paint and vinyl are visible on any part which is covered in this material. In this case, if a custom part is covered in this material, then the paint should appear correctly on it. The most common bugs found here are mistakes where sections of a part are wrongly marked as paintable or not paintable (e.g. being able to paint over lights or windows, which should be transparent or tinted). These materials and other parameters for a 3D model might be set up by a different person to the one who created the model; it could be a manual one-by-one process or the team could have even set up an asset creation toolchain to remove some of the repetitive legwork. Just like code features, the method of creation influences the likelihood of mistakes – and therefore bugs – with specific assets and combinations of assets.

When testing the vast paint colour options, each colour probably would not cause different bugs when applied to different parts. The goal would be to check that the 'paintable' sections are correctly defined, not that each individual colour is correct on each car. You *could* find a bug with a specific colour on a specific car, but it's unlikely. Based on this, you might decide that you don't need to include every paint colour in your combination matrix and so you could omit it entirely.

When I've tested racing games in the past, there were certain paint colours that had unique attributes, like chrome paints which had increased reflective properties and would react differently to light sources in the game. There were also some paints which were patterns instead of solid colours and where the pattern would repeat across the car panels. You could identify these unique groups as equivalent and then just use one paint from each group within your test matrix; using equivalence partitioning on the vast list of paints before feeding the reduced list into your test matrix.

Paint colours are a good example of not applying combinatorial test techniques blindly without considering the feature's context. Doing so would add a huge number of test combinations and other members of the team would likely perceive the effort as not a good use of test time.

This racing game example shows us how many different factors can influence the likelihood of bugs occurring and help the QA analyst decide on which inputs and values to include in their combinatorial testing. This example talks about customising cars, but the same type of testing problem can be found in customisation options for many other games, too. Multiplayer games frequently allow players to choose and customise their character model, adjusting everything from body type to hair colour to their clothing.

In addition, each character model would also need to hold and animate correctly with each item or weapon in the game that they are capable of holding. I've run tests in previous projects which test each animation for a character against each weapon that they can hold, which included both idle animations within the game menus and combat animations within a game session. This was the same process as our car example, a combination test matrix with three inputs: character models, animations and weapons. The movements within each animation would cause the weapon to swing around, sometimes colliding with the character model or with other objects in the scene (this was more of an issue in the menu or any scenes where the character was fixed in a scene with other objects and not under the control of the player).

I made a similar observation while watching my nephew playing the popular children's game, Roblox. Amusingly, the community-driven nature of the content meant that the quality bar for character customisation was pretty low, with many of the character clothing parts obviously clipping through other parts of the character model.

I'll speculate that this is an example where it wouldn't be worth applying formal test techniques; the number of visual bugs are so numerous and obvious that it wouldn't be worth the investment. Additionally, the issues appear to have a very low impact on the player base. Children don't seem to care too much about what it looks like!

Regardless, it proves the point that you don't have to look very far before you come across the similar scenarios in other types of games. Giving the player customisation and gameplay choices is such a common feature set that many test teams should be able to harness at least parts of this technique to make their testing more structured and efficient.

Orthogonal arrays and classification trees

These are two more combinatorial techniques that provide different amounts of test coverage if there is a requirement to test beyond a minimal set.

I want to give these two an honourable mention because they're more specialist: it's unlikely that game QA analysts will have a test problem that can't be solved with a pairwise test approach and some free tools to implement it. Additionally, you might have seen their names elsewhere and were wondering whether I'd mention them here. In the context of your testing toolbox, these two techniques are the highly specialist tools that you rarely use, but excel when you have the need to use them. As with the pairwise tools, the main benefit is to take the legwork out of creating the test matrix from the inputs.

Orthogonal arrays are another mathematically driven technique that produces an 'optimised' test set, creating a nice middle ground between a minimal (all-pairs) set and a full test set. Similar to the pairwise technique, you can use the number of inputs and values to generate a text matrix of the appropriate shape.

```
0000
0121
0212
1022
1110
1201
2011
2102
2220
```

Figure 4.22 – A raw orthogonal array with four inputs and three values. Some examples exist online where you can take the matrix and replace the numbers with your actual values.

Like pairwise, you can also increase the 'strength' of the matrix to increase the size of the final test set if it's required, too. The technique works by finding an appropriate format orthogonal array, given your inputs, and then replacing the numbers with your actual values. It provides a way of mathematically generating the output combinations.

My main problem with this technique is lack of support for generating orthogonal arrays. Creating tables manually or copying 'raw' examples (like the example above) and filling in your values is time consuming and error prone. There are some scripts out there (I found one on GitHub) to automatically generate a custom orthogonal array given the number of inputs and values, but you still have to replace the numbers with your own values, which is a huge chore. My recommendation is that you can safely ignore this technique unless you have a specific reason to use it.

Classification trees are a little more interesting to us. Firstly because there are tools that do all of the legwork for us, and secondly because they provide a unique visualisation to our complex combinatorial testing problems. The catch is that this technique is quite specialist and not something that you'll use often. It's also not free if you want to use an off-the-shelf tool.

In our examples so far, each input had a flat list of values within it; the 'visual upgrades' input in our example had a list of upgrades that should be included in the resulting test matrix. In many real projects, choices and customisations are sometimes mutually exclusive and other times choosing a value for one input impacts the available player choices for another input, complicating the ideal output matrix that assumes every value is compatible with every other value. In real projects, it's common to have sub-options instead of a set of flat lists, where making a choice opens a selection of further choices that the player can make. This is where the tree visualisation helps.

INPUTS

Cars	Visual upgrades		Liveries
	Full body kit	Custom parts	
2017 Acura NSX	Full body kit	Front bumber	Xbox classic
1979 Chevrolet Camaro Z28		Spoiler	Retro arcade
2005 Ford GT		Bonnet	
		Sideskirts	
		Wheel rims	
		Wheel arches	
		Full body kits	

VALUES

Figure 4.23

Let's expand on the racing game example with the inclusion of full body kits. Specific cars in the game may have racing body kits available (that exist in the real world) and transform the entire shape and performance of a car. When a player applies one of these full body kits, they usually can't modify the car shape further with any other individual custom parts, but they might still be able to apply liveries on top of it.

In this format, the testing inputs have essentially introduced the idea of sub-values. The player can choose either 'custom parts' or 'full body kit' as two choices, but choosing 'custom parts' provides additional choices for the player that need to be included in the testing. The classification tree structure enables the visualisation of options and sub-options much more easily than a table.

With this visualisation, you can still use the pairwise test approach, but you just apply it to the tree structure. If you have a large and complex system of potential choices or customisations, this approach might be worth the investment. In the example below, we still only have three cars and I've cut down the number of custom parts to just three for the sake of a clean screenshot, but you can easily imagine the scale of combinations that a full game example would present. It's a matter of organisation and visualisation of large and complex test data.

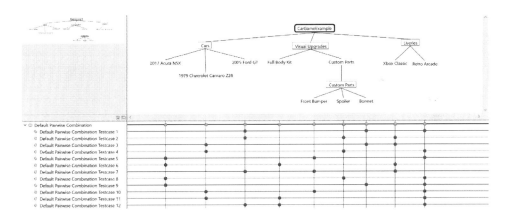

Figure 4.24 – A classification tree using the pairwise technique, generated by the licensed tool, TESTONA. The classification tree is seen in the top window with the test cases in the bottom section

If I was working on a new game project where we had several months of testing ahead of us before the game release, I might consider this tool. You could generate the tree once to organise your combination tests and then rely on it for the duration of the project. As I mentioned earlier, this is quite a niche tool and not something that most QA analysts will use. However, I'm sure that some large game projects will have test problems where this visualisation can be applied effectively. I wanted to include this visualisation into my list because it's likely that a mature project team would be able to see this visual style and build a custom internal tool to perform the same functions.

4.5.3 Tool support for combination test cases

Once you've used combinatorial techniques to identify all of the test combinations that you want to run, how do you import that test matrix into the tools you use to execute your testing?

In this section I'll briefly dive into test design before going into the full topic in the next chapter. This is particularly pertinent to combination testing because many test management tools have facilities built in to allow a test to be written once and then multiplied out across different configuration combinations.

As we've already discussed, combination testing, by its nature, creates large quantities of individual tests and it's easy to create a mess in your test management tool if the tests aren't organised correctly. The quick and dirty way to create the tests – and a method I've seen used far too many times by inexperienced QA analysts – is to write the tests that will be run against each configuration, copy them out to create a large list and then manually add a postfix onto each copy to mark which combination that copy is targeting.

- My set of tests – (Acura NSX, Bonnet, Xbox Classic)
- My set of tests – (Acura NSX, Spoiler, Xbox Classic)

Aside from being painfully time consuming, creating copies of each test prevents those tests from being updated (every edit needs to be made to *every* copy from that point onwards), stopping any ideas of maintainability in its tracks.

I've been using TestRail by Gurock over the last four years. It's a well-known test management tool which allows you to write, organise and run sets of tests. Its primary focus is manual scripted testing, but it advertises support for automated test results too. It has a handy 'Configurations' feature which works by defining lists of configurations, where each list contains the potential values for an input. You define a list title, "Custom Parts", and then can add items to that list, "Spoiler", "Bonnet", etc. Once the configurations are set, test suites (blueprints of tests) can be combined with a custom selection of configurations from multiple lists to create a set of executable test runs.

The tool is essentially making copies of the test suite blueprint to create a list of test runs and appending the combination postfix to each. The downside of this functionality is that the standard selection is a full test set, so you aren't able to easily configure an all-pairs or other intermediate test set within the tool. Regardless of the limitations, this is great functionality for virtually no additional effort and is great for the environment combinations I talked about at the start of this chapter, as well as basic gameplay combinatorial testing.

In my earlier years working on Microsoft game projects, we had two internal test management tools: one for writing tests and one for executing them. The test writing tool used a similar, but more powerful, version of the configurations feature within TestRail. As well as duplicating out tests and editing the title of each test, you could auto-merge the configuration names into the test steps themselves using special characters: "Go to your garage and select the {car}, then upgrade the {custom part}…"

Those of you using your own in-house test management tools may have this already, or a version of this functionality. If not, then you should consider requesting this as a feature of the tool. Standalone combination test tools are good, but combining them into your test management tools compounds the productivity boost massively. Whether you use your own in-house tools or an off-the-shelf package, find out if it supports basic combination testing and make sure you are using it to its fullest potential! With TestRail, I'm always surprised to see how many people have been using it for years without utilising this functionality.

4.6 Applied test analysis

Occasionally the teams I've been on have hired junior QA analysts who have stepped up from the tester role; or we've asked test leads (those that lead teams of testers) to step in and help us write some tests.

As a result of mentoring these junior test writers, guiding them through how I approach test writing and seeing their early drafts of test analysis, I've recognised that at least 50% of the test conditions generated during my test analysis come from my own ideas and experience. That's a lot of testing beyond what I would have derived directly from the feature details alone.

When I give feedback, I might say something like, "Have you considered how this feature will impact game performance?" or, "Will this feature have new telemetry events?". The test author will immediately grasp those points and begin to make connections with other information they have about the feature.

There will always be testing elements not explicitly mentioned in the feature details that will need to be considered during testing.

It usually only takes the mention of something like 'performance' and the test writer will begin to expand on that idea, asking the feature authors for their view on performance impact and then generating their test conditions for that sub area of testing. It just takes someone to have the idea, to remember it, and then include it as a consideration.

Sometimes the test writer will think themselves stupid for not having what appears in retrospect such an obvious idea. These test writers *aren't* stupid, because of course; everything appears obvious in retrospect. The point is that a great deal of a QA analyst's work in this area starts from a blank page and is conjured up from scratch, sourced from their past experience and ideas.

Put another way, it's a lesson on information recall, not on a lesson on deriving an answer from information given. Great QA analysts will consider things that no one else thought of, and the resulting tests will catch bugs that no one thought would occur. When done well, this is one of the core ways that QA analyst roles add value to the business. These tests aren't translated test cases based on the work of a designer or developer, they're brand new ideas of what should be tested for a given feature.

So, how do you increase your chances of thinking up good ideas? Project experience and actively practising test analysis will sharpen this skillset, building on these ideas each time you plan testing for a new feature. The important part of this practice is to dedicate time during your schedule to allow for test analysis and use the tools within this chapter to organise your work.

This needs to be a conscious effort by the QA analyst, to mentally store bugs and learnings for future test planning and then remember them at the right time. This improvement does not come for free simply by spending time writing test cases, as many people seem to believe. As for the tools in this chapter, defining test conditions and breaking down testing organises your thoughts and lets you focus on small problems individually, before having to think about the entire test plan holistically, making the task a lot easier.

In this sense, the content of this book can't give you the answers since every project and every feature is a different test planning challenge – but it can provide you with the framework, tools and mindset to help you solve new test planning problems that you face.

If you're still unsure about how you might generate ideas for the test areas on your own project, then hold on a moment. These ideas are driven by domain knowledge just as much as the tools in this chapter. That is, their effectiveness is directly linked to the depth of your understanding of each specific game area. Your knowledge of planning for environment tests isn't going to help when you need to plan testing for a new third-party SDK update. They require different test approaches, will utilise different techniques and will need different considerations made during test analysis. This is partly why much of my earlier career was spent exclusively planning tests for online services and multiplayer features, and before that it was video and music streaming apps for the Xbox 360, all heavily based on online connectivity. The considerations during test planning followed a pattern and could be more easily predicted with each test plan that I wrote.

Later on, in Chapter seven, **Major areas of game testing,** I'll be listing the main domains that QA analysts can work on and giving a summary on the method of test planning for each. The two chapters come together to provide the domain experience of planning tests for a specific area, together with the technical and process knowledge of writing effective tests in general. The two chapters combined should provide a solid foundation for anyone to apply test analysis in their own work.

Industry tales: Quick projects for fast learning

Before I was moved onto larger, single-release waterfall projects and, later, live ops mobile projects, there was a period of several months when I was exclusively responsible for owning the test plans for several smaller projects that would go live within the year.

I was working as a senior software test engineer (senior QA analyst-type role) as part of the Microsoft publisher test team to support first-party development studios. Because of that position, we owned the test planning for some of the Xbox first-party apps, websites and parts of the Xbox One dashboard where the development studios had no onsite test team. We had a direct relationship with the development teams and would be responsible for the holistic test plan of the project. By that time, Microsoft had teamed up with the test vendor, Lionbridge, and so we had some testers in Warsaw who would execute the test plans we made.

When the Xbox One was released, one of the selling points was that you could now capture and share screenshots and videos of your gaming directly on the platform without external tools or hardware. The console shipped with two apps, Upload Studio, a video editing app, and Upload Hub, an app for browsing and consuming video content. A few other test engineers and I owned the testing for both of those apps, dividing the feature set between us, and we were supported by a small team of remote testers. We were led by the test manager who oversaw all test activities for the studio. This was all pretty standard, but the projects immediately after this saw me own the test strategy exclusively for a number of smaller projects, conducting everything from the test analysis of the project to estimating the team size that we'd need from the Warsaw team and managing the execution schedule of the testing. I had everything peer-reviewed by the test manager and the development team, of course, and other support where I needed it, but the test approach for these projects was mine alone to shape. At the heart of this work was test analysis: choosing what we should test and making sure we'd considered everything for each project.

First up was a website version of the Upload Hub app. Having focused entirely on console testing previously, this was an interesting foray into PC and mobile testing for the website. The project shared common code with the app and so was completed within a few weeks.

Next up was an addition to the Xbox 360 dashboard – what we called a BDE, (branded dashboard experience). It was a sports hub that would collect and present thumbnails of key sports events that would deeplink into the relevant video-streaming app on the Xbox. This was really an extension of the type of testing I had done a few years earlier as a tester.

Finally, a larger project, an app for the Xbox One which would be a companion to the 2014 World Cup held in Brazil. It was called "Brazil Now". The app was designed to be snapped to the side of the screen and provide live stats, scores and tweets while the viewer watched the World Cup matches live in the main view.

It was another light client, populated entirely by remote data from various different sources. We had to contend with already-available data for things like player stats, but also figure out how to develop and test an application that would be receiving live data reported pitch-side and made available to the app through third-party services that specialised in live sports data. Luckily, we had some very sharp developers that were able to record, store and playback these data feeds in real time from previous matches. Even then, we had the data feed and not the corresponding video feed, so we spent all of our time watching the stats update without the corresponding match video feed.

When the time came to go live, we did have to stay late in the office and watch some friendly matches and the first world cup matches with the app snapped. There was very little we could do to test the full end-to-end flow without sitting through an actual game which had the stats being reported pitch-side. Sure enough, we had an interesting synchronisation issue where the Twitter feed would update before the live video feed because there was delay on the video. This meant every goal would appear in the Twitter feed comments first and then the video would follow – not a great experience. Luckily, we caught it during one of the early friendly matches and were able to fix it.

I'll always be grateful that my test manager trusted me to work on these small projects, because the speed of the iteration made for extremely quick learning. I was analysing what needed to be tested for a project and within a few months doing the same task again for an entirely new project. The 'blank slate' provided by new projects allowed me to try new formats for my work and tweak our testing processes, a rarity when I consider every other project I've worked on since has been mature when I moved to it and has come with legacy test baggage already.

Creating the test plan for an entire project, instead of sharing the planning with others also allowed the test process to be changed quickly and with flexibility, where a larger project would need consensus amongst the QA analyst team and a process for rolling the changes out to everyone else. Thinking about test analysis for an entire project also increased the scope of the thought process. Every single test task that we would need to carry out for the project needed to be captured during test analysis.

This put even more emphasis on the test analysis. It was no longer about planning for a specific game area, but instead was a much more generalised task. When I consider that for the single-release projects that I worked on, this project phase was followed by months of test execution and I found it much harder to remember and improve on my test analysis after such a long time.

These small projects also had small teams working on them – the team of testers, myself at the publisher office and the developers within the studio. This created very tight-knit communication and trust amongst everyone working on the project. It's much easier to build positive relationships if you only work with a small number of people.

I would highly recommend working on small projects if you are given the opportunity, especially if the project is so small that you're the only one performing your role – whether that's acting as a tester, QA analyst or test manager. Look for work where you are able to flex your test planning skills, try new methods and iterate quickly. Conversely, be aware of forgetting your learnings if you are working on longer projects. Write them down as retrospective notes or turn your documents into living versions so that you can update and iterate on them. Live ops projects can be good for iteration, since these types of projects release frequently and in a piecemeal way. However, live ops projects can release so quickly that it can prevent QA analysts from doing their best work.

Small, single-release projects, however, were a great sweet spot for me and taught me a lot. All of these online-only, video streaming, light client apps that I tested during this time, feed into my test planning ideas for new features even today. The projects I work on now are completely different, but much of the core technology and processes that drive communication with online services remains the same. We still use the same network tools to facilitate testing and I can still catch bugs using the same failure scenarios that I identified back then. Practise test analysis often and fill your toolbox with knowledge and experience that you can deploy again and again.

4.7   Test analysis: games vs. software

Test analysis, at its core, is the same process in games as it would be in any other software, so why have I included this chapter if you could get the same information from existing software testing books?

It's the practical application of test analysis within the games domain that teams find challenging; something that I've hinted at in each section of this chapter, showing first the trivial software example and then the more realistic and complex game project example. The translation into practical application within games is too big a leap for many teams to take, leading to the content of this chapter being woefully underrepresented within many teams. At the start of this chapter I described test analysis as the core of the QA analyst role and talked about the state of the role in the current industry.

> *The difference between games and other software for this chapter is quite vast, and also simple: I rarely see test analysis conducted at all in game projects.*

I find that most teams sit in one of two camps. Either they're somewhat aware of performing test analysis and the techniques involved, but find it difficult to apply this practically in their work, or they're not aware of it at all and instead are identifying what needs to be tested while the tests are written. In the worst cases, many game teams are just rewriting acceptance criteria from feature stories into test cases and leaving it at that.

In the former case, we've seen that many of the techniques appear to have evolved from the more generic software space where users are more likely to be entering values directly into the application and have greater rein to navigate throughout the entire application at their will.

To recap on this point from earlier, the main difference between games and other software regarding test input reduction is the format of player input into the application. Players are rarely entering number values or typing words directly into a game, instead interacting with values through player choices, progression and direct analogue input, like moving a character around a scene. The complexity of test inputs and combinations of potential inputs confuses the input reduction process, making it difficult to cleanly utilise during project work. While I can't give examples for every type of game, some of the examples and templates given in this chapter should apply to a broad range of game projects with a few changes, narrowing the gap to successfully applying these techniques and getting a good return on that invested effort.

The latter case is unfortunately quite common too, something I've seen through interviewing candidates from many different game companies internationally. Let's talk about that in more detail…

Industry tales: A lack of test analysis

We've had quite a few different QA analyst, QA lead and QA manager roles open at different times where I've been the main interviewer from the test discipline. In these interviews we've had a range of different candidates from across the game testing industry, both in the UK and internationally, in some cases we had candidates from outside of games too. During these interviews, I'm interested in the candidate's test writing experience and ask questions to understand who writes their tests, how they are written and who runs their tests. Even if a team doesn't conduct certain steps that I talk about in this book, that's fine, but I'm looking for an awareness of the steps and a conscious and logical choice if some, like test analysis, are skipped. Choosing to skip test analysis is very different from not conducting it simply because you don't know it exists. I've been surprised to hear, however, candidates say that they plan their tests directly from a feature spec, simply testing whatever is detailed in any documents that they are given. When I ask further, it seems many QA analysts plan tests that only cover the scope of what is defined within the documentation or feature story and then allow open exploratory testing to catch everything else.

This approach, while quick, lacks the independent assessment that test analysis brings; reviewing the feature with 'fresh eyes' and considering everything, not just taking it at face value and assuming the person who created it would have already thought of everything (and had the time to write it down). In the best cases, document creators might have been nice enough to include a risk analysis, some notes about the complexity of the feature or perhaps a list of existing game areas which the feature interacts with – though in my experience this doesn't come without a polite request from the test manager first!

Even worse, I've spoken to a number of interview candidates from large publishing test teams who base their testing on the game itself. They're given builds and are left to plan and create tests based on those builds. They explore it, break the game down into areas and create tests for each area, with no (or very little) documentation involved.

There are several problems with this setup. First and foremost, basing your testing on the game itself means that you're using the game as the 'point of truth' and any non-obvious bugs that exist in the game will be written into the test cases and become expected results. It's only effective at catching the most obvious 'low hanging fruit' bugs where you can assume it wasn't intended. Anything more intricate and you wouldn't know whether the bug is intended or not.

Secondly, the whole analysis of what should be tested is based on assumptions you're making about the game and how it should work; 'should the character be that colour? It looks okay, but it could be wrong'; 'should matchmaking take this long? it's not too bad but that could be wrong'; 'should that button be disabled in this state?' Not knowing what was originally intended by the design team and only knowing what was interpreted and built by code and other creators, doesn't allow testing to perform the function of cross-checking these two things.

This is alarming when we consider that one of the main reasons to test software is to check that what was built matches what was intended to be built in the first place. In addition to the details of how each feature is expected to function and how each part of the game is expected to look, this method of test planning provides very little supplementary information which would otherwise be used to help the team make many of the smaller test planning decisions, like testing the highest-risk or most unstable areas first.

As we've discussed in this chapter, contextual information about how the game is built is crucial to effective test analysis. Not having that information relayed from the game studio to the publishing team strikes me as a serious flaw in the holistic test strategy for the project.

At this point, my curiosity has peaked, and I ask how their test efforts fit into the testing of the wider organisation. Is there an embedded test team in the studio? Do they perform the same testing or does it have a different focus? Does it complement the testing that they perform in the publisher test team? Does the embedded test team forward information? These bigger questions mostly lead to uncertain and waffle-y answers, and so it appears many studio test teams aren't so hot at setting up their publisher test teams for success.

The answer I usually get is that they perform 'player focused' or 'end to end' testing and so their aim is to test everything that they are presented with in the game. Some even say that because it's from a player point of view, supplementary technical information isn't required for the testing to be carried out. This sounds to me like a combination of system level testing and user acceptance level testing, both of which I would correctly expect publisher test teams to be responsible for, but both are inefficient when conducted in such a loosely defined way.

Having acted in the role of a publisher test team on many first-party Microsoft projects, I know that the success of the system-level testing by a remote publisher test team hinges on the relationship and communication with the project team in the studio, and especially with the embedded test team (if it exists). We had weekly calls with the embedded QA lead, frequent documentation drops and project milestone updates from the studio which we could use to conduct effective test analysis and schedule the test execution at the right time. This varied from studio to studio, because we were the centralised team who worked with many different project teams, but in retrospect I'm thankful for those relationships which successfully enabled effective test analysis and design. I should also note that, at the time, I wasn't a manager or the driving force in those successful relationships, so I'm thankful to my managers who showed us all 'what good looked like'.

If you work in a remote publisher test team or a remote vendor test team where part of your role is to write tests, you have a greater challenge when it comes to test analysis. As with the examples I've described here, it's more difficult for these teams to gather the right information to identify the full scope of testing during test analysis, usually because they don't have direct contact with members of the studio development team or their information funnels through a single liaison within the studio team, usually the embedded test lead.

Even if they do have direct contact with the studio team, being remote doesn't create a close enough relationship to allow them to know who to speak to and what questions to ask. Gathering information for testing through reviewing documents and asking questions requires a level of cooperation, coordination and camaraderie with the individual designers, artists and coders that you're speaking to. You're asking them to stop what they're doing and assist you, so while you may get answers without a strong relationship, they might not be very good answers. Where a liaison or point-of-contact exists, sometimes that person isn't very good at relaying project updates, critical feature information, documentation locations or paraphrasing desk-side meetings. The reality of many modern game projects is that a level of information will only exist offline, through local meetings or discussions, making the information transfer to the remote teams even more challenging and often excluding them, intentionally or not.

My advice here is to set expectations with the studio team and let them know what you will need to carry out your testing effectively. All of the information you need might not be available, but you can at least set the expectation, find workarounds and establish channels for communicating. This might be weekly meetings to raise questions or discussions, a dedicated instant message channel or email group. It could also be requesting that you are added to project update announcements or at least that they are forwarded to you, so that you're always clued into the latest project information.

Request project updates and feature updates during sync meetings with the studio team liaison and ask clarifying questions on the details of those updates until you are clear on the details. Ask for a list of studio team members and their responsibilities so that you know who to speak to for what questions. Come to an agreement on how, when and where to ask questions which will aid test planning. Make sure the studio team knows who you are and what role your team performs, so that when you do reach out and ask questions, they're already familiar with who you are and why you are asking.

Any remote QA analysts who are responsible for test planning for specific game areas should become acquainted with the embedded test team member who also owns testing for that area. They should be attending all of the daily 'standup' and planning meetings for the sub team that are developing that game area. There will also likely be a primary developer or designer who is responsible for each feature that you plan testing for, and who will be the correct person to direct your clarifying questions to. Make sure who you know who those people are. Contacting the wrong person to ask them about code they haven't written is a little annoying, or worse, asking someone from the wrong discipline something that is outside their knowledge completely; both can be avoided once you have your point-of-contacts defined. For those remote QA analysts working on the same feature over many months of a project's development, you'll likely be contacting the same few people again and again, making this slightly easier.

To wrap-up this detour that we've taken: test teams should be extremely cautious about what source of information their testing is based on. If the answer is 'the game itself', this is a warning sign for poor test analysis and should be reviewed for improvement. Accurate analysis of test scope hinges entirely on the information available to the test team, and using the game itself provides a limited, player-facing view, reducing the effectiveness of test analysis. On the topic of career growth, conducting test analysis this way for a long time also prevents QA analysts from improving beyond the basic test breakdown of player facing components. Put it another way: the more complex and difficult test planning challenges are locked to QA analysts working in this way; challenges that might define the difference between a QA analyst and a senior QA analyst.

5

Test design techniques

5.1   An introduction to test design

So far, we've analysed what needs to be included in testing. Test design is the process of writing tests which define how testing will be executed.

For clarity, I'm talking about any type of test task that's written down and manually tested by a person who didn't write the task. This excludes automated tests, but does include all different types of manual test tasks, not just scripted tests.

These tests are the most visible work product of the QA analyst and will exist for the lifetime of the project. They will supersede much of the preparatory work carried out during planning and analysis, and creating them will occupy a majority of QA analysts time. Fear not: if the preparatory work is done correctly, then the hardest part of the process is over. Following a good plan during test writing makes the process a lot easier and, with some practice can become an autonomous activity – essentially just following your own instructions from earlier phases.

I've already discussed specific areas of test design in chapter one, with the introduction of the test design framework and the four quadrants: scripted verification, scripted failure, unscripted verification and unscripted failure.

Sections in this chapter will talk about the application of these types of testing, helping you decide when to use each type, and tips on how to set up effective tests for each type. Many of the test types listed in chapter three will also be relevant to this chapter, where I'll be describing how those tests are written. This chapter is intended to provide practical and specific examples of how to structure tests, as well as giving some examples of the common mistakes made by junior test writers and how you can avoid them. Where topics are specific to only one test type, I'll mention this explicitly, but the majority should be general to all types of testing.

I want to call out some of the skills QA analysts will be using when writing tests so that we can understand the attributes of good test design, before drilling down into the details of this chapter. The previous chapter on test analysis was focused on using techniques and experience to generate ideas, whereas test design is primarily driven by good organisation and communication; both very different skills from those making a good tester. Identifying and improving these skills is even more important for those moving from a role executing tests to one writing tests.

Remember these traits, because much of the guidance here deals with the effective application of these skills, meaning readers who are naturally organised, and to whom written communication comes easily, may see it as obvious common sense. This is why some testers I've mentored into QA analyst-style roles completely 'get it' from day one when it comes to the creation and organisation of tests. Left to their own devices, they would find a way to self-organise the large set of tests they are creating, anyway.

The difficulty of writing and organisation also depends on the feature under test. Some features present a clear and obvious organisation for tests, while others are much more of a challenge. Art and other content-driven features are generally easier to organise and write tests for, because you can see and interact with them directly, which makes the specific details of test steps and verification points easier to define. The wording of content areas is also more easily understandable to anyone reading the test – basic terms like particle effects, textures, lighting, reflections, animation are understood almost universally. I've found that junior QA analysts have an easier time with these areas when they are writing their first tests.

As you get into more technical areas of testing or where the method of verification is less obvious, the details within tests need to use appropriately specific and technical language. More complex test scenarios are also more difficult to describe clearly and concisely. This is where written communication skills come into play, especially when we consider that nearly every game test team I know operates internationally, where the language used to write the tests is not the first language of the testers executing the tests.

Effective test writing should aim to describe the test's intent as clearly as possible, removing any possibility that the instructions may be misinterpreted by the tester. Writing complex tests is difficult and writing them concisely is even harder. If you need to write an essay into your test session or scripted test to adequately describe your scenario, this will overwhelm or confuse the tester just as much as if you provided too little information.

Like the earlier test phases, the style of test writing is also orientated around the game area under test and plays a large role in deciding what test types to include in a plan. Some game areas will require more supporting documents as reference, like writing a test for a game item where there will be hundreds of similar items to test. A choice needs to be made whether to duplicate the test hundreds of times or whether to write the test once and direct the tester to execute it for each item in an external document.

Other game areas don't lend themselves well to scripted tests and will instead need to use more unscripted methods of verification, like the example of testing a large game environment that I gave earlier in this book, another instance where testing needs to be duplicated out massively and applied to a vast area of game content.

Additionally, there are always test tasks not associated with a feature test plan: one-off investigations, tasks to gather specific data instead of finding bugs, tasks to retest existing bugs to clean the active bug database, amongst other more customised reasons for writing a test task. Each of these will require a choice on the test type and written style to be effective.

QA analysts specialising in a specific game area, who write tests for it repeatedly, are more likely to develop a writing method that works particularly well for that game area, avoiding the organisational pitfalls. Those QA analysts who don't specialise have a greater challenge and need to remember to adjust their style of test writing to each game area they work on. In chapter six, **Major areas of game testing,** I'll be summarising the complexity and test writing approach for each area. If you're interested in the test approach for a particular game area, then head to that chapter and find the area closest to the one that you're interested in.

Lastly, this chapter is going to be tools-agnostic, meaning that you should be able to understand and apply the guidance regardless of what tools you use to organise and write your tests. The main focus areas will be structuring scripted tests, where tests are defined and verified on a step by step basis, and structuring unscripted tests, which include all other types of testing and is defined more loosely.

The majority of my experience for writing scripted tests has been using Microsoft Test Manager and TestRail, both of which have two fields for each step in the scripted test: an instruction for the tester (the step) and the expected result of that step (the verification). In addition to this, teams using spreadsheets to write their tests frequently also follow the same format of having a step and an expected result. While your own tools may differ from this, they should be close enough to apply the guidance here.

In many ways, the unscripted testing parts of this chapter will be even more interesting, because every team appears to structure these differently. I've written unscripted tests in a variety of tools: JIRA, MS Team Foundation Server, TestRail, even Word or just directly in an instant message. Because these tests are less granular, the tools usually provide you with a blank text field, forcing you to define the style of the task yourself. I've seen anything from a one-line statement ("Exploratory testing on the battle system") through to a test charter with a supplementary list of ideas to include in the session. I think there's a lot to be learned from seeing how other teams organise their unscripted testing and the types of test tasks that they run.

5.2   The goals of test tasks

The first words I write on nearly every single test are, "The aim of this test is to…". I do this regardless of the type of test — scripted, unscripted or otherwise. I do it to tell the tester straightaway what the goal or the intent of the task is, before they go on to read the more tactical details. I do it because it's simply not true that the goal of all testing is to find bugs, and I've had testers skip my task descriptions and whizz through a test, logging bugs which I didn't ask for or care about, only to ask them to read it again properly and re-run the entire task.

A basic example: in live ops games I've worked on, it's common to have bugs players have reported through the customer service channels that cannot be reproduced by either the code teams or the test team – complex bugs which only seem to occur for 1% of players on some strange device configuration that they are running. Sometimes we get exceptions and crash reports through live monitoring tools for which we don't have the repro steps. The code teams might investigate the code area causing the crash and add some defensive coding around the area without knowing exactly how the players are reaching that scenario. Then the test team will create a test investigation to gather common factors from the reports and try to reproduce the problem locally. The test team needs to reproduce the crash on an older build of the game first, before trying again on the newer, fixed build if they've got a hope of verifying the fix.

Such a test task has a very specific goal, with multiple stages. There's only value in trying to test the fix if the team can, first, reliably reproduce the bug on a non-fix build. Such a task requires detective-like skills, poring over many reports and data from players experiencing the issue, trying to look for commonalities in their profiles, their hardware, their region, anything that might link them together. This is a difficult task for the test team to carry out alone and needs input from the other disciplines, like the code and BI team, who can gather technical data or take a guess at how they think the issue might be occurring.

In this scenario, I don't necessarily care about new bugs and I'm not interested in the tester exploring other areas of the game either; it's a specific focus for a test investigation. In this task I might write something like this as the start of the task description:

> ### Task focus
> *The primary goal of this task is to use the collective data to reproduce the bug below on older builds and update the bug with the new data and repro steps. The secondary goal is to use that information to verify the bug fix on the new build.*
> ### Method
> *Inspect the CS reports below and the dev comments to aid your investigation. You should also consider the following…*

I would then list my own suggestions based on my assessment of the issue. This advice may sound obvious, but I've read a lot of other tests which are written in a notation format, without using full sentences, or that jump straight to the gritty details of the session without first spelling out the holistic direction of the test. Outside one-off investigations like this one, a majority of test tasks still have the primary aim of finding new bugs. However, the test may have a more specific aim. A smoke test run before a larger scripted pass might be described like this.

> ### Task focus
> *The aim of this task is to perform a broad and shallow smoke test of the feature before we commit to the verification test run. We're interested in major and blocking bugs that might prevent us from executing further testing.*

This lets the testers know they shouldn't spend test time investigating minor bugs, and also that deeper testing on the same area will be conducted soon, giving them the opportunity to revisit areas of testing more deeply.

Without specifying the purpose of the test, testers may spend longer on the task than you wanted, log bugs you're not interested in yet and test more deeply than you wanted to. So, even when the main goal of the task is to find bugs, there's usually a limit to the types of bugs you're interested in. Stating this clearly within the task is the first line of defence in making sure the task is interpreted correctly.

The examples I've given so far have shown how I would start a test task as entered into the project database (think JIRA / Team Foundation Server). But the same rule also applies if you're working at a lower level, on a specific test case. In test management tools, there's a field for a title and a test description before you start defining each test step of the scripted test. Some tools also have a field for prerequisites that are needed to run the test. I follow a similar style for the description field, stating clearly and directly what this test does.

> **Title:** *Cloud save – Cross device save synchronisation*

Description: *This test verifies the core flow of synchronising your save game profile from one device to another.*

Just like a task, communicating the intent of a specific test will help the tester correctly interpret each step of the test – which is more helpful the longer and more complex a scripted test becomes. I'll examine the level of detail given within scripted tests during this chapter, and we'll see that it's not possible to spell out every detail of what needs to be done for each test. The tester will always need to fill in the gaps during testing, and this is a lot easier if they know the intent of the test.

So, what are the different reasons to run test tasks? I've run a broad array of unique test tasks depending on each situation, but here are a few that I write most often.

These are just example snippets to give you a flavour. A fuller task focus would contain additional information, including describing the tactical details of the test. These examples are also generic; in real tasks I'm more likely to mention feature elements by name, include in-line hyperlinks and do anything I can to be as concise and precise as possible in the opening sentence of each task.

- **Verification / confidence building** – "The aim of this task is to verify that the core functionality of the feature is consistent with designs. Refer to the story and the design one-pager for reference".
- **Failure / bug finding** – "The aim of this task is to investigate specific points of weakness within this feature that might cause failures. Use experience from earlier verification testing of this feature and the guidance below to fuel your testing".
- **Early testing/smoke tests** – "The aim of this task is to perform an early test on the parts of this feature which are complete, and look for major and blocking bugs that might hinder later tests. This feature is still in development, so you'll need to stay strictly within the defined scope of the session."
- **Performance data gathering** – "The aim of this task is to gather and analyse memory and loading time data, to measure the difference between this release and the previous one. The test should analyse the data and produce a conclusion, not just produce the raw data".
- **Bug investigations** – "The aim of this task is to find the reproduction steps for the following bug which is appearing in our crash reporting tools for players on this device".
- **Remote data deployments (no code)** – "The aim of this task is to verify the data and assets for this live event. For this test, the primary focus should be the event data and assets. You can defer any bugs which also occur in the base game code".

- **Database cleaning** – "The aim of this task is to retest all of the active bugs in the database in the latest build and update them if their state has changed. The goal of this task is to make sure all bugs in the backlog are accurate and still present in the current game".

Benefits of discrete tasks

This is a brief side note to the different goals of test tasks that QA analysts will write, focusing on the benefits of organising testing into smaller, discrete tasks.

Many QA analysts don't create tasks like these at all, and instead will make informal requests to the test execution team asking them to self-organise around a task. This is particularly true for activities that are not scripted test passes. The QA analyst might request an investigation into a specific bug or an exploratory test session, for example, link the bug within an instant message chat and have that task assigned and reported entirely in chat. They may also have the testers create a task within the project database, but leave them to fill out the details themselves.

Other projects *do* create tasks for every feature or big piece of work, but will list all the test passes and activities inside the single work item. They do this even though many databases support sub-tasks, allowing them to be broken down. In all of these scenarios, there doesn't appear to be a space, or a requirement, to create distinct tasks in the project database and write the goals of each task as I've described in this section. I've been there too: short on time but needing to get many different tasks running as quickly as possible, so I've skipped writing up each task and requested it directly in a chat message. This is also common if the team has run a task many times before, and so should already know what to do without explicitly writing it down. It's easy and tempting to request a re-run of a task that the team is familiar with, without writing it out yourself.

However, I've consistently found that taking time to break down test activities into smaller tasks, and writing a short description for the task, has a measurable impact on the consistency and quality of test output. Separating tasks makes the goals of each one more distinct and trains the testers to expect tasks with different goals. Doing this removes mistakes made through assumptions by the tester – someone who will always be more junior than the person writing the task.

I think it's a mistake to assume every tester knows what the QA analyst wants from each task and that everyone on the test team has the same understanding of each task. Breaking down work into sub tasks also allows for easier assignment by the test execution lead, since discrete tasks can be more easily communicated to different members of a test team, rather than assigning the entire task to the group and having them self-organise which parts each person will run. Discrete tasks also allow for test results to be written separately, increasing the chances of the QA analyst getting the test output that they intended and not losing it in the output of a single larger test task.

To conclude this section, consider carefully the first words you write on each test and decide exactly what you want it to achieve. Be clear and direct in the language that you use and remember that there is always room to describe gritty details further down into the test description. Where possible, break larger tasks down into smaller sections so that you can more easily communicate the goal of each separate task.

I wanted to discuss this issue early within this chapter, because effective test writing starts with a clear focus for each test and QA analysts should endeavour to get this right before trying to improve other topics outlined in this chapter.

Industry tales: A mess of task assignment

This tale is partly about test design, but it also goes into more advanced issues around test implementation, including the organisation of the test execution schedule. I'll share what happens when individual team members lean too heavily on instant messages and email as tools for requesting test tasks.

Unlike my current projects, where we only have one or two QA analyst style test-writing roles per project, some of my past projects had five or more QA analysts owning testing for different areas of the game. This was the case when I was working on console and PC single-release games, due to the size of the game. Our method for scheduling tests was to use a joint spreadsheet resembling a Gantt chart, where each QA analyst would estimate the number of testers they required for their tasks on a day-by-day basis, which they would do several months ahead of time. The totals for each day from all the QA analysts were used to calculate the size of the test execution team required by the project for any particular week, with a contingency of a few testers for miscellaneous tasks. Despite this careful planning, we still had days where each QA analyst had additional work, so they would have to decide how to split the team resources and what work would take priority. It simply wasn't possible for multiple QA analysts to have more testers that they had estimated for that day.

These projects were an example of what good organisation in test scheduling looks like. All of the test tasks were planned and estimated for ahead of time, a contingency was available and conflicts would be discussed openly. We were able to make decisions and change task priorities accordingly in a way that was clear and obvious to the test team who were receiving these tasks. Thanks to this careful planning, the test execution sub-teams knew where to find their ongoing tasks each day and what to expect. They only had requests from the person who wrote their tests and could focus on those tasks uninterrupted. No (or very few) ad-hoc requests were made to the test team outside of the scheduled tasks, and when this happened, a test task was created and prioritised against the other tasks that were already assigned for that day.

As a contrast to this best practice, I've spoken to many frustrated test execution leads who receive test requests from different people across the project team: QA analysts, producers and developers. If test tasks aren't created as discrete work items in the project database and channelled through a single process for prioritisation and assignment, a mess of privately messaged test requests is created. This is akin to having multiple different bosses who are all messaging you at the same time and requesting something different, each one telling you that their task is of top priority and must be completed immediately. I've discovered this retrospectively in some cases when one of my tasks is taking longer to complete than I had estimated, and I start a conversation with the test lead about it, only to find out late that they've had other requests which have taken precedence and delayed my tasks. Apart from the obvious lack of coordination and transparency, the absence of written tasks for each request didn't allow anyone to compare current tasks and prioritise them correctly. The test lead had nothing to link to me and say "this is what we were asked to do" – they just sent me a copy of their chats with the person requesting the new task. At least if new requests had been written up in the project database, I would have been able to intervene and help prioritise them, then go back to the people requesting each task and let them know the decision.

In the worst cases of this bad practice, I've seen embedded QA analysts and QA managers forward requests from developers or make requests of their own, without written tasks and without appreciating how long the task will actually take the team to execute. This leads to the test team wasting huge amounts of time on tasks which aren't worth it. The person making the request simply didn't think enough about how the team would actually perform the task and what currently active tasks would have to be postponed. Almost as bad is when QA analysts edit the scope of an already active task, adding more and more to the original task or changing its focus. While in-flight changes to active tasks can be inevitable, all requests and discussions should be followed by an update to the task in the database itself. The task should remain the 'point of truth', not the parts of it scattered across instant messages and emails.

A lack of discrete tasks clearly describing the goals and priorities of the test, leads to the test schedule going off-track, or the test budget increasing through larger team sizes or the introduction of overtime to accommodate the increased work.

Another negative side-effect is that tasks are more likely to be wrongly executed or forgotten, because it's difficult to juggle a large number of different tasks if they're not all written down in the same place. I've seen instances where ongoing tasks have been started on one day, then deprioritised and not revisited, leaving them open and forgotten. Other times, tasks are requested and run, but then no-one follows up on them. If a task request isn't followed up, can it have really been that important? I don't think so. All of this creates a mess of active tasks and priorities for which no single person has the full picture. It also stresses out anyone who cares enough to try and organise it – usually the test execution lead or one of the QA analysts.

The solution to these problems comes back to our old friends, organisation and communication. It doesn't take long to write new work items into the project database for reactive test work, and doing so creates tracking and organisation for that new work. Task goals and priorities can also be more clearly communicated within the written database work items and referred to by anyone at any time. Private emails and instant messages should be scrapped entirely. If you need to make requests via these methods, they need to be made public and searchable.

5.3 Test granularity

Just before we move on to how to structure different types of tests, I'd like to introduce an idea which will get you to think about test types in a different way. I've found it's useful guiding principle when deciding what type of test to use and how to write tests.

Many test writers are accustomed to thinking of test types as binary, or 'digital'. A test has two options: scripted or unscripted. Some test writers might also split these out into sub-options, but regardless of this, the decision of which to use is entirely one or the other. The main characteristic of each of these types is the granularity of the instructions given to the tester. Scripted tests are typically very granular in the level of detail they provide, whereas unscripted (exploratory) tests are typically non-specific, providing much less detail. This begins to break down slightly with the introduction of things like session-based testing and player persona testing, which are exploratory but provide more direction than open exploratory testing. They're still generally thought of as exploratory test types, though.

The scale of granularity

Figure 5.1 – Different test types support different levels of detail. The length of the bar for each test type represents the range of granularity the test type supports.

*Instead of choosing a very granular scripted test
or a holistic unscripted test, we should consider test
granularity as a sliding scale and aim for each test type to
sit somewhere on that scale. The level of detail given within
tests should be thought of as 'analogue' rather than 'digital'.*

Test cases (tests with defined steps) are hugely flexible and can support tests which are driven by more holistic goals, much like focused exploratory tests which define a test charter. Likewise, since exploratory test types are usually written in open text format, they can provide as little or as much structure as the writer wishes to impose on the test. Some focused exploratory tests I've written provide just as much structure as some of my test cases.

The takeaway here is that test writers shouldn't approach all of their scripted tests with the same level of templated granularity for every test that they write – something which I've seen often. The style and structure of the test can be adapted to each test situation. This serves to differentiate free exploratory testing (or 'ad-hoc' as some call it) from more granular forms of exploratory testing which I've found to be so much more effective. It's an important reminder that test cases don't have to be a laborious marathon of extremely detailed test steps and can instead be written more holistically. I've seen many QA analysts forgo writing test cases because they take too long to write, and instead opt for focused exploratory sessions, even when a test case would have been a more effective approach for reusability reasons.

5.4   Test writing styles

Here I'll be walking you through how I format a typical task and subtasks for a feature test plan, as well as giving examples for the format and written style of scripted and unscripted test types. This covers both the tasks that I would write into the project database and the tests that I would write into the test management tools. In this context, tasks are the wrapper for our tests. All tests should be contained within a task, but not all tasks contain tests. As we see below, some tasks just organise smaller tasks together. The use of database tasks allows test teams to organise and structure their tests, as well as creating much needed traceability between testing and the feature stories defining the work being tested. The aim of this section is to show some styles which you can adopt directly in your own work.

5.4.1 Test task style guide

Most projects have test plans represented within the project database (JIRA, Team Foundation Server, etc.) where a parent work item is created at the highest level for the entire test plan, with other tasks that are part of the test plan organised under that parent task. Common work item types for this hierarchy are epics, tasks and sub-tasks.

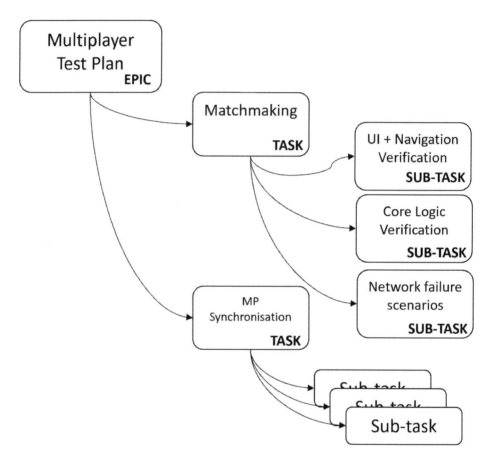

Figure 5.2 – Part of the work item organisation for a large test plan which might run for many months on a single-release project

Very large features can take advantage of the epic work item type to group tasks together, whereas smaller feature test plans can be organised just using tasks and sub-task work item types. In the example above, the test area of multiplayer is so vast that it's better to organise it into several smaller test plans, like matchmaking and multiplayer synchronisation. The breakdown of test conditions created during the earlier test analysis phase should feed directly into this task organisation, making the creation of this structure straightforward if earlier test analysis has been carried out effectively.

Epics and tasks are really just here to help us organise the sub-tasks and will be quite light in their descriptions. They also won't be executed by testers for this reason. The sub-tasks are the stars of the show: they contain all of the information the testers will need to run the task, including a link to the relevant test run within the test management tool if it exists for the test. I usually try to split sub-tasks by their goals and also order them chronologically, so that testers can work through them from the top. For example, I'd have a sub-task for an early smoke test, then another for the core verification of the feature, then another for a follow up failure investigation. Generally, you will want to run the core verification of a feature before moving onto more complex verifications, exploratory tasks or failure tests, because there is little use running more complex tests if the earlier tests are blocked or return major failures.

As a quick side note, I *do* still assign priorities to my tasks and sub-tasks, but these are used to compare the importance of sub-tasks between different test plans when there is a conflict in the test execution schedule, instead of ordering sub-tasks within the same test plan.

There is no strict right and wrong when it comes to test task organisation. While I use the test analysis as the basis for grouping the tests, considering the practicalities of the test execution during the design phase pays dividends later on when the tests are being run. This mostly comes with experience of executing tests with the same team of testers and learning from the specific way that they are working, but there is some general guidance that I can give.

- Consider the order in which the feature components will be delivered into testing. It may make sense to create sub-tasks which correspond to individual feature component deliverables, so that you can run them individually as each component is delivered into testing.
- Consider the relative risk and priority of each test within the plan. You could group all tests by their priority and then have a sub-task for each priority level. Many teams chose to execute tests in order of risk, with the highest first.
- Consider the complexity and stability of the feature when you begin testing. Most features for which I write tests don't require a smoke test, but larger features will be different. They will need more organisation within the tasks and increased vigilance against accidentally wasting test time. Introducing a smoke test into the plan is one way to prevent this.
- Consider which sub-tasks can be run in parallel and which need to be run sequentially. It makes little sense to run a smoke test at the same time as running the main verification, because the latter needs to follow the former,

but many features with vast areas of content can be run in parallel. Knowing that testing is running behind schedule may allow you to assign sub-tasks to multiple different groups of testers simultaneously to get the testing completed sooner.

- Consider which sub-tasks are difficult to set up or execute. Some tests may take several days to run because they're time-based or have external dependencies. Some tasks may require the test environment to be configured in a certain way or require certain test tools which are only known to some of the senior testers on the team. These are just a few of the practical limitations of test execution to be considered when setting up test tasks. Each of them will cause testing to be delayed or run inefficiently if they're not well organised.

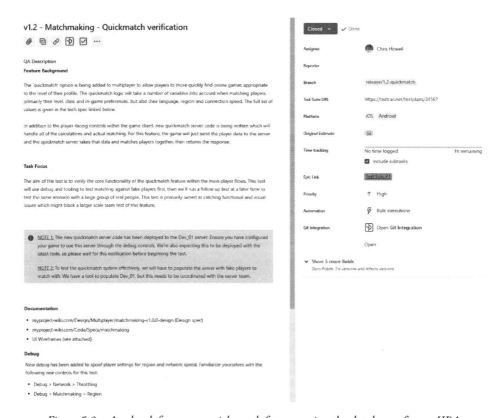

Figure 5.3 – A subtask for a new quickmatch feature, using the database software JIRA

Let's assume that I'm writing tests for a live game where a new quickmatch feature is being introduced to allow players to find matches more easily without searching manually. This tells us that the larger multiplayer system is already live and stable, with players currently searching through active games to join them, or joining games through friend invites. Even for an addition to an existing live game, it's a big feature and would require testing of multiple different components. This example shows the rough length of background description and task focus text that you should aim for when writing tasks. Some will inevitably be complex enough to need even more. I would advise challenging any task focus that extends beyond the screen and forces the tester to scroll. If the task focus is that long or complex, it's a sign that the task might need breaking down into smaller components or that it would be more effective to put that information into a separate document or into the scripted tests themselves. The more information that is added here, the harder it is for the tester to remember and consider it all while executing the tests. You don't want to write several paragraphs of task focus and then add a critical line of information at the end, it's likely to be lost in the noise and forgotten during execution.

With that example in mind, let's look at the key information within the task.

Title

Titles should include prefixes for maximum readability and use a consistent style throughout the project. In many locations where tasks are being communicated or listed, the title and the ID of the task are the only visible fields, making it very useful to add supplementary information.

Bad title styles

- JIRA-580: "Quickmatch" *(Too high level for sub task)*
- JIRA-580: "Primary player as match arbiter" *(A copy of a dev sub-task title / too technical)*
- JIRA-580: "CLONE – Quickmatch – 12/11" *(A sub-task clone without being renamed, in addition to the use of dates to label test tasks)*
- JIRA-580: "UI Verification" *(No reference to the feature name, it could relate to any feature, but does at least show test type as verification)*

Good title styles

- JIRA-580: "MP – Quickmatch – UI verification" *(Shows sub-task hierarchy, sub-task focus as UI, test type as verification and which feature it belongs to)*
- JIRA-580: "1.5.0 – Quickmatch – Network failure scenarios" *(Shows release version, sub-task focus, test type and which feature it belongs to)*
- JIRA-580: "1.5.0 – Quickmatch – Scripted regression pass" *(Shows the goal of the subtask as regression, also shows test type as scripted, as well as other best practices above)*

Feature background

This is something I've used more and more during my test-writing experience. The goal here is to describe what change has been made to the game to make this test necessary. It provides the test's 'why' reasoning before the tester reads the 'how' and 'what' within the task focus section. Understanding why the test is being run helps the tester make many of the small decisions needed during test execution and also helps them identify bugs when they occur. You might think that this section is superfluous and that the designs or technical specs should provide this information anyway. In my experience, these documents are too detailed or too technical to provide a sufficiently concise executive summary for the tester running the task. As we've already said, they may not exist a lot of the time, too.

On top of this, testers aren't normally well placed to correctly interpret all of the information given in the documents, partly because they're further away from the source of feature development and partly because they're more junior. They're not involved in any of the planning that leads up to the delivery of the feature, so part of the information I include here paraphrases discussions and decisions that we've made during planning meetings, or from email or instant message threads. QA analysts often ignore the basic details of a feature in this section because they've already been discussing it for several weeks, forgetting that the testers will be seeing all of this information for the first time. It's the role of the QA analyst to gather all of the details of a feature and condense that information down into the core facts that will be useful when reading each test task for the first time.

Feature background bad practices

- Directly copying a technical description from a developer (only do this if it has been summarised in a particularly direct style that you know the testers will understand)
- Pasting links to external documents or email/instant message history as the primary source of information, without explaining it first
- Using terminology that you know the testers won't be familiar with
- Referring to tools or processes that the testers don't have access or exposure to
- Describing something very detailed before giving a more holistic description

Feature background good practices

- Describing the 'story so far' by summarising the designs and final decision of all meetings on the feature. Include what has been done and what is left to do. I often add circumstantial information that will be helpful to the tester here, including practical limitations and gotchas!

- Describing new terminology or phrases inline within the summary when you can't avoid using them
- Using inline hyperlinks to bugs, tests, stories, documents and websites when referring to specific things, so that the tester can dig deeper if they need to. E.g. It's much better to link to a specific bug, "We need to look into this softlock bug", than to try and laboriously re-describe the bug within the summary.
- Paraphrasing technical reasoning and descriptions in your own words
- Providing your own assessment, thoughts and contextual information into the description. I use this space to add risk and complexity context from my own point of view. Tell the testers if you think the feature will be buggy, if you know that most of the code already exists and the new code addition is small, or if the feature will be difficult to verify in a reproducible manner.

Industry tales: Skipping the basics

When I was working on Fable Legends, the project was being developed at the same time that Windows 10 was being readied for release. Internal Windows 10 builds were already being dogfooded internally and MS had announced a public launch date for the operating system. We'd already been testing on the Xbox One, codenamed 'Durango', for some time and we had been told that the operating system was built to natively support games across all of the new MS operating systems. So, it wasn't a huge surprise when, only a year later, we discovered that all first party MS games would need to support both Xbox One and Windows 10 operating systems. For us, this included Fable Legends and, later on, Forza Horizon 3.

We started to ship in high-end PCs and set up the process for us to install work-in-progress Windows 10 builds onto the machines, which we would need to do regularly. This started within the studio development team for each game and they had a few months of work before there was a working build of the game for us to look at on these machines. By the time we started getting Windows 10 builds of the game, the code teams within the studio had already amassed a selection of technical documentation and how-to's to which we had access. Internally, the codename for Windows 10 was 'Threshold', so this was used across all of the documents, emails, meeting invites and other references to anything that involved the Win10 platform. So, for Fable Legends, we had Xbox One and Threshold as the two platforms in all of our tests and documentation too.

Just like the studio code team before us, we had a couple of months of test planning work to do before we could start assigning Threshold tests to our vendor test team working in Warsaw, Poland. We had set up several calls with them to work through the details of the testing and help them set up their own PCs so that they were prepared when testing was due to begin.

I remember one of the first calls we had with the vendor team, summarising what had happened so far with Threshold to get them up to speed. We needed to communicate a great deal of contextual information about the setup for testing, the problems we'd faced so far and what needed to be done next. With such a great deal of information to get through during the call, one of my colleagues began explaining the details of the topics that we needed to cover. A short way into the call, one of the vendor test leads stopped the flow and asked if we could explain more about Threshold because they didn't understand it. I cut in and said, "Threshold is the codename for Windows 10, any references to it are just referring to Windows 10. That's it". We hadn't explained the most basic piece of information – that this word was just a codename reference. After a moment of realisation and relief, we continued the call. We had a chuckle about it afterwards and my colleague thanked me for cutting in, he was about to respond by explaining it in even more detail.

It's easy to forget that remote test teams can't access the same level of information as teams closer to the source of development, and to skip some of the basic information when setting up testing. For this reason, QA analysts do well to put themselves in the minds of the testers and try to summarise features holistically, starting with the basics before going into the gory details.

Industry tales: Taking the initiative

This story comes from my work on mobile game projects. I've had some really great successes when the test team are kept in the project information loop, particularly when it comes to feature changes they will be working on. On this particular project, I am very proactive when it comes to providing information to our vendor test team in India, and setting them up to execute testing as independently and successfully as possible. As well as describing the feature context within my test plans, I set up calls to share my screen and explain details further when we're about to start testing a feature that is particularly complex. This extends to writing up 'how-to' pages on the internal QA wiki pages to aid testing and future tests in the same area. This all helps create a culture where the team is able to ask questions on subjects they're personally interested in learning more about. I try to answer all of the questions whenever I can or find someone else on the team to answer if I'm not able to.

I've found that many of the testers are very interested in understanding more about how the game is built and the processes that we follow to build it (essentially, sharing some of the insights from within the studio). Many are also keen to learn more about certain tools and processes that they don't frequently get to use during our normal feature testing.

I'm always happy to share details of tools and testing, that testers can take with them to other projects, even if we're not using them in our testing. Not only does this create a great relationship with the test leads and senior testers on the team, but it noticeably improves the quality of the testing that these testers produce. When I assign focused exploratory tasks and read through the session notes after a test session has been completed, there have been many examples of great test ideas from the testers; ideas that show a good level of knowledge about how the feature has been built and have uncovered some really interesting bugs as a result. This investment on my side has also encouraged the team to act on their own initiative and take action without it being requested, like staying late to finish an important task before a deadline, or reorganising tasks to prioritise more important testing and have it completed sooner. It's been great to see the team be so invested in the project and its success.

This is just a short introduction to an advanced topic about managing test teams and building relationships with remote test teams. It forms part of a greater ethos when building an effective test discipline across several different teams. For now, we can just recognise that there are many 'soft' benefits that come from adding contextual details to test plans and making sure those executing the tests understand under-the-hood details of features.

Task focus

This section describes what needs to be done for this task and, if there isn't a link to a test run, it also describes how the task should be executed. I start this section by first describing the highest-level goals of the task, then go into more detail.

The details of the task can take any form or length required. For tests that are run entirely from this work item (and don't have a link to another test management tool) – like a test session or bug investigation – all the information that the testers will need is outlined here. Test writers can add subsections to define supplementary information and organise the larger amount of information that will be required. Database tasks can be customised and should contain dedicated fields for common information, like which code branch to use, whether to use debug or non-debug builds, what server to use and whether the test needs to be run across multiple platforms. Any information that isn't input into a dedicated field within the test task will need to be added within the task focus.

For our current project, this includes a list of each discipline's point of contact for the feature, so that the testers know who to direct questions to. It also includes links to the relevant AB test within our live ops tooling, so that the tester can enable relevant game data for testing. Occasionally, a task will include tests that require the test team to coordinate with customer service agents, designers, developers or server engineers before they can begin running the test, usually to set up something specific within the test environment. I've known testers skip past this kind of information and run a set of tests against an environment configuration that yet to be set up, so it's really important to highlight special setups and prerequisites from the outset. More technical test setups will also be more difficult to describe clearly within the task and will usually still prompt a handful of questions from the test team (which I still prefer to the test team *not* asking questions and instead just running the task without fully understanding the goal of the test).

For tasks that have a link to a set of tests within a test management tool, the task focus section should still be filled out to provide supplementary information to the test run. The practicalities of testing mean that it's often necessary to tell the tester how they should interpret and execute the test run, or collection of test runs, linked to the task. Since tests are often reused for different purposes and test suites grouped into custom test runs, the tests themselves would likely not have been written explicitly for this task and so need added contextual information to supplement their smooth running for this particular instance.

Task focus bad practices

- Avoiding describing the actual goal of the task but stating that the goal is to complete the tests: *"The aim of this task is complete the linked test run"*. I see this a lot when people don't know what to write in this field or aren't actually sure why they're running the task
- Writing overly generic statements and just copying that statement across all test tasks: *"The aim of this task is to make sure the feature functions as expected"*
- Going immediately into the granular details of the task before describing it more holistically: *"This test is dependent on the cloud save service being down, so we will need to simulate this using the tool…"*
- Leaving this section blank and linking a test run without contextual information
- Not being explicit about whether this task needs to be run within this work item or within a test management tool

- Not being clear about where and how the test results should be recorded
- Updating existing tasks with new information while they're already being executed (there is a correct way to do this if it is unavoidable).

Task focus good practices

- Describing this task in relation to other tasks in the plan: *"The aim of this task to verify the core functionality of this feature before moving onto other failure and edge case investigations"*
- Supplementing the task fields with additional practical information that the tester will need to execute the tests
- Putting yourself in the shoes of the tester and considering everything they will need to know to run the task
- Highlighting special requirements by underlining or bolding them
- Creating subsections to define groups of task parameters like build numbers, links, contacts, tools, test accounts, etc.
- Putting the most important information earlier within the focus and providing further supplementary information later
- Defining what the output of the task should be and associating this output to the goal of the task: *"Performance data should be recorded in the linked spreadsheet"*, *"Record your test session notes below, include the areas you've covered and suggestions for follow up test sessions"*
- Highlight any in-flight task updates in a different colour and place them at the end of the existing task focus. I also add a date to the updated section, *"UPDATE – 01/11 – New information for this crash investigation shows us that…"*. These should also be communicated to testers running the test to refresh the task and see the updated section.

This guidance on task focus applies to all tasks regardless of the goal or test type. If you're looking for details on best practices for writing exploratory test sessions, then you can skip ahead a few pages because I'll be giving a specific style guide for test sessions which are run entirely from the task and don't have a link to a test management tool.

Depending on the maturity of their team, many readers may find that their team's test tasks don't follow any of these best practices. I've populated this list from my own experience of the most frequent problems I see in test writing. The consequences of these bad practices aren't immediately obvious. Testers may ask more questions when a task is assigned; they may also be forced to make more assumptions for a task which they probably wouldn't report to anyone as a problem. As I've hinted a few times already, failing to follow these best practices increases the chances of the tester logging bugs that I don't care about or providing results outside of the task objective, which also goes unnoticed if the QA analyst isn't actually reviewing and closing each task after it's been run. Simply having a blank task with a link to a scripted test run isn't necessarily bad, but it's not good either. It's just a mediocre approach.

Getting the test focus right by providing a concise summary of the task goal is a quick and direct method for increasing the chances that the QA analyst will get what they want from a test task. This is one of the most important takeaways from this chapter. I can't overstate the benefits. If you only make one change to your test tasks, let it be this.

5.4.2 Scripted test style guide

I'll now go into some detail about the style of scripted, step-by-step tests that are written in a test management tool or spreadsheet. These tests form the majority share of test activities for most projects, spanning hundreds of unique scripted tests over the lifetime of a project. They also have certain characteristics which make it important to write them effectively, especially given their heavy use.

As a start, unlike tasks and exploratory tests, scripted tests are reused repeatedly throughout a project, making reusability and maintainability crucial to their initial design. Many other test types (like focused exploratory sessions) are written in the knowledge that they are single-use, giving writers a degree of creative licence to make them as bespoke and as 'quick and dirty' as required. Scripted tests, however, need to be written with more care; reusability means that they can't be quick and dirty in style.

Unlike the unscripted test sessions I introduced earlier, scripted tests are defined through large numbers of small, individual tests. Because of this, the wording of scripted test titles needs to be concise and precise enough that you can browse a long list of scripted tests and pick out the ones you need. This also means that scripted tests need to be organised into agreed groups and subgroups, increasing discoverability when searching for a test set amongst the huge number of tests in the project. I've seen enough poorly organised test management databases to know that this is a frequent problem, even if it sounds like common sense to some readers.

I'll talk more about test maintainability and organisation later in this chapter, but it's worth mentioning here because much of the style exists to support these two attributes.

Let's look at a typical scripted test and I'll call out the key attributes of this style guide. I've given two examples below using the same quickmatch feature example I used earlier.

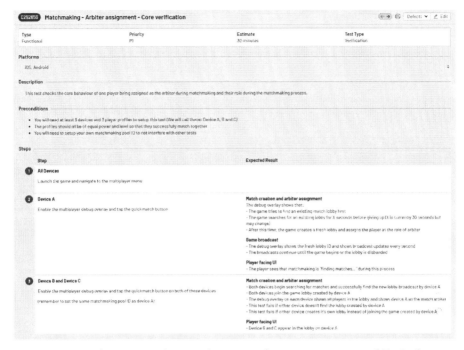

Figure 5.4 – An example scripted test using the test management tool TestRail,
covering the core flow for arbiter assignment during the matchmaking process

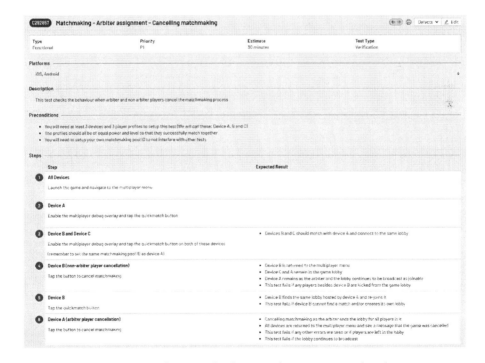

Figure 5.5 - Another example of a scripted test, written within the test
management tool TestRail. This one covers matchmaking cancellation flows

Title

Good style for scripted tests follows much the same direction that I gave earlier for test tasks. Just like tasks, scripted tests are usually viewed in long lists, sometimes with nested subgroups. They're also shared frequently in messages between the test team; a tester might ask a question and tell me the name of the test they're running. Because of this, titles should have prefixes to allocate them to groups and subgroups within the project. In the examples above, the titles tell us that the tests belong to the matchmaking test suite and are within the set of tests looking at the 'arbiter assignment' flows. The remaining section of test titles should be succinct, summarising the test scenario within a few words.

If a test can't be neatly summarised, this is a clue that the test is trying to cover too much and should be split up. For this reason, I write all of the titles first and edit them until I'm happy with the breakdown, then fill out the details of each test afterwards.

Because scripted tests are so often reused, it's a frequent occurrence for different members of the test team to be searching through the database, looking for applicable tests that can be run for their regression testing purposes. This increases the importance that tests are labelled clearly and use common terminology/keywords that the team has agreed on. Put another way: new scripted tests written by one QA analyst are added to the pool of shared tests that can be used by the wider team at any time; something that needs to be remembered when they are written. Here are a few examples of good and bad test titles.

Bad title styles

Title	Reason
"Prelude level"	Too generic, specifies a game area but not a test scenario
"Sniper"	Refers to a single item in a long list, commonly used for testing lists of assets. This should have a prefix or a description to describe what about the asset is being tested
"Performance verification"	Doesn't specify game area. Multiple performance tests could all exist in different parts of the game with this same title
"5.2.0 - Cloud save scenarios"	Refers to a specific release, which will hinder reusability, description is too generic
"Cloud save - Failure tests"	Too generic, don't just group all failure tests into one scripted test
"Test Case"	Contains no information on what the test is targeted at

Good title styles

Title	Reason
"Cloud save - Multiple accounts on one device"	Shows the test group with a prefix and succinctly describes the scenario that the test covers
"Sniper - Character model and textures verification"	Shows the test group and succinctly describes the scenario that the test covers
"Failure: Cloud save - Restricted network failure scenarios"	Agree a method for tagging scripted failure tests and/or create a subgroup for them. The failure scenario here is specific
"UI - Menu Navigation - Settings"	Good use of hierarchy to define the area that the test covers and the focus of testing. This style makes the long list of UI tests easier to navigate. This also can lean on the test analysis breakdown to define the hierarchy

Description

Because scripted tests are so numerous, I frequently see the description field empty, leaving the test steps themselves to show the tester what the test will cover. However, just because the test scenario is clear when the steps are being written, this doesn't mean it will be clear to the tester when they begin the test several days or weeks after it was written. Indeed, I've read my own tests several months or years later and have been left confused by what I'd written, forcing me to read through each step again before I understand what the test is trying to achieve.

In the best cases, understanding the intent of a test takes a little extra time to read through it all at once, and in the worst scenarios it makes no sense at all and requires a question to the original author.

This is all mitigated by a single sentence in the description field, written as plainly as possible, which describes what the test covers. Much like task descriptions which always start with, "The aim of this test is to…", scripted tests should have openings like: "This tests that…", "This test checks that…", "This test covers scenarios where…".

Once the intent of the test has been described in this field, you can still go on to add more specific and practical details for tests that require it. Complex scenarios may require additional explanation, document links, tool links, or special instructions if the tester won't be able to execute the test without support (Many of our tests require access to live ops tools which are only available to the embedded team, so tests are marked which require embedded test team support).

Lastly, the description field for scripted tests should be a place for detail which is specific to that individual test. Information which is common across many tests should be included at a higher level, either in the test suite within the test management tool, in the test task or even within accompanying test documentation pages. As with other fields, use of copy/paste when filling out scripted test descriptions is usually an indicator of inefficiency and the information should be placed in a single central location instead of copied across each test.

Preconditions

This is an optional field which appears in some tools and not others. It's not strictly necessary and can be left empty for simpler tests that don't require it.

This field is a great tool for maintaining brevity when writing larger, more complex tests. Like the examples I gave above, complex tests require a particular setup that the tester will need to execute before running the test steps. This setup could just be added to the test steps themselves, although it will bloat the test and make large tests even larger. Adding setup to the test steps also forces the setup to be described in more detail, increasing the unnecessary bloat.

Instead, test prerequisites can be added as a list in the preconditions field, separating the setup from the test itself. The preconditions list should also be populated relative to the domain experience of the testers. Unless a project is using crowdsourced testing, most testers should be working on projects permanently and should only need a top-level instruction in this field; there isn't any need to explain the setup further. In the examples I gave above, I've described that the tester should set up three profiles of the same level, but I haven't described how to do it. A more detailed explanation would be an unnecessary repeat of what the tester already knows, besides being applicable to all tests, so it would need to be written in a central location anyway. When used in this way, the preconditions field is a useful field for setting up the more complex test scenarios without writing paragraphs of explanation into your test steps.

Later in this chapter, I'll revisit the level of detail required within scripted tests. The successful use of each field relies heavily on striking the right balance of detail, between providing enough information to test effectively while not providing superfluous or repeat information that increases test writing and execution time.

The other powerful use of this field is to directly reference earlier tests, instructing the tester to execute an earlier test before running this one. Some tools, like TestRail, have rich text formatting which allows inline hyperlinks to the test, too. It's good practice to sequence the tests in the order the tester will run them, so I usually reference the test immediately before the one being run, which should have been the last test that the tester ran. This is a great time saver for tests that demand time-consuming setup, like those that require a player profile to be set in a specific way, or setting up multiple groups of players which interact together, like alliances or squads. This is also helpful when the test requires the game be in a specific state which is irreversible, like using a GDPR flow to request that the player profile data is deleted. The tests can be organised so that this needs to be done as few times as possible, whereas a badly organised test set might cause the tester to perform this setup more times than necessary.

Test Steps

The information given in test steps forms the core of what defines scripted tests, allowing the test writer to break down a test scenario into whatever level of granularity they see fit and get an explicit test result for each step. Scripted tests should share a common attribute regardless of whether they are written in a test management tool, a spreadsheet or a table. Each test step should have at least two fields: 'step', which describes the action to take, and 'expected result', which describes what they should see when they perform the step action. Additional fields can be added to each step in any tool, but any further information causes this approach to become even more heavyweight and in most cases isn't required, or isn't worth the added time investment when writing the tests.

Before diving into the guidance for each of these two fields, I'll first lay down some ground rules for test steps in general.

- Make good use of formatting like bolding and italics to highlight key information
- Use labels like 'device A' to clearly describe tests which use multiple player accounts, devices or player groups. The same style can also be used to describe other types of complex player flow.
- Add dividers and subtitles into the test steps to define sections within the test
- Avoid superfluous information and maintain precision for both fields
- Make good use of links which describe further information outside of the test
- Use bullet or numbered lists effectively
- Avoid all circumstantial information which would hinder reusability. This includes any references to setup or configurations which will no longer be accurate if the test is run at a later date (e.g. "Perform this step, then wait for the code team to update the event server with the latest data and relaunch the game," or "Run this step before the playtest, then wait for it to begin before continuing.")
- Avoid references to specific versions of the game where possible. This is common for tests that cover user flows like backwards compatibility. Instead of saying "Create a profile on the v1.3 client and then launch the v1.2 client on a second device and load the profile," try, "Create a profile on the current in-development game version and then launch the last game version released live and load the profile on it." Referencing specific versions in tests will confuse testers when those tests are being rerun and reduce reusability. If you can't

avoid this, make it obvious that the versions listed in the test are just examples and the tester should apply the logic to the current game versions under test.

All of these style guide points are intended to directly support either reusability, maintainability or readability. Your team may have their own methods to promote these same attributes – which is totally fine. Likewise, many readers may take the style given here as a starting point and build upon it to suit their project circumstances. Regardless of how exactly it is done and which styles are used, the focus should be on increasing the return on effort that goes into writing scripted tests. Having a complete and reliable set of scripted tests ready to be reused is a great asset during the later stages of project development and is essential for projects which make heavy use of regression testing.

Now I'll talk about the two fields which make up each test step. This is straightforward stuff, but you'd be amazed how often I see it done ineffectively.

Step

The 'step' field is the action that the tester must take. These fields should be a direct instruction for the tester to do something and, unlike the 'expected result' field, all of the steps should be either populated or removed from the test as there is no value having an empty field. The level of detail given to the tester is really important here, and test writers should remind themselves of the difference between a test script and a test case. The former is detailed enough that you could theoretically write it into code to automate it and, in nearly all cases, is too detailed for an experienced tester.

For example, you don't need to hold the tester's hand when navigating through menus if the details are irrelevant to the focus of the test (e.g. "Launch the game and tap the campaign button, then select single player, then select the 'Sapper' character..."). Tests should condense this into a single brief line or remove it entirely, instead skipping to the relevant game area where the test will take place. As a general rule, consider removing anything that seems to be a common boilerplate test step that appears across many of your tests. In all likelihood, they don't need to be included at all.

Conversely, relevant test steps should still refer to a specific action. They should instruct the tester to perform an action or a series of actions to reach a goal, like navigate to a game area, set up a profile, enable a feature toggle, attack an enemy, etc. For some tests which don't rely on player input so much, the action can simply be to draw attention to a specific thing, like a part of the UI or the game logs while some other game actions are occurring.

Steps that simply ask the tester to test something by using the word 'test' as part of the instruction should be avoided. This is a bit like trying to describe the meaning of a word by using the word itself: "The word 'test' means to test something". It's ineffective and doesn't instruct the tester on how to conduct the test effectively. Some of the poorest scripted tests I've reviewed read more like a checklist where each step asks the tester to test something and the expected result echoes the same fact without providing any more detail.

> *Step: Test that all the popup buttons have correct navigation*
> *Expected result: All the popup buttons have correct navigation*

There might be some circumstances where such a broad and non-specific direction is required, but I wouldn't recommend using the scripted test format for these tests. Providing too broad a focus leaves the tester to fill in all of the nuances of the test themselves, causing it to be run slightly differently depending on the tester – which is not a desirable outcome of scripted tests!

Scripted tests should guide the tester through a test scenario using the directions given in the 'step' field. Even if the steps are high-level, they should still guide the tester through the scenario. For test writers who haven't seen a running version of the feature yet, providing this level of detail can be difficult. This comes back to the problem of gathering sufficient detail from design documentation that's often never intended to define the design in such detail. When the details aren't available, it is tempting to write test steps like the example above. This should be avoided regardless. I usually speak to the feature authors while they are working on the feature to fill the gaps in feature knowledge. Often the designer also knows their intentions for a feature, even if all of those intentions haven't been documented formally, meaning that this information can still be gathered through questions.

Without further ado, here are some good and bad examples of test steps.

Bad 'test step' styles

Step	Reason
"Test that the menu functions correctly"	Too generic and also includes 'functions correctly' which should be part of the expected result and not the step
"Player is able to tap on the level icon without any issue"	Includes part of the expected result. Instead, this should be, 'tap on the level icon'
"Ford GT is in the race AND four players are playing AND the game gets a notification"	Several instructions are linked together here. You should either break this out into several steps or preface the test with information about how to interpret scenarios in this format

"Player state before level 12"	This should be written as an action, 'Inspect the player state' and have further instruction on how to setup the player and what game areas should be inspected
"Premium card pack #25"	Like some test cases, test steps are commonly written as long lists of game assets or components like this. There are better ways to organise large lists of assets, which I'll describe later in this chapter. Laboriously copying each asset into the test is time consuming and error prone
"Open the design one-pager for this event and verify all core features there against the build"	Too generic. Relies on the design too heavily. The steps should be broken down into smaller testable components, even if you still have to reference the design one-pager
"Launch the game and ask the internal team to check the Advertising ID"	Tests that include support from other teams should include details or links for what is expected from the other team members. Where is the Advertising ID checked from?

Good 'test step' styles

Step	Reason
"Tap the quest icon to see the goal for the level win conditions, then play and complete the level (don't use debug)"	Clear actions and added clarification for use of debug
"[Adjust Dashboard] Navigate to: Your app name>triage icon>all settings>testing console. Then input your advertising ID to search for it"	Clearly labels steps that occur outside of the game
"Use the debug to give yourself event points. Unlock each reward and check the score thresholds as you progress"	Direct and clear instructions for the tester to perform specific actions
"Setup Charles to monitor the network traffic to the device. Throughout the test, look out for the asset URL myproject.asset-server.com"	Direct and clear instructions for the tester to perform specific actions

"DEVICE A. Enable cloud save and download the profile that you set up in step 2"	Good use of bold and subtitles to mark important information in the task aiding readability
"Find the placeholder character and attempt to perform the following actions with it..."	This step would be followed by the list of actions. Words like 'attempt' are great for scripted failure tests where the action shouldn't succeed but you want the tester to try anyway
"WEEK 1. Use the debug to complete the daily chores and change the device time to skip forward to each next day's chore until you hit one that is locked. Then check the locked state of all chores in the list"	Good use of bold and subtitles to mark important information in the task. Let the tester know to use debug where it is allowed, preventing them from spending unnecessary time completing actions manually

Expected Result

The second field for test steps is 'expected result' which tells the tester what they should see after performing each action. This result is the point of truth with which they're comparing the running game to identify bugs. While the two fields have clear labels, I still see a lot of steps in the 'expected result' field and a lot of expected results in the 'step' field.

This field is more difficult to write because you frequently won't know exactly how you expect the feature to perform, particularly if you're writing the tests at an early stage of development. I'll admit that I sometimes get this far into the test plan and realise that I'm still missing some fine details of a feature and need to fire a few questions over to the designer to fill the gaps.

Unfortunately, it's common for the test writer to be forced to make assumptions about how the feature should function. In some cases, this works well, but in other cases it translates to lazy test writing and provides the tester with little concrete information. An effective example of filling in the gaps would be writing something like, "The game handles going offline gracefully and any error messages provide information which tells the player what happened and how they can fix it." Even if I don't know the exact errors that will be implemented, I can write the same result at a slightly higher level using the information that I have about how other parts of the game function. This way, the new functionality is at least consistent with the rest of the game. Consistency and standardisation is a good way to fill in the gaps if you don't have every detail to hand when writing scripted tests.

An ineffective example, something so common and yet so vague that it needs an immediate global intervention to bring it to an end, is writing 'functions as expected'.

I've seen many, many scripted tests that use this catch-all phrase as the expected result of test steps. 'The login option functions as expected'; 'Battle navigation functions as expected'; 'Switching weapons functions as expected'. It's easy because you can add the phrase to practically any test step's expected result and have it make sense. But this phrase is essentially saying 'make assumptions about how you expect this feature to work and then test it against those assumptions'. It doesn't give the tester a point of truth to base their testing on. These details need to be defined either in the test, or in a document or elsewhere; and the more specific they are, the more likely the tester will be able to identify bugs when running the test. Basing testing on assumptions will only catch the most obvious bugs, missing a majority of more subtle and intricate design intentions that the game might have.

Unlike 'step', this field doesn't need to be populated for every test step, which is another small mistake I frequently see. Tests should only include the expected result for steps that are the focus of the test case. If the target of the testing is a visual test for character particle effects, the first few steps of the test case might include instructions like 'Launch the game and navigate to the character menu,' and, 'Load the character and apply the outdoor camo outfit'. You don't need to write expected results for these steps because this test doesn't care if there is a bug while loading the game or navigating to the character menu. The focus of the test is specifically character particle effects. In this scenario, I often see test writers including boilerplate results like 'The game loads without issues' and 'The character menu loads when selected'. Not only does this mean the tests take longer to write, but it also adds superfluous information to the test case which dilutes the more important information and slows down test execution because the tester is now testing everything on the route to the focus of the test, as well as the focus itself.

The further consequence of this is that tests can fail even when the target of the test is healthy. If the test is targeting character particle effects but the tester sees a bug on the route to the character menu, they'll mark the earlier test step as a fail and the test will fail – even if no bugs are found for the character particle effects! This obviously gives a false representation of the test results and erodes confidence in the whole set of test data.

As a brief aside, finding major bugs on the route to the focus of a test is what triggers tests to be marked as blocked rather than failed. If you can't reach the target of the test, it's more accurate to say that the focus of the test is blocked. Practically, a blocking bug might also be assigned to a different team member because it's common for a feature to break another feature. These distinctions between bugs will surface during triage meeting discussions when the bugs are assigned to be fixed, so it's important that test writers get this right within the test cases.

To conclude this section, the expected result within tests should tell the tester what the player should see when performing each action and/or what the game should be doing. These should be specific and detailed. As you can see in the scripted test examples I gave earlier, multiple results can be neatly listed using bullet points and put into groups if many different things are happening simultaneously. As well as specifying what the tester should see, you can also specify what they shouldn't see. This still needs to be specific to the circumstance and not written as a generic catch-all statement. I like to start these lines with "This test fails if..." to make it clear to the tester what the fail criteria is for the test. Essentially, all of the expected results need to be true and all of these opposing results need to be false. Any other bugs found are still interesting to the project but wouldn't fail this specific test.

Bad 'expected result' styles

Expected Result	Reason
"Player customisation functions as expected"	Too generic
"No issues are seen and the feature is stable"	Too generic
"Navigate to each of the menus, they display with the updated HUD. Navigate to each popup, they are displayed on top of the HUD"	Includes instructions which should be within the 'step' field
"The grinding event matches the design document"	Too generic; relies too heavily on the design document for the entire feature test
"Performance is healthy"	A catch-all statement, usually added late if no separate performance tests were written. Avoid tacking-on results
"No other issues are found"	A catch-all statement; avoid reusing generic statements on every test

Good 'expected result' styles

Expected Result	Reason
"You get event points for activating items. You do NOT get event points for tapping rechargeable items that are not charged"	Describes both what should happen and what should not happen
"For each event reward, the visual asset is correctly updated according to the design for this event"	References the point of truth for the test, which is the external design doc and is specific in the verification point
"The data manifest file download fails but should be retried three times. Charles proxy should show three failed attempts to download the file"	Describes exactly what should be seen in the external tool for the test to pass. A good example of a non-player facing expected result

"No other graphical issues occur as a result of displaying this icon within this game area"	While this sounds generic, it references graphical issues specifically and also is specific to the use of the icon

Reference Images

Should you use reference images within scripted tests? Screenshots, concepts and wireframe designs can be a great visual aid when writing the expected result of scripted tests, particularly for UI and art tests. An image can communicate more than the most detailed list of expected results, showing the tester the rough position and orientation of UI elements – details that would be very difficult to describe. The same applies for a variety of art and content tests across games; level design maps for environment testing and concept artwork for character model testing are two examples.

Many test management tools allow you to include images in any part of the scripted test: description, steps or expected results. This allows test writers to include images directly into the expected result for each step. However, this often makes the test difficult to read and appear bloated. Some test writers also use this as an excuse to write insufficiently detailed expected results, either including the image without any text at all, or simply writing something like 'the popup should look like this' without calling out more specific verification points.

Images are a great addition to scripted tests, but should be used as a supplement and not as a replacement for written detail. Where possible, it's also more effective to link scripted tests to external documents containing the images, rather than copy each image into the test. Linking the test both saves time and prevents the images within the test from going out of date. I still receive questions from testers who are executing regression tests with old screenshots included in them because the screenshots include some UI component or feature which has since been removed from the game. These old tests border the line between being slightly outdated and completely obsolete.

5.4.3 Unscripted test style guide

This section covers all tests that aren't written in a scripted step-by-step format. The main focus here is on focused exploratory tests, sometimes referred to as session-based testing.* Some test management tools now allow for focused exploratory test types to be added and mixed into scripted test suites. However, teams will hardly ever use this

---

* True session-based testing is actually a specific type of focused exploratory test which puts emphasis on short exploratory sessions of a few hours and uses the output from earlier sessions to define follow up sessions that should be run. I take some pointers from it during this style guide but further detail into this technique is beyond the scope of this book.

feature and instead opt to write them directly into the project database work items so that the test instructions are embedded directly into the task.

Before I go into the details of the test session template, it's worth summarising the benefits of providing structure to exploratory testing. There are a good number of articles and books already published on the subject of executing exploratory testing effectively. A trait they all share is providing much needed structure to the testing while still maintaining the benefits that exploratory testing brings. Many teams run free exploratory tests because it's effective at finding bugs, allowing the testers to wander throughout the game, investigating whatever they feel like.

While being extremely easy to set up from the QA analyst side, free exploratory tests don't measure test coverage of the game or confidence in a feature, because the areas covered during testing and the depth of testing isn't tracked. Furthermore, exploratory testing has highly variable effectiveness when run by testers with different levels of experience, with only more experienced testers having enough good ideas to direct their own testing effectively. Testers lacking domain or technical experience will generally produce less effective results from free exploratory tests. Testers are also more likely to overlap each other's testing when multiple testers in a team are running exploratory tests at the same time, and, for the same reasons, are likely to leave gaps between the testing covered by each tester too.

The style guide in this section is my way of harnessing the power of exploratory testing within my test plans, but doing it in a way that can be controlled and directed to the areas that I'm interested in. A lot of the details I use are derived from other practices like session-based testing, persona testing and the use of test charters or mission statements. The styles of these test types overlap quite heavily, so we don't need to choose one and label it, but instead can use them as a guide to create our own focused exploratory tests.

Title and task focus

The task details should make it clear that the test type is exploratory. This immediately sets the tester's expectation of what is required from the test. Likewise, the task focus should make it clear that the test is to be carried out directly within the task and that there is no external link to a test run.

Test output

The task should define how and where the test output should be recorded. Sometimes this is in comments below the task, other times the test might call for an external document to be filled out. Scripted tests are easier for testers to report results because they always use a fixed format of marking each test with a dropdown of options like pass, fail, blocked, etc. Exploratory tests, however, need to provide more details about the output of the session. Is it intended to find bugs? Is it intended to gather information? Do you care about recording what areas the tester visited? Do you want ideas for follow up sessions?

v1.2 - Matchmaking - Arbiter assignment - Focused exploratory

📎 🔗 🔲 ☑ ...

Description

Test Description

QA Description

Background/Context

When players hit quickmatch, the logic first tries to find existing games which are waiting for more players to join before the game starts. If the logic can't find a suitable game after X seconds, it will create a fresh game with this player as the first in the new game, making it available for other players to then join too. This first player is assigned the role of the match arbiter, which isn't surfaced to the player.

During the matchmaking process before the game begins, the arbiter player is the host of the matchmaking process, broadcasting the open game for others to join. This creates some testing edge cases if the arbiter player chooses to cancel matchmaking or their internet connection drops. These types of actions -among others- will cause matchmaking to terminate for all the players in that pre-game lobby. e.g. If any other players leaves the game, everyone else will continue matching, but if the arbiter leaves, the pre-game lobby will disband.

Task Focus

The aim of this task is to investigate failure scenarios around the arbiter player during the matchmaking process, looking for any problems where the game isn't able to recover gracefully. In most scenarios the game should either continue on or be cancelled for all players.

> ℹ️ Debug: You can use the matchmaking overlay to show details of who is the arbiter and their current state, as well as connection timeout and retry logs. To be assigned the role of arbiter, the matchmaking service will need to have no available games to matchmaking with, you should use the dev_02 server for this test for this reason.

Use the ideas below as a rough guide for your test session and add your own ideas to it.

Test Guidance

- Try matchmaking as arbiter with a realistically poor network connection and then reduce gradually to zero, investigating the impact throughout
  - Note that you may seen different behaviour when the arbiter player has a poor connection vs. any other players having a poor connection
- Try using Charles/Fiddler to drop the connection only to the matchmaking service
  - Dropping the connection at different points in the matchmaking process may produce different results. Consider trying this before performing a specific action.
  - Dropping the connection for the arbiter will produce different results vs. any other player
- Try performing interruptive actions as the match arbiter during matchmaking
  - Be invited to another game and accept it while matchmaking as the arbiter
  - Suspend / resume the game while matchmaking as the arbiter
  - Terminate the game while matchmaking as the arbiter
  - Cancel matchmaking as the arbiter
- Try performing network and interruptive actions during different phases of matchmaking
  - Just when matchmaking fails to find a match and moves on to create a fresh session
  - While searching for other players
  - When the lobby is full and the game is about to begin
  - During the loading screen into the game

> ❌ **Example bugs**
>
> Here are some examples of the types of bugs that you might see
> - The match arbiter is able to leave a session and all other players are still waiting in the lobby
> - A matchmaking session stops broadcasting that it is available to join if the arbiter suspends and resumes the game during the matchmaking process
> - A matchmaking session has a free slot but is showing as full
> - No error is displayed when players are locked from a lobby where the arbiter has lost connection
> - The game crashes for all players if the match arbiter terminates the game during the loading screen into the session

Closed ▾ ✓ Done	
Fix versions	Test Version
Priority	↑ High
Assignee	🧑 Chris Howell
Branch	release/1.2-quickmatch
Test Suite URL	None
Reporter	
Platform	None
Time tracking	No time logged 15m remaining
Original Estimate	1w 3d
Automation	⚡ Rule executions
Git Integration	🔲 Open Git Integration
	Open

∨ Show 1 more field

Affects versions

Figure 5.6 – A focused exploratory test defined directly within a test plan sub-task and written in the database tool JIRA

Some of my focused exploratory tests, like performance tests, are framed as investigations where I'm less interested in the raw performance data and more interested in the conclusions that the tester has drawn from that data. I don't want the tester to mindlessly record the memory usage during their test and then just write down the number for me; I want them to consider it carefully and interpret the meaning of it. The average memory usage is 856MB for the session – so what? We need to know the memory budget and what the tester was doing during the session to make conclusions about whether that test result is actually good or bad. The format of the test output is closely associated with the goal of the test session. If you're explicit about both, and they align, then you're more likely to get what you want from the tester executing the test.

Because the output of exploratory sessions is always a free text field, the actual format and amount of detail can vary wildly from tester to tester. Writing that they 'spent three hours investigating the area and found no bugs' isn't a sufficient amount of detail to give me confidence that they tested the area as deeply as I had intended. Neither does it provide any clues about further testing. At the other extreme, writing vast paragraphs of notes makes it hard to pick out the relevant details. For the tester, it's a balance of providing enough detail to be helpful but not writing an essay of irrelevant details. In my experience, if QA analysts want to provide guidance and feedback on test output, it's best left to recurring meetings with the test team leads or instant message channels amongst the leads. While the QA analyst should set their expectations within the task focus, going further to include information that should be more 'best practice' is a waste of valuable space within the session template.

Test guidance

I always provide guidance beyond just the task focus during focused exploratory testing. It provides initial good ideas that the tester can use to navigate through the test. The test guidance can be as sparse as a single mission statement or test charter which sets the direction for the session but, in my experience, providing more information greatly increases the quality of the test output. Running a test session without something to kickstart the ideas is like asking a room full of people for ideas and getting nothing but silence: you need a spark to get the discussion going. Providing test guidance as a series of bullet points draws attention to specific points of interest which the tester can use as markers to navigate their way through the greater scope of the session.

When defining a task focus without follow-up ideas, the scope of a session is commonly too broad and testers can gravitate towards the familiar areas of experience without really considering what areas they should cover for the session. I've already spoken about how many testers see all failure testing as a brute force, button mashing, cable pulling activity. This is exactly the kind of output that I'm trying to avoid when adding test guidance into exploratory tests: it gently nudges the tester into a specific direction for a session, setting expectations *and* giving ideas.

A prerequisite of the QA analyst role is to be a great tester and know what should be tested. For this reason, QA analysts are well-placed to provide genuinely good ideas when writing guidance for focused exploratory tests. When I write these tests, I list the areas that I would test if I were running the session myself, I list areas and scenarios which my experience tells me are the most likely to find bugs.

I also add and explain scenarios which come from having a greater understanding of the game due to being embedded within the development team – scenarios the tester wouldn't be aware of. Some test ideas will have come from conversations with the feature authors or from reviews of the test plan too. This can act as a general educational piece as well as practical guidance, transferring knowledge to the testers over time.

Industry tales: The cycle of test experience

I created a short training presentation a few years ago talking about the development and transfer of testing knowledge around the team. The content described how testers see patterns in where and how bugs occur in their projects, that help the tester predict where bugs will occur again. The first time a tester finds a specific type of bug, they might have found it by accident or by following a scripted test case which told them to look for the bug. Some unique bugs occur once and are then forgotten. However, most bugs occur in patterns, occurring again and again. This isn't limited to a single project, with many games built using similar techniques; this phenomenon even spans across projects. Because of this similarity, they're all bound by the same limitations and share many common bugs.

Consider a typical functional localisation test. It will check for bugs like cut off text, or text bleeding out of its UI container. It might look for line-wrapping and font size bugs. It might also look for untranslated text, missing text, or have a check for languages that don't use the Latin alphabet. All of these common checks exist because every game project that I've worked on has used roughly the same technique for populating text strings at runtime from a localisation sheet. None of the text is hardcoded and the UI artist can't design all UI perfectly for every language. Because localisation is populated in the same way for each project, bugs can be predicted easily.

The second and third time a tester finds a specific type of bug, they begin to see this pattern and should remember the information when running tests in the future. Having experienced a similar scenario in the past, a tester can predict with some confidence, 'If I perform this test scenario then I'm likely to see this type of bug'. This is the root of test experience and what ultimately differentiates experienced testers and makes them so effective when running exploratory tests. Their experience of historical bug patterns allows them to better predict where bugs will occur again in future projects. The more successful this prediction is, the more effective exploratory testing becomes.

This happened to me during the first projects I worked on as a tester. We had a collection of Xbox 360 devkits that we could use for our testing. The first Kinect camera was due to be released and so we had many small booths setup in our office, with full height temporary walls, a small desk and home AV unit in each, complete with a TV and our devkits. The booths were added to accommodate the space that the Kinect camera required so that testers wouldn't be colliding with each other at their desks. It was normal to have more than one 360 devkit each and more than one TV too – we were able to run soak tests in the background or switch kits and continue testing while waiting for builds and crash dump uploads.

Having multiple kits and TVs in my booth meant that I was able to cover at least two different display types simultaneously. While most of the screens we had were early LCD TVs in widescreen aspect ratio (16:9), we also had a collection of older CRT TVs in normal aspect ratio (4:3) because they were still widely supported. My very first projects were apps for the Xbox 360 (not games), the Sky Player app and the Canal Universe TV app. Both of these had a similar UI structure and style of video streaming apps, and importantly, both showed the same types of bugs when displayed in 4:3 ratio on the older TVs. When I moved onto the next set of projects, I carried this information with me and knew that I'd always get a good haul of bugs from performing my testing on a 4:3 ratio screen.

The bug patterns occurred because widescreen was the primary display ratio the apps were intended for and the older CRT screens had a much lower display resolution as well as the different aspect ratio. Many of the bugs were fixed by configuring the display safe area for the older screens, which is a method for setting the visible area of the screen. Anything outside of the safe area was at risk of being off-screen on some displays. As well as the common safe area issue, there was also a pattern of small text becoming unreadably blurry on the lower resolution, another bug type I was always looking out for.

We went on to test several other apps for the Xbox 360 which would also exhibit the same pattern of bugs, allowing me to take that experience and apply it repeatedly and more efficiently for each new project.

My training explained how this experience of bug patterns can be transferred across a test team.

When a QA analyst writes a test, providing guidance and ideas to the tester from their own experience, they're essentially handing over their knowledge to the tester instead of performing the testing themselves. They are saying, "look here and you will find bugs".

By providing this information within focused exploratory tests, test knowledge and experience is transferred from senior members of the team to the more junior testers, allowing them to discover new bug patterns more quickly than they would otherwise. Common bug-finding scenarios are distributed amongst the team, balancing out the knowledge gaps and increasing the consistency of knowledge tester-to-tester. Rather than leaving testers to run free exploratory testing in their own silo, this method is advocating that the inner workings of exploratory tests are made transparent, documented and shared openly; something which can only lead to good things. Finally, some of these testers will move into QA analyst roles, writing tests of their own and handing their knowledge to the next group of testers joining the team, completing the cycle.

As a side note, it's exciting as a tester to investigate complex and interesting bugs. You might see clues that something has gone wrong before the full bug shows itself, so you need to pull on the thread to unravel the bug. As a test writer, I've spent much less time executing tests myself and more time planning and writing tests for others to run. However, the excitement of discovering bugs myself has been replaced by directing testers towards areas and finding out that the tipoff has uncovered bugs. It's a great feeling to have an idea when writing a test session and then have that idea come to fruition when the test is run.

Example bugs

I only include this field when a test session is complex or technical, and I want to double-down on explaining what the test is hoping to find. Providing examples helps the tester identify bugs when they occur, giving them clues about what to look out for during their testing. Not all bugs are obvious – the expected behaviour of technical systems within games is a common example of this. In the matchmaking-focused exploratory example above, I've used this section to provide some examples of incorrect behaviour of the matchmaking system: things that would be obvious to the developer who wrote the code but would likely be missed by a tester without this to prompt them.

This section is also a good place to provide some complex bug examples, planting the idea that bugs frequently occur when multiple different things are happening at once. See this example, "A matchmaking session stops broadcasting that it is available to join if the arbiter suspends and resumes the game during the matchmaking process". It reminds the tester not just to suspend and resume scenarios, but to try them as different players and at different times. It also sets the idea that even after you've performed the action (suspending and resuming the game), the bug might not be immediately obvious. You'd have to inspect the matchmaking logs or try other actions, like trying to join that game, after performing the first action.

The bug examples need to be specific and realistic for them to achieve these goals effectively. Much like the test guidance, they work best when they're driven by the test writer's experience of bugs that have occurred in past features and projects. Adding obvious or vague bug examples here isn't productive though, so don't be tempted to include things like, 'the game crashes when matchmaking starts', or, 'placeholder art is shown on the matchmaking UI' since these examples would be immediately recognisable to the tester anyway. Many focused exploratory tests won't require the level of guidance that this section provides, so don't try to force-fit it if it's not required.

Test estimate

An estimate for the focused exploratory session is the only other field that is strictly required. Adding an estimate provides a guide to how deeply the testers should be testing and how many testers should be assigned to the task. If I've described the test focus as a 'brief investigation', I follow this up with a corresponding test estimate to cement this expectation, typically one to two work-days. A more in-depth investigation might take a week for three to five testers, totalling at least three work-weeks. As an aside, I usually speak to the test leads who are responsible for tester task assignment and give them a hint on the number of testers I think each task would need. That way, they have some guidance during the daily task division amongst the team.

Importantly, the test estimate also tells the tester(s) when to stop testing. Unlike scripted tests which show clearly when testing is complete, exploratory tests are not so well defined and need this added explicitly. With test time nearly always at a premium, closely managing the time spent running these sessions is important. If a test isn't high priority, then don't let it overrun the allocated time.

All test estimates should be added in work-days for clarity and should be consistent across the entire project. This means a test can be run by one or many testers. For example, two work-days could be run by a single tester over two days or by two testers over one day. It's common for tests to run by groups of testers and for testers to be reassigned between different tasks too, so using work-days is important to capture the total test effort across the group.

Part of the reason to include estimates is so that the testers can record their actual time spent in the task. This comparison can be used to generate more accurate estimates for future tasks. When deciding estimates, they don't need to be precise to the minute. Rounding to the nearest half-day (four hours) is enough to make it a useful field without investing too much time calculating precise estimates and inspecting minor differences with the actual time spent. The practicalities of testers accurately totalling their actual test time is difficult too, making it unproductive to try recording test time with greater accuracy than four-hour blocks.

This process of providing accurate estimates and accurate test time is another area where QA analysts should be careful to only invest enough time creating estimates to make them a helpful addition. Incorrect or inconsistent use of this field is common. Many teams don't use it all because they don't see the value in it. Even if estimates aren't used to report on test progress at a project level or aren't requested from the QA lead in the studio, individual test writers can still include estimates in their own tasks for their own evaluation.

You might be wondering whether I'll give guidance on how to generate good test estimates for test tasks. Creating accurate estimates is a bigger topic beyond the scope of this sectioN. Test estimates don't just provide guidance for the testers; they're also used to generate estimates for the test execution schedule and predict project milestones, which are presented to the project leadership to roll into the project schedule. While I've introduced the importance of the test estimate field in this section, you should know that these uses delve into more advanced topics, covering things that test managers will care about.

5.4.4 'The detective' writing style

This section digs deeper into the writing style of focused exploratory tests. I frequently write mine using words and phrases that would be at home in some murder mystery show, using words like 'investigate' and 'clues' and telling the tester to lookout for anything 'unusual or mysterious'.

I do this because it's a super-effective mindset to adopt during exploratory testing, setting the tone for *how* the tester should be thinking during the session. Communicating to someone else how they should be thinking about something is difficult, and the analogy of approaching testing like a detective investigating a crime scene helps us do this for exploratory tests.

Conversely, test writers can include all of the components listed in this section and still have an inadequate exploratory test. Why? Because the writing style and words used have an impact on how testers will interpret the session. Using words like 'verify', 'test' or 'check' all suggest a direct verification with limited scope, which is counterproductive to the essence of an exploratory investigation which has unlimited scope and requires 'out of the box' thinking.

Experienced testers and test writers are likely to have developed their own mindset when conducting exploratory testing, but junior testers won't have developed this fully yet. Because of this, I sometimes find that my exploratory guidance has been followed like a scripted test, testing each idea exactly and then ending the test without thinking more deeply about the focus of testing. I also find testers that are accustomed to the test telling them exactly what the expected result *should* be and don't pick up on clues and unusual behaviour which might lead to a bug. In the best cases, the tester will be suspicious enough to message me and ask, but I've read many test session reports which suggest this hasn't happened.

When using this style my opening sentence will be something like this.

> *"The aim of this test is to investigate {TEST SCENARIO} using the clues that we've gathered so far, listed below".*

It's often implied that the tester should be looking for bugs, but since bugs aren't always obvious, I highlight what they should be looking for to set the expectation.

> *"Lookout for any anomalies, inconsistencies or irregularities during testing. Cross-checking them with the previous build will allow us to attribute them to the new changes".*

Often subtle differences in the behaviour of the game are hard to spot, but will indicate that something new is happening behind the scenes and lead to a bug if identified correctly. This analogy and wording prepares the tester to be looking for potentially small and subtle changes: the bugs aren't going to be obvious or easy to find, and the tester may only find one issue throughout the entire session.

There are a few detective tools that can be added to the wording to increase the chances that the tester will spot clues when they appear. Cross-checking with older builds before a change is a great way of performing side-by-side analysis to find new anomalies and attribute them to the change. For example, comparing two builds, one with a new feature and one without, allows bugs to be attributed specifically to that feature addition. Often, these investigations aren't looking for *any* bugs, they're looking for new bugs that were introduced with a feature. Checking for consistency between different parts of the game is another effective tool: testers can take screenshots or record details on a notepad and then compare with other areas of the game.

Lastly, the detective style should encourage testers to take a slower and more considered approach to their investigation, creating spreadsheets, tables or documents to track the clues and data for their testing – much like taking screenshots and then comparing the images is better than trying to just remember the details for comparison. Recording observations and data allows the tester the time to inspect and analyse the target of testing much more closely. When called out explicitly within the test, the tester is also less likely to get bored with not finding bugs, and test beyond the scope of the session in an effort to find them. Testers are often competitive about their bug count, which can be detrimental to a focused exploratory test run in the detective style. This isn't always the case, but it is something that test writers need to be aware of.

5.4.5 'The science experiment' writing style

This is another common writing style that I adopt when running focused exploratory test sessions that are geared towards collecting data and forming conclusions to answer specific questions. It's effective when paired with non-functional tests that look at areas like performance or stability. The goal of these sessions is to answer questions like these.

- Does the new feature have an acceptable frame rate across all of our supported devices?
- Does the game take too long to load?
- Is the current mean time to failure acceptable for release?

This style is also great for any questions which are subjective and so not easy to answer.

- Is the new event too difficult?
- Are the car engine sounds accurate enough?
- Does the dim lighting in this section inhibit gameplay?

All of these questions are difficult to answer and when they *are* answered, it's often complex and long, with caveats and follow up questions. Because of this, special care needs to be taken to collect the data in a controlled way. It needs to be well planned, like a science experiment, the general format of which is something like this: pose a question, form a hypothesis, gather the data, analyse the data, form a conclusion, evaluate against the hypothesis.

This is a good time to remember that the goal of testing is to gather information so the project stakeholders can make decisions on it. When doing this, no one will want to read through pages of performance metrics or read several paragraphs about the difficulty of an event. They'll just want the conclusion: an executive summary of the work. Gathering the raw data isn't enough, the test team needs to correctly interpret that data and form a conclusion from it. This is where our science experiment writing style comes into play.

The phrases used matter less: you can still ask the tester to 'investigate' the area.

However, the test focus should explicitly explain that the intent of the session is to answer a question and not just gather data or log bugs. For new sessions in this style, it's recommended that the experimental steps are listed to help guide the tester through the process. In addition to this, I talk with the test team about the intent of this style and place emphasis on the need to analyse and conclude the data.

Before I started using this style and talking to our current test team about analysing the data they produce, I would get completed performance tests returned to me with a vast array of data across different devices, profiles and performance metrics. I'd have to read through all of the data and draw conclusions myself. The tests were intended to check if the latest release had a negative impact on the game's performance and, if it had, was the impact severe enough that we'd have to log a bug and do something to fix it. This task wasn't just about recording the current state of the game's performance; it was a comparison with previous releases and an assessment of what we deemed as 'severe'. Being a mobile project, we also had to answer this question for a range of different devices and different player profile sizes, which would complicate the answer. Players with the largest profiles, who were playing on the lowest performance devices, would see the worst experience, so measuring the real impact of the data required it to be cross-referenced with analytics data on the number of real players with these setups.

I later adopted the science experiment writing style for these test tasks, and included instructions within the task focus to analyse the data and draw conclusions from it. The model output of the task is a conclusion followed by the full data set, in case readers want to dig into the details further. This forces the tester to think about what the data means and not just record it blindly so that someone else can figure that out. It also means that the tester is more likely to identify anomalous results during the task and either capture the data again or investigate the anomaly further. Before I used this style, the data set might have results which were clearly inaccurate, but the tester had recorded the numbers anyway, without really thinking about what it had meant. From this, testing is carried out with more vigilance and bugs are more likely to be found during the process of capturing the data.

To extend this style even further, test writers can ask the testers to form a hypothesis before running the test. Ask them what results they expect to see. This forces the tester to consider the inputs of the testing. When recording performance data each release, the tester should look through the features added during that release and consider the impact they might have on performance. New art content may increase build sizes or memory use; new visual effects may decrease frame rate. If I were running this test myself, I would do this mentally and not record it in the test. It doesn't need to be a deep activity. Having a hypothesis also forces the tester to think in a certain way during the test and helps them make sense of the data once they record it. When reviewing performance results alongside code teams, slightly reduced performance is often an expected and accepted result, since the code team knows that the results match the feature additions that were made during the release. It's frequently the case that the results are only good or bad when relative to the expectations of those results.

Lastly, many difficult test questions need to be approached in a structured and considered way. Science experiments keep all input variables the same and only change one variable at a time so that a fair comparison can be made. The experiment is setup in a specific way to allow for an 'apples to apples' comparison. Answering test questions is the same, tests need to be setup carefully so that fair comparisons can be made. It's very easy to mess up a test that aims to answer a question by not considering one of the variables, I've done it many times and have been forced to run the whole test again. The two main pitfalls are: not considering all variables, changing too many variables at the same time. Both of these mistakes can lead to a test investigation which either produces flawed data or produces a set of messy data that makes it difficult to answer the question. If you were running a test which answers questions on the realism of car engine sounds, a mistake might be forgetting to consider the number of audio channels you have connected, are you trying to answer the question for two-channel headphones or six-channel surround sound systems? The different setups would likely affect the answer. If you were testing the difficulty of an in-game event, a mistake might be forgetting that there are different configurations for the event because it's being run as an A/B test. The different variants of the A/B test would undoubtedly alter the results of the experiment.

5.5   Art and content-heavy test writing

Art and content testing within games presents a unique test writing challenge because of the huge number of assets to be tested. Consider every item in a game, every character, every car, every skin, every level. These content lists frequently span hundreds of items and are impractical to track within a test management tool without an alternative approach to setting up tests. As I discussed earlier, copy-pasting a test for every item in the list would be incredibly tedious and error-prone.

Tools that support combinatorial test techniques allow you to multiply out a single test across a list of items, eliminating a majority of the repetitive work, but the test writer still needs to get the item list from the game and into the test management tool. Some tools have implemented APIs (application programming interfaces) which allow you to write a script that does the heavy lifting of importing your asset list into the tool. However, most test management tools aren't designed to handle such large lists and the result is ugly when you try it.

Instead, a hybrid approach between a spreadsheet and a test management tool is required. The test management tool should still contain the test or set of tests that need to be run against each game asset, so the benefits of using a tool for these tests remain. But the tracking of those tests across the list of game assets can be done in an accompanying spreadsheet. This works particularly well when we consider that most design teams will use spreadsheets to set up the game's raw item data in the first place, allowing testers to copy the relevant data directly from the source files or even set up an active data connection between the spreadsheets.

For the setup of the accompanying test sheet, it should contain the list of items as well as any supplementary information that the tester will need to execute the tests. A recent project had a large list of quests all set up and controllable within the game data, so we used this approach to organise the testing. The test spreadsheet included details on the quest ID, name, description and reward. The tester would need all of this information to verify that the quest could be completed and that the correct reward was given. This shows how this method extends beyond just art and content: it's also beneficial when testing large sets of data like the quests in this example. Game data is set up in spreadsheets alongside the raw item data and presents the same test challenges.

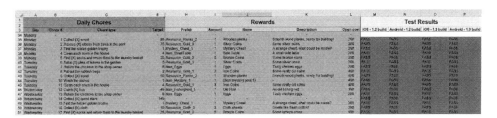

Figure 5.7 – A sample of a test tracking sheet for quests and their records, imported directly from the raw design data. This can include additional data like the prefab name which might enable testers to unlock the item or spawn it direct from debug for easy access.

The idea here is that the sheet supplies data specific to each item, while the tests describe the test method. Put another way, the tests define *how* to test and the sheet defines *what* to test.

The method of testing individual assets, like in-game items, would be very similar to this example. While the visual asset for each item (3D model, sprite or something else) obviously won't be stored in a spreadsheet, all of the metadata for the item will be. This will include all of the information about the item, both player facing and for use within the game code. Often this will include a unique ID for the item which the game code will use to find the corresponding art assets. Testers can use this information to spawn an item directly or use other types of game debug to reach and test each item more easily.

A further advantage of using the source game data files in this way is that they often contain a much more complete list of game content that the tester might see in the game. There can be legacy content which only old players will have, content that is only available through specific AB test game configurations and content that is present in the game data but just isn't made available to the player. This is a great way of increasing the scope of content testing to include those 'difficult to reach' assets that testers are unlikely to come across during their testing.

The test approach to art and content testing is important to get right because the testing requires a great deal of the team's resources. This increases the emphasis on good organisation of tests from the outset (it's extremely difficult to change your approach once you've started). Using a spreadsheet and having an efficient way of importing the design data into your test sheet also supports the focus on maintainability, reducing repeated manual effort when the design data is updated. To summarise, carefully consider your approach to art and content test writing before you begin, be cautious of copy-paste overuse and aim for reusability.

Industry tales: Open world environment testing

The Forza Horizon series is a great example of an open world game which has a huge amount of environment content that requires testing, as well as a long list of cars, each with unique visual, sound and data attributes.

While I was working on the third instalment in the series, we were defining new ways to categorise and organise our testing*. Through the process of improving our tests, all the QA analysts would meet to discuss the testing in their areas and how the new definitions and processes fit into their test plans. The QA analyst responsible for the environment testing had a different problem from the rest of the test plans, because a majority of their tests were unscripted, which in any other scenario would have raised concerns about the granularity of the test plan. As we know, unscripted tests can be very high-level and make tracking test progress very difficult. In addition to this irregularity, their work effort was divided differently, with much less time allocated to writing tests and much more allocated to where within the game those tests would be run and at which point in the project. So why was the environment test ownership so different to the other functional areas?

The game environment was a single open world map and the environment art team within the studio had broken it down into a grid of boxed sections, much like you would see on a real map. For all intents and purposes, each section of

---

*   See the section on the test design framework in chapter one.

the environment would be created and tested in the same way. Each section was created through a series of art iterations, starting with white box concepting and going through several rounds of placing final assets and polishing. The tests were written and scheduled to be run after each corresponding iteration was complete for a map section.

The test setup was unique because the test owner was able to write a single set of tests that could be applied to any of the environment map sections. While the complete process would take many months to create and test, much of the work from the test team was a cycle of repeating the same tests across all sections of the map.

The tests themselves would need to consider what the aim of the testing was for each art iteration. The first test runs of each section might only be looking for problems with the collision mesh and ignore anything like performance or visual bugs, while later test runs would be looking for these bugs, knowing that the final art assets had been placed already. Once the test runs were in place to test each environment iteration, the test plan was ready to duplicate out across all map sections.

Much of the QA analyst's time beyond the initial test writing would be spent organising the test schedule for each map section with the environment art team. The QA analyst would need to track the current state of each section and decide when the next iteration was ready to be tested. They then created the test schedule based on this, making sure that the environment testers wouldn't be double booked to work on two map sections at the same time.

While this might sound like an easy time, content testing raises huge numbers of minor polish bugs, driving the project's bug numbers into the hundreds and thousands. Retaining control on the state of testing for each map section and the bugs associated with it requires a much higher degree of organisation than standard functional testing. Bugs and tests would share common prefixes and fields (as defined by the QA analyst) to help categorise and associate them. Non-content test areas generally have low enough bug numbers that the test owner will be familiar with all of the bugs logged within their area of ownership. Content testing, however, creates so many bugs that oversight on all of them is impossible. Instead the test owner must rely on strict processes to make sure they're logged efficiently and consistently.

Testing and bugging at this scale creates unique risks to the test and project schedule. The huge testing resources that were taken up testing the environment meant that there was a sub test team that would be continuously executing the environment tests throughout the life of the project. Incorrect test estimations or test capacity problems with that team would have a directly negative influence on the final test complete date for the project. For this same reason, it was more critical that the progress of this testing was tracked closely to identify the earliest deviation from the plan.

Finally, the tests themselves were irregular and didn't fit the guide that we had put in place to ensure a good balance between the different test types: scripted, unscripted, verification and failure. We had agreed that test plans should use scripted tests for a majority of their coverage to ensure that testing was tracked and thorough, and to promote reusability for future titles in the franchise.

The environment tests broke this mould by needing to be unscripted. For any given map section, it wasn't possible to write a scripted test which would call out specifics like the locations of objects (like buildings or foliage for example). Writing tests which referred to specific objects would be both ineffective and incredibly tedious, 'Drive to the corner of the grid. A building is positioned at the crossroads and surrounded by five trees. Street furniture surrounds the crossroads junction and is orientated to face the oncoming traffic, etc…'.

Instead, the environment tests required the test writer to define a set of test criteria and then have the tester explore the map section and log bugs where the criteria was not adhered to. This criteria differed depending on the current iteration of the environment section but might include things like: 'All objects are level with the ground, not floating or sunk in', 'All trees have collision enabled but bushes and grass do not', 'All street furniture is textured and all light sources are in place'.

While these tests were unscripted, they had a strict focus defined by both the test criteria and by the map area that they were testing in, striking a balance between the bug-finding power of exploratory testing and the structure of scripted tests.

5.6   Test case abstraction

This technique is fundamental to writing test cases with reusability in mind and has been present in many of my examples so far, without being explicitly labelled.

Test case abstraction is the process of splitting up large test suites into smaller and more generic sets to allow those sets to be reused.

Instead of writing an entire set of tests with a specific feature change in mind and grouping them all together under the name of that feature, many parts of the test plan will be relevant to future feature changes, and can benefit from being separated into their own category and written in a more generic way. In other words, the smaller test suites are abstracted away from the feature for which they are currently being used.

To give a basic example: a new multiplayer custom match feature could use platform notifications to send invites to players. Some of the functionality to be tested is specific to the custom match feature, but much of it will be general notification functionality. If it doesn't exist already, the test writer should create a small test suite for notification functionality which makes no reference to the custom match feature for which it is being used in this instance. By choosing to write a generic notifications test suite, the test writer has set up those tests to be more easily found and reused by other test writers.

Let's assume another QA analyst is writing a test suite for a new game event type, and part of the functionality is a teaser notification triggered one day before the event is due to begin and again on the last day of the event. This test writer will have an easier time because notification tests already exist and don't need to be modified, because they don't reference a particular feature. The notifications suite can also be improved over time as other features make use of the new notifications functionality.

There is a balance to be struck, however. Abstracting a feature into too many parts results in important details being lost. For some tests to make sense, you need to refer to specific instances in use right now and avoid talking about them in a generic way. Applying the technique too much can make it difficult to organise all of the parts and look very messy when you group the parts into a single test plan. Choosing when to utilise test case abstraction and how to group tests requires practising with real features. The technique is a cooperative effort between anyone writing test cases on a project, and so only works well when all contributors are aligned on the approach. Starting to apply it when the existing test suites on the project aren't well organised can also be difficult, so don't be put off if you can't see an immediate benefit. The technique benefits are cumulative and will snowball the more it is used successfully throughout the lifetime of a project.

5.7   Pitfalls of test writing

In this section I'll group together all of the most common problems I see in tests so they can be more easily recalled during your own test writing. Some of these pitfalls I've mentioned already and are listed again here together for easy review, while others are new to this section. They have all come directly from working with testers and QA analysts, conducting peer reviews of each other's work and mentoring testers moving into QA analyst roles. This list isn't exclusive to the work of others either – some of the pitfalls are listed because they've been identified in my own tests, either by myself or by my peers. Like many skills, you're never 'done' when it comes to improving your test writing. There are always new pitfalls in areas of unfamiliar domain or technical test knowledge.

Copying design details directly into test cases

Tests should not just be a translation of design documents into test cases. While there will always be parallels between tests and designs, the scope of testing should always be larger. Tests will nearly always be more detailed too, aiming to expose small details not specified within designs. Try to avoid tests that follow this pattern: the design says, 'This feature performs this function,' and the test simply says, 'Test that this feature performs this function'.

Writing overly generic test cases

I see this one *a lot*. It occurs when test writers don't have enough information or time to write more detailed test cases, so they write tests on the sparse information that they have available instead. Test writers should recognise the root cause of this and seek more information before embarking on test writing. This is also a symptom of not conducting test analysis and/or test planning steps before test writing.

This can be identified by overuse of catchall phrases like 'functions as expected'. This also appears when the test step and expected result are just repeats of each other: 'Enter the battle and confirm that the units move correctly' as the step and, 'In the battle the units move correctly' as the expected result.

I also see tests that don't explicitly ask the tester to check anything, but instead define a breakdown of the feature. The test titles just read as parts of the feature ('unlocks', 'drag race', 'point scoring', etc.) instead of more specific test cases or scenarios. The test steps for these often read more like feature sub-parts or are copies of phrases from the design documents: 'drag races score race points when you win', 'new cars are unlocked when races are won'. While these phrases aren't incorrect, they aren't specific enough to provide effective test coverage and will miss important details of the feature.

Overuse of copy/paste to duplicate tests or test steps

Copy/paste is the enemy of maintainability when writing tests. I often see expected results duplicated for many steps within a test case. This is sometimes because the expected results include generic filler statements that could apply to every step in the test case, and other times because the test is iterating through a list. Where this is unavoidable, try instead to write the expected result only once at the top of the test and have a corresponding setup step like this, followed by the list of items as further test steps.

Step:
Spawn each of the following items and inspect the particle effects, animations and sprites on each. The following expected results should apply to all steps within this test case.

Expected result:
- *The sprite for the item matches the linked design*
- *Particle effects display in front of the item and are free from graphical anomalies*
- *All animations loop correctly and are smoothly played for each item*

The same pitfall applies to copy/pasting whole test cases. Sometimes this is unavoidable because two test scenarios are very similar and share many test steps, allowing you to copy them and make the small changes required instead of writing it from scratch. As well as creating maintainability problems, this also exposes the tests to copy/paste errors and the duplication of a single mistake. I've done this many times, accidently copying a mistake across a set of tests, which invariably leads to questions from the testers during test execution. Glaring copy/paste errors also make the tests look sloppy in the best scenarios and can completely confuse testers in the worst case, making them an impactful mistake.

Copying test cases many times is usually a sign that they could be organised or broken down more effectively. Many tests that are very similar could instead be grouped into a single test. Other times, test cases are duplicated to run them on different game configurations. Tools should be used to perform this duplication for you when a test run is created, removing the need to create duplicates of the original test case.

Remember that test cases are just templates where each test run is an instance of that template. You can use the tools to duplicate tests at runtime within each test run, but you should only ever have one copy of the original template test case. Don't be tempted to make copies of the original test case.

Writing tests so detailed that you never run them again

When a new feature is introduced, the testing needs to be at its most thorough and can be less rigorous if the feature is changed or requires regression testing in the future. While having a complete set of tests that are thorough and detailed is an asset, this kind of test suite isn't ideal if you require a lighter set of tests to run when the feature is changed in the future or if you want to add the feature tests to a set of regression tests.

While this is a complex problem to have, it's not uncommon. If you look through all the existing test suites for your current project, I can almost guarantee that you will find a few long-lost test suites for older features which are very detailed but are no longer relevant because the feature has since stabilised.

Often, the original tests were designed to be fairly heavyweight and time-consuming for the tester, making the total time estimate for the run quite long. When you run regression testing against existing areas, you usually want the testing to be broader and not as deep, since there can be a lot of areas to cover. So having overly detailed tests has the effect of reducing their reusability too. Test writers should be conscious of this when writing long and comprehensive tests, especially if they will take a while to run.

One way to remedy this in your project is a system whereby a subset of core tests within each suite is marked as priority 1. This subset of tests covers the core components of the feature that will be most helpful during future testing and doesn't include things like lengthy edge case scenarios. The test team can then build groups of regression tests, taking all priority 1 tests from each feature suite. Be kind to your future self and try to plan ahead when writing tests.

Adding expected results for the path to the focus of testing

Each test case should be targeting a specific game area, scenario or feature component. Each test should also only care about the state of that component and shouldn't be trying to verify things on the path to it.

Test cases don't need to include expected results for every step. For those steps that guide the tester towards the focus of the test, you can just leave the expected result blank. For example, you don't need to write 'the game launches without problems' as the first expected result of every test that you write. Likewise, you don't need to write similar statements when navigating through the game towards the area of interest.

Beginning test writing before planning the complete set of tests

Small features and changes require little planning before test writing begins and you can often get away with planning them on the fly as they are written. However, this doesn't work with larger, more complex features and I've seen inexperienced test writers get stuck trying to follow this approach.

A few years ago we had a tester from our outsource team join us in the studio and help us write some tests. There was a change which would be applied to a selection of different menus across the game and they had started writing for it. They wrote a set of tests for the first menu of the change and the tests looked good. However, I pointed out that there were about 20 other menu locations which would require the same set of tests and they'd need to write the same set 20 more times. The test steps were also customised enough that they wouldn't be able to easily use them as templates and copy them to each affected menu. They hadn't considered how they were going to plan the full set of tests before they began writing the first one and ended up putting too much detail into each test. Carrying on at the current rate would have seen the test writing take far longer than time would allow. I suggested that a better approach would have been to write slightly less detailed tests and plan for them to cover all of the different menus.

Beginning to write tests for a large or complex feature without a good plan in place first will always lead to an ineffective set.

Focusing on UI instead of the feature intent behind it

When test writers don't understand a feature well enough, this sometimes results in the tests wrongly focusing on the surface details of a feature instead of the underlying reason or logic. An example is writing 'an error popup appears' as an expected result instead of 'the game handles the failure, informing the player why the action failed'. Another example would be 'all players are displayed in the match list' as an expected result instead of 'all players successfully join the game lobby'.

Visual elements are the most easily understandable element to any feature, so it's natural for some junior test writers to walk through a flow and write the tests based on what they see instead of the underlying logic driving those visual elements.

Tests that describe the intent of a feature will better communicate what the test is trying to achieve and what the feature does. It also increases the chances that the tester will correctly identify bugs when they occur. Tests that describe the feature logic are also more resilient to small UI changes since the UI might change slightly but the intent of the feature remains the same.

Forgetting about live operations of a feature

This pitfall is specific to features that are implemented once but then used repeatedly once the game is live. It's most applicable to live service games that serve events, sales and other gameplay layers on top of the base game (plus seasons, booster days, visual themes and so on).

If you're writing tests for a new type of in-game event, then you'll require a set of detailed tests for the initial implementation for the code framework of the event, as well as a set of tests that will be used for testing each time that event type is run in the live game. Each instance of the event will use the same original code framework but will be driven by new data and artwork, which changes the risks and the types of bugs found. The live ops version of a test plan should be lighter and focus on the content within each instance of the event, not on the code framework that supports it.

If test writers forget about the live operations for a feature then they will have to two write two test plans: one for the code implementation and another plan to be run each time the event is used. With careful consideration, you can write and organise the test plan such that you can select a subset of the tests to be later used for the live ops testing, avoiding having to rewrite the test plan.

Forgetting the practicalities of what the tester will need to do

When test writers spend little or no time testing themselves, they're more likely to write tests that ask the tester to perform an action or set up a scenario without understanding how long it's going to take. Then during test execution they might wonder why the testing is taking so long. This sometimes also happens when the test writer knows that the test will take a long time but they're happy making the request since they aren't the ones who will need to execute the test.

Laborious or time-consuming tests can't always be avoided, but in many cases they can be reduced to when they are essential, and spending the time to set up the test is worth the time investment. Test writers need to know exactly how the tester will perform the action or set up the scenario that they are writing into the test, how long it will take and what tools or access they'll need. This is a common theme for time-based tests like quests that unlock daily or events that run for a week. A simple statement like 'wait until the event ends' might take several days without the right tooling and access to change the event timestamps.

Test writers need to be details-orientated when it comes to writing test steps, considering the 'how' carefully. Getting this wrong slows down test execution and will likely annoy the testers who are executing your tests.

5.8   Non-functional test orientation

Non-functional tests are frequently forgotten or added as an afterthought when writing tests, so I want to address this specifically here. As a reminder, non-functional tests focus not on what the feature does, but how well it does it. It includes areas like performance, stability and usability, each of which have several sub areas into which we can drill deeper.

I defined it earlier in chapter three, **Test Types and Terminology,** if you need a refresher. In that chapter I described how non-functional tests should be thought of as being orientated across all of the functional tests instead of being thought of as another game area in the list. How does this actually translate when you write your tests?

	FTUE - Performance tests	FTUE - Stability tests
FTUE - Tutorial dialogue tests		
FTUE - UI tests		
FTUE - Navigation flow tests		

Figure 5.8 – This is an area breakdown sample and shows the correct thought process for non-functional test areas. See that the non-functional tests of stability and performance slice across the functional areas

Many test writers remember late on that all of their functional tests need to consider non-functional testing, and write a final test step into every one of their tests. These include expected results like 'performance is smooth throughout the test' or 'no crashes or stability issues are seen'. Adding steps like these are an ineffective way to get test coverage on non-functional areas; testers aren't likely to be remembering to look for performance metrics throughout testing, especially if the details are only added at the end of the test. Generally, it's difficult to give your full attention to too many things at once and the same is true during testing. If you try to bundle too many things into the same test case, you will divide the tester's attention and they are less likely to give everything their full attention.

A further problem with this approach is it's often too generic and makes far too many assumptions. Most people instinctively think of frame rate when they see the word 'performance', but there are many more facets to it. You can't simply refer to checking 'performance' and expect the tester to know what you mean. It could be network performance, graphical performance, loading times from disk or memory utilisation, to name just a few.

Instead of this catch-all approach, specific elements of non-functional areas which have a non-functional risk should have been identified during the earlier test analysis phase, and the remaining areas dropped. If frame rate isn't a concern for the feature, then don't include it at all. Testing the combination of every functional area with every non-functional consideration (like in the table above) would take far too long and not be worth the effort. Early test analysis should have instead identified certain combinations that you want to focus on. Network performance might be a consideration just for the login flow, while memory utilisation might only be a consideration for late-game mature player flows.

These non-functional tests need to be written as separate test cases and not just tacked on to the end of functional test cases. They also need to be specific in their approach, targeting an area of performance and giving the tester guidance on what they should be looking for. They should have prepared the tools that the tester will need to measure the performance metric. Conducting performance tests 'by eye' can be effective in spotting issues that are the most jarring to the play experience, but tools are required to measure and compare different metrics over time. It's not possible to report, track or compare test results when testing is conducted purely 'by eye'.

The best performance tests will have accompanying spreadsheets to record and compare data over time, and they will have wiki pages on how to use and interpret the test tools. My performance tests normally follow the science experiment style that I described earlier in this chapter, explaining the goal of the test and setting the expectation that the tester needs to record some specific data and then draw conclusions from it. They're very targeted and very granular. While I included this style within the unscripted section earlier, I actually use it within scripted and unscripted performance tests.

In addition to wiki pages and test tools, performance tests are often complex enough that they require coaching the testers before the tests are run for the first time. Set up calls or meetings to talk through the details of the test setup and to highlight known pitfalls. I also advocate the use of role assignments where members of the team are assigned to be the performance or network experts, taking the lead on any testing conducted within these areas and answering questions from the other testers on the use of the test tools.

When we conduct our performance testing (currently including loading times, frame rate and memory usage) each test has quite a long list of considerations for correct test setup and pitfalls that can invalidate the results. The build type needs to be debug-free since development builds slow the game down; identical player profiles need to be used to ensure a fair comparison; live game events, sales and seasons need to be consistently enabled or disabled to ensure a fair comparison; the launch sequence needs to be consistent since the game would perform additional steps on a cold first launch of the game after installation compared with subsequent launches; and, finally, the game needs to be consistently online or offline since network activity affects the performance in indeterministic ways.

Only the performance testing experts on the team know how to correctly navigate all of the setup and pitfalls in order to record an accurate and fair performance comparison. The performance tests themselves are also detailed enough to include or link to all of these details. Writing a test to simply 'compare performance between a build with the feature and without' wouldn't effectively navigate the tester through these steps.

I've focused on performance testing here because it plays such a large part of the total scope of non-functional testing within games. There are many other areas of non-functional testing but I very rarely write tests for them. Usability is often driven by the design team and fundamental to many of the decisions that guide the creative direction of the game. Tests can be written to help gather usability data when it's requested, but this is unlikely and beyond the scope of this book. Other areas of non-functional testing like security and stability often also fall outside of the scope of manual testing. Even if these areas are applicable to the project, manual testing isn't an effective mitigation against their associated risks and so I won't include those here either. My advice here is to not try to write tests for these areas but instead speak to the test and code leadership about other ways to mitigate those risks.

5.9   Writing for your audience

Most teams I've spoken to have a team of QA analysts to write tests and another, larger team of testers who execute those tests. Sometimes they're in the same building, sometimes they're in a remote office in the same time zone and other times they're in a different time zone and are not working in their primary spoken language. Some test teams will work for the same company as the developer and will naturally have good domain knowledge of each game, while other test teams will be outsourced and will need to familiarise themselves with a style of game created by the developer. Smaller developers may use crowdsourced testing services which have no entry criteria for the testers to join, so the testers may have very little technical test knowledge. Lastly, small development teams may have QA analysts that write and run tests themselves, never handing their tests over to another person at all.

This variety of team setups requires tests to be tailored to each audience running them. Test writers need to consider both the domain and technical test knowledge of the test team when writing their tests. Where test teams are strong in both areas, tests can skip unnecessary details and proceed straight to the point of the test. This allows these tests to be written and run much more quickly, because there's a foundation of knowledge in place outside the tests themselves. Where these areas are weak (most commonly in crowdsource test teams), tests will need to be highly detailed and start with basic information such a description of the game and its major features. This information would go on to include use of debug within the game and finer details of the features under testing before the test can even begin to describe what it is trying to achieve.

Failing to identify the level of domain knowledge of the test team most frequently leads to false positive bugs being logged where the tester hasn't correctly understood the feature design. This creates additional work for the QA analyst and triage team to review all the false positive bugs. Failing to identify the level of technical knowledge of the test team will lead to a huge number of questions if the testers are aware of what knowledge they are missing, or worse, will lead to tests being incorrectly run and wrongly passed if the testers *aren't* aware of the technical knowledge they are missing. I've witnessed many instances of the latter where the tester has mistakenly thought they understood the test scenario. This is most frequently seen during more technical tests where the expected result is checked within the debug logs of the game, or within a network or performance tool – any tests which require the testers to understand and interpret the output correctly.

As an example, I frequently write network orientated tests since all of the games I've worked on have heavy online components. For these tests I include information boxes within the test tasks which describe key pieces of basic network behaviour, like how many times a game client will retry a failed HTTP network request and how long a game client will wait for a network response before trying again or giving up. I briefly describe retries and timeouts so that the tester is better equipped to look for problems while running the test. I've done the same for HTTP network error codes so that testers are confident in identifying a positive result and a negative one when browsing network communication. When writing these tests, I'm aware of the technical knowledge level that the testers have in this area and I'm careful to supplement this knowledge where it's required, and not blindly assume that they'll be able to follow all of it.

The use of technical and company specific terminology is also an important factor. Testers who work directly within a game studio are more likely to have access to company tools and the game code itself, so will have a fair grasp of the technical terminology that accompanies it. The following terms might confuse external testers but would be something internal staff might take for granted: game assets, sprites, prefabs, exceptions, telemetry, warnings, errors, animation rig, shaders, particle effects, textures, specular lighting, collision mesh, post processing layer.

These are just a few examples of course– there are many others you might use more often in your own team. Including a sentence like 'each pistol variation is the same mesh with different shaders applied, meaning that we only need to test the mesh once' assumes that the tester knows what a shader is and how it is applied to this scenario. QA analysts using external or outsourced test teams will need to do more to explain what these terms and phrases mean, or will have to write paraphrased tests and exclude them. Sometimes tests can be written from a player-facing point of view, avoiding 'under the hood' technical terms, but this often compromises the specificity of the test and shouldn't be used as a solution. Instead, the knowledge should be documented and/or included in sync meetings between the QA analysts and the test team. Some teams create fantastic testing 'cheat sheets' which contain lists of quick reference material like this, which is another solution to bridging this terminology gap.

Very small teams often have a single person who writes *and* runs the tests. This is a unique scenario where the test writer is their own audience and will have no problems understanding the tests. These setups present different problems however: often tests aren't written at all in this scenario since the person can save time by proceeding directly to test execution. Test writing is often seen as an administrative burden and there doesn't appear to be a need for it here. If the team does decide to write tests, they can often be of poor quality because they don't get seen by anyone else in the business – not through a peer review from another QA analyst nor a tester who is executing the test. This creates a problem when that person moves to another role where they *are* writing tests for other people to execute because they're aligned to a test style that only they understand.

For the purpose of this book, it's enough to recognise that writing tests for others will be different from writing tests for yourself, and take appropriate action if you're in this situation. Test writers should be aware of the domain and technical knowledge of their test team and write their tests with an appropriate level of granularity and supporting details.

5.10 Test organisation

Test management tools quickly get filled with huge numbers of different test suites throughout the duration of a project's lifecycle and can create a confusing mess if not organised correctly. This is particularly true for franchise games where tests are more likely to be reused from project to project, and in live service games which are continually improved throughout their many years of service. Much like test cases, test writers need to decide the granularity of their test suites. Do they have many small and specific test suites or do they have a smaller number of large test suites grouped by game area?

Test area groups

With the heavy focus on reusability and maintainability, test cases need to be in a place where they can easily be found, either by browsing or keyword searching. This means that the title of each test suite should make it clear which tests are contained within it and similar tests which are likely to be run together should also be in the same suite and not spread across multiple different suites. Let's consider all of the problems you might face when trying to find a set of tests for regression testing purposes, and would want to avoid during setup: valid tests mixed up with obsolete tests, tests for a feature spread across multiple suites, incrementations of the same test in multiple places, unclear groupings of tests within suites, incomplete test sets, suites that overlap each other.

Most often I see new test suites added whenever a new feature is added, and the suite copies the name of the feature as it is written in the development story. While this works for some project features, for many this approach results in a mismatch of different test suite names, all of which describe different parts of the same feature. As an example, if I'm looking for existing tests on platform notifications I might see the following already exist:

- Push notifications
- Notifications
- Notifications v2
- Image support for Android notifications
- Deeplinks

Since incremental improvements are made to features throughout the life of a project, the resulting test suites are too granular and each refer to individual improvement to the same system. Some of the suites refer to the whole feature, others refer to specific parts of the feature, while others refer to the feature in connection to some other feature area. It's very difficult and time-consuming to look through each of these suites, identify where they overlap and where they leave gaps in the feature testing, then cherry-pick relevant tests from each to form a complete regression test. The result of this common approach is a confusing mess of tests spread across multiple test suites, making reusability far more difficult than it should be and reducing confidence that the team has a complete and accurate set of tests which can be deployed easily for the notifications feature.

The first lesson here is a reminder to avoid copying the development story titles for your test suites and test cases. Test writers should also avoid creating fresh test suites when there is an improvement to an area. Adding a 'v2' will bloat the list and confuse reusability. If the old suite must be kept to maintain historical data, then prefix it with 'archive' or 'obsolete' to show that it should no longer be used. This also shuffles the suite out of alphabetical order and groups all similar obsolete tests.

Test writers need to more carefully consider the grouping of similar tests and the name that you give to that group (the test suite). In this scenario, notifications are a single feature within the larger group of platform integrations (the ways that the game integrates with the operating system that it runs on). Notifications and deeplinks are two examples of very similar features within the platform integration group, so it makes sense to place them together. Other features in the platform integration group include achievements/trophies, multiplayer game invites, platform voice chat, store purchases, reporting and blocking other players, game rating prompts, downloads and uploads. Many of these platform features will use notifications and share commonalities because they are also orientated around the integration between the game and the platform it runs on.

A better test organisation is to create more abstract groups and subgroups instead of directly copying the grouping that features arrive in. For platform notifications, this would either be creating a test suite for notifications or creating one for platform integration and including notifications as a sub area of the suite. The intent is that these more abstract groups provide more flexibility to be updated when the feature is updated, instead of creating the type of individual test suites I listed earlier.

This requires that test writers think ahead when writing new tests. They need to decide whether to start a fresh test suite or add to an existing suite. If they add to an existing suite, they will need to search through all suites and find the most logical place to add the tests – something which isn't always as obvious as it seems, particularly if previous test writers on the project haven't written their test suites with reuse in mind.

When writing new tests, I've sometimes had to first dedicate time to merge multiple old suites together into more logical groups before even beginning on my new tests. This added work can be frustrating because it's more effort in the short term for a longer-term reusability payoff. Test writers should be kind to their colleagues and future selves and make this investment so that they have an easier time in the long run.

In other instances, you might have to extend the scope of an existing suite to accommodate your tests, something which gets easier the more familiar you are with common feature groupings. Extending a menu test suite to include navigation is a good example of this. Since menus and UI navigation are so closely linked, it makes good organisational sense to group them together, extending a 'menus + UI' test suite into 'menus, UI + navigation'. It's perfectly fine to extend or reduce the scope of a group, but this should be done according to the size of the groups. Too large, and they become bloated; too small, and you meet the same problem I introduced at the beginning of this section.

Another common grouping I've seen on mobile projects is between the cloud saves, identities systems and profile conflicts features. A game will need some way of creating a unique ID for the player and storing it server side so that the player can download their cloud save profile to new devices. The system for tracking a player's identity is a separate system to the one doing the uploading and downloading of the player's cloud save profiles onto different devices. While these features are different, they are closely linked, so I create a suite for the full set and group them all together: 'cloud save, identities + conflicts'.

In chapter six, **Major areas of game testing**, I'll list many of these feature groups, providing a summary of each. This should serve as a good reference when deciding how to organise your test suites into groups.

Test case placement

One of the first questions I ask myself when I'm about to write tests for a plan is whether the tests are likely to be one-off or reused. If the test isn't going to be reused by myself or anyone on my team in the future, I'll write the test directly in the database task (JIRA in my current case). I do this even if I'm writing a scripted test: I simply list the verifications as bullet points in the task. This is because it's not worth the time investment to write a scripted test case into the test management tool if no one is ever going to use it again. It just adds to the project test bloat that I talked about previously. The first step to good organisation is being strict about not adding unnecessary tests into the test management tool in the first place. This means all tests within it are written with reusability in mind.

Test suite consistency

The ability to reuse test suites written by other members of the team relies on all of the suites within the project being consistent. While they don't all have to follow the exact same style, there are some key parts which greatly aid in reuse.

Consistent use of priorities for each test case creates an expectation for the importance of each test, quickly highlighting what subset of the total suite are the core scenarios. Often, when suites are reused for regression testing purposes, only the main verification tests are required; any extended verification, edge case or failure tests are dropped. Agreeing criteria for each priority (priority 1, 2 or 3) among the test team allows each member to pick only the tests they're interested in when reusing suites. I've seen QA analysts unknowingly select large sections of tests without realising that some hidden in the set take a very long time to run and would be excessive for the purpose they are intended for. This is either because all of the tests are marked with the default priority value, or because they haven't bothered to look through the test suite to pick sub-selection. Many teams do get by without setting their priorities so vigilantly, but doing so wastes valuable test time by re-running more tests than are required whenever test suites are reused. With testing time being such a limited resource, correctly setting test case priorities should be high on the test team's agenda.

To a lesser extent, consistent use of the test case styles in general will also contribute towards a healthy organisation of test suites written by different team members. Even if it's not the exact style I've described in this chapter, agreeing a consistent style to use across the test team will keep the full set organised. This includes consistent use of terminology and project phrases, as well as agreed use of test case fields. Each test writer should be able to search for keywords within the test case titles and find the tests that they're searching for. They should also be able to open any test and see fields like estimated time or applicable platforms populated if the team has agreed to use those fields. Consistent adoption of test suite and test case titles will also make the list of suites appear much more organised and ease browsing through the list.

Task and test plan traceability

Test management tools like TestRail allow test writers to create a custom grouping of tests from multiple different test suites into a single plan (the tool may call it a test plan, a test run, a test cycle or something else). However, I frequently see QA analysts creating a single run from a test suite – functionality which is intended as a quick one-click test run. Test plans allow test writers to collect custom sets of tests from different suites together into a single location, which is then linked to the database test task, creating traceability between the two. This functionality also allows the tests imported from each suite to be renamed and given customised descriptions, allowing the QA analyst to add supplementary information into the test plan within the test management tool without editing the original test suite.

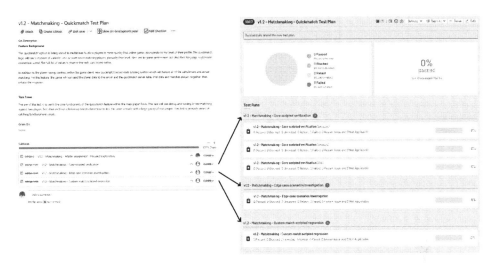

5.9 – A JIRA test plan, complete with subtasks, alongside the corresponding scripted test plan within the test management tool. Note that the JIRA subtasks share the same names with the corresponding parts of the scripted test plan to which they belong

Giving the test plan the same name in both tools creates a basic traceability between the two, even if no hyperlink is included within each. The sections of the test plan within the test management tool should also be renamed to correspond with each of the subtasks in the database. This setup allows test writers to create many sets of different test runs and still have them grouped into a single location, as opposed to simply creating a set of individual test runs from different test suites.

The shared naming of the subtasks and test runs makes it very clear which parts of the test plan correlate with each tool. When the test plan is divided up among the testers and the subtasks assigned out, the scope of each subtask is obvious and eliminates potential confusion. The example I've given above is a very small test plan, but this style pays off with test plans that are larger and expect to be tested by larger numbers of testers simultaneously. The clean and consistent use of names and breakdowns trains the test team into this traceability style and creates an unspoken association, even when no hyperlink is included.

5.11 Influencing factors

This section bookends the chapter on test design by talking about all of the things that can disrupt and influence test writing, throwing a curveball into the guidance given so far. It should prepare readers for some of the practical challenges they might face when applying these test writing techniques in their own work. Many of these influencing factors highlight the chasm between the theory of effective test writing and being able to execute that vision amidst the complex and fast paced work of real game projects. Many QA analysts feel that they aren't able to execute their best work because of these influencing factors, and some become disillusioned with it over time. They know what good test planning looks like, but their current project situation prevents it in some way.

I'll list each of these factors and give guidance on how to navigate them successfully. As a first step, even being able to recall and consider relevant influencing factors when beginning writing a test plan will make that plan more effective.

Time

Probably the most prevalent and impactful influencing factor when writing tests. The fact is, test writing takes a long time. Scripted tests, in particular, take a long time to write because they're so details-orientated. If QA analysts don't have enough time to conduct effective test planning before the test execution begins, then they should make this known during project schedule discussions, or raise it with their test discipline leads.

The best defence against insufficient time to conduct effective test writing is to have it tracked as a discrete activity in the project schedule, separating out the total test effort into two parts: the work of the QA analyst team and the test execution team. Unlike test execution, when test writing goes off track you have far fewer options to remedy it, like increasing the team size.

Test writers can also make tactical choices during test planning about which feature components they write scripted tests for and which they chose to test through test sessions and other formats. Scripted tests and focused exploratory test sessions written directly into the database are quicker to write than those within a test management tool, and can still be very effective when written well.

The trick here is not just to default to running open exploratory test tasks because you've run out of time to create anything more detailed.

A balance must be struck between investing equally across all tests within the plan. You can support this by exercising good personal organisation and practise estimating how long test writing will take. Junior QA analysts frequently underestimate test writing and start a plan with lots of detail, which then tails off sharply as they run out of time to finish it.

Test writing can also be tailored relative to the risk and priority of the feature. For lower risk features, I will allocate less test planning time and force myself to move onto the next feature. Even if I could write a more comprehensive test, I've chosen not to invest my time there. This is a good mitigation for those QA analysts who write test plans for many smaller features and need to divide their time carefully between them all. It would be regrettable to allow test writing for a low-risk feature to overrun and take time away from test planning for something higher risk.

This influence will create greater difficulties for some teams than others. When I worked in a publisher test team, we were only responsible for the system testing level and so weren't involved in the feature sprint deliverables. We were also not based in the development studio. The result was that we were left uninterrupted from much of the randomisation that you see within a developer office and were given a healthy time allocation to plan and write the system level test plans for the entire game. It still took a long time and required accurate estimations, but it was easier to produce my best test writing work.

When I compare this to working on smaller projects delivering new releases in three-week sprints, allocating enough time to conduct quality test writing was far more difficult. This is because of the greater number of distractions within the development office and the faster pace of delivering work. Test writing (like most writing) is most productive when conducted without interruption for long periods of time. QA analysts who have difficulty completing test writing on schedule should consider booking out blocks of their time where they can't be interrupted by testers or other members of the development team. This can be a few afternoons each week or a whole day once a week. Choosing to work remotely, to physically separate yourself from the development office, can also help this focus.

QA analysts who work on smaller teams will also be writing tests for a much larger range of different features, instead of specialising on one area for many weeks and months. These generalists will also have a more difficult time writing effective tests on time due to their constant context switching between game feature areas. Comparatively, those test writers who have a very defined feature ownership throughout the duration of the project can more easily pick up test writing and retain all of the background feature knowledge needed to write the tests effectively. Generalist test writers have to put a greater focus on choosing which feature tests to work on first and organise the test schedule to avoid context switching between different features. The aim should be to completely finish planning for one feature and have the tests ready to execute, before moving on to the next one.

Feature knowledge base

A common complaint among QA analysts is the lack of detailed documentation. Indeed, I commented earlier in this chapter that the tests frequently become the 'point of truth' for many of the small details of a feature that aren't defined within the feature one-pager spec. Other features driven by the design team may not have written designs at all, and the source of feature knowledge may be a designer on the team. For code driven changes (such as architectural changes and SDK updates) technical designs will also frequently not exist: the reason for implementing these changes isn't driven by design requirement or player needs, it's simply a requirement for the game to continue running.

If there isn't easily understandable supporting documentation you can direct testers towards, all of the background feature information needs to be included within the test tasks and test cases. The level of supporting information will vary from feature to feature and team to team. Regardless of this variance, the importance of describing the intent of each feature change to the testers remains the same. This variance will influence the level of detail added to test plans and test tasks, and should be accounted for in the test writing estimations. I frequently see QA analysts not fully understanding why a change is being made and proceeding to write tests for it anyway, describing it inadequately within the tests. This has a knock-on effect that the testers also don't know exactly what the change is or why it was added, making the entire effort far less effective.

If this sounds familiar, my advice is to allocate more time to speak with the feature author before test planning begins and ask them to explain in simpler terms what the change is and why it is required. If time is tight, a call is the quickest way to communicate this type of information. My further advice is to practise including the 'feature background' section in all test plans. I introduced this earlier within the test task style guide. Providing an executive summary to the testers is a way of taking all the unwritten information you've been told about a feature and describing it succinctly to the testers. Through practice, test writers can summarise more complex and technical changes in an understandable way, eliminating the reliance on detailed supporting documentation.

Tools

The use of any tools adds complexity during test execution, so the instructions to the tester need to be correspondingly detailed. Guidance on the general usage of a tool is often described on the company wiki pages. However, each test may ask the tester to focus on a specific usage of the tool, like looking for CPU throttling in a performance monitoring tool or inspecting certain network calls in a network tool. Unless the test is run frequently, you can't assume the tester will know exactly what information you are looking for, and will need to add instructions to help the tester navigate all of the information within the tool, particularly if it's quite a complex one.

If a test uses a tool, consider adding a small cheat-sheet section into the test task using annotated screenshots to quickly show the tester relevant details. Doing this also forces you to launch the tool yourself and perform a run of the test, which frequently highlights small problems which could trip up the tester when performing the test. This should be possible in most cases, even if the feature has yet to be completely implemented. Running the tool yourself like this is a great way to double check that the tests provide adequate detail and that the test scenario can be completed as defined.

It's not uncommon to write a complex test scenario only to find, when trying to execute it, that it isn't possible in the configuration intended in the test case. A common example might be trying to run a performance test on a non-debug build to get a more accurate measurement and forgetting that some of the test steps specify the use of debug commands. These types of practicalities need to be identified and fixed during the test design phase.

When introducing a new tool, time should be allocated to allow the testers to install the tool and become familiar with it before the test cases are assigned to them. There may be blockers like requiring IT approval to install the tool, which can take hours or days. The testers may also have installation and setup problems which require troubleshooting. If no members of the test team have previous experience of the tool, this also falls to the QA analyst to help them set up and be ready to run the tests. If a QA analyst is creating the necessity to use a tool through writing tests for it, then they need to take ownership for the setup of that tool.

Domain and technical knowledge of the tester executing the tests

I spoke about this influence in detail earlier in this chapter, so I'll only summarise it here.

Domain knowledge is knowledge of the game genre, game itself and components of the game. Technical knowledge is knowledge of the testing discipline and surrounding disciplines, like game coding and design.

Knowing the level of domain knowledge of the testers means that you can refer to systems within the game without explaining them further and know that the tester understands you. For example, referring to 'the loot system' or 'systematic upgrades' as components of the game within your test cases. Similarly, knowing when referring to something will confuse the tester and choosing to either explain it or remove it from the test.

Knowing the level of technical knowledge means that you can refer to types of testing and know that the tester has the same understanding as you and will interpret the instruction correctly. For example, asking the tester to perform 'regression testing against a game area' or stating that 'this is a system test'. Test terminology is a great way of precisely describing the work that needs to be done and cuts down laborious explanation; however it only works when the testers understand the term well. The same rule applies to other technical terminology outside of the test discipline.

Complexity of feature change

Many of the topics in this chapter on test design can appear obvious and trivial to implement when presented in small examples. The reality is that many game project features are large, complex and will test the QA analyst's ability to execute effective test writing. The process of test writing forces the writer to understand and explain each part of the feature through the tests, describing exactly what the expected result should be in each and every scenario.

Much like the test analysis phase, simpler feature test plans don't always require the rigorously effective test design described in this chapter. However, such test plans are a rarity and most QA analysts don't have the luxury to pick and choose which features they work on. The higher the complexity of a feature, the more important it is to double down on organisation and communication within test writing to avoid the tests being misinterpreted or confusing.

I've seen instances of junior QA analysts who have adopted a test writing style with a low level of granularity and write each test in notation format, leaving the testers to fill in the gaps. This approach would have been fine if it was a conscious choice, but they would use this approach for all features and struggle when presented with a more complex work.

QA analysts should assess both the size and complexity of a feature and choose their test writing approach accordingly. This includes deciding how to divide up the scripted and unscripted tests as well as any decisions on whether to write up further details elsewhere to supplement the tests. Performing these additional activities can also add significant time to the test design process and should be considered when providing work estimations to the wider team.

Alignment to the schedule and order of test execution

Because test design can be a long process, the choice of which tests to write first should be aligned with the test execution schedule and the project test strategy. One common strategy is to begin testing features in the order that they are made available for testing, while another is to test features in order of the risk they present. QA analysts should be aware when testing can begin and have their test plans ready for execution as close to this date as possible, they also need to juggle the different feature test plans they are writing and align them with the project test strategy (if there is one). A poor display of test design estimation would be to have a feature ready for testing but the tests are several weeks away from being complete.

QA analysts have the difficult job of needing to synchronise when a feature is expected to be ready for testing, when their test plan will be ready to execute and when the test team will have available testers to execute that plan. While the test execution schedule is a broader topic, all QA analysts in a team will need to provide estimations of how many testers they will need and for how long. This information is collected from all the QA analysts in the team and usually requires some work to smooth out the tester numbers for days where test plans overlap.

If a QA analyst has estimated a day to begin testing and there is a group of testers allocated to begin that plan, then they better make sure that the test plan is ready!

This impact is reduced if the QA analyst only owns one large feature for the duration of the project and the test plan is executed over many weeks and months. This setup allows the QA analyst to assume an almost constant allocation of testers. For projects where the QA analyst owns multiple different features and/or those features are developed in smaller iterations, the stopping and starting of each test plan will influence test design much more heavily. As a person who has worked on agile games-as-a-service projects for the last five years, I can attest to this!

5.12 Test design: games vs. software

Let's take a brief look at how test design in games compares with tests within other types of software. How much do they differ? The quick answer is not a lot. Many of the core characteristics that I talked about in this chapter are universal across all software testing. The same themes that make tests effective and ineffective remain true regardless of the domain application. Game industry QA analysts who have become adept test writers should be able to take those skills to other areas of software testing. In fact, many of my former colleagues have moved out of game testing and into other software testing industries.

One area which is more prevalent in games test design is the focus on art and content-heavy test writing. Game projects with lots of assets will occupy a large share of the project's total test cases – far more than most software applications. Because of this, many QA analysts within games will be faced with the challenge of writing tests for long lists of items and massive areas of content. Approaching tests for content isn't something that is mentioned in software testing academia, but I've dealt with some of the approaches that can be taken in this chapter.

We discussed the main theme to successful content testing as promoting reusability through abstraction. In other words, creating a set of more abstract tests that don't refer to any particular instance of content and so can be applied repeatedly, allowing scalability across the full scope of content.

6

Major areas of game testing

6.1   An introduction to game test domain areas

In this chapter I'll describe the main domain areas of game testing and their testing characteristics. This is essentially a top-level test analysis of an entire game, splitting the testing into areas that are most frequently owned by different members of the QA analyst team. With each domain area requiring a different test approach and having different challenges, this chapter also acts as a cheat sheet, providing a lookup for QA analysts to see the key information for a particular domain area. So, in addition to reading this chapter as a whole, I'd recommend referring back to specific areas within it when they arrive in your own project.

As I've hinted in various sections earlier in this book, some areas are more difficult to test than others and many require specialist tools or knowledge. Because of this, some are better owned by junior team members, while others require more experience before the test planning* is effective. For each area, I'll provide a difficulty rating and describe some of the challenges faced during test planning. It can be easier to write tests for player-facing and purely visual game areas because you can see the details on screen and interact with them, while more 'under the hood' areas might require a firmer grasp of the game logic even before the features are written into code. Furthermore, some areas (like game content) are easily accessible to any single tester and allow for simpler test cases, while others (like multiplayer or social features) require more test data setup and correspondingly complex test case steps.

---

*   I'm using 'test planning' here to refer to all of the work a QA analyst does during the fundamental test process.

These characteristics and many more all influence how the feature should be approached during each stage of the fundamental test process. The two main tasks – deciding what to test (test analysis) and how to test (test design) – can vary greatly from area to area and shouldn't be tackled with the same broad approach. For both test analysis and test design, the domain knowledge in this chapter should pair with the technical test process knowledge given in the relevant chapters earlier in this book and equip readers with all the knowledge required to embark on test planning for any of these game areas.

Not all games will include all of the areas listed here and some bespoke domain areas may not be included. For most projects though, this list is sufficiently comprehensive to allow you to place every game feature into one (or many) of the categories here.

These areas can also be used to help organise the distribution of work to a team of QA analysts with better tactical choices around who is responsible for which game areas. Similar and connected game areas can be assigned to the same QA analyst and smaller features can be grouped logically, owning them as a group instead of distributing them out amongst different team members. As a side note, it's the responsibility of the QA manager to perform this test analysis of the entire game to define the project test breakdown, making sure that all areas have been considered and that each area is assigned to a member of the team. This is a big responsibility, and you can see how this would be a natural progression from the QA analyst role. While QA manager work is beyond the scope of this book, this chapter provides a good template for this project breakdown, acting as a reminder for test areas that should be included within the project plan.

Specialisation

I mentioned before that much of my early career was spent owning the test plans for features within multiplayer and online services domain areas, while my recent work has been on smaller agile projects requiring me to own the test planning for a broad variety of domain areas. The company setup and project type will heavily dictate whether QA analysts need to be specialists or generalists for these domain areas. Specialists are required for waterfall projects and/or large single-release projects where the team is large enough for the game areas to be distributed amongst the team for ownership. Specialists are also common for franchises which release similar games on a set cadence. Smaller games, and those which operate as a continuous live service, are more likely to have smaller test teams who act as generalists and plan testing for all game areas.

Generalists have a far more difficult task because they need to be knowledgeable about all domain areas, something not commonly recognised in the industry when hiring for smaller teams.

I've seen enough junior QA analysts fumble through a test plan, performing only adequately because it's the first time they've encountered a particular game area, to know this is true. There are both pros and cons to the generalist role. The positive part is that, given enough time, this broad exposure gives generalists well rounded experience, equipping them to tackle a broader variety of testing challenges during future work.

On the other hand, generalists will find it much more difficult to hone their test planning approach for any particular domain area because they'll do the work once and then move onto a different feature. This constant shifting of test focus can prevent the test approach from maturing over time, blocking the whole test team from improving holistically. This is made worse if generalists don't share their learnings with each other, causing other QA analysts to stumble into the same problems for a particular area. The complexity of knowledge transfer and process improvement is avoided when specialists own test areas for longer periods of time.

This chapter should be particularly helpful for generalists, because they're likely to be writing test plans for many different (and new) areas in this list and should benefit from using this as a continuous reference throughout their work.

Bigger projects with larger test teams are more likely to have enough resources to distribute the feature area ownerships amongst a QA analyst team, usually for the entire duration of the project. Depending on the circumstances, the assignments are mostly chosen by the company, with the QA analyst having an input if they strongly object to the assignment. This is a great opportunity for individuals with an interest in a particular discipline of game development. Some QA job listings for embedded studio roles will even mention the specialisation in the job title. I've seen this mainly for audio and art QA analyst specialisations, and know past colleagues who have moved through these QA roles and into the corresponding content creation disciplines (audio engineer, artist, etc.), proving that these specialisations can provide a useful stepping stone. Technical and difficult game areas are commonly assigned to the most senior or technical QA analysts on the team; like art, it's not uncommon for QA analysts to have an interest in coding or automation, aiding their area of specialisation.

The good fit between the individual and the specialisation is also compounded if they've owned the test planning for the same domain area in recent projects. I've previously owned very similar domain areas across multiple consecutive projects for this reason. While it makes good sense to assign team members according to their strengths, the drawback is that it can cause specialists to become stuck owning similar areas for every project and never expanding their experience.

While specialist roles may lack broad exposure, they do provide a stable environment for permanently improving the test approach for a particular area. The longer period of continuous ownership allows QA analysts to invest more into processes and techniques because they have the entire duration of the project to see those investments pay off. This is particularly useful for complex and technical test areas which require a higher baseline of test effort compared with other areas. In this scenario, entering a new project already equipped with a good knowledge of the area can dramatically increase the speed, efficiency, and effectiveness of test planning.

Domain area characteristics

I've listed the main attributes of each of the following domain areas. The rating for difficulty and complexity refers to the entire test planning effort – everything from understanding the changes and gathering information, to breaking down the test areas and writing the tests. The discipline focus refers to whether the game area is primarily driven by code or content, where 'content' refers to all design and art game areas. This characteristic then influences what types of bugs are likely to be found and can sometimes also influence the test approach. Further notes are given for each area where this is applicable. Other common characteristics I'll cover include whether the area requires tool knowledge and the types of bugs that QA analysts can expect to result from their test plans. In addition to these main attributes, I'll describe the features within each area where this isn't clear and talk about the test approach for each.

6.2 Platform integration

Platform integration groups together all features where the game interacts directly with the operating system it's running on. Think in-game purchases, achievements, notifications, store links ('rate us' prompts, 'update game' prompts, DLC links, etc.), store pages, app icons, multiplayer invites, platform voice chat, device settings, parental controls, deeplinks and application lifecycle management (suspending, resuming and terminating the game). In addition to these common integrations, many more custom integrations exist for specific platforms too.

Platform integration tests are very likely to be re-run for regression testing purposes. This is due to their relevance in supporting compatibility across multiple versions of the operating system, and also for compatibility testing when taking updates to the platform SDK. Each platform's software development kit is the technology layer allowing the game to integrate with these features on the operating system. All games will need to update their version of the platform SDK to support future versions of the operating system. This is very common across mobile devices, consoles and PC.

Due to the high reuse of these tests, they should be written as scripted tests and be generic enough to be reused in different scenarios. These features should also be grouped in a single location (platform integration) and not split between different feature test plans. Without this group, test teams are more likely to duplicate effort, with QA analysts each writing their own tests for platform features which interact with different parts of the game, leading to inconsistency and sometimes missing areas entirely.

These features are often a high priority for the project and will likely be run as regression testing during system testing or against final release candidate builds, increasing their re-use.

Unusually, some of the sub areas here need to be driven by the test team, because they may not have corresponding feature work completed by the development team. Put another way, QA analysts need to identify, analyse, plan and execute tests independently because there is sometimes no explicit development work which would normally be the trigger for testing. This is because some of these features might come for free when the platform SDK is integrated. Others may be required to check compatibility with parts of the operating system, even though the game doesn't use them.

A basic example might be playtime limitations for child accounts, which interrupt gameplay when the daily allocation is up. The game should be able to handle such an interruption gracefully. Identifying these additional test scenarios requires some experience of this area before they are considered, making it tricky for some juniors.

Complexity/difficulty: Medium. While this area has a code focus, integrations with each operating system are well documented and standardised across all game projects. QA analysts who have previously written test plans for platform integration features can reapply the majority of their knowledge in the same way, since these features change little over time.

Take platform notifications as an example: a short message triggered by the game that appears on screen when the device is on but the game isn't running. Notifications function in a very similar way, even across different platforms. QA analysts who have previously written tests in this area can easily transfer it to future test plans with little feature change.

Tests can also be difficult to set up, since they frequently require the game environment to be configured correctly. Performing sandbox (fake money) purchase flows or triggering prompts to rate the game on the store page are two examples of this.

Discipline focus: Code.

Tools: Platform tools exist for some platforms (e.g., to trigger notifications).

Bugs: These flows frequently start within the game, then execute some code from the operating system before returning to the game. It's important for QA analysts and testers to understand here what parts of the flow are controlled by the game code and what parts are controlled by the OS, so they can avoid logging bugs against the platform code which can't be fixed from within the game.

6.3   Third-party SDK integration

This area categorises testing how the game integrates with other software it interacts with outside of the operating system itself. Most commonly, these integrations include social media platforms like Facebook, Twitter and Instagram, which are used as a method for logging in or sharing game content to those channels.

As an example, a game might use a player's social media account to connect their identity across multiple devices and allow saving to the cloud. Some games also allow connections to music streaming platforms like Spotify to play custom playlists during gameplay instead of the in-game radio stations. All of these require the game to install a software development kit (SDK) for each integration and then update it over time, adding complexity to the game's architecture.

Further examples of this include integrations with advert SDKs which allow games to serve ads and attribute new installs to adverts for the game (click-through tracking). Some common names include Google AdMob, MoPub, Facebook Ads, AppLovin and Unity Ads.

Third party SDKs exist for many other reasons, too. Games may use customer service products like HelpShift to manage player questions, requests and complaints, or chat apps like Discord to allow chat to be directly integrated into the game. Games will have SDKs for the graphics engine that they're using (Unity SDK and Unreal Development Kit are popular examples), as well as any other middleware they might be using. This is common for handling parts of a game like audio, UI or animation, but can include practically any game component.

Testers should understand that the code for these components are written by other companies and come with their own bugs, requiring updates over the lifetime of the project. Updates to SDKs are particularly difficult to test because they often have no player-facing changes, yet they still impact the entire game. We can describe them as 'system level' changes because this code underpins all of the individual feature gameplay code which is normally the focus of testing. These changes are often presented to the test team as being "nothing to test" as there are no player-facing changes to verify, or "everything should be tested" as they are used by many features game-wide. This leaves testers in a tricky situation and requires some experience of dealing with these types of changes. The reality is that updating these core parts of the game code are often risky, producing severe and unpredictable bugs.

Effective testing of SDK updates requires two things. One: the QA analyst needs to correctly identify game areas that are at risk of regression, and two: the project should have test suites for those areas which the QA analyst can reuse to form a new regression test plan. For this test area, having an up-to-date set of test suites pays dividends and means the QA analyst doesn't need to write fresh tests for every update – which would be a very inefficient strategy in the long run, particularly for projects which have a large number of third-party integrations.

The game area focus for the regression testing will depend on the type of SDK being updated. QA analysts should speak to the code teams to clarify the exact touch points within the game. In addition, the number of minor versions being skipped is a good indicator of risk, as well as checking if the SDK is being updated to a new major version (for example, updating an SDK from v1.0 to v2.1 would be an update to a new major version). The changelist from the update can also be reviewed to identify specific changes that might affect the game. It's helpful here to speak to the code team to understand how the game uses the SDK since it may not use many of the SDK's features referenced in the changelist, potentially increasing or decreasing the risk of the update.

Finally, third party integrations don't always have an SDK but are instead integrated into the project as packages within the graphics engine or development environment.

Complexity/difficulty: Medium-hard. These integrations create test scenarios which can be difficult to set up and understand because they impact the game at a system level. They're usually owned by more senior members of the QA analyst team, who know how to approach the testing without being prompted by other members of the team. As I described earlier, testers are sometimes told that there is nothing to test, and more junior QA analysts might take this at face value. These changes are also driven by the code team instead of design-led and, as a result, don't have the usual design documentation for the test team to use as a reference.

Discipline focus: Code.

Tools: Various. Many tools have web dev dashboards for testing purposes.

Bugs: Likely to generate few bugs, but those found are high severity. They are also frequently difficult to find and complex in nature.

6.4 Platform certification requirements

This area refers to criteria that must be met by a game in order to be approved for launch on a particular platform. The rules are defined by each platform owner, and how strict they are varies, with the big consoles (Xbox, PlayStation and Nintendo devices) having the strictest requirements and mobile platforms (Android and iOS) having more loosely defined and interpreted rules.

Releasing your game on Windows, Mac or Linux doesn't have such requirements, but if you are distributing the game through a store such as Steam, Origin or the Epic store, you will need to adhere to any rules they impose on game submissions. These rules will require negligible consideration by the game team compared with the certification requirements imposed by console companies.

This area is often referred to as 'compliance testing' or 'certification testing', sometimes even shortening this to 'cert'. It is testing to ensure the game complies with the platform requirements and will be certified once it meets those requirements.

The process here is for the final game build to be submitted to the platform company, who have their own compliance test teams. Their job is to execute the set of compliance requirements tests against each game submitted, which determines whether the game is approved to release on that platform. The test teams working for each platform will run the same tests back-to-back against each game submitted to them. For this test area, the role of game test teams is to perform these same tests themselves to ensure the game is approved first time when it is submitted. The requirements for each platform are published publicly, making the process transparent and allowing this self-check to happen before submission.

For franchise games and mature game teams who have released games before, this process can become just a formality and rarely raise any problems because they know the process so well. The same is true for games which operate as a live service: releasing updates and DLC to existing live games very rarely triggers compliance failures.

This game area is generally started later in the development lifecycle and nearer release time. It's not an area requiring continuous attention throughout development, unlike many other test areas. Live service games also need to identify which of their many game updates have compliance considerations, and only include this testing in releases when it's relevant.

Occasionally, an operating system update will introduce new functionality and force this test process even when the game has passed a previous submission. This is more common on mobile platforms due to the yearly cadence of operating system updates and new mobile device releases.

Some submission rules also appear to be enforced sporadically by some platforms, which can be frustrating for game teams. Just because a game passed its last submission and hasn't changed since, doesn't mean it will pass this time. It's unfortunately quite common for game submissions to fail based on long-standing functionality because the platform team had ignored it or not detected it during previous submissions.

Complexity/difficulty: Easy. Requirements for each platform are publicly available and oblige the QA analyst to identify which requirements apply to their project, and then include them into a test plan. The comprehensive documentation and absence of big changes allows game companies to write a single test plan interpreting the rules for their games, and then use those repeatedly over many years and projects. This is also the reason many big game companies have compliance testing teams who perform this testing for every project the company develops.

This type of testing can be repetitive and lightweight when compared with typical functional testing of new game features. It doesn't require test planning or analysis; what needs to be tested is already well defined. This can cause experience gaps for QA analysts who are moving from compliance testing to creating functional test plans for new game features.

Discipline focus: Code.

Tools: Some platforms have specific tools for their rules, but this isn't common.

Bugs: Test teams need to diligently categorise bugs according to their likelihood of causing the game submission to fail. Many testers wrongly categorise more minor compliance fails as critical and create a panic among the game team, only to later find that the game passes compliance review with the bug still active. The best compliance teams lean more on the trend in recent submission rejections than they do on testing strictly against the certification requirements.

6.5 Regulations and age rating compliance

This category describes specialist areas where a game must comply with legislation, much of which focuses on the player data stored by the game. The European General Data Protection Regulation (GDPR) and California Consumer Privacy Act (CCPA) are two examples. This requirement forces development teams to build and test functionality that allows players to see and delete the data that is stored about them, as well as opt out of future data being stored.

The Children's Online Privacy Protection Act (COPPA) is another US law games may need to adhere to if they have players under the age of 13 and are storing their data.

Along with data protection legislation, games must also comply with age rating systems such as PEGI, which are also enforced by law in some countries. On mobile, some app stores also have softer criteria which marks apps as 'designed for children', requiring a similar test approach if the development team is aiming for the game to be within this categorisation.

For PEGI age ratings, testing should be light. Many design teams will have already decided their target audience at concept stage and the game will be built with this in mind from the ground up. Game teams may perform some testing to make sure they stay within the target PEGI rating, but often this isn't relevant enough to require such specific attention from the test team. If the design of the game has changed drastically enough for this rating to change, then this is a problem larger than just the test team.

For compliance with regulations and law, test plans need to be extremely stringent due the high cost of failure. For this reason, peer reviews from other QA analysts are a must-have, as well as a review from the code team members developing the feature. Sharing the intended test coverage and getting wider team approval is more important for this domain area because compliance with data laws is often new ground for the entire development team and stakeholders are interested in all parts of the process, testing included.

If the game is being released in China, the regulations are so numerous and unique that many teams build a separate version of the game to release there, branching the entire project into a separate code repository. While not always enforced, game releases for China need to be submitted to the government to check that they comply with these regulations. This forms part of a larger publishing process whereby the game needs to acquire a serial number, called an ISBN, before it can be launched. Many teams outsource this entire release (and all testing involved) to a registered Chinese company familiar with the process, handing over their code base to be modified and submitted on their behalf. Other teams choose to pair with a publishing company specialising in preparing games for the submission process and outsource some of the work. Like the earlier examples of regulatory law, any failures have a high impact, with ISBN submission rejections being final, no resubmissions allowed.

Complexity/difficulty: Hard. Test planning for these areas can be a very dry topic and requires extensive reading of external documentation and interaction with company leadership and legal teams. Unusually, the test team will have two sources of information to work from: the external requirements documentation by the regulation provider and the internal specification documents, which detail the features to be implemented to comply with the regulation. Test plans need to consider not just that the feature implementation is correct according to the design, but also that the design satisfies the regulation criteria. Often testing unveils small nuances in the game that weren't considered during the design phase and need to be included.

The cost of failure can also be extremely high if bugs escape to the live game, with maximum GPDR fines in the tens of millions of Euros. Likewise, failing a submission to launch in China could block the game from ever releasing in China, jeopardising an entire country's worth of potential revenue.

This type of test planning is a far cry from the exciting and interesting domains of game content. Many QA analysts and testers would much prefer to be working on the latest game mode or the latest level layouts, especially because most don't have experience working in this domain area and find it difficult to apply the more game-orientated techniques they're so comfortable with.

Discipline focus: Client code, server code, legal.

Tools: Various. Teams may build in-house tools to manage data requests.

Bugs: Bugs are often complex and difficult to set up. They are typically few but high in severity.

6.6   UI, menus and navigation

I've grouped UI and navigation together because these domains are so closely associated that organisation of tests is easier and more efficient than planning for them as separate feature areas. This grouping is also desirable because navigation isn't always highlighted as a feature area in its own right, causing it to be underrepresented during test planning. While easy to test and find bugs, these domain areas are sometimes overlooked because QA analysts either don't consider them at all, or think that the testers will find these bugs naturally on the path to the feature that is in testing. While this is sometimes true, such an approach provides very inconsistent test coverage and is likely to only catch the most obvious of UI and navigation bugs.

The design details of game navigation aren't always explicitly labelled within design and tech design documents, particularly when the game is already live and new features are being added. Navigation to those features is often assumed and, as a result, missed during testing as an explicit check. This demonstrates the pitfalls of basing testing entirely on the scope defined within the design documentation and not thinking about the wider considerations of a feature. Experienced QA analysts will not only include direct navigation to any menu or feature, but also think about different entry points to that menu, include special cases like the 'back' button on Android devices or consider whether the player can navigate using different input methods.

For example, many games support multiple input types (controller, touch, keyboard, VR, hand gestures, etc.) which can sometimes be handled differently by the UI. All of these additional details need to be tested but won't be referenced within the wireframes or design documentation.

On-screen button prompts and the button legend will also update in real time if the player switches between input types (for example, between controller buttons and keyboard input), cementing the association between UI and navigation. This means it's not just navigation that needs to be tested with each input type – the UI does, too.

On the topic of UI and menus: these are separated because UI has a larger scope, including elements like the game heads-up-display (HUD) and popups that appear in certain scenarios and in different areas of the game. For this reason, test plans should separate the primary menu structure away from other UI elements which often have different functionality.

Test considerations include different screen types due to the prevalence of visual compatibility bugs (aspect ratios, display resolutions, mobile screens with notches, ultrawide screens, etc.) Visual compatibility is another angle not mentioned within UI wireframes, but should be included within the test plan and is likely to yield larger numbers of visual polish bugs.

Surrounding areas such as UI sound effects and localisation can also be included as an option in this test plan, because they share all the same touch points within the game as the UI test plans.

Complexity/difficulty: Easy. Interfaces and menus are one of the most documented and cleanly broken-down features within games. They're also entirely player-facing and easily understood. These attributes make them great for junior QA analysts to own, resulting in a straightforward breakdown during the test analysis phase.

Template tests for a single menu/popup type should be written and then reused across the entire game, reducing the volume of work for the QA analyst. Reusability of tests is very important for this area. Trying to write a unique test for every popup or menu would take far longer than the available test planning time. Furthermore, the QA analyst needs to make good use of combinatorial test techniques to inject the different display configurations and input types into the test plan. This domain area contains a lot of tests that follow the style: 'test list X attributes against list Y game areas'.

Discipline focus: Mixed. Built from a combination of text strings, UI art, UI code and code logic behind, QA analysts should expect bugs to be assigned to many different team members and will have different fix difficulties. Being able to differentiate each type of bug allows the QA analyst to make better decisions when speaking with testers during test execution, knowing the severity and root cause of each.

Tools: None.

Bugs: UI additions and changes typically generate a large number of low-severity visual bugs. These are usually obvious 'low hanging fruit' which can be explained with a single screenshot, which also makes this an ideal area for test execution by less experienced testers.

6.7   Game environment

Game environment testing includes everything within the game-world canvas but excludes any heads-up display UI, characters or other items that populate that environment. It has a strong art and visual focus since it is almost entirely driven by art instead of code, influencing the type of bugs found and the test approach. The scope of this area ranges from a manageable test effort for small 2D games to a colossal test effort over many months for open world 3D games.

Game environments are commonly made up of several layers and phases, each of which needs to be included within the test plan. Some layers, like the collision mesh (invisible geometry which prevents moving characters from going through objects and the floor) cannot be seen by the player, while other layers and phases are combined to form the environment visible to the player. Assets are built by artists and placed throughout the game world by level designers.

Any environment test plan should understand how the environment has been created and seek to leverage this within the plan. If a post box asset has a visual bug, that bug will be present everywhere that post box is placed within the environment. In this example, testing should log a single bug and understand that the fix would also be global across all post boxes. Conversely, some bugs will be due to how assets have been placed within a specific world location, and not a problem with the source assets themselves.

The creation and testing of game environments can include many unique components depending on the game and complexity of the environment. Most teams build custom tools that allow their designers to create entire locations more easily, without placing every individual asset and texture. Roads and paths, for example, could be placed using a tool which automatically calculates which junction texture to use at the point where each of the roads meet. The corresponding test plan might use this knowledge to focus on the road junctions. Other unique elements might include things like pedestrian and vehicle routes, animations, special surfaces, particle effects, lighting, weather and day/night cycles.

Environment testing lends itself to focused exploratory tests. These define what testing should be looking for and then leave the testers to explore each area of the environment. Trying to achieve test coverage through more granular scripted testing (defining the placement of every asset within the environment) would be an impossible task.

Focused exploratory testing is also used because, unlike other domain areas, there isn't a detailed design for the environment that testing can use as a source of truth. Instead, game environments are built from concept artwork and improved upon throughout development. The creation process is often iterative, with major changes occurring during early development and tapering off to fine adjustments during the latter stages. This creative process forces an adjustment in test approach away from scripted testing, which might seek to document specific details of the domain area even when they're liable to change.

Performance is the last consideration to mention here and, while it's important for all environments, it's critical for larger 3D environments due to their sheer size. Performance testing of environments is multi-faceted and should consider framerate, memory usage and loading times.

For framerate, the density and complexity of individual assets placed within the environment will cause varying framerates depending on where the player is. More built-up areas of the environment will cause the framerate to drop. The main goal of testing this is to find hotspots where the framerate is particularly poor so that the assets used in that area can be adjusted to improve it. While searching for hotspots manually is effective, mature teams often develop their own tools to automatically capture framerate and map coordinates of all testing conducted through network telemetry calls. This data is then used to create a framerate performance heatmap of the entire environment, which can be used to identify and monitor hotspots automatically and repeatedly.

For loading times and memory usage, testing should seek to understand whether the entire environment is loaded in one go or whether it is loaded and unloaded as the player travels throughout it (sometimes called 'streaming'). As a general rule, these operations should be invisible to the player, providing a good benchmark for any testing. This testing will seek to exercise the loading and unloading of environment assets through different entry points and whether the player is likely to notice it. This testing will also use a worst-case scenario for this task, finding the lowest spec device that the game supports and coupling it with a large player profile.

Complexity/difficulty: Easy. For the QA analyst role, test writing is limited and based around repeatability, executing the same test approach for each area or level. Testing may still take a very long time and require good organisation, but it's a predictable test effort. This area is also entirely player-facing and visual, causing both the tests and the bugs to be much more easily understood than some of the more complex code areas.

Mature test teams will also have tests from previous projects which will fit closely with the new project, further reducing the test writing burden. Franchise titles may even be able to use existing tests without modification if their environment is built using a known toolset and process.

Discipline focus: Content. Various artist specialisations and level designers.

Tools: Various in-game debug overlays are used to display hidden geometry and meshes which the test team can use. Debug can also be used to hide or show different visible environment layers, allowing them to inspect specific components independently. Further tools or debugging can be leveraged to automatically capture bug information, such as map coordinates, a screenshot of the problem and the names of the assets involved. Some teams chose to log only visual bugs that can be seen by the player, while others extend testing with the use of a free camera debug, allowing testers to inspect art assets more thoroughly from different angles.

This area lends itself to automation for games that have an AI already built in to control non-playing characters. Bots (computer-controlled players) can be set to wander the world aimlessly or to play a multiplayer match. The development team can detect when those bots fall outside of the world or get stuck. Since the code to control the players exists in the base game already, this is often an easy win that can reduce a lot of the manual test burden.

Bugs: Environment testing creates huge numbers of low-severity bugs, requiring a custom approach to fixing and retesting. Environment designers and artists frequently won't fix bugs on a case-by-case basis, but instead schedule in polishing passes for sections of the environment, marking all bugs in that area as fixed in one go. Unlike code bugs, content bugs are often very predictable and simple in nature, eliminating a lot of the follow up, triage and general back-and-forth questions that frequently accompany logical code bugs. This results in a much simpler bug life cycle.

Due to the number and style of bugs, this area requires a unique and well-defined bug style from the outset, as well as an agreed bug lifecycle process. The test and environment teams may agree, for example, that clipping bugs only require a screenshot and the map coordinates within the bug, since further detail such as reproduction steps and reproduction rate is superfluous in this scenario. Custom bugging rules allow the test team to save valuable time writing up bugs and lets them log the huge number of bugs within a shorter time.

Retesting follows the same style, running a test pass against an area instead of retesting each bug individually. Testers will test the area and then close the bugs in bulk, without explicitly checking each one. The lowest-severity bugs are sometimes closed without a retest because they are so numerous and trivial that retesting them isn't worth the test effort.

This domain area is also unlike most functional testing of code in that many of the bug resolutions are not binary (i.e. fixed or not fixed). Bug fixes here can be subjective improvements, like tweaking the position of a tree to not clip so heavily into another nearby object, or improving the appearance of a stretched texture by altering the geometry of the object slightly. If the test team intends to retest these bugs, reasonable expectations and processes should be in place to decide the correct definition of 'fixed'. Indeed, I've seen many disgruntled artists and designers whose bug fixes have been sent back to them with a 'fix failed' result because the tester has observed that the original problem still occurs, at least to some extent.

On the subject of the test effort, this domain requires a granular test schedule and good test estimations. Projects with large environments should expect to allocate a sizeable portion of the test team to environment testing for the duration of the project. These test passes should also closely synchronise with the schedule of the environment creation team.

6.8 Content (Characters, weapons, items, etc.)

This category comprises multiple domain areas that make up the content lists within the game. These areas aren't labelled as 'content' but are instead referred to by the name of their groups and sub-groups, and will be different for each project. For racing games this test area will be the cars. First person shooters might have several content lists like character models, weapons, outfits and items. This can also include object lists within the game, like chests and other consumable items.

All of these pieces of content share the same characteristics that each object is made up of art assets to represent it visually and data to define its behaviour and attributes. Complex objects, like characters, might have multiple art assets like a model, textures, rigging and animations. One of the defining attributes of this domain area is that adding new content doesn't usually require new code to be written, which affects the test approach that must be taken.

A code framework is still required to handle how the content is going to function, but this is a one-off development effort. The game is developed assuming each object type contains predefined attributes in data, and then uses those attributes to perform whatever on-screen action necessary. This means that new content (like cars in a racing game) can be added without writing new code, as long as they're defined using the set of attributes the code is expecting. New code only needs to be written if new functionality is being added or if the format of the data is being updated.

Before beginning a test plan for this domain area, QA analysts must consider what the goal is. Is it to gain confidence in the code framework functionality, or in each piece of content? There's a requirement for both in every project but, as I've described above, they require different approaches. It's valuable to separate the two test goals within the test management tools, creating one test suite designed to be rerun against each piece of content in the list and another, deeper test suite designed to focus on the functionality provided by the code.

When writing tests for content lists, they should focus on what is defined in data and shown in the art for each object, and not test the underlying code framework repeatedly. As an example, all items might have a sellable value represented as an integer in the data which shows how much currency is given when selling each item. Testing each item should verify that the sale value is correct for each, but not cover different selling scenarios and edge cases, since they are part of the underlying code framework and not unique to each item. While testing should cover various selling scenarios, they don't need to be run for *every* item.

Tests for content lists should heavily leverage reusability for test writing to be maintainable and efficient. This means writing a single set of tests that can be applied to all objects in a list, rather than separate tests for each content item. Even writing the tests and then copy/pasting them for each item creates a maintainability issue if the tests need to be updated at a later time. QA analysts can use the test design techniques I described earlier to organise testing for long lists of content and avoid this problem.

Another reason to set up tests this way is that it's safe to assume all content will be expanded in the future, even if it isn't on the immediate project roadmap. This approach allows the test team to invest early and save a lot of time later in the project when more content is added. In the best-case scenario, new content can be added, and no new tests need to be written at all.

So far I've described content as flat lists of objects. In reality, content objects are more likely to fit into tree structure of groups and subgroups due to their varying characteristics. For example, characters in a game might be split into different classes, each with their own unique data types to support their separate class abilities. These subgroups might then be split into separate lists even further. For this reason, it's not always possible to write a single set of tests which are applicable to every object, so the test suite must be broken down. I recommend writing a core set of tests which *do* apply to every object, and supplementing it with additional test cases which are more selectively applicable. When the tests are duplicated by the tool across the list of content, you can make a custom selection of the tests for each content object, selecting those which are applicable to each.

Complexity/difficulty: Easy-Medium. The difficulty and scope of this test area is highly dependent on the amount and complexity of content within the game. Generally, content areas are easily understood due to their strong player-facing visual focus. While there can be more complex facets to the testing, a large part of the test effort is often searching for visual problems, which is usually a straightforward endeavour. Since this domain can encompass multiple major content areas for any project, the ownership is spread across multiple QA analysts, with only the simpler content going to the more junior members of the team. Where games have multiple content lists which interact with each other, the test approach can become far more complex and require a more experienced approach.

In some projects, a list of content can be tested individually, testing each item without further consideration. Take the example of testing a list of possible reward chests. The visual look and contents of each chest can be checked without needing to test them in combination with other items.

However, many game objects interact with each other and other parts of the game in complex ways, making it difficult to define the scope of testing. In these cases, QA analysts will need to make extensive use of combinatorial test techniques to identify where content lists need to be tested in combination with each other. For example, do I need to visually check each character with each weapon and each outfit, or can I just check each content list separately? Characters, weapons and outfits are all separate lists of content with their own visuals and data definitions which will need to be tested, but they interact with each other so closely that both visual and data bugs may be found when they are used together.

This combinatorial testing of game content is an area which won't be defined in any design document on the project. The correct combinatorial considerations need to be identified by the QA analyst during the test analysis phase of test planning.

Discipline focus: Mixed. Can include work from a variety of disciplines: art, code, sound and animation.

Tools: In-game debug tools for spawning and inspecting each asset.

Bugs: Content testing creates large numbers of low severity bugs. Most content bugs are visual issues, but a smaller set of more complex data bugs can also be found.

6.9   User generated content (UGC)

This area is specific to projects which allow players to create content and then share it with other players within the game. Allowing players to generate any type of content creates new complications beyond normal game content, like managing storage and censoring explicit material.

Consider the most basic form of UGC – a player choosing their multiplayer name by typing it into a free text field. The player can type whatever they choose and, since other players will see it, even this would need a profanity filter to prevent it being abused. A multiplayer chat feature can be considered a slightly more complex form of user generated content, giving players more freedom to create longer messages, perhaps containing images or emojis, and share it with other players. This content also needs to be censored, stored somewhere and scaled as more players send messages.

One of the defining characteristics of this domain area versus other game content is that players can create as much or as little UGC as they wish, and the game needs to handle it. This could include in-game controls which allow the players to manage their content, giving options to create, move, share, report and delete individual pieces. It could also include server-side scaling to store and provide access to the content as players interact with the feature for the first time after the game is launched. Until the game is live, it's often difficult to estimate how much engagement there will be with UGC features, creating a challenge for server engineers to estimate the storage capacity and speed of access.

The other defining characteristic of UGC is that it's the only part of the game that isn't carefully curated by the design and art teams. Players can use UGC features in weird and wonderful ways, often taking their use in a direction that wasn't originally intended by the development team. In many ways, these features allow players to influence the game direction, which can be both damaging and beneficial to the overall game experience. This is particularly true because all UGC features are designed to be inherently multiplayer features. Creating your own in-game content has no value if you can't share it with anyone.

In real projects, we don't refer to multiplayer chat as user-generated content, the name is reserved for more complex UGC that can come in the form of player created 'skins' for weapons and items, spray tags, car liveries, character setups, video and audio recordings, custom modifiers, even whole levels or game modes. Indeed, some games are entirely built around user generated content (think LittleBigPlanet and Minecraft).

For this area it's particularly important to consider failure scenarios and edge cases. The core flows will likely be straightforward to verify and yield few bugs, while the more interesting test scenarios will require the QA analyst to apply some 'out of the box' thinking. You should ignore how the feature is intended to work and instead explore how the feature can be used by the player for other purposes, malicious or not.

UGC is nearly always intended to be shared with other players as a social feature and so needs to be stored server-side. So this test area requires network and online services test knowledge, and will link to online services test ownership. Any UGC test plan should seek to understand the limitations of the feature and then include those within the plan. What is the limit on the amount of UGC any single player can create? Are players able to report each other for abuse? Are there file size limitations to the content that can be created?

Under-the-hood details should also be understood and included in the plan. When during gameplay is new content uploaded to the server? When and how is content from other players downloaded from the server? Does the player need to be online to create new content?

UGC tests should also include scenarios where the server is populated with huge amounts of content, with at least a representative sample of what it will be when the game goes live. Many performance and UI bugs can be missed because the testing is conducted on a development server where there is very little content saved and/or the server is being erased frequently.

Some network performance bugs may only manifest when there are large amounts of data that the game is trying to download. As an example, when a player enters an in-game menu that allows them to browse and apply content created by other players, the game may try to download all of the content immediately upon entering the menu, or download content in smaller batches, triggered by the player scrolling down the list. These nuances in how the game handles downloading content can only be experienced during testing when there is enough content populated on the server, making this an important consideration during testing.

Likewise, some UI controls and features only appear when large quantities of content are available. Large content lists can display a scroll bar when the content goes past the bottom of the viewable window, or they can implement pagination and show buttons to navigate forwards and backwards between pages. These UI controls are often dynamic, showing as hidden or visible when necessary. For example, a 'next page' button should only appear if there is another page of content beyond the current one. Testing can use this knowledge by populating different amounts of content on the server to test different UI configurations. What happens where there is no content? Do the first and last pages have special considerations? How much content is required for the UI to create a separate page?

Complexity/difficulty: Medium. A small domain area for most games, but has some interesting testing challenges that requires the QA analysts to think like a player and explore the boundaries of the content creation.

Requires a good understanding of network testing, client-server relationships and how the content is being handled behind the scenes. Also requires the QA analyst to understand the difference between storage and memory, and be able to include storage considerations into the test plan.

Discipline focus: Code.

Tools: Network proxy tools used to test content being uploaded and downloaded. UGC content debug tools can also be created to allow the development team to populate the UGC server with spoof data for the purposes of testing.

Bugs: Many *potential* bugs are generated here: problems that players could face if they were to use these features in a very specific way. These bugs can have a high impact but a low likelihood, and the project team needs to triage them carefully, because we all know players often interact with the game in strange and unpredictable ways. What may initially seem a low likelihood, can become a big issue when the game releases.

Bugs found in this area may be considered by other members of the development team to be outside the scope of interest and not worth investigating. While QA analysts shouldn't blindly pursue an agenda to have these bugs fixed, they would do well to impress the potential for UGC to be abused through these bugs so that the triage team can make the most informed decision.

6.10 Game modes (campaign, co-op, skirmish, etc.)

This is another area which isn't labelled as 'game modes' during project work but is instead divided into the applicable modes for the game. For many this is simply the single player campaign (sometimes called 'story mode'). Other modes that would be included here might be features like skirmish modes in strategy games or endless/survival modes which continue until the player dies. Any minigames (games within the game) would also be given their own area here.

This domain area takes an end-to-end perspective of an entire game mode, focusing on all the highly scripted milestones that lead the player through the game mode. This includes gameplay components like triggers, cutscenes, quests/missions, scripted sequences, transitions and unlock flows. The primary aim of this test plan is to focus on the sequential flow of the game mode, scene to scene, level to level, moment to moment. In this area, many of the other game features come together to form the complete flow, and a surprisingly large number of bugs can be found because of it.

This area should include all variations of the core game modes, too. Many games allow you to play them from the perspective of different characters with unique dialogue, or they allow you to choose good/bad paths. Many even have complex choices and multiple endings. Any elements which are unique to the game mode and don't fit neatly into other test domain areas need to be included within this test plan.

Complexity/difficulty: Medium-hard. This test area cuts through many other game test areas making it difficult to define the scope of testing. QA analysts testing the campaign should only include game components that are unique to the game mode, and ignore anything already covered by other test areas. Because this area is where so many other game features culminate, the test writing needs to be particularly careful not to include verification points for other game areas, overlapping the test effort. A little overlap is fine, and sometimes required, but a lot can introduce harmful inefficiencies.

For example, testing here shouldn't include visual checks for the character models and their standard animations, since they'll be covered by other content testing and are not specific to this game mode. However, if the game mode contains one-off custom animations for those characters (during cutscenes, for example), then this would need to be included. For this reason, the tests need to be precisely worded, and the intent of each test made clear to the tester. It may also help to explicitly define what is in scope and out of scope for each of the tests within this plan, cementing the goal of only focusing on components which are unique to this game mode.

In addition to this difficulty, this domain area requires a heavily scripted and details orientated approach, because the campaign mode for many games is itself so heavily scripted. There are many small and unique gameplay elements to each game mode which are important to the flow and need to be called out within the tests. The main game mode often contains a tutorial section at the beginning which holds the player's hand through the early gameplay mechanics, unlocking additional features at predefined trigger points. Depending on the type of game, the tutorial is included within this test ownership, and for other projects it's split out into a separate area. Regardless, it's a good example of how heavily curated some game modes can be, guiding the player's every button press.

As well as requiring well-written scripted tests, the highly scripted nature of this feature area causes it to be fragile and susceptible to breaking after it has initially been developed and tested. Experienced QA analysts recognise this trait and include continuous regression testing of the primary game mode, even after its initial development. I'll talk more about this next.

Another reason this domain area is difficult to test is because the primary game mode can be incredibly vast, requiring many hours for a real player to complete naturally. Even with debug and tools to aid testing, a single playthrough of a game mode can take several work-days, causing the overall test effort to be very large. On the topic of test estimations, the key test consideration is to estimate how long it takes a single tester to test the primary game mode end-to-end.

The test execution strategy for the primary game mode (campaign/story mode) is often to organise the campaign test team such that each main section of the campaign is tested by at least one tester on any single day. This can be achieved by staggering when each tester begins their test pass by a day or so. For very large games, the campaign test team may be big enough to allow sub-teams of testers to be organised in the same way as individuals.

This strategy provides three important benefits. The first is that each sub-team can perform any bug retests for the area of the game mode they are currently testing, instead of assigning bug retests back to the tester that originally logged the bug. This dramatically shortens the retest time for bugs because the alternative is to wait for the creator of the bug to begin their next campaign test pass and reach the same area of the bug, which could take several days.

The second benefit is that new bugs and blocking issues are found throughout the campaign far more quickly because there is always someone looking at each section of the campaign. Without this approach, some bugs would go undiscovered for several days until the team progressed through the test pass again to the point of the bug.

Finally, this approach provides continuous and repeated test coverage of the entire game mode, allowing testing of newly created sections and regression testing of already completed sections.

Discipline focus: Mixed. Includes work from a variety of disciplines.

Tools: In-game debug tools only.

Bugs: A mixed bag of bugs are likely to be found that need fixing by different disciplines within the feature team developing the main game modes. Bugs for surrounding features may also be found incidentally during this testing and assigned out. Due to the scale of the main game mode, this is a large area that generates a lot of bugs, both code and content.

6.11 Game progress and retention

This area focuses on the core game loop and metagame systems behind the game modes, whether a single player campaign or a multiplayer focus. Games that operate as a live service (and particularly those that are free to play) will have many features that are developed as retention features – meaning features that are intended to retain the interest of players and keep them playing. Live service games often have a development pod that is dedicated to create many different features with this same goal. As a result of this organisation, they won't be called 'retention features' during project work.

Other subdomains within this area cover game economy and core loop changes. These areas include many data driven changes that influence the game balancing: levelling up, technology/skill trees, upgrades, modifiers and the rate of player progress throughout the duration of the game. Another subdomain can include testing of different difficulty settings.

Game economy and balancing data is usually automatically calculated by the design teams using formulas and tooling, due to the huge number of values that are required to drive the game balancing and rate of progress. This data is entered into spreadsheets, and scripts are used to convert the data into a format that can be read by the game code at runtime (some teams even build their own toolchain which then commits the relevant files into source control and deploys them to a content server if one is used). This allows design teams to repeatedly update different components of the game economy with ease, preventing having to manually curate every single value each time a change is required.

Consider a game that provides ten different locked chests for players to acquire, with higher levels providing greater rewards. Design teams will be able to control the chances that different level players will get each chest and the value of the rewards within each chest. The increase in values from chest to chest can be represented on a graph showing the deltas between each chest. This type of item is often designed to provide large increases in value during early levels and exponentially fewer increases in value towards the higher levels.

The process used to produce the game progression data influences both the test approach required and the bugs that are likely to be found from such testing. Since the values are so susceptible to change, tests should never reference them directly and QA analysts should also use caution when making copies of design data spreadsheets. Because of the automated creation process, testing is very unlikely to find missing values or individual values which have been incorrectly entered due to human error. Instead, it's more likely that testing will identify more subjective bugs relating to playability and difficulty.

On the subject of difficulty balance testing, this area needs to be a joint endeavour between the test and design teams. It is not an opportunity to provide a personal critique of the game balancing, unless it is asked for. Where balance testing is required, bugs should be captured in a data-driven way, by recording the number of hours played against current progress for example (Free-to-play games often have a defined currency conversion between hours played for free against the hard currency value you need to spend to achieve the same progress). Rotating testers away from other test areas also provides a useful 'fresh eyes' perspective for game balancing, increasing the chances of finding subjective feedback bugs.

Complexity/difficulty: Medium. This area overlaps with many other test areas and is heavily associated with the main game mode. Defining the scope of testing can be difficult and, if planned wrongly, tests can easily include verification points for other feature areas, becoming very unwieldy and time-consuming to execute. QA analysts owning this testing require a firm grasp of the underlying game systems.

This test ownership is ideal for QA analysts who are aiming to move into design discipline roles due to the strong focus on gameplay loops, game economies and meta systems.

Discipline focus: Mixed. Should be primarily data-led by the design team.

Tools: In-game debug tools only.

Bugs: Bugging balancing issues can be difficult to define due to their subjectivity. Close communication with the design team is essential to agree which type of bugs should come from this testing, and when it should be conducted. The data-driven characteristics of this area mean that logical bugs are less likely, and incorrect or badly-designed data is more likely.

6.12 Online services

A game doesn't need to have a multiplayer mode to require some kind of online service component. Indeed, even the simplest single player experiences will likely have telemetry events that are sent to an online database to understand how players are interacting with the game. Online services can be developed and maintained by the game team or be third-party services which the game interacts with. Regardless of the approach, integration with online services requires a unique test approach and includes considerations not seen when testing more player-facing features.

Having spoken to QA analysts and testers from different studios and outsourced companies, it's clear that this is an area of confusion for many and can be daunting to plan testing for, as much of it is 'under the hood' of the game. Online services also break many normal test processes, causing further confusion. A lack of updated code for new builds installed onto the device is a good example of this. Server code is instead updated and deployed remotely to a server, often with little visibility to the test team, making it difficult to know what code is deployed and whether the current setup being tested contains a specific bug fix. Because of the increased unknowns, it's even more important that testers understand what online services are, and how they differ from traditional multiplayer features regarding their test plans.

An online service (sometimes called a web service or microservice) is software deployed to a remote server (it does not exist on the player's device) with which game clients interact, sending and requesting data to and from the service. Online services operate a one-to-many relationship with the game clients installed on players' devices, meaning all game clients will connect to the same single service deployment. Game clients communicate with online services through a series of requests to URLs which are defined by each service. These URLs are called 'endpoints' and will provide a response back to the game for each request it receives.

These requests and responses nearly always use HTTP/S protocol, which operates synchronously, keeping the connection open and waiting for a response from the service before giving up*. Because of this trait, all game clients have two values which help them reduce unnecessary failures. The first is a timeout value which defines how many milliseconds the client should wait for a response before giving up or trying again. The second is a retry value which defines how many times the client should retry the request silently before reporting back to the player that the operation failed. These common behaviours eliminate fragility when the network connection is poor.

Here is a basic example of a game login request-response flow between a game client and an online service. An online service is created by the game team to store the player account and all its details. It has several endpoints implemented which provide account functionality: login, edit and deletion. When logging in, the game wants to retrieve the account information so that it can display the details within the game UI and use it for other purposes during gameplay. When the player enters their login details (username and password) the game sends this data in a request to the login URL (e.g., https://mycoolgameservice.com/login) and the service responds to that request with a response. If the login request information was correct, the response back to the game client contains the player account information. If the login request was incorrect, the response back to the game client would contain an error code. The exact same flow is seen whenever you visit a webpage. By navigating to the page, your browser is making a request to the website URL which is responding back with the contents of the page so that the browser can display it on your device.

One of the defining characteristics of web services is that they sit idle and do nothing when no clients are making requests to the service. This pattern of doing work and being idle helps us understand how they respond during load and stress testing. Compare this with a multiplayer server which needs to continuously send network communications to every player in the game many times each second, broadcasting

---

*   This is an important distinction which separates the behaviour of online services with the network behaviour you see for a multiplayer game server.

the coordinates of each player and the state of the game, even when the players are idle. I'll talk more about this in the next section.

HTTP proxy tools allow us to view and modify each network request, providing much needed transparency into this test area. These tools not only allow testers to see what endpoints are being contacted, but also block the requests so that no response is sent back to the client. Blocking network requests is the most basic test that can be done and will exercise the timeout and retry behaviour of each request, as well as checking how the game handles the failure. However, these tools provide far more complex features, allowing testers to modify a request before it goes to the service or intercept responses before they reach the client and instead provide a customised response.

The main 'gotcha!' when testing online services is the uncomfortable truth that manual black-box testing isn't a very good mitigation against the risks that exist there. QA analysts should coordinate closely with the server team to find other ways to identify bugs within online services code. The best server teams may write unit tests and test their own work extensively for exactly this reason. When manual test teams conduct testing using HTTP proxy tools, the goals are often to gain confidence in how the client handles failure scenarios when communicating with online services, *not* to test the service code directly. The tools are great for forcing specific failures to occur, providing a more precise version of the common network cable-pulling offline scenario.

Finally, load testing of new online services is notoriously difficult to estimate accurately without testing it with real players. Everyone has heard of at least one game or website which goes offline on launch day due to overloaded servers. This is another area which can't be tested through standard black box testing and requires the use of specialist load testing tools, usually set up by server engineers. The other effective test approach is to use scale beta tests with real players to measure a sample of the total load that a game or feature might have before it launches. Both approaches illustrate the type of abnormal thought process required by QA analysts owning the testing for this domain area.

Complexity/difficulty: Hard. This area is usually owned by senior QA analysts. This code is developed by server code engineers and deployed as remote services which the game connects to, making this area difficult to understand for many testers because they can't see it or directly interact with it, like they can other game features within the client software. Server code updates are also deployed remotely and independently of new client builds, confusing the normal bug fix retesting flow of updating to a new client build to get the latest changes and bug fixes. QA analysts need to be familiar with server environments and how these changes are delivered into testing so that they can relay this to the test team.

Discipline focus: Server code.

Tools: HTTP proxy tools (Charles, Fiddler), network monitoring tools (Wireshark), Debug overlays.

Bugs: Few in number, but often have a technical nature and can be difficult for testers to understand and retest.

6.13 Multiplayer

This is a big area for many projects, containing numerous sub areas that fall under the MP umbrella: Game modes, matchmaking, synchronisation, voice chat, text chat, banning, blocking, reporting, friend systems, invites, leaderboards, ranking systems, rewards and more.

The unique challenge underpinning all test writing, planning and organisation in this area is that much of the testing requires the coordination of multiple testers together. Practically all other areas in this domain list allow testers to execute each test independently, and mostly on a single device, providing flexibility during test execution to run the testing with a single tester or shorten testing by assigning a group of testers to the task. Multiplayer test plans, however, need to consider the minimum number of testers that are required to run each test and then factor this into the test estimations. In this area, adding more testers doesn't speed up test execution time; it's simply a requirement to run test cases, period.

As well as thinking about test estimations in this different way, the tests themselves also need to include supplementary instructions on how the testers should organise themselves before running the test and, when it's required, which tester should perform each step in the test.

The former can easily be communicated through an opening statement in the description of each subtask or test suite, setting the expectation that all the following tests assume the testers are working in teams of ten, for example, and will enter each multiplayer game with five testers on each opposing side (assuming a team vs. team game). QA analysts owning this test area should also set this expectation ahead of time with the test execution lead, planning the team size and general organisation. Because of the organisational burden of coordinating a team of people towards a common goal, it's also common for a senior tester to be assigned as a local point of contact amongst the test team. This person acts as both a knowledge holder for the domain area and a coordinator during test execution, remembering that the QA analyst is often not working at the same location and not involved in the testing themselves.

The latter is required when testers on the team need to take on specific game roles, such as the creator of the custom game, the leader of a squad, the player who gets banned or the player who drops out of the game due to their bad network connection. Test instructions for individuals amongst the group can be extremely confusing if they are not written clearly and use the style guide I spoke about in chapter five.

On the topic of test estimates, the test schedule should include a generous contingency for the time required to run multiplayer tests. If a tester within a group of ten needs to stop the test to log a bug or look up some information, the other nine testers need to be able to continue executing the test in a reduced capacity or find something else productive to do with the time. Multiplayer bugs are sometimes left to the end of a test session for this reason, allowing all testers to finish the test at the same time and then log bugs individually.

In other cases, a tester needs the help of others to reproduce the scenario again, creating opportunities for the team to break out into smaller groups to log bugs before joining together to finish the test. These are just a few examples that show us the huge potential for wasting time through poorly organised test execution when running multiplayer tests, making this problem high on the priority list of QA analysts owning this area.

Tooling and debug can make multiplayer tests more bearable when they are available. Many games have built-in computer-controlled players which can be repurposed to populate entire multiplayer games easily, allowing a single tester to enter a game on their own and reach areas without the assistance of other testers. This debug can help testers access areas that would usually require multiple devices, but not necessarily multiple active players. Note: computer-controlled players can also become a nuisance if testing needs to set up a specific multiplayer scenario, varying their usefulness.

Another major consideration during multiplayer testing is the association between the game clients, the multiplayer server and online services used for multiplayer features. It's another area which can be confusing to many testers and creates uncertainty knowing which component a bug is in – the services code, the client code or the game server code. I'll introduce the key differences here.

In the online services area, I spoke about how services are always running and are idle when no requests are being made to them. Multiplayer servers for synchronous games behave very differently to this in multiple ways.

Firstly, multiplayer game servers don't operate a one-to-many relationship with the entire player base like online services do. Each new instance of the game server is run for each concurrent game session and destroyed once the game finishes. More players playing in multiplayer sessions means more game servers running simultaneously. All of these 'game servers' are programs running on physical servers, with each being able to handle many 'game server' instances in parallel, like running many versions of the same program on your computer.

Developers and testers can also run the game server locally on their PC and use debug to direct their game clients towards it. This local setup allows easier access to debug and logging of the game server. Multiplayer bugs often require testers to retrieve client logs from each player as well as the log from the game server to show a complete picture of what occurred during the lead up to the bug. Having one log without the others is akin to having only one side of a conversation.

Secondly, the network communication during multiplayer game sessions is different. It doesn't use the request-response HTTP/S style I described in the previous section for online services, and so can't be tested in the same way or use the same tools. With online services, the network communications were transactions (they explicitly fail or succeed) where the game would wait for the response before deciding what to do next. These HTTP/S network calls use a reliable network protocol called TCP because it handles errors and doesn't tolerate lost data.

Conversely, synchronous multiplayer sessions require each client to repeatedly send their world coordinates and/or other state data to the game server, which then broadcasts out the state of the entire game to all players. It does this many times each second for the entire duration of the session, even if all players are idle. This continuous broadcasting of the game state requires a much quicker method of network communication; it can't wait for a response each time and it doesn't care if network errors occur. Because of this, synchronous multiplayer game servers use a different network protocol called UDP, which is quicker and tolerates data loss. If a player has a poor network connection and doesn't receive a broadcast from the game server, it doesn't display an error, allowing the player to continue and then pick up the latest broadcast when the network recovers, ignoring any out-of-date broadcasts that it missed. Players will perceive this as 'lag' or 'skipping' in the game, where other players may skip from their previously known location to the location given in the latest broadcast from the game server. UDP sends out these broadcasts without ever getting acknowledgement in return that they reached their target device, essentially trading off reliability for speed.

This difference in network protocol means that this network data can't be seen in HTTP/S proxy tools because they're not built to detect and display other network protocols. Instead, testers must use more universal network packet monitoring and throttling tools such as Wireshark. These tools are powerful but are complex as a result and so require training before testing begins.

Testing here should include how different network characteristics impact the game session. Network latency, packet loss and bandwidth can all have a slightly different impact, requiring testing to go beyond basic low bandwidth configurations. This area of failure testing is often not defined within technical specs and should be generated entirely by the QA analyst.

Complexity/difficulty: Hard. While the area does have a selection of player-facing features that can be approached in a regular test planning way, much of this test area focuses on 'under the hood' logic and requires heavy use of debug and tools during testing, as well as a good understanding of the relationship between the game client, game server and online services. This area can be technically difficult and requires the QA analyst to both understand it and be able to communicate that understanding through well-written tests and documentation for the test execution to be effective.

Test design and test execution is more complex to set up, requiring groups of testers to coordinate on a single test or tools which allow a single tester to execute some of the tests alone using tools and AI to populate the rest of the multiplayer session.

Discipline focus: Server code, multiplayer code. These teams will usually be different specialisations, separate from the gameplay code team that other QA analysts would speak to most often.

Tools: Network packet monitoring tools (Wireshark, Windows Network Monitor), Debug overlays, local multiplayer servers.

Bugs: Most multiplayer bugs will require additional attachments so that they can be diagnosed and fixed. This includes network logs or a set of client game logs from all players, as well as the corresponding game server log. It's vital that the testers are able to accurately document the series of events leading up to the bug, from the point of view of every player in the session.

6.14 Live events, sales and AB tests

Many games now operate as a continuous live service and punctuate their calendar with competitions, sales, seasons and other events which refresh the gameplay. In addition to these retention features, live service games also release these events, normal features and economy changes as AB tests, only deploying the change to a subset of the total player base to measure the impact when compared with the standard game configuration. All features in this 'live ops' group are particularly common amongst free-to-play games, often with a sub-team of the development team dedicated to it.

While some games require a game client update to run these events, many successful teams have built code frameworks allowing them to deploy data and content remotely 'over the air' without the need to write new code and release it as a game update. These frameworks give live ops teams a huge amount of flexibility and power, allowing them to make substantial changes to the base game for all players instantaneously.

This is possible because much of a game's content is driven by data and art. Each new event type requires a one-off implementation in code and then it can be reused with fresh content each time it is run.

Any testing within this domain area needs to consider what the goal of the testing is. Is it to check the content populated within each rerun of the event type, or is it to test the underlying code framework? I described the difference between these goals in the **Pitfalls of testing** section in the previous chapter. There's no value in testing the code for every event if it's not changing. Likewise, the focus on art and content means that you may be able to cut out compatibility tests if testing is usually duplicated across multiple supported platforms.

For example, event testing is unlikely to yield bugs specific to the Android platform that don't occur on iOS, so testing doesn't need to be duplicated across both of these platforms. The same logic applies if multiple game versions are live at the same time. Any event test plan should consider whether the event is likely to yield bugs that are specific to one version of the game code. Often the answer is 'no' and testing only needs to include a light sanity check on players running older versions of the game. Depending on the circumstance, other efficiencies can also be made here, helping the test team gain confidence in each event while keeping on track with the demanding live ops schedule.

Additionally, the more each type of event is run, the more confident the team running that event will be. Over time, the setup and deployment can become near autonomous, generating very few bugs or none at all. Testing should consider this and reduce the testing required where it's appropriate.

Owning the testing for live ops event reruns involves very little test analysis and design since the tests already exist in most cases. A lot of the work here is instead organisational, due to the fast pace and continuous deployment of changes to the live game. Mature games have events run as often as every week, overlapped with seasons, AB tests, sales and more. With many events based around national holidays and key dates in the year, the highly time-sensitive schedule sometimes requires a more quick-and-dirty test approach. QA analysts will need to protect against project time pressures and plan accordingly by cutting out unnecessary tests that I've mentioned here.

Complexity/difficulty: Easy. A good area for juniors. This area is highly repetitive as in-game events and sales are frequently re-run throughout the year, allowing QA analysts to follow the same set of live ops tests again and again. Only when a new event type is written into the code does a new set of corresponding tests need to be written.

These tests already exist for many established live service games. They can be handed to new juniors coming on to the team to duplicate each new test run and organise the testing. Very little test analysis and design is required on a day-to-day basis.

Discipline focus: Product, design, live ops.

Tools: Custom event data tools are required to enable and disable events, sales and other in-game configurations. Further tools are often needed to check the state of remote event data.

Bugs: Testers and QA analysts should be careful to focus on those bugs that are within the data for each unique event and not spend time investigating code bugs that are within the event framework of the client build. While still valuable, these code bugs can't be fixed remotely and will be raised repeatedly against each event until the next game update is released. Understanding the distinction between the code framework and the data that uses it to build events and sales is an important lesson in making this test area effective.

6.15 Audio, music and sound effects

These areas can be extremely important for certain game genres such as simulation or racing, with a huge work effort going into the production and testing of all audio. For a majority of other console and PC games, audio testing holds a similar importance to other functional test areas, but some smaller and/or mobile projects put much less emphasis on it.

Complexity/difficulty: Mixed. Can be an easy area of ownership for junior QA analysts on mobile projects. However, games with a heavy focus on audio will require a specialist or senior QA analyst who understands the technical details of the audio production pipeline and the different components of audio, like music, sound effects and dialogue. This area can be good for audiophiles and those who aspire to move into the audio production role.

Discipline focus: Audio engineers, code.

Tools: In place of digital tools, the primary requirement for audio testing is a range of hardware. At the very least, test teams will have to consider dual channel audio output (e.g., headphones) and multi-channel audio output (5.1 and 7.1 speaker systems).

Bugs: Testing frequently produces a moderate number of easy bugs that detail areas where sound effects aren't played or where music is cut off or jarring. Compatibility issues can also be fairly obvious for certain hardware setups. However, the best test plans will also dig deeper to identify more nuanced sound balancing and accuracy bugs. As ever, a close relationship with the audio production and engineering team is crucial to understand what users should expect to hear.

Test considerations: Sound design frequently goes undocumented or severely under-documented, making it difficult to identify when audio is missing and leaving the test team to guess what is expected. This should be avoided.

On projects where audio isn't a strong focus, the QA analysts should agree whether a dedicated owner is assigned to all audio or whether each feature owner will test the audio in their areas. If the latter, the team should coordinate to ensure a consistent test approach.

6.16 Player profiles and file I/O

This group includes all features that read and write files to the device storage. Most commonly, this will be the player profile (their saved progress), but some games allow the player to create objects which are stored independently of their own profile. The user generated content I mentioned earlier is a good example of this. Some games will also allow players to download items, content and other data from the game or other players, increasing the storage allocation for the game.

For player profiles, QA analysts should understand how and when the different parts of the profile are saved by speaking to the code team developing the feature. Many games display a visual indicator on screen during saving or loading, providing a clue when this is happening. Knowing how the player profile is broken up allows the QA analyst to write tests for each part of the player profile, verifying that each piece of profile data is being saved correctly. For example, multiplayer mode levelling could be captured at different trigger points during gameplay and saved in one of many files that together make up the player progress.

A lost or corrupted save file is one of the worst bugs a player can experience, because their time investment is gone forever. Crashes can be fixed with a game update, but progress loss is permanent and will likely cause the player to put the game down and not return to it. For this reason, profile test plans need to include well-considered failure test scenarios to probe ways the player might experience progress loss. This could be through bad design, such as not making it clear when automatic saves are happening, or poor messaging when the player exits the game.

Progress loss can also occur through technical failure caused by destructive actions when the game is performing file IO and vulnerable to such actions. Players can unknowingly terminate the game while it's loading or while a save operation is happening, and accidently corrupt or overwrite their progress.

I've grouped all of these features under file input/output because they all share common test cases relating to when these files are read and written to the device storage. All these tests will have to consider the minimum and maximum file sizes and how those files impact load times. Do very large player profiles cause loading problems? Do large player profiles experience bugs that smaller profiles do not?

Interaction with the device storage also introduces complications for devices which have removable storage (i.e. most of them). When I started testing, these tests would include removable Xbox 360 memory cards, as the game needed to cope with the card being removed at any point, or a loose connection. More modern devices might still include tests for removable storage like micro-SD cards, USB sticks and removable hard drives. All of these are still common across mobile devices and consoles.

Device storage is still a limited resource, with many players quickly filling up the storage on their phones and consoles with media and games. Because of this, all file IO test plans need to consider full storage scenarios. What happens when the player creates a new item or starts a new save game when the storage is full? Such testing might also highlight bugs with the design, like checking that the game provides an option for the player to delete and manage their game files without uninstalling the game.

This area requires the tester to know the difference between temporary memory (RAM) and permanent storage, and the relationship between them. I've occasionally seen testers fill up the device storage when they're running memory tests and vice versa. It comes down to the confusing use of the word 'memory' to describe both of these areas. Remember that the device storage is where files are permanently stored on the device, even when the device is powered down. The temporary memory only stores game data when the game is running and uses it for quick access. The loading screens you see are the game transferring data from storage to temporary memory, ready to use it.

As a brief aside, consoles and mobile devices have the same main components as standard desktop computers. If you want to understand more about each component, building a computer or watching videos of people building computers is a great way to do that. The knowledge can be applied throughout testing, regardless of the target device.

Complexity/difficulty: Medium. For many projects which are built on a mature code base, this area can be very simple and yield almost no bugs, eliminating it as a dedicated test area. However, for new code and updates to existing code, this is a high risk and potentially complex test area.

Discipline focus: Code.

Bugs: Bugs specific to a profile should have the affected profile attached to the bug wherever possible, or provide a way to retrieve it.

6.17 Identities and cloud save

This test area is closely associated with the player profiles area. The key difference is that it only applies to those game projects that are either online-only, or can be played offline and have an optional cloud save feature. Allowing players to upload their save profile to remote storage (on a server) introduces a surprising amount of additional logic and test considerations.

QA analysts need to identify when game data is uploaded to the cloud during gameplay and perform both verification and failure tests against those upload points. Because the files are being uploaded and downloaded, this testing needs to introduce network considerations, checking how the game behaves when the network speed is poor or if the connection drops during play. Additional UI is sometimes added to indicate to the player that the network connection has dropped and the game is trying to perform a network action, introducing some visual tests to the plan.

Aside from backing up the files, the main use case for cloud save is to move the profile data between devices. Players can play on one device and continue their progress on another. This, in turn, requires a method of linking devices together through a common ID that the game can access. Online-only games usually implement their own system and have the player create a username and password for the game, while other games use the platform account (Steam account, Apple sign in etc.) or a third-party social media account to link devices (i.e. Facebook sign in). The identity system is a separate game component to cloud save and should be given independent test focus, particularly if it's a bespoke system developed by the game team.

These systems introduce more complications during development and testing. The game needs to be able to handle switching between multiple accounts on the same device and between devices with the same account, being logged in with the same account on two devices simultaneously, and handling conflicts when the local save file doesn't match the file on the cloud.

Where games are both online and offline, players can begin playing locally and then choose to enable cloud save and upload their game at any point during play.

If they sign into an account which already has a different save file uploaded, the game may force the player to choose which data to continue with or provide UI to allow them to maintain multiple save games associated with their account.

Finally, the introduction of multiple devices introduces the possibility that players will have updated the game to a higher version on some, but not all of their devices. Transferring save files from higher versions of the game to older versions requires a compatibility check by the game, which also needs to be considered during testing.

Test plans need to consider all these core scenarios as well as a much longer list of potential edge cases that exist within each of these flows. This area requires a strictly methodical approach, using scripted tests to make sure no scenarios are missed during planning. Test cases here also require very clear language and consistent style so that complex scenarios can be easily understood by the tester during execution.

Complexity/difficulty: Medium-Hard. The test scenarios are often complex and require multiple devices with test accounts setup and network tools running. Some teams will also need tools to view the identity data on the service itself to see the save files associated with each account. Much like player profiles, both the testing and test planning for this area require a good understanding of the hardware interaction 'under the hood'.

This test area is most frequently owned by the more senior QA analysts on the team and requires strong test analysis and test design skills.

Discipline focus: Code.

Bugs: Bugs in any of these scenarios could cause players to lose their game data entirely, and I've seen many customer service tickets from annoyed players to whom this has happened. Because of this, fewer bugs are found compared with other test areas, but they are generally high impact and either cause cloud save not to function properly or cause progress loss for the player. Much like the test cases, testers need to log bug repro steps diligently when multiple devices and profiles are used, making it very clear which step relates to which profile or device.

6.18 Hardware and peripherals compatibility

This test area includes testing compatibility between the game and the device it runs on. It also includes the compatibility of any supporting hardware, like screens and input devices. Consider the huge number of mobile devices, PC hardware configurations and even different generations of consoles and variations of those generations.

Then add screens and input devices into this mix: 4k screens, ultra-wide aspect ratios, VR headsets, cameras (Xbox Kinect / PlayStation Eye), steering wheels, controllers, keyboards and a myriad of other bespoke input devices.

Many games release across multiple platforms, making it necessary to consider each platform for all testing conducted across the entire project. While a lot of confidence can be gained simply by assuring all testing is spread across each platform, there is a lot of value in assigning hardware compatibility as a dedicated area of ownership. Testing is rarely as simple as testing one or two hardware configurations in isolation (a PlayStation release and an Xbox release), but instead requires consideration of many combinations of different hardware setups together (device variations, screens and peripherals). Because this compatibility is game-wide, it can demand a substantial (and wasteful) test effort if test direction has not been chosen wisely.

Effective and efficient coverage of supported hardware requires the use of input reduction test techniques to cut the number of unique configurations down to a smaller, manageable set. It's impossible to test every configuration of hardware, and equally impossible to test every feature against every hardware configuration. Teams often get this wrong by taking a simplified approach, such as running every test against every supported platform (iOS and Android for example, or PlayStation, Xbox and PC). This approach is likely to mean the test estimate balloons far beyond the available time due to all tests being run twice or more.

QA analysts owning this test area should instead consider which domain areas are most likely to generate platform-specific bugs and require test duplication. This data can then be used to develop a more targeted hardware compatibility test plan. Historical bugs are a good source of guidance when they're available. Information can also be gathered by discussing the platform test coverage strategy with the code team to identify the highest risk areas.

Side note: a top-level plan for device coverage might have already been decided by the QA manager early in the project, because it often requires the test team to order new test devices to use throughout testing. As a result, any finer detail planning will have to work within these limitations. There are a finite number of devices and peripherals available, and they may not be easily portable between testers.

Many gameplay-orientated domain areas in this chapter are hardly influenced by which platform they're running on, making platform-specific bugs very unlikely. These commonly include areas like game modes, tutorials, telemetry, audio, environment, game progress and retention, content, live events and online services. Consider a test-heavy area like the environment. Duplicating the entire test plan across each supported platform would exacerbate an already burdensome test effort. For these areas, any testing can be divided across supported platforms, not duplicated. This guarantees that each supported platform or device is included in the testing, but each test is still only run once. As a basic example, half of an environment test team is testing on PlayStation devices and half on Xbox. They split the testing, each taking half of the test plan. They don't *both* run the entire plan.

Conversely, some domain areas are at high risk of generating platform-specific bugs because they interact directly with the system or are influenced by it. These areas commonly include performance, platform integration, third-party SDK integration, platform certification, regulations, UI, navigation, multiplayer and file IO. Some areas have different functionality for each platform and so require separate tests per platform and, by definition, need to be duplicated out. Other areas have the same player-facing functionality for each platform but require a separate code implementation.

In these cases, the same test can be used but must be duplicated, because each platform is handled differently by the code and is therefore much more likely to yield platform-specific bugs. Lastly, some of these areas don't have a separate implementation but are still highly influenced by the device or platform. Performance is an obvious example of this and will generate different test results for each supported device.

These lists of test areas may change from project to project, but the goal remains the same. Use past bug data and team expertise to identify which test areas are likely to yield platform-specific bugs and then focus on those areas.

On the topic of test input reduction. This involves taking an entire set of available devices and reducing them down to equivalent groups, and only testing one device from each group. A basic example of this would be taken when approaching performance testing on mobile. It would be impossible to run testing on every mobile device available on the market. Instead, we can group them into roughly equivalent performance groups (low-end, mid-range, high-end) and test one device from each group. Similarly, PC testing would not test against every available graphics card and processor but would instead bracket them into the major manufacturers and architectures.

For different screen types, testing on console and PC requires, at least, coverage across both 1080p and 4k resolutions. This frequently also includes other screen attributes which are known to affect the game visuals, such as refresh rate, aspect ratio, safe areas and proprietary screen technologies like FreeSync and G-Sync. Display hardware and configurations are likely to cause hardware-specific visual bugs, particularly within the UI and text, making this domain an important crossover with other areas of testing that have a visual focus.

Lastly, input peripherals should have their own set of tests written to structure their testing. It can still be valuable to have test team members who always conduct their testing with a particular input device, but different input devices are likely to introduce bugs within the UI and navigation.

Complexity/difficulty: Easy-Medium. This area doesn't require heavy test writing and instead requires more organisational work with test owners of other domain areas. The tests for different screens and input devices are easily understandable and player-facing.

The more challenging side of this domain comes when applying test input reduction to hardware groups. The QA analyst must be confident with the different attributes of devices, knowing when they are equivalent for each test. In some cases, devices will require grouping by the amount of memory they have. In other cases it might be the texture compression or the chipset architecture they use. Such decisions require a good working knowledge of the device hardware.

Discipline focus: Code.

Bugs: Testers should make good use of process-of-elimination to identify if bugs are specific to a device or multiple devices with a specific attribute.

6.19 Tutorials

A small test area, often called the OOBE (out of box experience) or FTUE (first time user experience) which covers the highly scripted tutorial flows that players usually see during the first few hours of play.

Tutorials often have unique functionality not seen elsewhere in the game, and demand special attention during testing: functionality which disables advanced features and unlocks them at specific trigger points. This might involve visual changes like disabling UI, hiding UI, displaying arrows/pointers or displaying highlight effects that draw the player's attention to an area of the screen. These flows might also include some form of tutorial tooltips or 'talking heads' to explain the game features to the player, again triggered at certain points during play.

Unlike the rest of the game, tutorial flows follow a granular click-by-click flow, hand-holding the player to each next feature or action. The uniqueness and high granularity of tutorial flows creates a fragility, causing easy breakages as other parts of the game are implemented. Hidden dependencies in the code to other parts of the game can cause seemingly innocuous changes, like renaming or reorganising UI components to break the tutorial flow fantastically.

As the complexity of the game code increases throughout development, these hidden dependencies are easily forgotten. Coupled with the tendency to debug-skip past the first few hours of gameplay during other testing, these breakages can go unnoticed.

The OOBE is so named because this area can include anything that is unique to the first launch or install of the game, and refers to the 'journey' of unboxing and setting up the game. Some games provide a 'streaming install' where the player can play a small part of the game while the full game is still installing or downloading. Any features like this, which only occur on first launch, can be included within this test area, increasing the complexity of the feature and its testing considerations.

Complexity/difficulty: Easy. A very player-facing area which has limited size, ideal for more junior members of the team to own. This area lends itself to scripted tests, mimicking the scripted nature of the feature. They are also simple to write, following easily understood flows. While there is potential for failure scenarios where players are able to break out of the tutorial flows accidently, these failure tests are more easily identified than some other domain areas.

Due to the high fragility of the area, regression testing needs to be scheduled to return to the area after the initial verification has completed. Some teams may even be able to predict which new features and changes are most likely to break the tutorial flows, and schedule regression tests alongside verification tests for those changes. Furthermore, some smaller projects choose to include the tutorial flow within their build verification tests, covering it against every new build.

Discipline focus: Code, design.

Bugs: Bugs are often obvious functional and visual breakages in the tutorial flow that can be easily found by playing it through. There is a higher-than-normal chance that bugs will completely block the player flow, preventing access to other parts of the game during testing. This is another reason to include these flows within the build verification tests.

6.20 Telemetry and analytics

This domain area covers all features which remotely record data from the game. This primarily includes recording game actions and state from each player, allowing business intelligence analysts on the project team to analyse it and understand how players are interacting with the game.

Much like other software, every menu seen or button pressed will trigger an associated event, sending some data for that action to a remote database which collates data from the entire player base. These events contain a payload of data captured from the player profile, the current game state and/or anything else that the team wants to capture for each action. They allow the project team to build a picture of what players are experiencing, generating statistics such as which menus players are visiting most, how many players have progressed to each stage of the game, what error messages players are seeing, what in-game packs players are purchasing and the average amount of resources each player has. These are just a few examples from an almost infinite list that the project team may want to monitor.

This data is particularly crucial to enable free-to-play games to operate profitably, increasing the importance that the data is accurate. It allows the team to track player retention over time, monitoring how long players stay in the game after initial install. Games often track this as a percentage of the number of players who have stayed in the game at day 1, 7, 30, 60 and 90. In addition to retaining players, other KPIs track how and when players pay for in-game content.

Common KPIs include daily active users, average revenue per daily active user, non-payer to payer conversion rates, cumulative average revenue per user during the first seven days, cost-per-install for advertising and average return on advertising spend. These are just a few examples; many more primary KPIs exist. In addition, soft currency data is captured to monitor the game economy, generating secondary KPIs that influence primary revenue and retention stats.

The aim of testing for these telemetry events is to verify the accuracy of the data and that events trigger at the correct points during play. While there is potential for failure scenarios like duplicate or missing events, the majority of testing is data verification. Many telemetry events are written into the code in one location but apply to many areas throughout gameplay, creating an uncertainty that the data will be successfully captured at each trigger location.

For example, game economy events are triggered whenever a player acquires or spends soft currency*, changing their resource balance. While code for this event is likely only written in one location, there can be a huge number of game locations where the player is able to spend or acquire soft currency and trigger this code. As well as recording the change in currency, the code will also retrieve the game location and action that triggered it. These economy telemetry events allow the BI** team to see all inflow and outflow sources of each currency, allowing them to balance it as they desire. Testing can find bugs where the player's resource changes for a particular game location, but doesn't trigger an event, or where the data is incorrectly populated

---

*   Soft currencies are secondary resources (gold, wood, food, etc.) that a player acquires freely through play and cannot generally be used to purchase new game content. In comparison, hard currencies are primary resources (game dollars, diamonds, gems, etc.). They are very rarely given away freely and must instead be purchased with real money. Hard currencies are used to purchase new game content within the game.

**   Business Intelligence. Team members that are responsible for gathering and analysing game telemetry

for a game location. Other bugs could incorrectly classify a game location, or even incorrectly record the resource delta value. Like in this example, telemetry events often trigger in many entry points throughout the game, each providing a different test result.

In addition to these game analytics, which are implemented entirely by the project team, this test area can include advertising and attribution analytics events that are implemented by integrating with third-party attribution tools. Free-to-play games, which advertise on an app store and allow players to click an advert to install the game, will want to attribute installs of valuable players to specific advertising channels. The value of players installing from each advertising channel can be recorded through triggering game progress or purchase events for each player for a set time period after install. These events tell the team if these players are installing and playing the game or just installing it and then quickly losing interest. From a testing perspective, these events are similar to those above but will be sent to a third-party service such as Adjust. Event verification can be carried out by visiting the game's dashboard for that supplier and searching for the player.

This area can also include tracking of game crashes and exceptions. Most games use third-party tools to collect and monitor these from players in real time. When a player launches the game for the first time after experiencing a crash or exception, an event containing the data is sent to the service provider. Examples of stability analytics tools include Firebase Crashlytics, BugSnag, Backtrace and BugSplat. Testing integration with these services involves triggering exceptions and crashes, then verifying that the event has appeared on the service dashboard with all of the correct information populated. This isn't a heavy area for testing and often functions well out of the box, but there can still be the occasional requirement for it.

Complexity/difficulty: Medium. A non-player-facing test area that requires some understanding of the reason for capturing the data. A close working relationship with the project team members analysing the data will allow testing to be more effective, identifying bugs within the data more easily. Testing can be carried out via a network tool to monitor the events as they are sent from the device, or it can be checked through access to the destination service's dashboard (if it exists).

BI analysts will build SQL queries to gather data from the database. Some more technically-minded testers with access to the database are also able to test this way, without the need to go through a web dashboard. As a result, this is a great area of ownership for any QA analysts who have experience with SQL or who have an interest in free-to-play game economies.

Discipline focus: Product managers, business intelligence, code.

Bugs: Bugs should include the event name affected as well as a log or snippet of the data payload of the event. While some bugs may be obvious during testing (missing data, incorrect data, events not triggering), many more subtle bugs can be missed here if the test team don't have an intimate knowledge of the events and the data within them.

BI team members may still identify bugs even after testing is complete because they are the end users of this data, using it throughout their daily work. (This is essentially user acceptance testing.) These more subtle bugs could be finding multiple events that use different formats to record the same data, making it difficult to collate the data together. It could also be that the data recorded is too abstract and requires more granularity for it to be useful. The requirements for the data can also change over time, generating change requests to add new information to each event. To mitigate these problems early, the test team can engage with the BI team earlier and ask them to review the events generated during testing in the development environment instead of checking the production data once the change is already live.

6.21 Anti-cheat and security

Cheating is a huge problem for multiplayer games because it erodes confidence in the game when legitimate players see it happening. They are less likely to engage fully or spend money in-game if they see that they're competing against players who are clearly cheating. For single-player experiences, cheating still impacts revenue but has a much lower and more isolated impact.

While cheating and security can be a high-risk area for many games, the harsh truth is that manual functional testing isn't an effective mitigation against these risks. It's very difficult for generalist testers to identify opportunities to cheat beyond basic gameplay exploits. Because of this, these risks are instead mitigated through proactive measures by the engineering teams, often spearheaded by the server code team. These anti-cheat server-side features have similar test characteristics to the online services domain I described earlier, in that they're also difficult to test manually and require a technical understanding of the interaction between the game client and the server.

So, how do players cheat and how can we stop them from doing it? Cheating is nearly always done through the game client because it's the part of the game code the player has access to. If you have visions of players hacking their way into a game server to change their score, then this is going to be a let-down. Nefarious players with the right skills can reverse-engineer the game client and modify it, adding cheats and making modifications to the game. They can then sell the hacked version to other players, or make high level game accounts which can then be sold.

Cheat tools also exist which can be installed and used more easily by any player, not requiring the same time and skillset. GameGuardian is a good example of this. It's a tool for iOS and Android devices that allows players to modify in-game values like experience points and resources. The tool isn't available on the app store and so requires the player to either jailbreak (iOS) or root (Android) their phone so the app can be side-loaded onto the device. The player runs the tool alongside a game and performs an action on the resource that they want to modify. The tool monitors when data is written into the device memory and can identify the section within the memory where the resource is stored. Once the association is saved within the tool, the player can then use it to modify the resource to any value outside of the game. Importantly, this modification is still only local to the player's device.

Unlike these modifications to the client game, the game server code and databases are nearly always hosted by large third-party suppliers such as Amazon Web Services (AWS), Google Cloud Platform (GCP) and Microsoft Azure. These third parties handle all the server-side security, transferring risk away from the game team and making it difficult for anyone to gain unlawful access to the game code and data stored there.

Because of this, we can generally assume that the game server and data is trustworthy because it's secure, and that game clients and their data are untrustworthy because they are insecure.

Online games wanting to prevent cheating by modification of the player profile can implement features server-side to validate the data coming from clients. If a player changes their profile locally and then launches the game while online, the server and client will have different versions of the player profile and the server will need to either trust or reject the version of the profile presented by the game client. An architecture where the server validates and potentially rejects changes originating from clients is referred to as being 'server authoritative'. These features prevent cheating from spreading from individual clients to the wider online and multiplayer game which is seen by the rest of the player base.

From a testing point of view, these features are difficult to test and require either debug or tooling to modify the client profile to exercise the server validation. However, testing can also verify that false positives don't occur during server validation, i.e. that legitimate changes aren't wrongly rejected by the server. Because of the large range of game features which change the player profile, regression testing for this area requires an equally large scope. Bugs can be severe too, because a rejection by the server means the profile will be rolled back to a previous state.

Another way games can prevent cheating is to generate statistical models of how quickly legitimate players make progress, gaining more resources and levelling up their profile. These models can then be implemented into server-side code to automatically flag players who are progressing more quickly than the game allows. This means that even if cheating data is accepted by the server, it can still be filtered out and removed. The list of players can either be automatically banned from the game or passed to a separate team to inspect each profile more closely before deciding what action to take. The test team may be able to help verify the functionality of the tool and validate the assumptions made within the statistical model. False positives can occur here too: in-game exploits or overpowered items can cause players to be wrongly flagged for cheating. While testing can help a little with the deployment of such a tool, the initiation of this work and the majority of the effort towards it is outside the ownership of the test team.

Lastly, this domain area includes testing the reporting and blocking flows. Functionality is provided for players to report others when they see them cheating, which then appears within a customer service tool. The CS team can use tools to inspect the player profile and take action, often applying a temporary or permanent ban. Testers will need access to the CS tool to verify this flow works. Testing here can also explore ways that players might be able to circumvent a ban.

Complexity/difficulty: Medium-Hard. This area is heavily orientated around server code and non-player-facing code features. Most of the testing also uses either custom debug or tooling which requires setup and training for the testers executing the testing. Anti-cheat features and logic are also complex technical topics and can be difficult to understand for testers if they aren't explained well.

QA analysts owning this test area should be aware of the limitations of manual functional testing and suggest more effective risk mitigations, if they're available. We can say that testing reduces the likelihood of cheating risks by identifying bugs early and taking action against them. If these preventative measures aren't possible, the team can instead employ contingency measures to reduce the impact of cheating when it does occur. These concede that the risk will happen and focus on reducing the impact when it does occur. For cheating, this can include introducing features to separate cheaters from legitimate players, placing them in their own multiplayer games together or giving cheaters their own leaderboards. On a previous project we had a feature which delayed giving out leaderboard rewards at the end of each competition. The delay was several hours and allowed the project team to manually remove cheaters from the leaderboards and shuffle legitimate players up the board before triggering the rewards.

Discipline focus: Server code, client code

Bugs: Bugs in this area are not clear cut and are often improved rather than fixed completely. Many bugs here are also difficult to triage whether players will actually use the bug to cheat or not, making priority assignment difficult.

6.22 Settings and configurations

This test effort required for this domain area is often binary, either requiring no effort at all and being folded into the menus ownership, or requiring a large test effort and being separated into several subareas. This depends on the number of game configurations available and how much they influence other game features.

Depending on the type of game, this area can include a myriad of miscellaneous settings: graphical and display settings, language and region, notification settings, colour blind modes, sound settings, purchase limits, themes, gameplay preferences, subtitle toggles, amongst many others. This area also includes sundry features that reside within the settings menu: terms of service and privacy policy links, custom service and FAQ links and website or forum links.

On the topic of large subdomains in this area, the most immediate example is the array of graphical settings that many games provide, changing the gameplay experience throughout the game. PC games provide the biggest range of settings here, allowing players to balance visual fidelity with performance on their device. Graphical configurations and display settings can be given their own domain area or are sometimes included within the performance test area due to their close association. Either way, this testing has far-reaching considerations and affects almost every other feature. Graphical configurations have a particularly direct influence on the non-functional test areas of stability and performance, introducing crashes and other stability problems that are unique to certain configurations or even combinations of configurations.

Localisation and region settings are common here – another configuration that requires game-wide test consideration. Functional localisation testing doesn't consider the actual translations during testing, but instead checks for hardcoded strings that don't have translations at all, functional bugs switching between languages, functional bugs importing the chosen language of the device and UI problems with translations, like text bleeding out of the UI container. It's also possible for language settings to cause other functional problems detected during this testing. Regional settings and/or player billing region can change what currency purchases appear in, requiring testing to check in-game purchases using different billing regions.

Complexity/difficulty: Easy-medium. This miscellaneous domain area shouldn't be forgotten when test ownerships are assigned. It requires a careful division of work due to the heavy overlap with other game areas. Once the work is clearly defined, however, test analysis and design are fairly simple to work on.

Discipline focus: Mixed, depending on the test configurations.

Bugs: There isn't anything particularly noteworthy about the bugs in this area; they're often player-facing and easily understood. The structure and detail of bugs will vary depending on the sub-area but won't require any special considerations when they are logged.

6.23 Performance

This non-functional domain area covers the entire game, not testing *what* each feature does but *how well* it does it. A feature could technically work, fulfilling all its acceptance criteria, but still be slow and unresponsive. Because of this attribute, this test area overlaps all other areas in this list, making it potentially very large in scope and difficult to define. Does each feature owner test the performance of their individual features or does a single performance testing owner cover everything as one? The answer depends on the circumstance, but it should be a conscious choice.

Without clear performance targets, performance bugs can also be very subjective, making assignment of severity and priority difficult. Contrary to marketing boasting that games run consistently at 30 or 60 frames-per-second, the reality is that many scrape through this target and even have areas which dip below it. Often the target is only for the highest-end supported device and doesn't apply to other devices. Because of this variability, defining what is acceptable and what should be bugged as not acceptable can become difficult depending on each circumstance, requiring a subjective assessment from the tester.

Project leadership and test teams can agree on quality bars to combat this subjectivity. For example, agreeing that all instances of FPS (frames per second) below 20 are bugged regardless of circumstance, or that the game should never take longer than 3 minutes to load. Even with these measures in place, there might be worst-case scenarios which cause the FPS to plummet far below this value, but aren't fixed due to their extremely low likelihood. Minimum supported devices for the game will also stress these quality bars, often falling well below them in areas and requiring the project team to reassess their accepted quality. For some teams, this might be building the game to run on the previous generation of consoles; for others it might be trying to support as many mobile devices as possible, including the very low end. Lastly, performance values higher than the quality bar can sometimes still present noticeably poor visuals in certain circumstances, requiring testers again to make a subjective assessment to log the bug even though the data shows it technically meets the agreed quality bar.

Performance testing in games includes three key metrics which are commonly measured: framerate, loading times and memory usage. Framerate is the measurement people think of first when they say the word 'performance', and is most relevant to games that use 3D models and therefore require a lot of graphical processing power. Measured in frames-per-second, framerate represents how quickly the on-screen image updates and indicates how smoothly the player perceives movement and animation. To update the image that the player sees many times each second, the game needs to do a huge amount of graphical processing. The more objects that are in the player's view, the more processing is required. In addition to this, other effects and post-processing occur on every frame, polishing the final image displayed on screen. Understanding some of the technical details of what affects FPS helps us identify interesting areas to test within this domain. It also helps us know when we can begin testing. There's no value in recording performance data if visual layers are disabled or still in development.

Loading times are a consideration, both when launching the game and when transitioning between game areas. Long loading times which are not accepted by users of other software are seen in games because they are so content-heavy, requiring large file sizes. Loading times can be measured in seconds using a stopwatch but, for a more accurate measurement, loading milestones can be written into the code and recorded in milliseconds. Adding this automated recording in the code has the added benefit of providing more granular data to see which steps in the load process are the most time-intensive – a handy insight for diagnosing and improving this metric.

When testing loading times, considerations should be made to test the game on the first launch* and subsequent launches, since the behaviour can change. Games may perform unique processes on first launch, like downloading assets, checking for previous save data in storage or performing a one-time migration or other process. Testing should also identify the difference between 'warm' booting and 'cold' booting the game, where warm boots refer to when the game is already running in the background (i.e. suspended or paused).

Some games also check for updates or download content when they launch, increasing the loading time when remote content is available for download. This is something else testers need to consider when recording loading times, and will dramatically increase recorded time as the game downloads the files. I'd recommend using tools to monitor the network utilisation to identify when content is being downloaded, and discard these results.

These are just some of the variables that can affect the loading times and skew the results of any test if they are not accounted for during test setup. In fact, setting up a clean test to record loading times is often the most difficult part of this test.

Some games also provide more advanced logic, which performs loading and unloading operations in the background during play. These systems try to predict what

---

*   Some teams also refer to the first launch as 'hard' booting.

assets the player will need next and load them ahead of time in preparation. This can be seen in open world games as the player moves from area to area. Some games also provide the same logic when the player moves from scene to scene, providing a load-free transition. These advanced loading features require a more thorough approach and should be tested separately from game-wide performance.

Memory usage is included in this shortlist due to the large file sizes that must be loaded and unloaded into memory as the player transitions around the game. This metric has the interesting attribute that it doesn't impact play until the device runs out of free memory, at which point the game terminates and the player is badly affected. Player impact is very binary in this respect, and any testing should be aimed at preventing out-of-memory crashes and not simply detecting them when they occur. Put another way, it's helpful for testing to measure and report how close to the memory limit the game is running. This limitation on temporary memory is the reason the game can't load all of the assets when it launches. Instead, it needs to continuously load and unload different assets into memory during play, all the time keeping below the limit.

Some project teams will have planned this into the game design ahead of time, making it less of a consideration during testing. Franchise project teams releasing on console will be more experienced in building the franchise game successfully to the limitations of the target consoles, because they've done it before using the same code base. New games, or games releasing on multiple platforms, are more likely to accidently push their development to the limits of the hardware causing out-of-memory crashes. When a project begins to use too much memory in areas, the team will need to take optimisation measures to reduce the memory again to eliminate the bugs; not always an easy feat. I'll speak more about the style of performance bugs shortly.

Other facets of performance are included in some projects but are less common for manual functional teams. Network and server performance are good examples of such areas. Since these are more specialist, they are beyond the scope of this introduction.

On the topic of project relevance for this domain area: contrary to what some believe, performance is a significant and critical area of consideration for all game projects regardless of their target platform – PC, consoles or mobile. This is due to the inherent nature of games to push the boundaries of whatever platform they're running on. 3D games are likely to have complex 3D geometry, impacting framerate most on any platform, while 2D games are more likely to have high resolution 2D assets, impacting memory usage most. Even seemingly simple mobile games are pushing the limits of mobile hardware; they just do so in a different way to their console and PC counterparts.

The question is not whether performance is an important consideration for your project, but what area of performance should be considered most important.

Complexity/difficulty: Medium. The main components of performance testing are well understood by most QA analysts. Even basic performance checks will probably find bugs in any game project. The metrics and tools for this domain are also widely used and understood by many testers and QA analysts, requiring little or no training.

The hidden difficulty isn't apparent until you get into the details on a real project. The challenge is setting up a fair and controlled environment in which to record the performance data. As a first step, all performance testing should be conducted on a non-debug build because the addition of debug code worsens performance stats. Beyond this stumbling block are the numerous game settings and configurations available. Which devices should performance data be recorded for? Which graphics settings should be used? Which display hardware should we test with? Which characters should be selected for the testing? Which versions of the operating system should we test on? Are other apps or games running on the device? The list of variables is huge and often difficult to fully identify.

The influencing factors don't stop with the variables that you have direct control over, either. When executing performance testing on mobile we found that hot devices begin to throttle their own processor, influencing the framerate sporadically. Older devices with poor batteries do the same thing. Cleanly recording performance data becomes a ritual of charging the device before the test and waiting for it to cool if it's been active for a long time running other tests. Other background processes within any operating system can also make a mess of your performance data, like automated updates that begin downloading data in the background, anti-virus scans and other scheduled processes.

I've seen many testers unknowingly record bad performance data, concluding that a performance metric has drastically worsened since the game's last update, only to later identify that the data was skewed by some other variable and the game is fine. I've also seen testers 'chasing ghosts', trying to reproduce an instance of particularly poor performance, then later conclude that it was a result of a background process running for a short time, and nothing to do with the game code.

To conduct performance testing effectively, tests and testing should adopt the science experiment style I defined in the previous chapter. Just like a science experiment, this testing should define all input variables and keep them all the same across all tests, so that all of the data adheres to the same baseline. For many games releasing updates or adding new content, the goal of this testing is to compare the new update with the existing game and deduce whether the additions have degraded the game performance. Having a consistent baseline allows fair comparisons to be made. Much like a science experiment, testing changes only one variable at a time. In this case, it's the build version.

Discipline focus: Code.

Bugs: Understanding performance bugs presents another challenge during testing because these bugs break the normal process and cause testers to action them differently. Here's the headline:

Performance bugs aren't ever fixed, they're just improved.

Unlike most other bugs which are binary, broken or fixed, performance bugs require the project team to optimise areas of the game, a task which is often complex, difficult and time consuming. Some optimisations may improve performance a little, some a lot. Many optimisations also trade off one metric for another, like decreasing framerate to decrease loading times. This improvement forces good communication between the fixer and the tester within the bug comments to describe the actions taken on the bug and what the tester should expect to see from the 'fix'. I've seen enough performance bugs marked as 'fix fail' by testers to know that this often isn't the case.

6.24 Tooling and debug

While the vast majority of testing is against features which are destined for the player, the path to creating this product often begins with building tools, debug and automating processes to aid the project team. Just like the end-product, bugs can exist in these tools, which in the best scenario causes the tool to fail, and in the worst scenario causes covert bugs to be passed on to the game through use of the tool.

A variety of bespoke content creation tools are built early in development to make the creation of game content more efficient and hide the technical code details from artists. Test teams embedded within game studios may be asked to help test these tools if they're particularly large or complex. Since these require access to the game code and content repositories, this testing doesn't extend beyond the local team. It's also common for this testing to follow a more casual process, not requiring strict bugging guidelines and often discussing problems face-to-face during team meetings.

Tools are also used later in development, too, and get continuous use throughout the lifetime of the product. Customer service tools are a good example of a tool that the game team will create themselves and needs to be included within test scenarios. These tools allow a CS team to both inspect player profiles and edit them based on requests from players. Common actions might be to award currency and items for players that have experienced a bad bug, like making an in-game purchase and not receiving the items they purchased or finding out that their profile has lost progress and rolled back to a previous state.

Other examples include tools to automate the creation of in-game sales, competitions and events. Instead of these being created in data by a design team each time, tools can help ease the burden of running frequent events by automatically generating data templates, eliminating human error. One project I worked on had a toolchain which generated JSON data from an event spreadsheet, committed the data into source control, built a 'patch' for the event and then deployed the patch to the development server. To make an event available for testing on the development server, the designer needed only to create the event within the spreadsheet and then run the tool. In these cases, testing can help build confidence in the tools by checking the resulting live event or sale that the tool has created. This may be as simple as running an existing test suite for the event. A more comprehensive test approach would be to use the tool during testing to create many different events, testing different creation variations.

Testing against internal tools requires a different mindset for the tester. The tools don't need to be highly polished; they just need to work reliably and be understood by the team members using them. As a result of this, the test team should agree with the project team what type of bugs and feedback are helpful and what information they need within each bug. This means major functional bugs only. Bugging components like untidy UI is likely to be superfluous, annoy others and bloat the database. Likewise, performing destructive testing to probe the limitations of the tool may not be necessary, since the users of the tool will be informed of its limitations and may even be given training on the correct use of it.

Lastly, while I've used the word 'tools' here, these can take the form of both a standalone application or embedded within the game, surfaced through debug.

Complexity/difficulty: Medium. This domain area is much more like regular software testing than any other areas in this list and so can be difficult for QA analysts who are accustomed to testing gameplay features. For testing to be effective, this test area also requires a technical understanding of what the tool is doing and what problem it is solving.

With the process of creation being much more casual than player-facing work, it's much less likely that good documentation will be written for internal tools. This makes test planning difficult and relies on the QA analyst involving themselves within the right conversations and meetings, as well as asking the correct questions to build their understanding.

This domain area is also a great example of one where the QA analyst should think 'does this require testing?' and 'what risks does this carry?' instead of 'everything needs to be tested'. Many internal features and tools don't require such a comprehensive approach, with bugs being surfaced and fixed naturally through their use.

Discipline focus: Code.

Bugs: Bugs should be light in detail and include bespoke details relevant to the tool. The scope of bugs should also be limited to core functional use and exclude failure scenarios and edge cases, which are unlikely to be triggered by the internal project team.

7

Test management

7.1 An introduction to test management

In this final chapter I'll introduce some holistic processes and strategies to manage testing throughout a project. These management processes are usually defined and driven by QA lead or manager roles, a full exploration of which is beyond the scope of this book. Instead, I'll touch on some parts that QA analysts need to know and provide a brief introduction to some of these larger topics. While QA analysts don't define these processes, they do provide input into many of them.

This chapter also highlights some key differences in seniority, knowledge and experience between the QA tester role and QA analyst role. While the work of testers is primarily directed by their test leads, the work of QA analysts is predominantly self-directed, fuelled by the knowledge given in this chapter. The analyst role requires a much broader understanding of the project and its test strategy, which translates into the test management activities discussed here. Incidentally, this step-up makes it more difficult for QA testers to move up into the QA analyst role because they're often shielded from wider project activity, making this chapter particularly helpful for any readers who are not privy to this in their current work.

Estimates for the required size of a QA tester team throughout a project are calculated from the combined test plan estimations from each QA analyst. The testing duration for a release or project phase is also, at least partially, defined by the combined feature testing schedules of each QA analyst. Since teams of QA analysts are far smaller than their QA tester counterparts, the accuracy of the contribution from each QA analyst is magnified, increasing the importance placed on conducting test estimation effectively.

In addition to providing some guidance on how to estimate testing, I'll also describe the difficulties faced with synchronising the availability of testers, the readiness of tests and the readiness of the feature to be tested. Failing to align these schedules can result in a huge amount of wasted time and budget.

I'll give some guidance on producing meaningful reports and describe how the data from QA analysts frequently feeds into the reporting and tracking for the entire project. Unlike QA testers and their leads who produce reports for others within the test discipline, QA analysts produce reports for other disciplines within the wider project team who want only summaries and who are often more critical of the usefulness of each reported metric. This reporting is less like the many-templated daily and weekly reports that are produced by QA tester teams, and more on-demand, bespoke and orientated around testing as part of the wider business. Unfortunately, it's often the case that QA analysts don't report their test data at all and the result of testing is seen as 'no news is good news', with bugs being the only output.

Lastly, I'll outline the most common structures of the test discipline within a project, defining each team and their responsibilities. This will cover remote outsource test teams, publisher test teams and embedded test teams (sometimes called 'dev qa').

This chapter will explain why these separate teams exist and the differences in their testing. Many testers, particularly in publisher and remote outsource teams, aren't exposed to the wider team structure and aren't aware of the different testing roles available. This section will provide some clarity to help make day-to-day work more effective, but also provide a map to aid career progression.

7.2   Test estimation

Whether a project is using an outsourced testing company or its own team of testers, it will still need an estimate of how many testers are needed on a week-by-week basis throughout the lifetime of the project.

In both cases, the company will spend huge amounts of project budget hiring testers or paying outsourced vendors: a sum in the order of tens of thousands or even hundreds of thousands of pounds per month.

When QA analysts estimate how long their testing will take and how many testers they need, they are indirectly spending a portion of the company budget on those testers.

Test estimations should be viewed in this light. Booking a team of testers to be available, and then failing to have the tests written on time, wastes that expenditure while they are unable to work. Likewise, estimating when testing will begin, and then not having the feature available for testing, gives the same result: wasted budget.

Underestimating creates the opposite problem: not enough testers to complete the work within the project deadlines, either impacting the schedule or causing overtime crunch. In some cases, with outsourced vendors, overtime testing during evenings and weekends will also be charged at a higher rate and can exceed the cost of a larger test team being booked in the first place, resulting in both budget problems *and* overtime. In some cases, the team of testers can be increased as and when required by moving testers from other projects or by onboarding new recruits. However, this isn't always possible, and lowers test quality in the short term as the new testers familiarise themselves with the project.

QA analysts aren't alone in this task. Test managers will use their experience to make the final decisions, reviewing the estimations and adding contingency to the total number of required testers. The test manager will also collect and organise the individual estimations into a schedule, negotiating what each QA analyst has requested against what is available in any given week.

Test estimation is actually a two-step process. The first is estimating how much test resource is required to execute all the testing, and the second is fitting those estimations into a test schedule so that the availability of testers aligns with the readiness of the features and test plans. I'll explore the second step later.

QA testers, senior testers and leads who organise teams of testers will all need to provide test estimations as part of their work. These estimations are used to answer questions like, "When will I/we be done testing?"

These estimates nearly always focus on the progress of a single test pass in isolation, providing short term feedback on test progress. Rarely does a tester need to consider the bigger picture of test progress beyond the immediate task they are working on. They don't usually take any action on these estimates either – they just report them. Because of this, there isn't much accountability when testers provide test estimations. Test progress is included within test task comments or within a daily report and is forgotten unless someone comments on it.

When we compare this with the QA analyst role, test estimates need to be a longer-term prediction and be given in work days*, because they feed directly into the decision about how many testers to recruit or request. By providing test estimates in work days (or even work weeks or work hours, depending on the chosen granularity) they consider how many testers will be working on each task in parallel, and how adjusting that number impacts the final completion date for that task.

---

*   A unit of one day's work for one person

For example, a test pass taking five work weeks could be completed in one week by a team of five testers. Because test execution is always conducted in teams, this approach is a strict requirement for holistic test estimation. Test estimates can't be given in the number of days alone.

Practically speaking, when I provide estimations for my test passes and tasks, I look at the number of testers available and the size of the task, using both to provide an estimate in work days. When I do this, I've already got a good idea how many testers I expect to be working on the task in parallel, because I know the team capacity and which testers are going to be working on other tasks.

There are many factors feeding into the time required to execute testing, many of which are unique to the circumstances of the project and the test domain area. Because of this, it's difficult to provide a globally applicable list of things to consider for your estimations. Instead, I'll give guidance on how to measure and refine test estimates for any project. I've used this process for all the projects I've worked on: it's lightweight and provides good estimates over time, irrespective of the experience of the QA analyst.

When calculating the numbers, test estimation requires a data-driven approach and can't easily be judged on experience alone. As an individual contributor, you know very well how quickly you work and how difficult you expect the task to be, making experience-based estimation easy. But when other people are involved and the work is more extensive, the number of unknowns increases and requires a more comprehensive approach.

The best way to measure test execution time on your project is to estimate each task and have the testers submit the time it took them to execute it. This can be recorded through two fields within the test subtasks, named 'estimated time' and 'actual time'. This provides continuous feedback to the QA analyst on the accuracy of their estimations, allowing them to provide more accurate estimates over time. It's not an issue if some tasks take longer than planned; the important thing is that a more accurate estimate can be provided next time that type of task is run.

Over the course of a project, QA analysts will build a knowledge base of test execution times and won't have to refer back to their data, making this a hybrid of experience-driven and data-driven approaches. As this process matures, the administrative work required reduces, and creating accurate estimates becomes easier. For it to be effective, the QA analyst must remember to review the 'actuals' data during test closure, something which is usually forgotten. The testers must also be briefed on how to enter their allocated time, logging the total work-hours of all testers contributing to the task.

As a side note, test case management tools have fields for estimates for individual test cases, the values for which are usually recorded in minutes or hours. These are more helpful in giving the tester a guide to how long the test should take but are far too granular for the purposes of refining holistic test estimates. You can provide estimates to the testers here for each test case, but I'd recommend not using it for any other purpose.

Holistic test estimation for the test execution schedule is best conducted in days within the higher-level subtasks and tasks of the plan, striking a balance between added administrative work and level of detail. This level of detail more easily allows all of the test tasks to be combined into larger estimates for entire test passes or releases.

Industry tales: Parallel testing fallacy

When we include the tester team size in our test execution estimations, the question arises, "Do I book a larger team of testers to execute the testing in a shorter time or do I book a smaller team and accept it will take longer to execute?"

Completing work in a shorter time is nearly always preferable but there are practical limitations when moving large groups of testers between tasks. Let's assume a scenario where the entire test execution team is large enough to assign a team of any size to a specific feature by moving testers from other areas. What is the limit on the number of testers that can be assigned to one task or test pass? Would it be possible to assign so many testers that a 30 work-day test is completed in a single day?

This is exactly the thought process of many producers and project managers when the project schedule inevitably goes off track. Because testing is one of the last phases of the development pipeline, it's common for it to have a reduced timeframe if earlier phases are delivered late. As the project team begins to look for solutions to execute testing in less time, the first option is always to increase the test team size or introduce overtime. There is a fallacy amongst non-test disciplines that all test execution can be parallelised infinitely and still remain effective. If we double or triple the test team size, the same amount of work can simply be completed in a shorter time. This seems an attractive proposition when you aren't the one organising the test resources for the project.

However, we know that even if the testers were available, only certain types of testing can be parallelised, and even then, there are limitations. Much like coordinating any type of work amongst a large group, work efficiency drops as more people are added and the number of coordination mistakes increases. After all, there's no value in speeding up testing if it results in missed bugs.

Some domain areas lend themselves more to parallelisation than others. Content testing is a good example of something that can be easily divided up because it's so vast and repeatable, like testing a thousand game items or hundreds of levels. Many testers can repeat the same templated tests on each content item in the list without fear of overlapping their efforts or miscommunicating who is testing what.

These are exceptions though. Many tests against logical code domain areas don't lend themselves to parallelisation at all and trying to pile more testers into a task would only add more work for the existing testers as they stop to explain the feature logic and test approach to the newcomers. This is particularly true for technically complex testing. The test setup and method can be difficult and time consuming, again requiring help from the testers currently running the test. Even less technical tests often require the tester to have a specific player profile state or have made game progress to a point within the game. This makes it costly to move testing between tasks, adding a 'time tax' each time a tester is requested to switch focus.

Many tests simply take a long time to execute. A game playthrough can't be shortened, nor can features which have real-world time restraints requiring the player to wait in real time, like a daily login bonus or an in-game GDPR data request. Many individual tests like these can't be divided up and parallelised, but instead require the time of a single tester over a longer period.

Finally, many test plans I write are designed for the same group of testers to proceed through the entire plan. They often begin with an early smoke test, followed by core flow scripted verification tests, then progress to edge case scripted tests, failure exploratory tests and other lower priority scenarios. The earlier tests familiarise the testers with the feature and show them the core flows covered within the scripted tests. When these testers follow up with exploratory failure and edge case test sessions, they're well-equipped to know what hasn't been covered by the scripted tests and often have generated good exploratory test ideas through earlier scripted testing. Time constraints have sometimes forced me to instead assign all subtasks to different groups of testers to execute in parallel. This results in less effective exploratory and failure testing because the test session notes show these testers have spent more of their test session checking the core functionality – essentially duplicating the work of the scripted tests – instead of investigating deeper failure scenarios.

If your producer or project manager has ever said to you, "Can't we just get more testers?" consider how effectively the testing can be parallelised before giving your answer. You should also recommend that the team takes proactive measures to avoid the situation in the future, and back that up with some context as to why this 'reactive' approach isn't effective and sometimes not feasible at all.

There are two footnotes to this introduction to test estimations. Both provide some context to applying estimations in real situations.

Firstly: many teams don't estimate their test tasks at all. They have a fixed test team size and simply ask them to perform exploratory testing when no tasks are scheduled. This is most common when the company employs their own test team and can't change the team size quickly. Because of this, test estimates don't appear to be required at all, and the QA analyst assigns their task to the team as soon as it is ready.

This approach is very lightweight and works when the project schedule is accommodating, and the work doesn't all arrive at the same time. However, it doesn't give the QA analyst any experience handling test resourcing on projects with a more complex schedule and requiring a more structured approach. This is particularly necessary on projects which have many QA analysts working on different development sub-teams and assigning tests to the same team of testers. If you're accustomed to this lightweight approach, don't make the mistake of applying it to all new projects and companies you work on: many will require a more formal approach.

Secondly: test estimates and test scheduling are far more important when many QA analysts are sharing the same test team. This scenario doesn't only require accurate estimates, but also needs the tasks to be drafted onto a schedule, so testers are not double-booked on any given day.

The goal is to avoid the situation where one QA analyst cannot execute their testing because all testers are tied up working on other tests. This kind of delay is recoverable if it lasts only a few days and occurs early in the lifecycle of the project. As any project enters the final phases before release, the focus of the entire project team shifts from development to testing, bug fixing and polishing. It is during this time that any delay in testing will have a direct impact on the project schedule, and the cause behind the delay will be scrutinised. Any weaknesses in test estimations and scheduling will undoubtedly be highlighted during this critical phase of the project.

To make these later phases worse, work is more likely to be ready for testing late or all at once. This creates spikes in the resource requirements for testing, meaning the affected test plan needs more testers over a shorter period. Such spikes can be accommodated by using up a contingency of 'extra' testers that was planned earlier. If multiple features arrive late and cause multiple spikes, this is when the real resourcing problems begin, since QA analysts can't all rope in additional testers at the same time. The spikes have a compounding effect and ultimately result in either delays or overtime crunch. Experienced QA analysts and managers may have seen this before and will not just plan estimates diligently, but also plan for the worst-case scenario and assign a contingency in case work arrives late.

7.3   Managing test execution

The work of the QA analyst doesn't stop when the tests are written and assigned to the test execution team. The team may need support throughout testing, clarification on the details of the tests and help with some of the more technical test setup procedures. Even the most expertly written test will benefit from a brief catch up when it is run, not least because of the many small complications and choices that arise during testing.

When I introduced the fundamental test process earlier, I grouped test execution, monitoring and control into a single stage. I chose this grouping because, in my experience, all these activities occur at the same time and are linked to one another. While the lion's share of this work is done by the QA tester (execution), QA analysts still have the monitoring and control work.

A side note regarding questions during test execution: if an early build of the feature is available, I strongly recommend that QA analysts run complex tests themselves while creating them. This helps the analyst identify complications and address them before the testers hit them. This can dramatically reduce the number of questions during execution and increase the accuracy of the test details. Conversely, writing tests based on early documentation and specs is more likely to result in small test case details that don't align with the final feature built into the game. All differences between the test cases (derived from the specs) and the game will need clarification so that either the specs or the test cases can be updated.

As well as clarifying questions, the test team will need guidance on which tests to execute first, and exactly when each test can begin and is expected to be complete. They may need to know any prerequisites before some tasks can be run. As I described in the previous section, there are many components that need to be ready before testing can begin (entry criteria). With the rapid pace of development, the state of the project changes daily, so QA analysts should get the test team up to speed with the latest progress when execution begins. Some book kick-off meetings for this handover, whereas others write the information in an email that can be distributed around the team.

The start of test execution is also the right time to consider running smoke tests and to ask the team to familiarise themselves with the feature. Both activities can warm up the team before the planned testing is due to begin. As I discussed in earlier chapters, smoke testing allows you to get an early read on feature health before committing to a larger test effort. Any obvious blocking bugs can be identified early. No one wants a carefully synchronised start date to be derailed by a blocking bug which causes the whole team to stop work while they wait for a fix. Familiarisation can include running exploratory testing against an earlier build, reviewing the feature documentation, or reading through the test plan. All of these activities will help iron out questions and problems *before* testing begins, saving valuable time later on.

Task allocation

There are two methods for day-to-day task allocation and prioritisation – the push method and the pull method. With the push method, the team of QA analysts assemble a list of the tests that are to be run each day or week, prioritise them, assign tester numbers for each task and send this list to the test team leads to execute. This method creates more work for the QA analysts but provides granular control over the exact task allocation. Where many smaller test plans are being executed by the same team and randomisation of tasks is very likely, this method is preferable to prevent tasks being missed or forgotten. It also helps control the distribution of testers across tasks from different QA analysts, making sure that each QA analyst is using the team resources they had originally estimated. Any resourcing conflicts can be negotiated amongst the QA analyst team first.

The direct assignment of an ordered list can also provide much needed clarity on the state of each test when they are volatile, being stopped and started due a myriad of causes. Without this method, I've often seen lower priority tests being postponed and then not resumed once other tasks are complete. While the test team lead should be able to organise this, input from the QA analyst team provides a welcome oversight.

The pull method is more common. This involves the QA analyst team marking their tests as 'ready' within the project database when they can be picked up by the test team. The team then pulls their tasks from this list in priority order on a weekly or daily basis, distributing them amongst the testers as they see fit. This method is more likely to be used with longer test passes or where dedicated feature test teams are set up (i.e., an environment test team, a multiplayer test team, etc.) These teams are less likely to move between many different tasks or be randomised during their day-to-day work, allowing them to focus on the list of open tests for their game area for longer periods.

Choosing the most effective method depends mainly on the type of project under test. Larger projects have bigger test teams and longer test passes, generally requiring fewer day-to-day updates and less micromanagement of the test schedule. On the other hand, smaller projects or those which operate as a live service are more likely to have smaller test teams which move between many smaller test plans and require more management.

Monitoring and communication

Regardless of the task assignment method used, the QA analyst team needs to communicate the latest feature and project updates to the test execution team leads for them to make the correct task assignment decisions. In the most mature teams, the test leads are responsible for organising all of these details, leaving the QA analysts free to focus on test planning. But for this to be successful, the leads need to be set up for success with the right information. Do they know the priority of each test task? Do they know when each test needs to be completed? Do they know the dates of the current release milestones? Do they know which features are to be included in the next release and which features are being deployed server-side? The answers to these and many other questions should be provided (proactively where possible) by the QA analysts. QA analysts have the choice to either set up test execution teams to have more agency in their work or manage it themselves.

Testing also raises questions about the intended designs for a feature – small details which are too granular to be included within any documentation. The tester has made an observation during testing and needs to know if it's intended: not all bugs are obvious, after all. Without clarification, testers are left to guess how the game should work and log bugs against their own assumptions.

While text execution should be managed by the leads on the test team, much of its success depends on this information exchange with the QA analysts since they are often the sole line of communication to the rest of the project. Some project types demand less continuous interaction during test execution while still being effective. Even so, a QA analyst can rarely assign tests and forget about those tests until they are complete. Heavily repetitive testing, like live events or game content, can sometimes be executed smoothly for long periods without questions, but these tests are the exception. For all other features, if the test team doesn't have support, they are forced to make assumptions and interpret tests in their own way, leading to mistakes and missed bugs.

Many teams don't do this at all: they assign tests to testers and simply leave them to conduct the work in isolation, leaving the testers with extremely limited information on how the game should and shouldn't behave. Some projects are also set up to conduct testing overnight in a different time zone, so that a development team can start work each day with fresh bug reports from the previous day's work. While this sounds ideal from the developer's point of view, it severely limits the effectiveness of the test team and will likely result in only the most obvious, low-hanging fruit bugs being raised.

Industry tales: Fire and forget task allocation

I've met many QA analysts who provide poor support to the test teams executing their tests, knowingly or not. They assign out their tests and then forget about them, waiting for the resulting bugs to appear within the project database. This has been particularly evident when the QA analyst is working in an embedded studio team and assigning their tests to a remote team. The pressures and priorities of work within the game studio mean that QA analysts are far more interested in writing their next test plan and hitting the next sprint deadline than they are in seeing through the execution of current plans. This is seen more with embedded team members because their work is far more randomised and varied than the standard test writer within a publisher's office.

When part of an embedded team, QA analysts will put more effort into requests and work from various studio leadership members who make a contribution to their appraisals and career advancement. Even when this isn't done for a direct benefit, they're still more likely to form relationships and carry out work requested from people they see in person every day than they are to spend time supporting their remote teams. Furthermore, performance reviews for QA analysts rarely seek feedback from remote test teams to measure the support they are getting from the QA analyst, reducing any remaining accountability to support test execution.

During one of my own performance reviews a few years ago, my direct manager was our executive producer and because he only had our immediate relationship on which to measure me, I asked him to gather 360 feedback for me. This is a process of gathering performance feedback from team members who report to the person, are peers with the person, and to whom the person reports. In my case, I asked to include the test leads from the remote vendor team we worked with, because I was primarily responsible for maintaining the relationship with that team. Because we were their clients, they would never have provided honest feedback without a direct invitation to do so and a promise that it would be given to me anonymously.

The reality is that many vendor and publisher test teams conduct their work without any of their pain points ever being heard or improved, either through the nature of the client relationship, internal company politics or simply due to a poor communication process. I'm referring here to the many questions, doubts, complications and blockers that occur during everyday testing and require outside information before they can be worked out.

I would like to see more accountability within the industry regarding this management aspect of the QA analyst role. Managing test execution and the relationship with test teams is very similar to having people directly report to you, making it important to recognise the management skill set of the QA analyst role within job descriptions and performance reviews.

While test leads, managers and directors are ultimately responsible for team management at the top level, QA analysts should be responsible for managing the tactical details. They cannot assign their tests out and expect the testers to execute them effectively without some level of support.

The guidance I give here is to allocate time to support test execution, including that time in any sprint planning estimates, so that it can be accounted for. QA analysts should make themselves available during the opening days of executing a new test task, when support is most likely to be required. Avoid booking time off during these phases or starting a new task during a period of heavy meetings where you cannot provide timely support. Test execution should not be planned optimistically, hoping that no complications will be encountered during testing. As the cliché goes, plan for the worst and hope for the best. If there are indeed no complications, this will be a pleasant surprise.

7.4   Test reporting

I'm including this section here because test review and reporting are frequently neglected by QA analysts, with bugs often seen as the only useful output of testing. When test execution is complete, QA analysts don't always go back to review any of the results, observations or other comments from the testers. This may be because they're mostly interested in the bugs, but it's also because reviewing test results and collecting the data into reports takes valuable time that they would rather spend writing the next test plan.

Why is test reporting important for more than just bugs? Earlier in this book we said that the goal of testing was to capture data so that the project team could collectively make decisions on that data. More specifically, this data provides continuous feedback on the current health of the product.

The problem with only reporting bugs is that the feedback loop is broken when testing is executed and no bugs are found.

The wider project team doesn't know why no new bugs have been found: was it because no testing was conducted or because testing was conducted but found no bugs? These two explanations for the lack of bugs provide very different conclusions on the current state of testing.

"No news is good news" is not good enough when it comes to reporting. This highlights the fact that reporting on the progress of testing is as important as reporting on the product itself, because it provides much-needed context, shows whether more data is likely to arrive and when it will arrive. It lets the team know when they can expect to have a complete picture of the product's health. Other team members also care about test progress because the feedback from testing needs to be given promptly, giving others enough time to take action on negative results. Finding critical bugs on a feature after it's been deployed to production is not helpful. Although the information is captured, it is too late to be helpful during the correct phase of development. So, feature stakeholders are interested in both the results of testing and the current progress of testing.

Let's give a practical example. Picture a QA analyst within a development sub-team working on a new feature. The sub-team will have a range of different disciplines building that feature together, organised by a producer who is responsible for the schedule. All of these team members are stakeholders of the feature and could be impacted by the results of testing, and are interested in knowing the test progress and when testing is complete. Once their initial work is complete, team members will want feedback (bugs and test results) as quickly as possible so that they can begin working on fixes. It would be frustrating to wait a long time and not hear any feedback, only to then get a spike in bugs right near the end of the release phase or sprint, causing that person to rush their work and resolve the bugs within the shortened time frame. The sub-team producer also has a particular interest in everyone's work because they want to know that work is on track to be completed by the agreed milestones. Any deviation from the plan needs to be raised with them. Deviation from the plan is actually very common during testing because blocking bugs, complications or large quantities of bugs are just some of the influences that slow down testing and can push progress off track. As before, this feedback needs to be timely. The producer will not appreciate learning this information on the final day of the development phase.

This helps us remember that testing doesn't directly improve the quality of the product and that the result of testing always generates additional work for others on the project team. For testers, their work is done when the tests are complete and the bugs are logged, but this is just one step in a larger process for everyone working with the project teams, QA analysts included. Bugs need to be triaged, discussed and resolved, all of which takes time and effort. When we think in this way – considering the impact that testing has on others – the importance of communicating test progress is more appreciated.

Once we have a better understanding about why test reporting is helpful to others, we can better refine how we communicate the test information. Many testers and their leads produce daily and weekly reports filled with many graphs, data points and bug lists. These reports are often so heavily populated and frequently sent that it takes some dedication to read and digest them all. Critical information can easily be lost amongst the greater set of data. These types of reports also require the reader to analyse the data and draw their own conclusions, which is acceptable because the audience for these reports is always within the test discipline.

For QA analysts reporting to the wider project team, a more concise and casual approach is often more effective. Other disciplines don't have the time or inclination to read through pages of test data in an email; they only want to know the highlights concerning their own work. As a result, test reports can be given verbally or through instant messaging tools to a specific group of interested parties, instead of the whole studio. In this frame, we're using the term 'test reporting' very loosely. This activity requires less formal reporting and more casual feedback of key information. When QA analysts consistently deliver helpful data back to the correct stakeholders of each feature in a timely manner, the appreciation of and reliance on test data will increase in future work.

I say 'helpful' data because test reporting requires a tailored approach. The stakeholders might be interested in your intentions when testing to confirm you have included areas and scenarios they've identified as being important. They might be less concerned about bugs and more interested in other types of data, like performance or stability information. The point is not to report every single bug and test progress update, but instead to understand what is helpful and relevant to each stakeholder and report on that. Team members will quickly become disengaged with your work if you share uninteresting or irrelevant data, and miss the good data hidden within future reports.

Communicating the details and the output of testing has the added benefit of providing insight into the test process for other disciplines who aren't familiar with it. Many QA analysts forget that other disciplines within the studio don't know the details of their work and can only make broad assumptions about how and why testing is conducted. This applies to both holistic topics, like the goals of testing, and specific topics, like the bug retesting flow. When QA analysts share what they plan to test, how long it's going to take and when they'll get the results, they are making the details of testing visible to others, allowing feedback and indirectly getting others interested in their work. Project stakeholders can't become engaged and interested in testing if the details are kept private. If QA analysts share their work and the results of it regularly and consistently, it has a compounding positive effect on stakeholders, causing them to respect and appreciate test work more.

In practice, I've seen (and been part of) quite a few test teams that didn't practise good test reporting. Either the team members didn't know they could be reporting test data beyond bugs, or they did know what needed to be done but just didn't have the time to do it. The latter scenario is unfortunately quite common within game studio test teams, particularly when the project is practising agile development or is a live ops project. Agile projects are particularly difficult because the focus of feature test work can change from sprint to sprint, leaving very little time to invest in longer term test reporting. To put this another way, the test data we report this sprint might not be valuable next sprint. In these cases, the test team needs to be careful about how they invest their time in test reporting processes and tools, making sure that the reporting remains relevant for as long as possible.

Industry tales: Test reporting

An example of a project schedule I've worked on, used two-week sprints, releasing every four weeks. It was a mobile game running on Android/iOS and a live ops project running the games-as-a-service model. This tight turnaround to develop, test and release new features in four weeks left little time to perform non-critical activities if the embedded test team didn't manage their time effectively. There was nearly always pressure to release on time or to move onto the next sprint's work. Releasing frequently like this can create a feeling of there being no respite. This was a stark contrast to the 18-month-release console game projects I had worked on in previous years.

The testing for our mobile game captured a lot of data because we ran many test sessions and investigative tasks whereby test comments, observations and sporadic numerical data were captured from the team of testers. The project leadership also had an appetite for including as much as they could in each four-week game update, and there was always some critical feature or bug fix needing to go live. Under such business pressure, it was normal that completed tests wouldn't be reviewed properly (or at all) by the analysts writing them, and instead the team just focused on the bugs that arose out of those tests. Daily work became a quick-and-dirty version of the fundamental test process, with QA analysts writing tests back-to-back and sending them to the team of testers as soon as each one was drafted. I'm pretty sure there were a lot of insightful tester observations and added context that would have been valuable and were missed. Added context can change the output of a test entirely and some small, apparently insignificant observation could suggest that the tester was close to finding something big, but simply needed more time to run the test session again. This reviewing and assessing of the test results should all have been part of the test reporting activity but wasn't. In hindsight, we were saved by the close communication between the remote team of testers and the embedded test team: summaries of the outcomes of testing were escalated and discussed in the instant message chat channel.

The focus on test writing comes from the fact that, from the outside, this appears to be the core of the QA analyst job, where all of the surrounding activities outlined in the fundamental test process are unknown to other disciplines in the studio. QA analysts will also be asked for estimates of when they can expect to begin testing a feature, which can only start once the tests are written. These estimations (whether intended or not) can have the effect of inducing the QA analyst to begin writing their next test plans instead of reviewing the test results of existing completed plans. It's extremely important that embedded test teams within the game studio manage their time to avoid these scenarios and manage the business pressure correctly. The embedded test team are the test experts and should know that allowing time to conduct thorough test results analysis will save time in the long run. It's up to them to reinforce this value when discussing with other disciplines on the project team.

My advice is to constantly remind yourself of the fundamental test process and review how closely you are following it in your work. This self-review will help you assess which sections are being neglected. I also find it helpful to allocate a slot in my day to review my tests that have completed. For me, this is first thing in the morning, before I get distracted and interrupted by other activities going on in the studio.

Why does it take so long?

For statistical data, good test reporting takes time to collect the data and present it in a useful format. This usually involves built-in bug database plugins/tools or some process which exports the bug data out to a spreadsheet or other data visualisation tool. The same is true for other types of test tools. This can be difficult because there are already technical limitations that the QA analyst has to overcome. The right tools need to be available for the bug database and then the analyst has to acquaint themselves with the tooling to make effective use of it. So even before the test data can be analysed, there's an overhead of work to be done. An example of this is the common database tool, JIRA. This contains a set of off-the-shelf graphs, but it isn't able to support more specific analysis, nor does it effectively support custom bug fields within reports. For more specific analysis, a plugin is required, or the data needs to be exported into a spreadsheet or other tool. The same is true for test execution tools like Microsoft's Test Manager or TestRail: only specific data styles are available, and they may not always be what you want.

My advice is to take the time to learn the more advanced features of common project tools so that you can reduce the setup time needed to analyse a new set of test data. Understanding how to manipulate graphs and data in spreadsheets is also very helpful and will serve you well in your test career. When you are short on time, you don't want to be wrestling with reporting tools and spreadsheets for hours.

Finally, I'd advise giving test reporting a higher priority within your work week, and allocating time to invest in it. Remember that many non-test staff within the studio won't have set expectations of the test team (they aren't testing experts like you!) so they won't know the value of good test reporting until you provide it.

7.4.1 Reporting metrics

Within the test reporting compartment of your personal toolbox, there are four sub-compartments in which you will be storing your knowledge. These compartments are easy to remember as the '*The Four P's*' of reporting metrics: project, product, process and people.

This section introduces more advanced topics that are most relevant to the work of test leads and managers, since they include managing people. However this is still a useful introduction for QA analysts, since it provides a good framework to categorise these metrics.

Project

Metrics relating to progress of the project. Anything involving dates, deadlines, milestones and the velocity of completing work goes into this category. Test execution velocity over time is a good example of this, i.e., how quickly is the team completing tests and when are they expected to finish? The test schedule will feed into the project schedule, which is usually owned by the producer or product manager roles. When reporting progress metrics, it's common for the test team to work closely with the production discipline on these metrics and to rely on one another when reporting progress and planning schedules.

Product

Metrics relating to the state of the actual game itself (or other product of work being created). Lots of test metrics fall into this category, with bugs being the primary data source showing product health. The amount of data in bugs is vast and can be cut in various ways to give different kinds of meaning. Common metrics derived from bug data are things like count of active bugs, active bugs by severity, active bugs by code or content discipline, average age of bugs, number of bugs found in the live product, active bugs by game area, etc. Since the data captured within bugs can be customised, the ways to cut and display bug data is almost limitless.

Process

Metrics relating to process measure how efficiently the team is operating, showing areas of potential improvement. A good example is the average time between a bug being introduced into the game and being found by the team. Bugs found quickly suggests higher testing effectiveness. Another example is the average time taken to retest bugs after they've been resolved. A longer average time shows that the test team isn't completing all retesting before the end of the day, and some bugs are waiting longer for the retest to occur. It's worth noting that metrics in this category are difficult and sometimes time consuming to measure. For this reason, they aren't used that often in practice.

Consider the example given above relating to finding bugs soon after they've been introduced. To get accurate data on this metric, you would have to retest the same bug on older versions of the game to find the version where the bug was first introduced and then manually record the difference between this and when the bug was actually found. Such an approach is extremely time consuming and usually not worth the effort. It's more likely that a test team manager would initiate one-off activity to confirm suspicions they already have about process inefficiencies or ineffectiveness. These metrics are good at showing the maturity of a test team and highlighting the potential for improvements.

People

This metric is mainly for test leads and managers and is also the most frequently forgotten when reporting. All metrics within this category measure the team and individuals on the team. An unhappy team can have a huge impact on the effectiveness of work, with events like team redundancies and overtime being contributing factors.

Team polls capturing individual happiness are a good source of data for this, as are manager one-to-one meetings for understanding individual motivations. Practically, this is another area of data which is difficult to measure and requires certain processes to be set up at a company level. Personal evaluation scores and happiness ratings are good metrics to understand the current skill level and state of the team.

Further detailed data can be captured on individual specialist skills across the team to understand where the team is strong and to analyse gaps in the skillset. This can easily be captured by the test lead and be very helpful as a guide when interviewing for new hires; using this data, test leads can build well balanced test teams. This is true for both teams of testers and QA analysts. I won't go into more detail in this book, since it strays into the much larger topic of building test teams and looking after your people – something for test leads and managers specifically.

These Four P's of reporting don't just apply to written reports, but can also act as helpful reminders when more informally discussing the state of the project. When someone asks you "how are things going?", you can consider all of these categories in your response. Perhaps the quality of the product is good because bugs are being fixed at a good velocity and the team is on track to hit the next date, but the rate of work isn't sustainable due to the team doing overtime and becoming unhappy. Without the people metrics, this scenario shows an incomplete, falsely positive picture.

Another good example I see quite frequently is positive data for product and project metrics, but warning signs being shown in the process data. This is because the team has some poor processes and discipline, but so far has been lucky enough to have avoided failure. Well-presented process data in this scenario can show the team that they're taking risks through poor processes and should fix the issue before a failure occurs. Unfortunately, it's also true that many teams need a sufficiently big failure to occur before they actually take note and invest time in improving their processes.

7.5   Test team structure

One of the first questions I ask when interviewing for QA analyst roles is to ask how their work fits into the larger organisation and test strategy for the project. I ask this because, unlike QA testers who can execute their work successfully in relative isolation and ignorance, QA analysts play a much larger role in the holistic test strategy and so require a more complete understanding of the wider testing pipeline. This applies even more when the QA analyst is embedded within the development studio, because this is the source of all test decisions on the project. Many strategic and resourcing decisions start here with the QA director or manager and filter down to the immediate embedded team, publisher test teams and external vendor test teams. QA analysts take the lead in executing this strategy across the project through writing and distributing their test plans. For these plans to be successful they need to know the vision of the QA manager above them and how each testing sub-team contributes to that vision.

In this section I'll lay out the most common team structures for game projects across embedded, publisher and vendor test teams and describe the most common ownerships of each team. I'll also give a brief overview of the different job roles that exist in each, and how they differ from each other. The test discipline has multiple roles with the same title who actually perform different work, causing some confusion when you start on the career ladder. QA leads, for example, might exist in each team, but one QA lead might manage a team of testers while another manages a team of QA analysts – two very different roles. Similarly, testers who are embedded within the game studio may perform testing within sprints and have a much greater exposure to the source of development when compared to a tester working in a remote team.

To confuse things even further, many game companies request their QA testers to perform different work depending on their project structure. Some testers will be asked to write test cases even if it technically isn't in their job description or experience. In other cases, the testers will be asked to execute tests written by QA analysts. External test vendors accept both types of work in an effort to win and maintain business with their game studio clients, even if their testers are inexperienced in test writing. This situation means that the work of a QA tester or QA lead can vary greatly even within the same team type.

Because of this unfortunate state of affairs, it's even more important that all testing roles understand their own ownerships and responsibility, as well as how they fit into the project strategy and how they compare to the rest of the industry.

7.5.1 Testing sub-teams

Embedded test teams

Sometimes called 'dev QA', these teams work directly within the game studio alongside other project disciplines. They most often consist of a QA lead or manager who manages a team of QA analysts. Where the studio develops multiple projects, a QA director or 'head of QA' role also exists to define the test policy for the company, uniting each project strategy. While some studios *do* hire QA testers to execute testing directly, this isn't very common[*]. Instead, QA analysts occupy a majority of embedded test team roles, working alongside other disciplines and developing new features within the sprint structure. It's common to hire a QA analyst for each sub-team[**] within the development team. On larger projects, sub-teams are orientated around domain areas and will include specialist roles, like a multiplayer team, a server team, a gameplay team, an environment team, a character team, etc.

This style of work gives embedded QA analysts a lot of exposure to the software development process, the work of other disciplines and technical details about how each game component is built. Delivering work in sprints also sets a fast work cadence, something which is felt much less in remote test teams. The mix of disciplines also make game studio offices more chaotic; team members are more likely to get randomised during their work through being invited to meetings, playtests and general desk-side discussions or by direct requests from others on the project team.

Embedded test teams are the only test team who will have access to the source code and assets, allowing them to build and run the game project on their PC/Mac. Embedded team members will have access to asset creation tools that the art disciplines will be using – so they can load and test assets without running the game – as well as bespoke in-house tools. This exposure provides both technical insight and a source of truth to base testing on. Direct communication with other project team members and direct access to the game files makes the embedded team the best equipped to gather information that drives testing for all test teams working on the project.

For smaller projects not supported by publisher or external vendor test teams, the embedded team will complete all levels of testing for the project, writing and

---

[*]   There are logistical and financial reasons for this, but it's beyond the scope of this book
[**]   Also referred to as 'pods' or 'Scrum teams'

executing all of the testing themselves. While this provides great end-to-end exposure of the test strategy for an entire project, the work is often lightweight and conducted in a 'quick and dirty' style that wouldn't be effective on more complex projects. Any moderately sized project requires a separate team of testers and large projects need multiple teams of testers performing different levels of testing simultaneously. For these projects, the QA analysts working within the embedded team write test plans for each new feature as they are built within the sprints. These test plans are then executed by teams of testers either in a publisher test team (if the studio is owned by a major game publisher) or an external vendor team. I'll outline some of the different models later in this section.

Publisher test teams

These are large, centralised test teams situated within a main publisher's office that provide testing support to multiple game studios working with that publisher. In most cases the publishing company owns the development studios and, because it supports many projects across different studios, it can hire and manage a huge team of central testers, moving them between projects whenever required. Some big names who support these types of teams include Sony, Microsoft, Sega and EA, to name just a few.

These teams perform their testing at different levels to the embedded test team. Whereas the embedded team tests individual features at the component test level, the publisher test team tests the entire system once those features have been merged into a single build (system-level testing). They also perform other test activities requiring many testers, such as multiplayer playtests.

Generally, these teams rely less on understanding the internal workings of the game, because they don't have access to the code or easy access to the studio team members. Therefore, system-level testing is ideal for this team. It takes a player-facing view of entire game sections and is likely to catch bugs which weren't picked up in earlier testing of each individual feature.

QA analysts within the publisher team will write their own system-level tests, separate from the embedded tests created during each sprint. As they work remotely from the studio team and are surrounded by test-discipline team members, QA analysts here are less likely to be interrupted or rushed in their test writing. In ideal circumstances, this should result in a more comprehensive and well-written set of tests, particularly when the embedded team is accustomed to a more casual way of working (sometimes not writing tests at all).

However, due to the lightweight nature of modern agile game development, many design and technical specs don't exist for the publisher team to base their testing on. Since they don't have direct access to the code or to conversations within the studio office, the QA analysts on this team have the difficult job of extracting feature details from the documents they have available and filling in any gaps by speaking with the embedded test team. When the embedded and publisher teams have a strong working relationship, this information exchange works very well and the publisher team can be very effective in supporting the embedded team within its larger team sizes.

Publisher teams also have other roles parallel to the embedded team. They have test managers for each studio the publisher team works with, managing the relationship and planning test team numbers. Unlike the embedded test managers who are test discipline experts, these roles are sometimes more business-orientated, people management roles. This is particularly true for very large publisher test teams which hire hundreds of testers. In these cases, there is enough work for multiple full time test managers purely hiring and managing the workforce. Due to their size, publisher test teams are also likely to have department heads who manage the entire team.

These teams have many test leads who organise test execution for teams of testers. This is a different role to either a test manager on this team or a test lead within the embedded team. Test leads in publisher test teams organise the testers under them, distributing tests from the QA analysts and acting as a first-line support for questions and problems during test execution. They're also responsible for onboarding and training of testers, as well as performance appraisals. These test leads should be experts in test execution and the organisation of it but will have little knowledge of test plan writing and more holistic project test strategy.

Finally, these teams have a selection of QA tester roles, sometimes called test technicians or test associates. They are given numbers or prefixes to denote seniority: junior tester, tester, senior tester and assistant lead. The role of the testers is to execute the test plans created by the QA analysts and distributed by the QA leads.

The benefits of publisher test teams come from being part of the same company as the embedded test team. Both teams will be able to work more seamlessly together because they use the same tools and IT infrastructure. Being within the company also means that both teams can see confidential project and company information. Because of this, a lot of 'red tape' is avoided during day-to-day work. The company is also more likely to spend resources on training and welfare for the publisher team, something which isn't seen for outsourced test teams.

Outsourced vendor test teams

Specialist game testing companies set up these teams and provide their services to game development studios. These teams are the furthest from the source of development, frequently not having direct communication with other disciplines on the development team and having limited access to project tools and data. While their primary goal is to execute testing, they are used for a wide variety of testing and test writing work.

As a result, they're mostly made up of test lead and QA tester roles, following the same format as publisher test teams. However, in recent years, some test vendors have begun offering QA analyst services too.

The work varies quite widely for these testers. Some smaller development teams don't have any test staff at all and require the vendor team to handle all aspects of testing and prerequisite planning. The vendor's other customers ask them to perform playtesting and provide design feedback; a very different role to the functional testing we've been talking about in this book. The most common model is for the customer to provide the tests that need to be executed and for the vendor team of testers to execute those tests. They either support game studios directly or they act as auxiliary teams to the publisher test team. In some cases, the publisher team is a mixture of locally hired testers and remote vendor testers that together form a single team.

This variability means that testers can find themselves performing very different types of work depending on the customer and project they are working on. Some projects will use all of the techniques and terminology covered in this book, giving the tester useful insight and experience in their work.

However, playtesting, or free exploratory testing over many months without guidance, can be very stifling for the tester's career. The same applies to the level of exposure that each tester gets to the wider test strategy from the publisher and embedded test team. Many testers on vendor teams aren't privy to this information and so have limited learning opportunities. Again, this varies depending on the customer they are working with.

Test managers within these teams are nearly always business-orientated roles, responsible for managing the relationship with each customer and organising the team size and experience to meet the requirements of each project. These roles rarely get involved in the details of test execution or strategy. Much like publisher test teams, test lead roles within these companies lead teams of testers and are knowledgeable about managing test execution. They don't usually lead QA analysts and aren't experienced with wider test strategy and test writing. I will mention that despite this, many game teams *do* still request that these leads and testers write tests and execute them. While this serves as good practice for the testers and leads, it has the effect of throwing them somewhat into the deep end.

7.5.2 Common team structures

Here I'll list the most common organisational split between these three sub-teams and describe the responsibilities of each team in each scenario.

Embedded, publisher and outsourced vendor team structure

This is a very common structure for many medium and large projects: they require multiple levels of testing, and the split allows each team to be responsible for a different test level. In this structure, the embedded 'dev QA' team is responsible for component testing, (i.e., testing each feature in isolation on its own feature branch). This team is ideal for this task because they can test any work-in-progress branch on their PC/ Macs, instantly syncing fixes and changes from the rest of the project team without the need to create new builds for the target devices. Often, the embedded team is orientated towards providing a very tight feedback loop to the other disciplines, catching early bugs and raising them in daily meetings. Testing and bugging at this stage of development is restricted to newly added features, and many bugs are ignored because each feature is still considered to be a work in progress. Testing work is focused on those areas that are helpful to the rest of the project team.

Because the embedded test team restricts itself to the latest individual feature additions, they have no opportunity to consider the wider game experience during their work. This is where the publisher test team contributes. It is responsible for integration and system level testing: writing and executing tests that focus on how all of the features interact together to form the complete product. Critically, the publisher team needs to understand that new features have already gone through one round of testing and that their role is not just to test these new additions again. In some cases, the embedded team hands over its tests to the publisher team, showing which tests were not run due to time constraints within the sprint. The publisher team can then pick up this progress and run those lower priority tests.

Unlike the component testing level, the testing conducted by the publisher test team is executed on a 'no exceptions' basis, where all bugs observed are logged in the database. Because of this, the publisher team might only receive builds for new features once they are feature-complete and the project team is ready to receive any and all bugs found. This also simplifies the setup for the publisher team. It can receive builds from a single game branch with all the features together, without the confusion of testing features on multiple different branches. Logging bugs against anything identified within the game also simplifies the testing instructions to the team, removing any danger of logging bugs against work in progress.

The inclusion of outsourced vendor teams varies slightly with this model. Some projects use them to supplement the publisher with the same task of executing tests at a system level. In other cases, outsourced vendor teams are included near major release dates, once all game features are complete and only bug fixing remains. In either scenario, outsourced vendor teams add flexibility to the testing effort, allowing the project to scale up at the critical testing phase of the project. These teams sometimes perform acceptance testing on the near-final game, which is very close to playtesting.

Many teams also conduct a phase of 'release testing' which is an extension of the system testing phase beginning once all features are complete. The fresh perspective of the outsourced team is a good opportunity to identify even more bugs which might have been overlooked by earlier testing.

In this model, the feature-complete build is given to the vendor team to conduct release testing and the publisher team is free to move onto the system testing for a future release in parallel.

> **In this way, the embedded team is the start of the testing pipeline, the publisher team in the middle and the outsourced team forms the end.**

Because of the multiple teams and test levels working together, this structure is the most complex and requires the most planning, organisation and communication. Each team must be aware of its ownership and how it plays into the wider test strategy. Due to the distributed teams, knowledge isn't circulated as effortlessly as it is within a game studio. These teams need to coordinate their testing efforts, handing over knowledge from team to team. For the same reason, test processes within these projects cannot follow the lightweight and casual style that many smaller teams are accustomed to.

A variation of this model includes just the embedded and publisher teams, without any outsourced team involvement. With this setup, the split of test ownership is very similar, but the publisher test team performs all testing through to release instead of handing it over to the outsourced team.

Embedded and outsourced vendor team structure

This is another very common team structure for many game studios that don't have a supporting central publisher test team but are still large enough to hire their own embedded test team. Many large game companies also choose not to create a centralised publisher test team, instead providing each game studio with the test budget to control however they see fit, which leads to this arrangement.

With this structure, the outsourced team takes on the testing of more test levels or the test levels are merged, rather than being conducted as discrete activities (many teams don't label these levels so formally anyway). Where the embedded test team is well established, it is responsible for defining what should be tested and writing all the tests, and the outsourced team is responsible for executing those tests. Smaller embedded teams may lean more heavily on the outsourced vendor team, asking them to contribute to the testing writing as well as the execution.

One of the key differences versus the previous model is that testing of different stages isn't executed in parallel. Here, it's more likely that the two teams will work through each test level together, with the outsource team being involved in testing much earlier in the creation of new features. With direct access to the embedded test team, the outsourced vendor team has better visibility of project information and a deeper involvement in the holistic test strategy. For example, the outsourced team is more likely to be testing across multiple feature branches during the component testing level and will transition their testing to a single branch later in the testing pipeline. Testing multiple work-in-progress branches requires the outsourced team to understand the details of project lifecycles that I mentioned in chapter two: a much more complex working arrangement than being sent a single build from the same branch and logging any bug that is observed within the game. This is just one example: there are many other practical complexities that make this arrangement more challenging for the vendor team.

This illustrates that even within the same roles in the same teams, the complexity of the work conducted varies wildly depending on how the project is organised. The embedded team roles will change the least, but the outsourced vendor team forms a much bigger part of the total strategy in this scenario. As with the previous model, some smaller embedded test teams will also ask the vendor team to write tests, adding more responsibility to its role. In this scenario, the embedded test team might only consist of a single QA manager or analyst who acts as the QA point of contact for the entire project and doesn't have the time to write all of the tests themselves.

Some small studios using this team configuration don't have QA analysts within their embedded team and instead have a small contingent of testers executing testing directly, supported by a larger outsourced vendor team.

Embedded-only team structure

This team structure is common amongst small, mobile or indie game studios where the testing requirements are very light. While these test teams are working on the smaller projects, they're responsible for the test effort across the entire project and so develop a broad and holistic view of all test activities. QA analysts and QA testers working in these teams have very well-rounded experience because of this setup. Unlike the earlier team structures, these roles have no problem understanding how their work fits into the wider project plan, because it begins and ends with themselves.

Due to the smaller size of these teams, they are less likely to have a hierarchy of test roles (leads, QA analysts and QA testers) and more likely to consist of a flat team who report directly into company leadership, instead of a manager within the test discipline. These roles are heavily self-directed, performing the entire fundamental test process themselves.

This test team will have a strong understanding of technical, business and release processes as a result of first-hand involvement in every aspect of project life. The team will also gain the greatest insight into other disciplines, sometimes even having split roles where an individual is both a tester and a producer. The same applies to all other disciplines within the project team. This is another common scenario where individuals begin their career in the test discipline and are able to easily move across to other disciplines within game development.

The flipside of this team structure is that these testing roles gain no experience working on larger and more complex products, limiting their domain and process knowledge. These test roles are also more likely to conduct their work in a very lightweight fashion, sometimes not writing tests, logging bugs or producing reports at all. While this work style is efficient for small teams, it prevents honing techniques and processes that are a strict prerequisite of testing on larger projects. Anyone moving from these roles into companies with larger projects can have a shock as they adapt to more rigorous work processes. Unlike these singleton teams, larger projects also require a conscious effort of written communication and organisation not seen within small teams.

Outsourced-only team structure

This team setup exists when game studios don't hire anyone from the test discipline directly, usually due to their very small company size. Instead, they seek outsourced vendor teams to provide testing support on an as-required basis.

Unfortunately, these projects frequently don't have the test experience to provide clear requirements for their testing. They don't know what they need for their project situation and the outsourced vendor managers don't have enough testing experience to provide suggestions. As a result, testers can spend the entire project performing exploratory testing and logging bugs, with no guidance at all. In other cases, testers are asked to perform playtesting and provide qualitative feedback, which really is playing the game and not testing it.

While this might keep the client happy, it's damaging to the profession because it provides a distorted view of what game testing is. Testers can perform this testing for a long time and never acquire any new skills or experience. There is an enormous delta of skills and experience between these testers and a tester that you might find working embedded within a game studio. These two extremes show just how different the same role can be.

Industry tales: Career Advice

With such a broad range of teams and roles, which one is right for you? How difficult is it to move from a QA tester role to that of a QA analyst? Should you move into a management role or continue as an individual contributor?

For new testers, embedded test teams may seem like the best choice for their breadth and depth of knowledge; however, they rarely hire entry level QA tester roles. Most embedded teams are looking to hire QA analysts who already have experience not just in testing but in test writing. Publisher test teams are far more likely to hire entry level testers who have no experience at all, often on short term contracts during busy testing phases. Outsourced vendor teams also have low entry criteria with many just requiring the tester to pass an English language proficiency test with no technical interview at all.

As I've demonstrated in this section, the work that testers perform can be the luck of the draw. Some projects allow new testers to learn and grow more than others. On large and well organised projects, testers can see what good test plans look like and begin to have their own ideas about what should be tested for any given feature. The test direction a tester takes during exploratory testing paves the way to write those ideas into test plans when they move into a QA analyst role later in their career.

Other projects can pose a serious danger to the career progression of testers, keeping them in a rut and sheltered from more interesting work. Testers can be asked to perform playtesting or exploratory testing for weeks without further guidance. While this may catch some easy bugs, it doesn't teach the tester any new skills or provide any feedback for their work. The same applies when testers are working on unstructured projects with a badly organised schedule and poorly-written tests. The lack of exposure to a more mature testing process doesn't equip the tester to learn enough to move into the QA analyst role.

Testers working in publisher and outsourced teams should try to recognise when they aren't learning anything new from their current project or when they've been performing the same type of work for too long. I've interviewed testers like this, who have several years' experience but who don't interview strongly because they have very little to show for their years. Remember that experience doesn't come for free simply by spending time in the workplace. Like any other job, testers need to make an effort to improve and be in an environment that allows them to do that. If your current environment is stale, then move on. Unfortunately, outsourced teams are at particular risk here because they are more likely to be isolated from wider project knowledge and work for longer periods without accumulating experience and insight.

As a basic example, when I was a contract tester at Microsoft I once spent four weeks playtesting multiplayer horde mode for Gears of War 3. While it was great fun, it didn't teach me a lot (apart from how to get good with the Longshot weapon!) Had I spent any longer performing that task, I would have become bored with the lack of actual testing I was doing.

What can testers do to solve this problem? With the large size of publisher and outsourced test departments, asking to move to another project without leaving the company is a real possibility. Afterall, not every project is equal. If this isn't an option, testers should move to a new team closer to the source of development, either amongst publisher test teams or embedded test teams. Generally speaking, publisher teams will be more involved than outsourced teams, and embedded teams even more so. Moving closer to the source of development has other career benefits. In these teams, testers are more likely to be offered full time roles with greater company benefits.

Similar dangers apply to QA leads on outsourced and publisher test teams, too. These are people management roles and do not participate in test execution or test writing. When senior testers are promoted into the outsourced lead role, ironically, they stop practising those very skills that secured them the promotion, and do not participate in test planning either.

If your goal is to pursue the management career path within an outsourced team, this experience will serve you well. However, it's easy to accidentally become pigeonholed in a management role that will not help you apply for any QA analyst or embedded management role because of their requirement for practical test experience. If an individual spends several years in this role, they will find it difficult to return to any other role that requires hands-on test experience. This is another interview scenario I've unfortunately encountered quite a lot. Candidates who think they're experienced and have multiple years under their belt, but still don't have the hands-on practical skills required for the role.

Afterword

With this book I wanted to start from the ground up and define a solid foundation before delving into more complex topics. It was important that we took the time to look at the core principles of game testing in the earlier chapters and remind ourselves why testing exists as a discipline. So often, this is misunderstood.

In my view, the key learnings about QA versus testing need to be written in permanent marker on the walls of every game team office worldwide. I hope that individuals of all seniority levels can use these core principles as pillars to guide the QA vision of their teams in the future. If they are not understood by everyone, much of the knowledge that builds upon them will be ineffective. To put it another way, there's little value in discussing advanced topics if the fundamentals aren't first understood.

Aside from the core principles, we looked in detail at creating effective test plans for game features. We explored the technical knowledge required to define *what* should be tested and *how* it should be tested and followed up with the domain knowledge of game areas to include into the mix. The combination of these two knowledge areas is the key to effective test planning and, therefore, effective testing. Find opportunities to practise these different skills and the quality of your work will improve. Likewise, find opportunities to increase the breadth of your domain experience and you will be better equipped to tackle new testing challenges in the future.

While this book doesn't cover the work of test managers above the QA analysts or the work of testers executing tests, the creation of test plans are so integral to the success of the whole system that improving them will have a significant impact on any project. This is one of the reasons I chose to write about this first. Test plans organise, structure and guide the test effort. If the test discipline for a project was a body, the testers would be hands and eyes, with a role to interact and observe; and the QA analysts would be the brain, instructing the hands and processing the observations made. Without structure and direction, even the best game testers in the world are limited in their effectiveness. Therefore, I chose to focus here first, before writing about test execution techniques.

In many areas of the book, I've talked about the testers' 'toolbox' of knowledge. Remember that the techniques and topics here don't all need to be utilised immediately. They are simply tools to store in your toolbox until you face a test challenge that requires them. I hope that this book has defined many new compartments for your toolbox and began to fill them with knowledge (tools) which can be used in future work. Readers should endeavour to remember these compartments and continue to fill them as they practise and hone these techniques in their work. Only through conscious practice, retention and recall can skills be improved and used again.

Looking forward

Because this is a foundation of knowledge, we're several hundred pages on and have only scratched the surface of what a best-in-class game testing discipline might look like. Many areas of the book cover topics broadly to provide a holistic view, but in doing so I wasn't able to provide a full explanation of every area of the work. To reach the widest audience, this book specifically covers only topics that are applicable to all teams, leaving many more specialised topics to be discussed in further detail.

Large AAA games, in particular, have many deep and interesting feature areas that occupy the time of a QA analyst for many months over the entire duration of the project. Documenting the test strategies for game domain areas in detail could fill an entire book on their own. Such a book could give sample test breakdowns for each area, bug and test templates, and a more detailed list of pitfalls for each area. To document the real work of QA analysts and avoid talking theoretically, we would have to interview domain specialists from across the industry and record their accounts. It's very difficult for a single person to gain such deep and broad experience across many game areas naturally through their work. The only way to acquire this depth and breadth of knowledge would be to acquire it elsewhere, through books and training. I would love to write such a book.

Applied testing also presents many complications, 'gotchas' and 'exceptions to the rule' which diverge from theoretical and academic publications. Even the content within this book won't apply to some situations. During its writing, I explored some of these rabbit holes* with you and talked about some of these exceptions depending on the project circumstance. However, I still left many of these diversions out of

---

*   I use the term 'rabbit hole' here because these topics devolve into deep discussions with many different viewpoints. So often these complex topics are at the centre of debate in online forums and social media.

this book because they are advanced topics that would require many more pages to give them the full consideration they require. An advanced QA analyst guide might introduce static analysis techniques, the role of automation in games and the idea of quality at source (AKA 'shift left') as well as other hot topics that many game teams strive towards.

An advanced guide would also speak to the interpersonal soft skills that embedded QA analysts require working in cross-discipline development groups. As well as being technically competent, the most effective embedded team members share the common traits of strong empathy, trust and communication. They understand that other disciplines in the team have their own objectives and deadlines. While QA analysts have the responsibility of test planning through gathering information from other disciplines, they don't have the authority to formally request the information they need. Where juniors become frustrated at the apparent lack of documented information, seniors understand the importance of building strong working relationships that are mutually beneficial to each individual. Because testing gathers information for feature creators, asking them to assist in its planning is a bit like 'helping me to help you'. While the importance of collaboration and soft skills are important to many roles, testers need to speak to almost every other team member to conduct their work, making this particularly important.

Finally, I see the discipline as split into three types of roles: QA managers and leads to organise teams and projects, QA analysts who define strategies and write test plans, and testers who execute those test plans. This book focuses on the work of analysts because their individual contribution is the most critical to project success and the most undocumented. This leaves test execution still to be documented and is the next book to be written. If one person is considered to be a better tester than the next person, what attributes make them so? How do they differ? When a tester follows a process of elimination to determine the nature of a bug, what questions do they ask themselves? What test techniques does a tester use to structure their exploratory testing? And, importantly, how does game testing differ from software testing? What different skills are required? These questions and many more are left answered when it comes to test execution within games.

While it's unfortunate that I couldn't cover all of these topics within this book, it shows the massive scope of unpublished areas within the game testing profession and the remaining potential for us all to share, learn and improve even more. This isn't a definitive guide to game testing, but is one step towards a more appreciated, respected and documented profession.

Printed in Poland
by Amazon Fulfillment
Poland Sp. z o.o., Wrocław

32472772R00222